Elvis Cinema
and Popular Culture

Elvis Cinema
and Popular Culture

by DOUGLAS BRODE

McFarland & Company, Inc., Publishers
Jefferson, North Carolina, and London

LIBRARY OF CONGRESS CATALOGUING-IN-PUBLICATION DATA

Brode, Douglas, 1943–
    Elvis cinema and popular culture / by Douglas Brode.
      p.   cm.
    Includes bibliographical references and index.

    ISBN 0-7864-2526-1 (softcover : 50# alkaline paper) ∞

    1. Presley, Elvis, 1935–1977 — Criticism and interpretation.
    2. Musical films — United States — History and criticism.
    3. Popular culture — United States.   I. Title.
    ML420.P96B75   2006
    791.43'75 — dc22   200612340

British Library cataloguing data are available

On the cover: Poster art from the 1957 film *Jailhouse Rock* (MGM/Photofest)

Manufactured in the United States of America

McFarland & Company, Inc., Publishers
  Box 611, Jefferson, North Carolina 28640
   www.mcfarlandpub.com

Once again,
and as always,
for Sue

Table of Contents

All Singing! All Dancing! All Elvis!

During the three decades that have elapsed since Elvis Presley's death (August 16, 1977), practically every aspect of his life and career has been scrupulously studied. Of primary significance is the music. And with good reason: Presley inarguably rates as the most influential performer of the twentieth century's second half; if not the first of his ilk, he certainly stands as the most notable singer to fuse white rockabilly with black rhythm 'n' blues for a sound initially referred to as The Big Beat, retitled "rock 'n' roll" by disc jockey Alan Freed.[1] Even if Elvis wasn't the original white recording artist to achieve commercial success by singing black music — Bill Haley and the Comets' rendition of "Rock Around the Clock" (July 1955) preceded Elvis' "Heartbreak Hotel" (March 1956) onto the pop charts by eight months[2]— Presley was the primary person to achieve *mainstream* superstardom by doing so.

His records sold in the multi-millions during his lifetime (and afterwards); Haley (though not his breakthrough hit) was all but forgotten before the following decade had a chance to unfold, if more recently rediscovered (and rightly revered) by rock historians. Still, it was Elvis' fundamentally consistent yet subtly modified vocal style (transforming from the raw blues ballads of his early Sun recordings to a more sophisticated orchestral styling that marked the RCA era) which set the pace for virtually all American music to follow. Not surprisingly, then, the ups and downs of The King's behind-the-scenes activities, as well as his incendiary personal life, serve as source material for numerous biographies, fair or exploitative.

Varied books on Presley's accomplishments (and, sad but true, failings) and the apocrypha surrounding both the good and the bad reached a watershed with the publication of *Elvis Culture*[3] in 1999. This academic volume analyzed the symbolic resonance of Elvis memorabilia, from the first crude album covers to recent black-velvet wall hangings, which posthumously project his physical semblance. Still, one element of "Elvis Culture" remains virtually untouched by scholars: The movies, 31 B Westerns, lowbrow musicals and romantic melodramas released between November 16, 1956 (*Love Me Tender*) and January 21, 1970 (*Change of Habit*),[4] as well as two documentaries in the 1970s.

The best known tome to offer even a feeble showcase is *Elvis: The Films and Career of Elvis Presley.*[5] But that book is by and large a picture album — images augmented by brief (and often inaccurate) plot synopses. Its only value is in its abundance of stills, assembled scrapbook-style for the delectation of Elvis devotees. The "text" (honoring it with that term seems more kind than correct) is composed of obvious commentaries, as well as cast and credits (surprisingly limited for a volume of this type) for each entry. Missing, even on a superficial level, are any "making-of" vignettes or gleanings from newspaper critics, *de rigueur* for such volumes.

Significantly — and perhaps surprisingly — the authors, Steven and Boris Zmijewsky, never attempt to analyze the films as an *oeuvre*; i.e., a body of work composed of individual *texts* which, closely scrutinized, form an organic whole. There is no sense that their book resulted from an intellectual search for any ongoing themes or emerging techniques that might justify their referring to the included motion pictures as "the films *of* Elvis Presley." All the Zmijewsky brothers have to say:

> Just as there were such easily recognizable commodites as "the Jerry Lewis film" ... there was something called "the Elvis Presley film." By the time *Blue Hawaii* appeared in 1962, they had become so individualized that they were a category unto themselves.[6]

By "individualized," the authors may possibly mean the opposite of what they state. In their opinion, the films, at least after the first five, could no longer be perceived as in any way "individualized" since they became *generic*, produced according to as rigid a formula as, say, the very different though equally schematized James Bond movies.

They continue:

> The plots were little more than thinly-veiled vehicles designed to carry Elvis into a recording studio to produce another album of songs.... [W]hen in doubt about the plot development or dialogue, *sing*! Add plenty of girls with shapely legs and healthy bosoms and picture postcard scenery to distract from the feeble storyline, and you have an Elvis Presley film.[7]

What they express is, at the very least, a general attitude about the movies that has been long held by the public and, perhaps surprisingly, even many diehard Elvis fans.[8] At the time of its release, each Presley vehicle was either dismissed ("shrewdly and cynically tailored for the express purpose of exploiting that most peculiar of contemporary phenomena ... Elvis Presley," *America* noted about *Loving You*[9] or damned with faint praise ("wholesome mindless spontaneity," *Time* commented on *Viva Las Vegas*).[10] In-depth analysis of Elvis films did not take place at the time, nor has it (as with many other B movie genres, following the popularity of auteurism in the '70s and such critical-academic passing fancies as Structuralism and Semiotics since) after the fact.

From the beginning, Col. Tom Parker, Elvis' lifelong mentor (some less kindly tag the man as a corrupter, Mephistopheles to Presley's Faust) steered his star away from those ambitious films offered him (*Thunder Road; The Fugitive Kind; Sweet Bird of Youth; Baby, the Rain Must Fall; A Star Is Born*)[11] and toward synthetic projects designed to sell records in an economically rather than aesthetically oriented process, on occasion described as "synergistic opportunity."[12] As one student of Elvis' career commented, "To the Colonel the movies were just one more plum in the pudding, a promotional tool which could sell the music and which the music in turn could sell."[13] Further — and, for many, more damning still — there is evidence Elvis himself eventually came to believe the films were worthless: "All they're good for," he reflected, "is to make money."[14]

Most observers — including those who go out of their way to treat Presley with kingly respect in all other avenues — would agree. "Cornball specials"[15] is how Princeton University professor Benita Eisler writes off the films, if not Elvis the music-maker. "An infinite succession of tripey flicks"[16] are the kindest words University of Colorado (Boulder) Fine Arts professor Erika Doss manages to muster. This, despite her ability to find substance and significance in such other Elvis artifacts as T-shirts, plastic purses and trading cards. Few cultural arbiters would disagree with Greil Marcus' insistence that the only way to comprehend the essence of Elvis's genius is by listening[17] — forming interpretations from what one *hears*. In view of the impact Presley's music exerted on performers as diverse as rock poet John Lennon ("Before Elvis, there was *nothing!*") and retro roadhouse performer Dwight Yoakum (who recorded a revival-homage of "Little Sister"), Marcus' theory might strike us as bedrock fact.

To a degree, Marcus is correct — obviously so. Elvis' recordings changed the history of modern music; it's only right that musicologists continuously study any aural treasures they discover on scratchy artifacts of what now, in the age of CDs, can quaintly be referred to as American hot wax. Listening is *a* valid way to appreciate Elvis from our perspective. Few would dare to argue against the belief that it ought to be the primary way. Marcus errs, though, in arguing that it's the *only* way. So the purpose of this volume emerges: To assume an alternative approach, based on the heretofore largely unexpressed belief that an equally effective means of grasping Presley's importance is through a close textual study of the considerable cinematic canon.

Is there any sound justification for proceeding in this vein? First, anyone contrarian enough to dare and argue that Elvis Cinema has something of value above and beyond unambitious mass entertainment ought to consider the largely ignored fact that young Elvis' motivation for pursuing a show business career was *not* to become a singer. "What he really wanted from the start," David Halberstam notes, "was to go to Hollywood and be a movie star like James Dean or Marlon Brando, a rebel up on the screen."[18] A local singing career was the only way a poor Memphis teen could attempt that leap. Marty Lacker of "The Memphis Mafia" concurs: "When Elvis first went out to Hollywood, he was tremendously excited about being an actor. He wanted it more than anything. More than being a singer."[19]

As to the reality that Elvis achieved at best only a dubious form of screen stardom after setting off a radical revolution in popular music, Halberstam ironically notes that it "was almost as if the music that shook the world was incidental"[20] to Elvis, whose dedication was to a film career. A few perceptive onlookers did notice Elvis' potential to become one of the new rebel stars before he appeared in a single film. "He's a guitar-playing Marlon Brando," comedian Jackie Gleason remarked after catching Presley's act for the first time.[21] The comparison was one Presley himself consciously nurtured from the first day he, a virtual unknown, stepped on-stage. Having seen Marlon in *The Wild One* (1954) and James Dean in *East of Eden* (1955), young Elvis — when not singing his heart out at country fairs in provincial Tennessee — sought out and re-viewed those films at revival houses. After countless screenings, he came up with his own theory as to what made those performers — as well as their forerunner, Robert Mitchum, the first to bring a counterculture-ish idiom to mainstream Hollywood during the postwar period — click with their audience of disenfranchised youth.

Elvis would not, in his upcoming TV performances and eventual motion pictures, smile too much. That would rule him out as an icon for an exploding youth subculture. A 21-year-old Presley explained to close friends, "You can't be a rebel if you grin."[22] So was born the laconic manner and arrogant attitude. When a rare smile did appear, he made sure it was sardonic. Elvis soon had little competition for the status of "rebel king" to the era's youth audience. Brando deserted such roles for the likes of Mark Antony in Shakespeare's *Julius Caesar* (1953). Dean would disappear from the screen after smashing his Porsche, while driving at 86 miles an hour on a California road, into another car on September 30, 1955. Not, however, before filming *Rebel Without a Cause* (1955), released posthumously and hungrily devoured by millions of young fans. The timing couldn't have been better: Bill Haley's original rock anthem, which had reached the number one spot on the music charts a month earlier, remained solidly in the Top Ten; *Rebel* held a similar position at the box office, even as Elvis performed on the Dorsey Brothers Saturday evening TV show.

In part, Elvis' overnight superstardom derived from an uncanny ability to fuse Bill Haley's big beat with James Dean's vulnerable but ornery image — something he couldn't have done had radio still dominated the world of home entertainment. Remarkable as the records were, we should recall they hit "huge" only after (and, to a large degree, as a result of) the broadcasts turned on teenagers while bringing down the parents' wrath. Clearly, Elvis had to be *seen* to be fully appreciated, or — at that time — condemned. Those swiveling hips, not the syrupy voice that recalled Hank Williams by way of Dean Martin (Elvis idolized and imitated them both), were what caused the censors to lash out against the overnight sensation.

Here, Col. Parker made a key decision which insured that Elvis would remain not only the king of rock 'n' roll but also an ongoing *commercial* draw. Following Presley's spring 1960 homecoming appearance from the military, hosted by Frank Sinatra, Parker insisted that his protégé would never again perform on television. He held to that decision for the better part of a decade. If you wanted to see Elvis, you had to *pay*— which meant attending live concerts for those few able to do so. For the millions of other fans, this meant buying a ticket to the movies. An impressive number of people were willing to do just that (the quality, or lack thereof, of any one film temporarily set aside) owing to their implicit understanding that a full appreciation of Elvis demanded he be viewed as well as heard:

> [I]t was more than just the music. It was also the movement and the style. And a great deal of it was the *look*: sultry, alienated, a little misunderstood, the rebel who wanted to rebel without ever leaving home [emphasis added].[23]

In fact, Elvis was far from the first rocker to reach theater screens. Early in 1956, young consumers could catch an assortment of low-budget musicals (some produced by disc jockey Alan Freed) including *Rock Around the Clock*, *Don't Knock the Rock* and *Rock, Pretty Baby*. No one performer, however, dominated these exploitation items. Acts arrived on-stage, performed for five minutes, then made way for the next. For many of them, a move to the big screen backfired. Haley, who appeared in two such movies, was revealed to be a balding, plump, good ol' country boy, as sweetly likable as he was unfit to qualify, once visualized in larger-than-life terms, as a sex symbol. Anyone able to combine all the elements — rockabilly rhythms with matinee idol charisma — couldn't help but emerge as a monumental figure.

As historian J. Ronald Oakley notes, "In 1955 teenagers had their music, their movies, their idols ... but as yet they had no one who combined all three of these and served as a focal point for their growing consciousness as a subculture."[24] To coin a phrase, if Elvis hadn't come along precisely when he did, someone would have had to invent him. There are those who argue that Elvis' personal Svengali did precisely that. Revealing a natural genius for Madison Avenue–style marketing while choosing to remain below the Mason-Dixon line, Col. Parker created a persona that had it both ways. After the initial controversy surrounding Elvis' overt sexuality subsided, he simultaneously played to the angry young men and women of the late 1950s while neatly avoiding the hardcore juvenile delinquent image that might incur ongoing resentment from their parents.

Influential people like Ed Sullivan, who initially claimed this "throwback" would never appear on his show, took note of competitor Steve Allen's rocketing ratings when Presley guested, and reversed his decision. On the nation's most beloved variety hour, the aging King of Sunday Night embraced the youthful King of Rock 'n' Roll, insisting this was "one fine, decent young man." After the first tenuous films in which Parker and Presley felt their way toward what would become Elvis' official screen image, they found their *métier*. From that point on, the movies ceased to be individual filmmaking endeavors, instead conceived as a means of promoting this dual personality:

> the image of Elvis the Pelvis, the rebellious, sexy, rock 'n' roll singer joining with the kids in rebellion against the sexual and social conventions of the time, yet a young man who was, conversely, an all–American boy who did not smoke or drink, did not hang around nightclubs, was religious and patriotic, polite to his elders, and loved his parents.[25]

The Broadway musical *Bye, Bye, Birdie* soon savagely satirized the process by which the roughhewn rural performer had been turned into a non-threatening commodity for mass market consumption. Less discriminating movie audiences bought it. The films made money (if in ever-decreasing amounts) for the better part of 15 years.

In retrospect, pop-culture critics begrudgingly accept that what began as a mere image transformed into a movie-star icon. "The Presley tough guy," James L. Neibaur explains, "was a mere caricature throughout the sixties: sexually attractive, a good singer, able to throw a few good punches and subsequently win the girl."[26] Not everyone had such (relatively) kind words. British critic George Melly complained, and not without justification, that an appealing "angry young bull"[27] was artistically castrated by Col. Parker and Hollywood's powers-that-be. Did Elvis indeed conspire to destroy what was greatest about himself— that pre–Hollywood aura of excitement edging toward anarchy? If perception actually is reality, then that remains true enough for those who accept it.

One could also argue that Elvis moved in precisely the direction he'd always hoped to take, abandoning the temporary means (wild rockabilly sensation) to achieve his desired end (movie star) if on a limited, compromised plane. Had he clung to a countrified image, Presley (like Jerry Lee Lewis or Conway Twitty) would have ruled himself out as a Hollywood star in anything other than inexpensive flicks of the sort they both did, *High School Confidential!* (1958) and *Platinum High School* (1960) — raunchy exploitation flicks for schlockmeister Albert Zugsmith. Considering that film stardom took precedence to musical artistry in Elvis' vision for himself, he did achieve (on a modest level) precisely what he wanted most by toning down his hostility level to win acceptance as a box office attraction with "legs."

About that roughly 15-year run of movies, there remains a difference of opinion. For one author, Presley's "longevity as a cultural icon is largely due to his *flexibility*— his willingness to take the shape of what we most wanted to see."[28] Perhaps "flexibility" is a less appropriate term to describe Presley's dexterity at what might best be noted as a fascinating gift for *accommodation*. Elvis' image is what film aesthetician Louis Giannetti has defined as an "open form"[29]— allowing every viewer to read into it, and derive from it, whatever he or she chooses to see. Another observer draws a similar conclusion: "Elvis's image changed during the two decades his fans eyed him in the flesh — from flashy rocker to sleek soldier,"[30] from rock 'n' roll rebel to Jesus in a jumpsuit.

In actuality, though, did Elvis arc at all? Some thought not. In its openly condescending review of *Speedway* (1968), *The New York Times* insisted, "Music, youth and customs were much changed by Elvis Presley twelve years ago; from the twenty-six movies he has made since he sang 'Heartbreak Hotel,' you would never guess it!"[31] A more charitable consideration of that aspect might reach the conclusion that this hints at a deeper truth concerning his on-screen aura. We might find some social significance in noting that Elvis the pop icon, as embodied by Hollywood during an era of striking transition, remained essentially the same — other than the unavoidable aging process — while the world at large continued to shift around him. Thus understood, Elvis can be viewed (or in contemporary terms "received") as a touchstone — one of those rare permanent objects in a mass-media environment that alters since, by its nature, it can do nothing else.

Such a "reading" of Presley comes closer to the manner in which he perceived himself. Lest we forget, he insisted to a crowd of loyal Memphis fans on August 2, 1956, the eve of his entrance into the epicenter of our national consciousness, "I just want to tell y'all not to worry — them people in New York and Hollywood are not going to change me none."[32] Though it's widely assumed that immediately thereafter he began to compromise himself, possibly Elvis *was* true to his word: The Beverly Hills hotel suites and Vegas white-satin jumpsuits were what, in his heart, Elvis always coveted. Likewise, those grass roots fans! Embracing commerciality signified (to them as to him) not descent into corruption Eastern intellectuals are wont to read into the absorption of tacky luxury but completion of a white trash dream. The only difference between himself and any other dirt-poor Southerner who shared such fantasies was that Elvis was one of the rare few who got to live them out.

Like the cast of characters in the CBS-TV series *The Beverly Hillbillies* (which premiered shortly after Presley achieved full stardom, only to be cancelled at the same time he ceased making movies), Elvis dove headfirst into all the luxury items money could buy without turning his back on the po' boy values he carried within him. "Elvis' image as an intimate, as someone who shares their secrets and listens to their problems," it's been claimed, "not only drives the devotion of his fans but shapes their sense of self."[33] That's only partly true. The situation can be viewed from an opposing perspective: Elvis in movies sets off significant shifts in the real world, his rock-solid image like the chipped statue of some revered Confederate hero in an old town square which remains the same while nearby buildings are razed to make place for high-rises.

More specifically, he in his virtuoso solidity foil-like reveals the ways in which the ever-altering American scene surrounding his rock-like presence impacted on the moviegoing audience. For by and large, loyalists perceived Elvis as a romanticized — and, after his death, *mythologized*—vision of themselves, solid and certain in a world that revealed itself to be neither of those things. It seems fair to say that

> Ascribing to Elvis the honesty, decency, humility, generosity, respect, politeness and familial devotion that they ascribe to an idealized American working class, many fans see Elvis as one of them, as a "blue-collar guy in blue suede shoes."[34]

Most of those long-term fans were teenagers, happily screaming the very first time they saw Elvis gyrate. Many were, 15 years later, early-middle-aged parents, cringing in horror when their own offspring worshipped the likes of Mick Jagger and Jim Morrison as the pop-cultural compass came full cycle. Aging Elvis fans, like their hero, became in large numbers Nixon supporters.

As in Presley's case, this was less due to the notion that they had changed, than to the fact, that they remained much the same while a world they could no longer comprehend shifted gears. These fans may choose to see the situation as actor Charlton Heston does. When this scribe once asked the granite-jawed performer why he moved politically from liberal to conservative, he answered, "I didn't change; the world shifted around me." Values considered radical in 1955 (such as assimilation of minorities into the mainstream) appeared reactionary in 1970, as the emerging notion of multi-culturalism largely replaced the concept of integration. Now, many members of ethnic groups steadfastly defended their right to diversity instead of becoming part of the country's "consensus"—a concept now relegated to a bygone middle-of-the-road liberal past. In this light, the makers of Elvis' movies—again, perhaps unconsciously—rightly assumed the films would play to a specific if ever smaller audience. Such an approach allowed them (Parker and Presley ranking as collaborating *auteurs*) to build on key issues from one installment to the next. Viewed in this light, the films amass into an ongoing saga set to music.

Under a series of names and guises, Elvis—shifting from contemporary settings to one place or time period and then the next—portrays a continuing *persona*. This legendary character brings lessons learned (by him, and by the audience for which he serves as a surrogate) to the particular situation faced in each film. When Elvis began making movies, the Civil Rights Movement was relatively new, led by such non-violent spokesmen as Martin Luther King; when Elvis' career ended, that movement had hardened due to bitter disappointments. With Dr. King dead, black power rested in the hands of H. Rapp Brown, who held that violence was as American as apple pie. At the time of Elvis' screen debut, teenage mores had been frayed to the point that high schoolers stayed out until midnight, and co-ed colleges dared allow students to visit each other's dorms; as Elvis less than gracefully retired from the screen, high schoolers discovered "the pill" their elders had picked up on a decade earlier, while co-eds *shared* dorms and, in time, even rooms.

By then, a considerable number of 1955's young rebels, the first generation to rage against the machine and insist on freedom, had hardened into conservatives who complained that enough was too much. This was equally true of their most cherished youth-cult figure. Scrutinized by the F.B.I. in the mid–'50s as a potentially dangerous influence, and found guilty without trial of encouraging youth's delight in reckless abandon, Elvis Presley visited Richard Nixon at the White House—begging for a badge and, like James Bond, a license to kill to help eliminate "undesirable" elements.[35] All of which returns us to this book's stated approach. Far from the agreed-upon notion that a Presley film consists of nothing more than a single story, told over and over again with little modification other than variable settings, costumes and leading ladies, the films serve as an effective barometer of our ever-changing social, cultural and political landscape.

Viewed chronologically, they offer a vivid cinematic canvas that portrays America in the process of renewing and redefining itself in ways Elvis himself apparently was incapable of comprehending. His persona, thusly viewed, obliviously passes through a complex world in constant flux. Like the blithe spirits of Keats and Coward, Elvis solipsistically maintained a personal vision in order to isolate himself ever further from a world-at-large he felt increasingly disconnected from—even if he had set most of those changes into motion. Or, at least, solidified them as no one before him had managed to do. When perceived from this oblique angle, the films appear less so many isolated pieces of commercial hackwork than a vivid panorama — revealing in step-by-step order where we came from and, in sharp contrast, where we eventually found ourselves — as a people, as a country and as a culture.

None of this is meant to suggest that all critical attitudes about the films' quality should be reconsidered. The best — *Jailhouse Rock, King Creole, Viva Las Vegas*— are good indeed, at least when judged on the modest level of their ambitions. The vast majority — particularly *Kissin' Cousins* and *Tickle Me*— do rate as some of the worst films Hollywood has ever produced — at least from any standard criteria of judgment (that is, the Ebert-Roeper position that a film can neatly be pegged as a thumbs-up or -down). Still, aesthetic judgment has a way of changing with time. Who would have guessed, half a century ago, that Roger Corman's *Little Shop of Horrors* and Ed Wood's *Plan 9 from Outer Space* would eventually rank as revered works of their era, screened at lofty museums, while many Best Picture of the Year Oscar winners (*All the King's Men, The Greatest Show on Earth*) are long forgotten?

"Popular fiction, more than great art," Eisler notes, "gives us the texture of its time and place. The people are plastic, but the period — its values and style — lives."[36] The professor's comments, intended as a means of assessing literature, hold equally true for film. Today's ephemera become tomorrow's collectibles and, the day after that, valuable antiques. "The most important signs of the way a society lives," Warren I. Susman once observed, "are often the simplest, most ordinary artifacts of its culture."[37] That well describes the Elvis Presley films: Simple, to say the least; ordinary, at best. Their appeal on the drive-in circuit, shortly before that uniquely American form of moviegoing succumbed to sex and violence, makes clear that the Presley musicals were, in Susman's phraseology, ordinary and simple artifacts produced roughly between 1955 and 1970 — one of the most remarkable periods of the twentieth century.

No grandiose claims will be made, then; no implication that here is a myriad of overlooked masterpieces awaiting rediscovery. Nonetheless, there are alternate aesthetics to be considered other than what, at any point in time, is deemed to be "in good taste." Sociological film criticism has long insisted that the "best" (i.e., most valuable) films are the ones that reveal the most about the moment at which they were made. Considering their initial lowbrow appeal — speaking directly to H.L. Mencken's great American unwashed — these motion pictures offer an unfolding populist presentation of the country's soul and spirit at that time.

"Ours was the era," it has been noted, "that launched the first teen cult, rock and roll, complete with ... new young stars like ... Elvis."[38] That the central figure of 1950s youth revolution could, a mere 15 years later, appear a symbol of conservative mainstream values seems an aberrant situation. Nothing could be further from the truth. The paradox of Elvis Presley — damned by Nixon in '55, embraced by him in '70 — offers a variation on a continuing theme while signifying a recurring trend in our society. Lest we forget, John Dos Passos — *U.S.A.* author and firebrand radical of the Depression — supported arch-conservative Barry Goldwater for president in 1964.

There are those who may think it strange Elvis could be viewed as a reactionary in 1968. Only recall then that a significant number of 1968's own "revolutionaries" — rock balladeers Bob Dylan and Neil Young, presidential hopeful Eugene J. McCarthy, political satirist Mort Sahl, black separatist Eldridge Cleaver, film director Dennis Hopper and yippie leader Jerry Rubin, among others — all fervently supported Ronald Reagan's 1980 bid for the presidency. In their case, it took considerably less time for the reversal to occur than with Elvis. This suggests that Alvin Toffler's theory of "Future Shock" may be correct: Changes now occur so quickly that we barely have time to adjust to the new order before everything alters again.[39]

Today's radicals are tomorrow's reactionaries, less owing to any about-face on their part than because, by holding true to their original ideals, others who observe them undergo the illusion that they have changed. More correctly, the entire *zeitgeist* has shifted, causing us to perceive them from an altered line of vision. Nowhere is that so true, so obvious and so significantly revealed in our popular culture than in the films of Elvis Presley.

CHAPTER 1

Elvis Died for Your Sins

◆ *Love Me Tender* (1956) ◆

Love Me Tender had, in its initial form, never been conceived as a Presley vehicle per se — Elvis and his music were a happy afterthought. The working title for Robert Buckner's script was *The Reno Brothers*, changed during the production to emphasize that Elvis, recently signed to a Hollywood contract, would play a role and perform several musical numbers.[1] It's highly unlikely that yet another of the era's B Westerns would have become a box office sensation if released as conceived. *Love Me Tender* scored financially because, for the first time since Elvis's earliest national appearances on *The Stage Show*, young fans were able to *see* something that had been denied them in later performances on *Steve Allen* and *Ed Sullivan*. In an age when such theatrical films as *From Here to Eternity* (1953) and *Peyton Place* (1957) dared challenge all existing sexual boundaries while testing the limits of the Motion Picture Code,[2] Elvis seemed relatively tame — however horrifying his gyrations might be for the more conservative medium of television.

Ostensibly a genre piece, the film strikes many observers as an anomaly: interesting, certainly, though a far cry from the later "formula" for Presley musicals. In fact, like the star turns to follow, this film functions (if implicitly) on an autobiographical level. *Love Me Tender* also reflects the era when it was made, other than as a visual portrait of the then-current social scene owing to its period-piece orientation.

As one keen observer noted:

[T]he nation was ... undergoing dramatic social and economic changes. Perhaps nowhere was this better illustrated than in the shifts occurring in the distribution, composition, and size of its population. Americans were moving from farms and small towns into cities and suburbs ... getting married in larger numbers and at earlier ages than they had for decades, and having children at a record rate that defied all the predictions of experts. In short, the United States was experiencing a demographic revolution that would profoundly affect its history for decades to come.[3]

For the past century and a half, the social identity of the United States had perched precariously between large rural areas and growing urban centers. Now, however, pollsters estimated that a whopping 83 percent of the population had shifted to recently created *suburban* tracts.[4] Across much of the country, housing developments modeled after William J. Levitt's original experiment-in-living on Long Island sat sandwiched between newly built shopping centers. Thanks to FHA loans, returning veterans could, rather than renting living space, move their families into "standardized, low-cost housing" that would sacrifice "variety and style for affordability and function."[5]

While the birth of suburbia was greeted with applause by the burgeoning middle class, intellectuals — convinced that form follows function — claimed that people living in such suburban sprawls would quickly become "just as uniform, unimaginative, and boring as the houses."[6]

For better or worse, by 1955 an entirely new way of life had come into being. Such social (and, with it, cultural) conformity occurred almost everywhere *except,* for the time being, in the South. There (and, to a degree, the West), people resisted the tendency toward a national conformity owing to a headstrong nature — the *rebelliousness* for which the South had become famous (some would say *in*famous). This holdout mentality only increased middle class hostility toward a notably regional culture that the newly affluent (and, like the milk they bought, homogenized) citizens associated with poor Southern whites.

Little surprise, then, that many suburbanites derided country music as crude, preferring middle-of-the-road crooners like Perry Como. Initially, this new class of Americans felt certain that their kids — the second generation to inhabit a reinvented America and the first to be born there — would simply follow suit. Youth, though, invariably rebels against the status quo. Instead of accepting their lot, this new youth grew nostalgic for what they'd never known: The wild, free days of rich *regional* possibilities. This partly explains why young people became addicted to Westerns. "Western Movies," an early rock 'n' roll song, was an example of the new music commenting on youth's parallel enthusiasm for this particular (and particularly American) form of drama. Likewise, country-western music, when abetted by a modern big beat of the sort Bill Haley and his Texas-born Comets provided, at once became their preferred music — in comparison to the whitebread-mainstream perception of country-western as a quaintly primitive if slightly embarrassing regional sound.

Tellingly, then, in *Love Me Tender*, the Reno home (a poor-white farm) is located in *East* Texas — an area as Southern (perhaps more so) in its orientation as it is *Western*. In the opening sequence, a squad of Confederate cavalrymen, unaware that the Civil War is over, ambush and kill a group of Yankees. A trio of brothers (Richard Egan, James Drury and William Campbell) return to their humble home, where their mother (Mildred Dunnock) and younger brother Clint (Elvis) have for the past four years steadfastly farmed the land.[7] From that point on, the characters exist as much in the South as in the West — if, properly understood, an intriguingly *new* South, strongly informed by the *old* West. In this historical-geographical context, Elvis' sideburns proved as acceptable as they were controversial when glimpsed on TV (belonging to a contemporary pop singer). Everyone knew men of the previous century wore their hair long.

Love Me Tender thus glorified that area of the country which in the 1950s had come to represent "what the west once did: the self-sufficient, the inaccessible, the fiercely independent soul of the nation."[8] Some discouraged adults wondered how their kids, fans of Fess Parker's *Davy Crockett* only a year earlier, could turn away from such an acceptable role model to instead idolize Elvis. Actually, the situation represented not a conflict but a continuum. Parker had been a Texan playing a Tennessean; Tennessean Elvis portrayed a Texan here. In each, west and south collapsed into one another.

Though the popularity of Elvis is often cited as the key reason why suburban teenagers cultivated Southern-style sideburns and wore cowboy boots, he actually furthered a trend already in existence. The affluent L.A. boys in Nicholas Ray's *Rebel Without a Cause* (1955) sport just such a look, though the film was written and directed nearly a year before Presley's first national appearance. In *Love Me Tender*, Clint — more than the other Reno Brothers — signifies a distinctly *Southern* mentality. When the veterans arrive home, they spot their youngest brother as the audience enjoys its first big-screen glimpse of Elvis. The older brothers look like the Rebs in a typical post–Civil War Western for example, *Santa Fe* (1951) with Randolph Scott, featuring a nearly identical plot. But Elvis' appearance is not as the *cowboy* image he would in time embody, but that of an itinerant *farmer* in dirty overalls, pushing his plow behind an old mule. This correlates to Elvis' first "appearance" in life, his earliest memories those of a farmer's son in Tupelo.

Plot-wise, a romantic triangle develops. Vance is unaware that his fiancée Cathy (Debra Paget) has married Clint — the two had believed the rumors that the three brothers were killed in combat — so he sweeps Cathy up in his arms. Clint stands back, uncertain what to do. The difference between Vance and Clint is virtually the distinction that, in the '50s, existed between John Wayne, Charlton Heston or Burt Lancaster and James Dean, Montgomery Clift and the young Marlon Brando. However unconscious on the part of those who constructed this modest movie, *Love Me Tender* posits the two major variations of the American male during the twentieth century's second half. On the one hand, there remains the traditional male, rugged and ruthless in his pursuit of women; on the other, the newly arrived male role model, sensitive and wounded. The old-fashioned heroic movie star faced off against a postwar anti-heroic alternative.

After viewing *East of Eden* (1955), Pauline Kael wrote:

> There is a new image in American films, the young boy as beautiful, disturbed animal, so full of love he's defenseless. Maybe the father doesn't love him, but the camera does.... [W]e're thrust into upsetting angles, caught in infatuated close-ups, and prodded, "Look at all that beautiful desperation."[9]

In this context, we must note that the Reno father died during a Union raid. This qualifies Vance not only as Clint's older brother but also the head of the household and Clint's father figure. The violence that eventually erupts between Vance and Clint seems unduly melodramatic so long as we perceive the two as siblings. How much better to consider their duel — emotionally if not biologically — as an Oedipal conflict. As such, it plays off a theme introduced to the screen when father (and old-fashioned hero) Wayne and (adopted) anti-heroic son Clift battled it out over, among other things, Joanne Dru at the end of Howard Hawks' seminal Western *Red River* (1948).

Like that classic, *Love Me Tender* placed the then-emerging notion of "the generation gap" in a period-piece setting. In such a context, young Westerners could be re-imagined as 1950s-style juvenile delinquents, suffering in "the era of Momism."[10] James Dean's major problem in *Rebel* had been the dominating personality of his mother, the father reduced to a cipher. In *Love Me Tender*, Mildred Dunnock is listed in the credits only as "The Mother," though every other character (even minor ones) was assigned a name. This allows Dunnock to serve both as a universal symbol of American motherhood, 1950s style, as well as a substitute for Elvis' own beloved Mother Gladys.

The love demonstrated for Dunnock by *all* the brothers is intense, at times perversely strong. When, after the long absence, Vance steps down on home ground, his initial instinct is to hug his mother. Then — and *only* then — does he move on to beautiful Cathy, the girl he left behind. This is paralleled by Clint's feelings. When Elvis sings the title song, he's directed by Robert D. Webb to do so in an unexpected way. The family relaxes on their porch after the brothers' return. All encourage Clint to sing; to the tune of the folk ballad "Aura Lee," he performs the slightly modernized "Love Me Tender." Like Vance with his pecking order for homecoming hugs, Clint offers the song up not to Cathy (at least not initially), but to his *mother*. He sings of eternal love to Dunnock. As an afterthought, he turns to Cathy, at last half-heartedly dedicating a chorus to her.

This directly parallels the star's own situation. Elvis first recorded his voice when, on July 1, 1953, he paid three or four dollars to record several songs for his mother on 10-inch acetate for her birthday present. He did not know studio technician Marion Keisker had turned on a tape machine and made a note of his (Elvis') phone number and address, which she passed on to Sun Records' Sam Phillips.[11] As in the movie, Elvis' "mother was very possessive of him," a writer for *The Memphis Press-Scimitar* noted following Elvis' death;[12] Jay Cocks likewise claimed that Elvis was "fanatically and unabashedly devoted to his mother."[13] Such respect, even devotion, to a parental figure suggests that Elvis' early critics were misguided in perceiving him as a threat to American values that they hoped to retain and pass on to their own children, Elvis fans all:

> He was an odd mixture of a hood — the haircut, the clothes, the sullen, alienated look; and a sweet little boy — curiously gentle and respectful....[14]

Nor did Elvis present a sexual threat, despite the strong sensuality of his movements. This is reflected in *Love Me Tender* when Cathy becomes uncomfortable in her relationship to the boyish, almost saint-like Clint. She longs for a *real* man who knows how to hold her and, in bed, satisfy her — rather than treat her as a mother figure, desiring only to be cradled in her arms. For all we know, the Clint-Cathy marriage may not have been consummated. This predates and parallels the situation that developed a few years later between Elvis and Priscilla when, before their marriage, she moved into his home, where they cuddled sensuously but did not engage in the sexual act. Or after marriage and the birth of their daughter when Elvis proved himself unable to accept Priscilla as a total woman — lover, friend, mother (to their child), wife (for himself) — and destroyed the relationship.[15] From the moment Lisa Marie was born, Elvis perceived his spouse in a narrow sense — solely as *mother* to his child.

He projected emotions associated with his own deceased Gladys onto Priscilla; he could continue cuddling with her, as he had Gladys, even if he found the concept of sexual penetration as odious as if Priscilla had *been* Gladys. To Elvis, *a* mother (*any* mother) was an incarnation of the very *idea* of "mother" — for him, if only on some unarticulated level, *his* mother. In frustration, Priscilla became involved with her traditional masculine karate instructor — a "Vance" type. All of this is rendered more fascinating still if we consider the striking physical resemblance of Paget to Priscilla. The adoration of his own mother, and mother figures in general, had somehow become associated in Elvis' sensibility with Mary, mother of Christ. More religious than rebellious, young Elvis — when his first royalty check arrived — at once purchased a picture of Jesus, which he presented to his mother — who then dutifully hung it in her bedroom, where she and Elvis continued to curl up together and warmly cuddle.

At the time of *Love Me Tender's* release, Elvis was quoted as saying that he "would have been a preacher" if he hadn't gone into show business.[16] However much the star's unique style of performance was initially perceived — angrily by adults, giddily by teenagers — as a means of affronting Establishment pillars (home, family, church), there is no suggestion (in life, in his music, or in this or any other film) that his "gyrations" were intended as such. Neither did he hope to foster juvenile delinquency, though he was widely accused of promoting such activity. No sooner had Elvis achieved fame and fortune than, upon returning to Memphis, he financed a school and youth center to help *remove* the causes of teenage crime — with, of course, the ever-adoring Gladys' blessing.

Likewise, when Clint sings publicly, giddily dancing (Elvis and Clint all but indistinguishable), he does so to raise money for the new schoolhouse. Half-completed, this bastion of conventional virtue stands down the street from another iconic place — the archetypical whitewashed small-town church. Clint performs for a crowd that has attended service at the latter and is raising money to complete the former. His screen mother gazes on, Gladys-like, equally proud of her boy's motivation and talent. The pelvic movements are intended only as his humble contribution to the community. This is precisely how they are accepted by the other characters in *Love Me Tender*. Elvis' early TV performances appeared horrific to mainstream American because his manner had been removed from its true and proper Southern context.

As made clear by this film's setting, Presley's performance was a *regional* style — *not* that of the entire Southland, only the remote portions of Dixie (the two-room, "Shotgun" ramshackle homes of poor whites from Tupelo, Mississippi, to Memphis, Tennessee). Their gospel style — less country-western in the neo-commercial roadhouse sense than authentic hardcore hillbilly — had suddenly (and, for the first time, visually if not aurally as with earlier radio broadcasts) been seen by the entire nation. "The offense" existed "in the eye of the beholder, not in Elvis's intentions."[17] His gyrations were rooted "in roistering responses of some fundamentalist congregations"[18] — offensive to the mainstream because it differed from the recently emerged, "polite" suburbanite norm for religious expression.

In addition to expressing early Elvis, *Love Me Tender* also offers a glimpse of the later Presley, who in time would become fascinated with weapons in general, guns in particular.[19] Clint, initially taken by the sword that Vance brought home, dances around the humble kitchen while waving it in the air. Here, we experience an echo of a similar scene from a more ambitious post–Civil War Western released earlier that same year, John Ford's *The Searchers:*

Ethan Edwards (John Wayne) returns to his own Texas home (likewise carrying Yankee money, obtained by dubious means) and gives an all but identical saber to a young family member, also an unofficially adopted son. Later in *Love Me Tender*, Clint grabs a gun and almost kills his older brother-foster father, regretting the act a moment later. In actuality, no sooner had Elvis become a full-fledged Vegas performer than he grabbed a gun and fired into a television set on which Robert Goulet — unofficial father-figure to all lounge acts — was appearing.[20]

At movie's end, Clint strikes out blindly at a world that has unwittingly wounded him. In due time, Elvis would record "That's When Your Heartbreak Begins," one of his best-loved ballads, which describes such romantic melancholia, updated for the twentieth century and given a regional twang. How fortuitous, in this light, that Elvis' breakthrough record on the national scene had been *Heartbreak Hotel*. In truth, "The whole amazing story of Elvis is *about* heartbreak," Jack Kroll noted, for this was "the man whose great contribution was *feeling*,"[21] (emphasis added). This truth about Elvis and his music fuels *Love Me Tender*'s narrative; Clint's intense *feelings* justify the near-operatic histrionics more than the conventional plot mechanics. The drama focuses on an attempt by family members to avoid Clint's eventual heartbreak, even as it becomes (in large part *because* of their collective best efforts) all but inexorable.

The film is as much about society as self. The War between the States remains (Vietnam not withstanding) the most bitter military action in American history, if only because all casualties were American. The botched reconstruction policy following Lincoln's death led to a lingering sour tone. Sour is also the term most often employed to describe the aftermath of the Korean Conflict. This combat began on Sunday, June 25, 1950, when North Korea unexpectedly invaded South Korea along the 38th Parallel. Included in the arsenal were 150 Russian tanks, leaving President Truman to assume this was not a local issue but the first serious Cold War "testing" of the free world by a growing Communist block. The public wasn't sure they were willing to have their sons risk life and limb in a "limited" conflict referred to as a "police action." When our forces withdrew in 1953, the loss of American lives totaled 33,629. TV's daily depictions of the un-winnable war ushered in the first wave of a new sort of widespread cynicism. Precisely such a social sensibility is at the heart of *Love Me Tender*. With its divisiveness of Americans, the Civil War here effectively serves as an objective correlative for the national nightmare of Korea.

Likewise, the issue of corrupt capitalism — or the potential for capitalism to corrupt, a theme that would dominate Presley films — is essential here. In the opening sequence, Radwell's Rangers — a cavalry outfit modeled after John Singleton Mosby's outfit — attack a Greenwood, Louisiana, railroad station. They kill numerous Yankees stationed there and seize $12,250 in federal funds, which Vance plans to turn over to their commanding officer. Even before the Rangers learn of the armistice, a sense of greed pervades their thinking. It isn't the resident bully, Mike Gavin (Neville Brand), who first voices such opinions. Vance intones, if with sardonic humor, "What a pity it don't belong to *us*." Those words will haunt him when they learn from stragglers that Lee turned over his sword to Grant at Appomattox Court House several days earlier.

From that moment, greed is the key motivating factor. "The surrender changes *everything*," Vance muses. "We've got to talk this over." What we witness is not a character who expressed only patriotic attitudes toward the money so long as he believed the war winnable. Vance eyed the money all along; the look in his eyes upon learning of the South's defeat is less disappointment than fascination with the chance to live out a dream — a corrupt (and corrupting) version of the American dream. He can seize the cash (or at least his "fair share") without incurring disgrace, or so he convinces himself. Despite the period trappings he relies on the *modern* notion of situation ethics, and strikes a difficult moral balance between democratic capitalism and socialistic considerations. The men, a community for four years, divide the money equally; their leader gets no more than any of the others.

At that point, the group — formerly fighting for the greater good, without personal consideration, dissolves. Each man, all at once a rugged individualist, goes his separate way with $1,750. "Instead of going back empty-handed," Vance muses, "I've got this *money!*" Just such a dramatized discourse on whether capitalism corrupts or frees those who succeed within such a system will reappear in virtually every Presley vehicle.

Elvis — at least *early* Elvis — is often interpreted as a revolutionary, perhaps even Marxist hero. In large part, this is because in life — and more often than not on-screen — he projected an image of the American proletariat, Southern style: "the lower or working class people," according to Linda Ray Pratt, "who saw in Elvis some glamorized image of their own values."[22] Still, Elvis (at least after he had fallen under the Svengali-like influence of manager Col. Tom Parker), rated as the complete capitalist, eager to abandon rockabilly and be a pop balladeer. But perception is reality, and the initial perception of Presley — enhanced and forwarded by the crude polemics in *Love Me Tender*— appealed to a Marxist mentality despite what we now know was the highly commercial shape of things to come.

Shortly after this film's release, an American journalist returning from Russia noted that "the singer is the latest craze of the Soviet zoot-suters, of *stilyagi*."[23] Once the "corruption" (or *perceived* corruption) of Elvis began, *Harper's* reported that "from a strictly Marxist-Leninist viewpoint, you probably realize that he is a typical example of capitalist exploitation."[24] Likewise, many middle Americans who initially feared and loathed Elvis saw the supposed threat as part and parcel with the era's Red Scare, a singin'-dancin' allegory of Soviet subversion. One letter from the Diocese of La Crosse, Wisconsin, mailed directly to F.B.I. director J. Edgar Hoover, insisted that this young man represented "a definite danger to the security of the United States."[25]

It's necessary to note, then, that *Love Me Tender* veers from the formula for a genre Western into less traveled cinematic terrain. Ordinarily (as, say, in the aforementioned *Santa Fe*) the former Confederates refuse to give up the money and are relentlessly pursued by Yankee lawmen. Such a scenario posits that the money represents the very heart of the matter. Precisely the opposite happens here. Though Vance initially is tempted by the Mephistophelean money, he in time changes his tune. At the aforementioned open-air party, even as residents celebrate in an anachronistically rock 'n' roll–influenced variation on John Ford's communal celebration of simple American values from such upscale Westerns as *My Darling Clementine* (1946), famed frontier lawman Charles Siringo (Robert Middleton) arrives.

The living legend makes clear he knows that the Reno Brothers have hidden the government money. Vance and his brothers deny it. Clint angrily defends his family, insisting that Vance's words are true. Actor Richard Egan's eyes make clear he has unwittingly corrupted his innocent younger brother (and virtual son). "So you *did* rob the payroll," Clint literally cries upon realizing that Vance lied — the first onscreen expression of Elvis' essential heartbreak. "Why didn't you just tell the *truth*?" He signifies the '50s' younger generation, stunned to realize the hypocrisy of supposed grown-ups.

Clint's outburst, as well as the realization that Siringo will drop all charges if the money is returned, causes Vance and his brothers to reverse their initial position. From that point on, *Love Me Tender* concerns their attempts to give the money back rather than, as in generic Westerns, keep it. Fascinatingly, they remain blocked at every turn: by former squad members, corrupted by the cash and hoping to hold onto their shares; and by federal troops who, unlike Siringo, do not trust Vance and plan to shoot him on sight. There is a sense of relief when the money, after many mishaps, *has* been returned. Vance remains haunted, though, by the realization that this — even more than his thwarted love for Cathy — triggers Clint's death. Spurred on by innate jealousy and vicious gossip, Clint wounds Vance, then is himself shot by a former Reb.

How much better things seemed when, at the fund-raising party, everyone gave what little they had to benefit all. Such an ideology appealed to young moviegoers, offended by their parents' submission to the self-serving orientation of the 1950s sensibility. The film's conclusion conveys a fatalistic sense associated with Greek tragedy. There, unspoken sins within the family unit are essential to a bittersweet final act which combines the sacrifice of an innocent with a revitalization of all surviving family members and, on a grander scale, society. Dying, Clint is cradled by both Vance and Cathy; they appear, despite their own relative youth, to be his parents.

This is precisely what moviegoers perceived at the end of *Rebel*— including youthful Elvis Presley. There, James Dean and Natalie Wood, little more than children, become parental figures to Sal Mineo as he, under similar (if contemporary) circumstances, died. In *Love Me Tender*, the emotions are even more complex since the "son," through circumstances beyond his control, apparently slept Oedipus-like with his virtual mother. Vance and Cathy assure Clint (though they know he's about to expire) everything will be all right. Understanding the moment's full implications, Clint changes the cadence of that phrase as he repeats it — realizing Vance and Cathy were meant to be together, even managing a warm smile before "passing over."

Clint smiles again after performing a final chorus of the title song, via a ghost-like rendering of his image. This is superimposed over a shot of the family, mourning Clint at his burial. "A dead but evanescent Elvis," Greil Marcus noted about the mental image fans have retained since the King's passing.[26] However unawares, the faithful borrow that vision from the conclusion of Elvis' first film; in a quasi-religious way, the ending was thus present from the beginning. In an ambitious shot, the camera closes in on Clint's face while pulling back from a panorama of the family farm. This creates the sensation that Clint — now, apparently, in the company of God — closely and forgivingly observes the action below, as members of the Reno family make their way up the hill to the house.

It was not one of those new suburban tract homes to which so many young moviegoers returned after the movie ended, but the *traditional* home of the *rural* American family. Such a house might have been found more or less anywhere in America previous to the postwar era, if now linked to the South and the West. The mother suffers the greatest loss, yet even she seems able to accept Clint's death as a part of God's will ("little do we mere mortals know...")— something that *had* to happen if a semblance of order was to replace the chaos visited upon this cursed family unit since the return of the prodigal brother(s). The tableau conveys our first on-screen hint of the star's eventual spiritual significance.

Twenty years later, reporting on the growing fascination with Elvis after his death, the BBC's religious affairs correspondent noted that this seemed "nothing less than a religion in embryo."[27] Writing in *The New York Times*, Ron Rosenbaum added that the behavior of loyal followers of Elvis "transcended the familiar contours of a dead celebrity cult and has begun to assume the dimensions of a redemptive faith."[28] That eventual occurrence, in the aftermath of Elvis' life, had been predicted in the first film's ending. Sorrowful, Vance and Cathy move closer together, clearly under the spiritual guidance of Clint. The metaphysical incarnation of the youth smiles down on them, accepting that through his death as sacrificial innocent, others (the world, or at least their rustic demimonde, serving as a humble microcosm) can continue, rebuild and, in time, mend.

So long, at least, as they maintain their faith and continue to seek redemption. Even at the inception of his film career, the ultimate truth was in evidence: Elvis died for our sins.

CHAPTER 2

Alive and Well in TV Land

♦ *Loving You* (1957) ♦

What most strikingly separated Elvis from earlier pop music stars of the twentieth century — beginning with Al Jolson, running through Rudy Vallee, Bing Crosby, Frank Sinatra and even Johnny Ray, who predated some of Elvis' melodramatic movements — is that an attractive, gifted singer alienated adults as intensely as he appealed to young people. This phenomenon had no precedence: "For the first time, idols our own age embodied cool, glamour, sex; more radical still, they showed us that rebellion and defiance were rewarded with fame and glory."[1] Presley did not, as Maureen Orth (among others) has asserted, "create the Generation Gap."[2] What he *did* do was crystallize that already existing great divide during the watershed cultural juncture that was 1955-56.

Or, to view the star from a social perspective:

> This was the new, wealthier America. Elvis Presley began to make it in 1955, after ten years of rare broad-based middle-class prosperity. Among the principal beneficiaries of that prosperity were the teenagers.... [A]s the new middle class emerged [it created] as a byproduct a brand new consumer class: the young.[3]

Scholastic magazine estimated that during the mid–'50s, there were 13,000,000 American teenagers. They possessed a solid income (hefty allowances for the well-to-do, paper route earnings or jobs as soda jerks for the less affluent) of $7,000,000,000 annually.[4] "As they had money, they were a market, and as they were a market they were listened to and catered to; Elvis was the first beneficiary"[5] of what Madison Avenue perceived as America's original Youth Culture.

By 1958, in a virtual revolution in the merchandising of entertainment products, more than 70 percent of all records purchased in the U.S. were bought by people under 20.[6] Here then was a "unique postwar phenomenon," since the emergent American teenager "had no counterpart anywhere in the 'Free World.'"[7] These savvy kids quickly realized that television, already the favorite medium of their suburbanite parents, had little to offer them. The initial Presley appearance on *Stage Show* (January 28, 1956) did reveal their beloved performer in all his pelvis-swinging glory. By the time the overnight star who replaced the late James Dean as their favorite anti-hero was allowed to perform on *Milton Berle* (March 28, 1956), *Steve Allen* (July 1, 1956) and finally *Ed Sullivan* (September 9, 1956), producers — eager to draw in teenage viewers while concerned about angering their parents — watered down the impact. On Sullivan's show, the camera showed Elvis from the waist up. Angered by the compromise — something they had come to associate with the older generation — Elvis' legion of fans sought out ways to see him uncensored. *Love Me Tender*, despite its genre trappings, featured the *entire* Elvis performance.

Meanwhile, the youth-exploitation film was being invented. Such quickly shot low-budget items as Roger Corman's *Rock All Night* showcasing Elvis wannabes played at *declasse* downtown theaters or rural drive-ins. Such films appealed to kids with hot wheels and money to spend. Col. Parker nixed any inclusion by "his boy" in such nominal quickie flicks. Yet Parker warmed to the idea of such a film if produced on a bigger budget, featuring Elvis as a variation on himself and appearing as the sole (male) musical performer. The result was the first wave of Presley musicals (1957–59), beginning with *Loving You*— which, among other seminal elements, directly addressed the TV medium and its unique relationship to rock 'n' roll.

In the opening, we are (despite the contemporary setting) promptly returned to that part of the country where *Love Me Tender* took place: East Texas, as Southern as it is Western in attitude and orientation. This location takes on symbolic as well as geographic meaning: "With the taming of the West completed, only the deep South retains a comparable aura of mystery, of romantic removal from the concerns of a steadily urbanized and cosmopolized America."[8] The opening occurs in a remote hamlet where rhinestone-bedecked drugstore cowboys earn a few bucks singing for a paltry crowd. Their leader, Walter Warner (Wendell Corey), resembles Hank Williams (Sr.) minus the genius. As a performer, Walter failed to find his own unique "sound," becoming an imitator of others. Walter bills himself as "Tex"— a *faux* cowboy, half-heartedly playing the country role. Shortly, he will encounter the real thing.

His partner, press agent, former wife and current mistress, Glenda Markle (Lizabeth Scott), makes this clear when Deke Rivers (Elvis) offers an inspired amateur performance, then hurries away. "Hold on, *cowboy!*" she calls after him. Though there is nothing overtly cowboyish in Deke's outfit, the phrase fits him perfectly. For here is an itinerant Southern boy, always on the move, whose car has replaced the earlier horse. Deke is the twentieth-century equivalent of the cowboy hero (in popular mythology, movies included) of an earlier era. This may seem unlikely as, in some respects, Elvis represented the era's Beat Generation, translated from hipster poetry to popular music.

Social historians have defined "a tradition of new American rebel that would include James Dean and Jack Kerouac"[9] as well as Brando and Elvis. Nonetheless, a member of that subterranean subculture who hung out with Kerouac might have been speaking of Elvis: "In 1957, in the excitement and hope of that moment, in what was real and strongly believed and truly lived out — there seemed the possibilities of enormous transformations."[10] Scruffy anti-heroes from *On the Road* (1958) on initial glance appear to have little in common with beloved singin' B-movie cowboys heroes. In fact, they are all but identical.

In the novel hailed as the Bible of the Beat Generation, Kerouac described his uneducated friend and personal idol, Neal Cassady (fictionalized as "Dean Moriarty") as a "young *Gene Autry*—trim, thin-hipped, blue-eyed with a real Oklahoma accent — a sideburned hero of the snowy *west* [emphasis mine]."[11] The 1950s hipster did not offer the polar opposite of America's previous cowboy hero; he revitalized the same substance via a nouveau style. Properly understood, the beatnik was the singing cowboy re-imagined for an altered American scene — likewise carrying a guitar, if now an electric one. "Here's that rock 'n' roll cowboy," an announcer gleefully shouts while introducing Deke. That he is a modernized redux of Autry and Roy Rogers is made clear when Deke performs "Lonesome Cowboy." The term here has less to do with the specific nature of a cowboy's work than a state of mind which Presley will, in due time, totally embody.

Important too is what one critic — writing about the decade's other key sex symbol, Marilyn Monroe — has called her "appalling innocence."[12] Elvis has been recognized in retrospect as "the male Monroe"[13] — serving the same function for female viewers that Marilyn did for male. The concept of an "appalling" innocence equally applies to Elvis — particularly the desire he elicited from women to protect him from a harsh world. Deke is a radical innocent, utterly untutored as to the raw capitalism (a key recurring theme) that will shortly overwhelm him. "He'll *pay* me for that?" Deke gasps when Glenda asserts that Walter will shell out money for Deke to do what comes naturally.

In the past, Deke took blue-collar day jobs to support his music. Walter's equally "appalling" corruption is evidenced when commercial success causes Walter to separate himself from the Western element. "No more '*Tex*,'" he announces after their first financially successful concert, slipping out of his phony cowboy duds. At that very moment, though, Walter wants to push Deke *into* just such a costume: not real cowboy clothing, which Deke would relish, but the false facsimile even then being marketed to naïve suburban kids hooked on TV Westerns. Embodying the authentic cowboy spirit, Deke refuses to play the part. "I will *not* wear that Hopalong Cassidy shirt," he insists.

Walter, meanwhile, eagerly steps into a business suit. Walter's failure as a manager derives from his inability to grasp that the country sound (and sensibility) is on the verge of catching on with the emerging youth audience. The great paradox is that Walter wants to escape country music marginalization and stand at the heart of what he considers to be mainstream American popular music — even then fading in popularity. This becomes clear when Susan (Dolores Hart) attempts to entertain a youthful crowd with her rendering of the recently popular "Detour" by Patti Page. The kids cannot relate, though Susan's voice is lovely. Then Deke performs and the teenagers go wild. What he offers is not merely regional rockabilly but early rock 'n' roll.

The theme of raw capitalism is further developed, as money — and *only* money — motivates Walter and Glenda. This is clear from one of the stylish, cynical woman's first lines: "I haven't had a *check* in three weeks." Walter believes that by commercializing the area's indigenous culture, he can achieve financial success. "Folk music is big, and getting bigger," he smugly asserts. "All you need is the right *gimmick*." That, of course, will be the hard-edged rhythm which Elvis' character instinctually adds to the existent country-western sound. In truth, it is no mere gimmick but the true, pure, original "voice" that Walter, in his early artistically ambitious years, failed to find. Still, Walter's casual line links Elvis-Deke's emergent musical form with an older tradition. Folk artist Bob Dylan lauded rocker Elvis, however commercialized and corrupted that performer might have appeared by the mid-'60s.

This can be traced back to *Loving You*. In 1957, Dylan was still Robert Zimmerman, high school student. Elvis was then honing his image in the mold of his own heroes. Surprisingly, they included not only folk or country artists like Williams but also Frank Sinatra and Dean Martin — "old guard" performers who, misunderstanding Presley, nastily dismissed him. One possible reading of *Loving You* presumes that Presley is represented on-screen not solely by Deke but also by Walter-Tex. In this light, the film confronts us with a moral dialectic between Elvis's antithetic instincts. The two characters represent the polar sides of his personality — the raw rockabilly "real thing" and the glitzy neon Vegas sellout.

This inner conflict would in time lead to highly destructive self-loathing, causing Presley's entire life to become a "Faustian scenario of sell-out and corruption."[14] Yet the vast audience for the film — including upscale suburban kids — mostly ignored this aspect. Teens preferred to emotionally interpret Elvis as the latest incarnation of '50s anti-heroes they had discovered in *The Wild One* and *Rebel Without a Cause*:

> the first of the new rebels from the world of entertainment and art. Soon to come were many others. If there was a common thread, it was that they all projected the image of being misunderstood, more often than not by their parents' generation....[15]

That element dominates in *Loving You*, as Walter and Glenda become adoptive parents — only to corrupt Deke for their own financial benefit. Hungering for parental love (we later learn he has been an orphan since childhood), Deke will be tempted and tested in a modernized morality play until he, like other youth heroes, finally explodes, rebelling against the adult Establishment. Elvis' own false father was of course Parker, who manipulated the star (not that Presley resisted much) into leaving the purity of Sun Records to become one more crooner for RCA. In an autobiographical interpretation, Walter stands in for Parker.

Always, though, Elvis' on-screen expression of self is balanced by a depiction of his relationship to the surrounding society. Suggested, however tentatively, is a civil rights theme. In the opening sequence, friendly looks pass between Deke and a young black worker. Momentarily, it appears as though Elvis might be gazing into a mirror; in this town of hucksters, fools and loafers, the only other diligent working man is Deke's non-biological brother, in every sense of that term. Though white, Deke (like other early Elvis characters) feels at odds with the world around him — precisely how one of the rare blacks in such a setting would perceive himself. This is forwarded when Deke first performs. The gathered adults fail to respond (they don't "get it") but the young people do. *White* young people, seen together in a collective long shot. Also included is a close-up of a small black child, at one with Elvis' music. Deke "turns on" Anglo teens with something totally new to them; he speaks to the African-American child in an alternative artistic language the two implicitly share.

Simultaneously, Norman Mailer penned an influential (in Beat circles) "underground" pamphlet, "The White Negro." Mailer described the era's hipster — alienated from suburban whitebread society yet at one with the African American soul.[16] Though Mailer referred to "serious" jazz musicians (Bix Beiderbecke) and rebel writers (Kerouac, Allen Ginsberg), no single white artist of the time (though rock 'n' roll was decidedly *not* yet perceived as art, even in avant garde enclaves) more perfectly embodied Mailer's concept than Elvis. Though the theme is taken no further here, it shortly would be — in *King Creole*.

Meanwhile, the hopeful minor talent Susan realizes she's in the presence of a major artist. At once, Susan sets her career aside to offer Deke the virginal girl-next-door variety of woman. In so doing, Susan sets in place another element that will be found, with numerous variations, in films to follow. Though a key sociological critic was writing about James Dean in *East of Eden* and *Rebel*, but might as well have been referring to Elvis' persona when he noted, "Sullen and sulky, he was still worthy of redemption if only the properly tender girlfriend could be found to mother him."[17] Mothering, of course, is what Elvis had desired from Debra Paget, the slightly older (and sole) leading lady in *Love Me Tender*. From this point on, Paget's archetype would be broken down into two distinct and separate entities: early Elvis Cinema's dichotomization between an experienced older woman and the young virgin, the two competing for the right to mother this James Dean–like, vulnerable man-child.

In *Loving You*, standing between Susan and Deke and their healthy-happy coupling is Glenda, a southwestern Jocasta in embryo. The ensuing triangle, despite its quasi-realistic grounding, conveys a curious fairy-tale quality: the beautiful ice queen competing with innocent Snow White for a countrified, working-class Prince Charming. While Glenda happens to be attractive, age-wise she could be Deke's mother. Here, then, is the ongoing Oedipal theme, suggested in *Love Me Tender,* the mythic element now more openly asserted. Glenda likes to have Deke call her "Mama," even as they flirt; Elvis called Gladys that while sweetly cuddling her in bed.[18] The Oedipal element is re-asserted by Walter: "You're the kind of boy any man would be proud to have as a *son.*"

Self and Society are not necessarily kept separate. Shortly, the (personal) Oedipal and (public) capitalist themes will conjoin. In addition to the sexual allure Glenda employs to keep Deke from leaving, she offers hard, cold cash (which could be used to soup up Deke's hot rod, in need of work) to seduce him into joining the combo: "Costs *money!*" The film's initial conflict, then, is between Deke, a pure singer who humbly accepts money for doing what he loves, and the adult couple, corrupt parental types for whom money is not a means to achieve valuable things but an end in itself. They hope to live off of—and in the process destroy—their "son." Walter sounds like the worst sort of father when he mutters, "I think the kid's gonna *make* it" and "put *me* back in the *money.*" Whenever Deke is disgusted by the corruption, the hard-nosed businesswoman turns coy, charming him into staying.

Susan remains sidelined, unable to compete with such a sexual power-house. She can only hope (and, one assumes, pray) that Deke will see through Glenda's smothering "love" and in time return for her softer solace. It's not for nothing, then, that when Deke sings "Mean Woman Blues," he's thinking of Glenda. Essentially, Deke, like Elvis, is an arrested adolescent—an overgrown little boy, perhaps even a male virgin — who, in an incredible irony, emerges as a potent sex symbol. Certainly, star and character become interchangeable when Deke wins a Teddy bear for Susan at a carnival; later, Deke sings Elvis' song "Teddy Bear" to her, making clear that what he most wants (from her or any woman) is to be cuddled — not as a prelude to sex but for its own sake. "Elvis is more about romance, intimacy, and friendship," one observer stated, "than about passive participation in some masculine wet dream."[19] Though sexy, he is not truly sexual.

One band member — referring to their mascot (a bird) following a disastrous concert — tells Deke, "Matilda did something you've never done — laid an egg." That line can be taken two ways: He never bombed before in a show; he's never consummated a relationship with a woman. Deke's physical "innocence" becomes clear after he turns on young women during a concert. On stage, he is "the master of the sexual simile, treating his guitar as both phallus and female, punctuating his lyrics with the animal grunts and groans of the male approaching an orgasm."[20] But *only* on stage. His act is just that, an *act*. One girl, Daisy, corners Deke backstage. When he pulls away, Daisy realizes he's all braggadocio. "You are *afraid*!" she laughs, amazed. Perceptive if cruel, Daisy adds: "You don't *sing* scared, but you *are*. You're a *phony*!" Deke's eyes make painfully clear she's hit the bull's-eye.

Sociologists have written of an "age-old sexual injustice, the male burden of performance, with all its attendant ego risk."[21] Eustace Chesser, the 1950s' most perceptive analyst of that era's un-liberated male-female relations, insisted the man was expected to "educate" his woman one step at a time in the "art of joyous mating"; he had better perform that task well, Chesser continued, owing to a "strange intuition of woman" which "warns her against the nervous lover."[22] Elvis-Deke is just such a male. No sooner are Daisy's words out than Deke grabs the girl and kisses her — as if to prove she's wrong, tacitly making clear how right she was. Image, apparently, is everything — to Deke in the film as it was to Elvis.

Before his marriage to Priscilla, then again after their split, Elvis hosted lavish parties in which members of his Memphis Mafia had sex with whichever women Elvis didn't want. The King always took the most beautiful female present into his bedroom and, after casting a knowing wink to the others while closing the door, promptly went to sleep — before anything sexual could occur.[23] In *Loving You*, Deke seems incredibly relieved when journalists interrupt the tryst. He pretends to be disappointed that the illicit lovemaking can't continue. As to that cinematic moment's relevance to real life, we ought to recall that in 1972, Elvis admitted: "The image is one thing and the human being another." In time, he sadly stated that he'd always found it "very hard to live up to an image."[24]

In the film, Deke gets a charge out of the newspaper photograph that publicly presents him kissing Daisy as the only part of the "interlude" that could, in the name of decency, be shown — when in fact it was all that occurred. Deke prefers a pastoral interlude in which the Presley persona returns to his roots, accompanying Susan home only after she mentions that she hails from the country. "*Farm*, huh?" he muses. The line references both Presley's own origins and those of his only previous screen appearance, creating a character continuum. Deke at once reverses his decision to stay with the band and volunteers to drive Cathy home, meeting her parents. When Elvis performs the title number, it is not exclusively or even primarily to Susan but to her entire *family*. Everyone — grandparents, small children, even farm animals — crowd around — a decent (and natural) community, far from the madding crowd, gathered in God's good land.

In light of the earlier comparison to Autry and Rogers, Presley, properly understood, was more conservative in implication than critics of the time (who saw him as a menace to American society) grasped. He does despise the homogenized, suburbanized postwar lifestyle. What he embodies — and what his teenage fans, listening on the radio or watching this movie — responded to, qualified him (and them) more as reactionaries than radicals. Here, Elvis offers, if in a ridiculously romanticized form, a return to the basics, the good old days of the family farm when people put down roots, supporting (and loving!) one another. Watching Elvis, '50s teens made clear that, like Thomas Wolfe's embittered heroes, they wanted to go home again — if to a home they'd never experienced firsthand, to an American mythic realm.

In an entirely other context, Richard Schickel addressed this social-cultural phenomenon of the mid–twentieth century: "a popular nostalgia" for "an imagined past" which "informed much of the new popular culture."[25] No wonder the song "Loving You" plays in context more as spiritual than sensual. Or that the following exchange of dialogue occurs:

SUSAN: I never heard you sing like that before.
DEKE: I never *felt* like that before.

What Deke most wants, as he dimly realizes, is not fame or fortune (though one side of Deke-Elvis does pursue that) but old-fashioned family values. This desire to remain pure — or later (after the fall) to be born again, re-achieve purity — was crystallized early on when Walter and Glenda considered changing Deke's name to something trendy like "Tab" or "Rock." Angrily, he replied: "What's wrong with 'Deke Rivers'? It's *my* name." Such a country name connects the bearer to a way of life, a sensibility that Deke (like Elvis) hopes to remain true to, even while paradoxically pursuing the bitch goddess of success.

A refreshing complexity derives from the fact that Deke Rivers *isn't* his real name! In a moment of self-revelation, we learn he took it from the grave of a man he never met and who died in 1934. "I don't know any more about him than I do me," the man born "Jimmy Tompkins" admits. Jimmy assumed that name and set out to recreate himself when he ran away from an orphanage, then happened upon Woodbine Cemetery. He's a B-movie version of "Jimmy Gatz," at once profoundly proud and yet deeply ashamed of his simple origins, turning himself into the great "Gatsby" in F. Scott Fitzgerald's best loved novel — if here an American Dreamer who lives closer to the Pecos River than Long Island Sound. When Walter and Glenda attempted to force a false identity on him, Deke's resistance was a performance. Long ago, he traded one identity for another — the concept of image once again an all-important theme.

Numerous bits are basic to the ongoing creation of the star's screen iconography. At one point, Deke plays so heatedly before an audience that he breaks a guitar string, which sets the kids to howling with delight. An endless parade of rock 'n' rollers to follow would borrow (steal?) that gesture. In a bar, Elvis performs an impromptu number for gathered teens, then fights an obnoxiously jealous guy. This is the first of many such bouts that quickly became a staple. He receives a Cadillac, a car that would be important to Elvis in real life — symbolizing for the blue-collar working class he hailed from the ultimate in "making it big time."

Most telling is the manner in which television becomes, in *Loving You*'s final third, the focus. One aspect of modern media, the motion picture, provides a commentary on what in the mid–'50s had become its chief competitor. In the film as in life, a regional phenomenon is about to go national via a network broadcast. Quickly, a protest develops. The key to understanding the vitriolic reaction from parents to early televised Elvis (or, in the film, Deke) had less to do with the man, the music or even the wild movements than his initial medium of impact. Late in 1955, "Elvis Presley was working the American home, and suddenly the American home was a house divided."[26] An institution suburbanites had come to trust had now, they felt, violated their sensibility; "television compounded the jeopardy [since] Elvis could come lurching into any living room."[27] What parents reviled above all else was the honest, open sensuality in Elvis's performance.

During the age of Eisenhower,

> sex in general [was] a taboo topic. The 1950s were profoundly conflicted about
> the body and sexual display: *Playboy* was first published in December 1953
> (with the era's other sexual icon, Marilyn Monroe, as its first centerfold
> offering), but sex itself was viewed as something dangerous and explosive.[28]

Mojo Nixon overstated the situation when he argued that "Elvis wiped out four thousand years of Judeo-Christian uptightness about sex in fifteen minutes of TV."[29] Still, that statement offers something of the situation's reality, as Elvis's TV appearances

> intimidated the adults of America and drove their kids into a frenzy. Parents said Elvis was suggestive, lewd, a greaser. To kids that was just the point.... He used his music as an open invitation to release, and [young people] took him up on it.[30]

Years later, a book about the youth culture would be titled *We Are the People Our Parents Warned Us Against!*[31] That began when Elvis first appeared on TV,

> a critical moment for the whole society: The old order had been challenged and had not held. New forces were at work, driven by technology. The young did not have to listen to their parents anymore.[32]

Not listening to parents began with not listening to their parents' music. All this is schematized, if necessarily in simplified form, in *Loving You*. Adult protest causes the upcoming broadcast to be cancelled, at which point Walter complains about "a real issue — freedom of speech."

He tells a gathering of dubious little old ladies, "You're the same people who were criticized for doing the Charleston 30 years ago." People *were* attacked during the 1920s for dancing to jazz at a time when syncopation seemed as controversial as rock would later become. *Loving You* states the obvious (though important) in pointing out that the kids who love rock 'n' roll were criticized by middle-aged people who believed *their* rebellious forms of music and dance were okay though the latest ones weren't.

The challenge to such a prejudice — in life, as in the film — would grow strong. Less than a year later, wholesome Dick Clark would (for better or worse) tone down Freed's raunchier rock 'n' roll and eliminate the negative stigma via his daytime dance show *American Bandstand* (ABC–TV). That series debuted late in 1957, a seminal year: "the last moment of a uniquely regional culture and its heroes, the [final stage of an] era before the great leveler — television — changed American culture forever."[33] In *Loving You*, the show does go on. Walter muses on what most matters: "Loyalty, gratitude ... and *money*." This may seem cynical — except that he has finally begun to put money *last*. In the movies to follow, money would never signify the root of all evil. The messianic presence of a young martyr to rock (another early instance of Presley's religiosity) allows Walter to arc, causing the huckster to admit, "Something's happening to me. I'm *changing*."

"Ask Americans to judge" is the broadcast's motto, restating the then-popular defense of Presley: "Fifty million Elvis fans can't be wrong!" Before performing, Deke steps into his old jeans, setting the rhinestone cowboy persona aside to reclaim what he was — redeeming himself from any compromise committed along the way. *Loving You* then concludes on an upbeat note as Deke has it both ways, winning national success while remaining true to his roots, As he sings the title tune, this soft ballad is balanced with elements of rock 'n' roll. Like Elvis, Deke integrates the new music with the old and, in so doing, redefines popular tastes forever — in life as on-screen.

In the final shot, Walter and Glenda come together again, as a couple with other things than money on their minds. Susan waits for Deke. It's clear the character, like the star who plays him, isn't dangerous after all. *Loving You* makes plain that Deke-Elvis is not the enemy of all things American (one minister had proclaimed that Presley was "morally insane"[34]). He is only a youthful moral conscience, hoping to spur the misguided adults to frayed but worthwhile (and American) standards with which, in the suburban society, the older generation lost touch.

Peter Biskind has noted that in the '50s, the values most stressed were "conformity and domesticity."[35] Even as Elvis opposes the recently enshrined former, he champions a return to the latter. "I'd like all of you to stay together," he tells his entire entourage. "All of you are ... *friends*." More than that, the group now surrounding him — adults and young alike — represent a makeshift, non-biological version of what the character, and the man playing him, loves, desires and (as Sly Stone would assert 11 years later at Woodstock) desperately *needs*: We Are Family!

CHAPTER 3

Of Music and Money

◆ *Jailhouse Rock* (1957) ◆

Principal shooting for Presley's third screen vehicle, *Jailhouse Rock*, commenced on Monday, May 13, 1957. The script had been fashioned between mid–January and late April of that year by Guy Trosper, from an original story by Ned Young. This gestation period paralleled the first six months of Dwight D. Eisenhower's second presidential term, which began with a private swearing-in ceremony on Sunday, January 20. Pat Boone, most wholesome (i.e., least black) of the "new" singers, performed at the inaugural;[1] the notion of Elvis (most black) being invited would have been greeted by jeers — particularly from then–vice-president Richard Nixon, who roundly condemned Presley as representing all then currently wrong with America's youth.

At the time, the two were not only men but metaphors. No one in the country more effectively served as symbols of the era's polarized attitudes than Nixon and Elvis — who would, 15 years later, meet and embrace. That was a future no one could have imagined. A true understanding of *Jailhouse Rock's* implications necessarily proceeds from a review of 1956-57 as a precise moment in time that bore witness to the beginning of the end of an economically prosperous if otherwise complacent period. The initial Presley vehicles, *Love Me Tender* (released November 16, 1956) and *Loving You* (July 9, 1957) reflected attitudes already in decline, the early '50s era shortly to be considered a golden age.

A recession — its initial signs in evidence soon after Ike's second term began — sorely strained the business sector eight months later. It set to rest any naive belief that the country had entered into an unending era of industrial expansion. In "the worst economic downturn since World War II,"[2] unemployment lists skyrocketed to 5,000,000 (seven percent of the labor force). Despite his legendary "likability," the president's popularity plummeted.

Though 79 percent of the public approved of Ike's performance when he took office for the second term, such support crumbled owing to our "crises of confidence," "the decline of the Eisenhower consensus" and the necessary beginning of a "search for a [new] national purpose."[3] That journey would steer youth even further away from safety-in-conformity — the legacy their parents hoped to pass on.

Such turmoil is implied in *Jailhouse Rock*'s subtext. The film's opening does not seem notably different from that of *Loving You*: Elvis is here cast as Vince Everett, a young redneck with a hot temper and an untapped singing talent. At once, though, director Richard Thorpe organizes on-screen elements to create an iconography that reflects an altered financial (if not geographic) environment. At a construction site in some unnamed Southern state (this setting, thanks to repetition, already taking on a meaning), a group of men halt their activities as the paymaster arrives. All are middle-aged, ranging from late twenties to early forties. Snippets of dialogue reveal much:

> FIRST WORKER: This will make the last payment on my car.
> SECOND WORKER: Yeah, but it's all worn out!

What initially appears to be realistic banter offers something more. Presented "throwaway style," the dialogue effectively sets up an oncoming cynicism about what, a few years earlier, was accepted at face value. This is, we later learn, 1954. Though their work may be strenuous, the men are well-paid. Nonetheless, they have unknowingly slipped into a tender trap: Buying cars (the first material object mentioned in the movie and, some 96 minutes later, the last) and other items on the installment plan. Now they discover such products deliver little lasting satisfaction owing to a planned obsolescence developed during the postwar years. These men have, in the past, perceived themselves as capitalists and, as such, active; now, they realize, they are reduced to passive consumers.

Though the 1954 characters laugh good-naturedly, the 1957 audience — watching the incident after a recession put many such people out of work — bristled. Just then, Elvis' alter ego tears up on a truck, other *Southern* men making way for the *youngest* member of their company. This distinct image of Vince as an individual, tolerated by group members though not fully a part of their community, is established kinetically. Vince wildly interrupts sedate conversation among what, a decade later, would come to be called "the silent majority." The sole teenager present, Vince is something of a maverick. He alone plans to use his pay to "buy me a line of chorus girls, make 'em dance on my bed!"

The difficult business of Elvis' relationships with females (on-screen and in his personal life) comes into full play, building on his problems in the first two films. This clearly necessitates a consideration of feminist attitudes. Having summarily dismissed *all* the films as "stupid," one noted female observer complained that *Jailhouse Rock* and the other movies "bluntly projected conventional ideas about gender difference and heterosexual male mastery."[4] Yet on close examination, this film does not so much enshrine the era's "conventional ideas" as it subverts them. Early on, Elvis-Vince does "bluntly project" a 1950s macho image, later in the film making every heterosexual male's fantasies come to vivid life on-screen; the results are, significantly, disastrous. While he does dominate the film and the women in it, Elvis hardly seems to serve, considering what happens to him because of his embarrassing attitudes, in any way as a role model. He's more a tragic figure whose hubris (regarding women) must be replaced with humility.

The work's moral vision will be expressed by the *female* lead, Peggy Van Aden (Judy Tyler). She insists that Elvis-Vince (and by implication every teenage boy in the theater) must *un*learn all such conventional "wisdom" while grasping an emerging value-scheme from the modern woman. Vince eventually rejects all retro-male dreams to complete a necessary journey and become a whole person, an adult — perhaps even enlightened — male. Though Vince does in the film's third act live out a chauvinist fantasy, his final rejection of it suggests that *Jailhouse Rock* proceeds from a pre-feminist sensibility, expressing ideas not accessible in "serious" literature until the publication of Betty Friedan's *The Feminine Mystique* in 1963.[5]

The film's put-down of arrested adolescent behavior stretches beyond Vince's relationship with females. Before Peggy's appearance, Vince (paycheck in hand) heads for a roadhouse, where he unsuccessfully attempts to best the bartender in a bout of friendly arm-wrestling. A seemingly minor incident, this establishes Vince's desire (but inability) to live up to a then-prevalent John Wayne image. A pop rendering of "Red River Valley" (the theme for numerous Wayne films) plays on a Wurlitzer, establishing a Western as well as Southern idiom: "Buy me a drink, *cowboy*," a female barfly asks, though Vince wears no Stetson. As in *Loving You*, the Marlboro Man need not be glimpsed on horseback to be recognized as such.

Gender relations solidify as a focal issue. Vince's tenuous involvement with this unnamed woman serves as a catalyst for his incarceration: After rejecting the barfly's advances, Vince protects her from a middle-aged man (husband? fiancé? lover?) who berates the woman. This type of knight-like behavior will earn an Elvis character the nickname "Kid Galahad" in an upcoming film. Always, though, Elvis' uncritical acceptance of macho codes will draw him into danger. The two men engage in a fistfight — Vince once again unconsciously attempting to live up to the Wayne image — which Vince wins. Up to this point, the film in no way appears critical of its protagonist's actions;

the physical abuse of a woman should never be tolerated. Then, as the bartender calls out, "He's had enough," a darker side of Vince (Elvis' facial expression alters) dictates that he deliver one more (and, importantly, unnecessary) punch.

In so doing, Vince accidentally kills the man, at this point not in his traditional role of gentleman-knight but out-of-control macho male. Adhering to studio convention of implying rather than depicting violence, Thorpe cuts away before the moment of impact. By not showing the final punch, Thorpe transforms violence into a serious subject rather than allowing his film to become superficially violent. When the unnamed man falls, his head hits the jukebox's metal rim. As he dies, early-'50s pop goes with him; the record ceases playing. Though grounded in reality, the situation serves a symbolic function. This is indeed the day the music — at least, the *old* music — died. Shortly, a new music will emerge, Vince (Elvis) giving birth to it.

Thorpe cuts to reaction shots of various characters. Vince is horrified, as is the bartender and, notably, the barfly — negating any suggestion she might represent the "evil woman" stereotype of the twentieth century's early years. Her actions were guileless, understandable considering this young man's appeal. The sequence is not as simple as it initially seems, allowing a genre innovation. At the time, rock 'n' roll exploitation flicks were equaled only by juvenile crime movies — *Rumble on the Docks* (1956), *The Delinquent* (1957), *High School Hellcats* (1958) — in their popularity with youthful moviegoers.[6] Never had the two been combined in a single feature; *Jailhouse Rock* was the first significant hybrid.

The continuing pressure on Elvis' persona to conform emerges. In prison, Vince sets arrogance and ego aside, learning modesty by referring to the warden — local arm of the Establishment — as "sir." In an indelible moment, Elvis sits still as his locks are shorn by a prison barber. This dramatic situation is informed by the audience's awareness that adults had, for the past two years, demanded a cutting of his hair. While watching, teen audiences bore witness to the beginning of the end of Elvis' early "wild stage" and, in surprisingly short time, their own.

At this point, a *deus ex machina* allows Vince his detour into the world of commercial music. Cellmate Hunk Houghton (Mickey Shaughnessey) turns out to be an oldtimer in more ways than one. In addition to a wheeler-dealer behind bars, Hunk is a former country performer whose little-used guitar enjoys a place of honor in their living area, alongside photographs of such legendary balladeers as Hank Williams. Hunk serves a dual function, introducing Vince both to music ("You'll never make a guitar player") and money ("I run a business"). The two — folk-art and financial success — soon fuse for the impressionable youth. "You made all that *money* just *singing*?" Vince asks incredulously. Prison is not an isolated situation but a metaphor for modern life: When it comes to cigarettes (in their microcosm, the equivalent of cash in the macrocosm), Hunk explains: "You buy 'em, you steal 'em, you trade for 'em — just like on the *outside*."

Before the film reaches its conclusion, life will have become a prison for Vince. The world — even on its most glamourous level — proves as much a trap as did his small space in stir. Because Vince listens as closely to Hunk as Elvis did to Col. Parker, the character can be taken as a stand-in for Parker.[7] Thorpe effectively establishes the complex nature of their emerging relationship — Hunk well-intentioned mentor *and* cold-blooded manipulator — through montage. Whenever one or the other sings in their cell, the camera focuses on the performer, denying the audience any image of the listener a few feet away. This suggests the degree to which Hunk sets Vince free to be himself. On the other hand, whenever Hunk offers Vince further lessons, the camera remains in two-shot, Hunk dominating — visually insisting on his Machi-avellian side. Hunk's duality, like that of Parker himself with Presley, becomes basic.

The ongoing issue of men's tenuous relationships to women re-emerges even in this all-male situation. Hunk, we learn, was imprisoned for robbing a bank; he did this for "a *woman* ... she got used to bonded bourbon." A key parallel is established between the film's two males. In each case, the man acted rashly, on his own accord, to impress the female through macho action. Such an immature attempt to win attention, as opposed to anything evil in the woman's nature, led a man of each generation down the path toward *self*-destruction rather than, as in retro-films, destruction *of* the male *by* a woman. Though Hunk (representing the male as well as the music of the twentieth century's first half) may be too old to learn new tricks, Vince (the embryonic male of the century's second half) is a different story.

The theme of art vs. capitalism temporarily takes center stage. At first, Vince resists Hunk's suggestion that he use cigarettes for money; on the other hand, Vince is anxious to learn how to play guitar. This duality suggests a naive personality. It makes sense that Vince's first musical effort is a love bal-lad, one which Vince (as a child) overheard an uncle singing in the country. This simple ditty *hails* a woman — a traditional earth-mother — who will be "forever young" (though her looks will fade) and beautiful (beyond the phys-ical) owing to her innate goodness, and the corresponding intensity of a man's ongoing unconditional love. Again, we encounter the idealized image of Gladys.

Hunk's moral ambiguity is rendered disturbingly clear by two key plot elements. Hunk teaches Vince the essential chords so he can play in the prison talent show. But when letters from female fans pour in, Hunk uses his influence to keep Vince from receiving them, so the youth — unaware of his potential — will continue turning to Hunk for guidance. We are made aware, though, that Vince (like Elvis with Col. Parker) learns from Hunk in more ways than one: "What's the *percentage* of singing for a bunch of cons?" he asks, following an invite to perform. Only when Hunk mentions that the show will be telecast to a vast national audience does the young man becomes excited. Since this occurs early in *Jailhouse Rock*, we may choose to read it as a film that thematically begins where *Loving You* left off.

The filmmakers quickly establish that Vince has not given up his old macho ways. Before his release (Vince leaves jail prior to Hunk), the youth becomes involved in a riot over rancid food. Firmly but politely returned to his cell, Vince unnecessarily hits two guards. The sequence, with no clear relationship to the story proper, could be dismissed as a contrivance allowing for exploitation in which Elvis is stripped, bound to a rack and whipped. Mainstream-kink may have been a motivation, yet the sequence functions on more significant levels. The same hot-headedness that landed Vince in jail is the cause. No matter how insensitive the adult world — "the system," to fifties rebels — may appear, it would not (according to the film) arbitrarily single Vince out for cruelty. Brutal treatment is applied only after Elvis, the New American Teenager incarnate, engages in antisocial behavior. The star's total turnabout in social attitude has begun.

The situation doesn't end there. Hunk, Vince learns, attempted to buy off the whipping with cigarettes but didn't have enough. "Lesson to be learned," Vince mutters, hearing this. "Without *money*, you're *dead*." The incident cements Vince's already-hardening attitude toward cash. It's this jaded incarnation of Vince that shortly will be released into the world. Still, nothing we have seen justifies Hunk's willingness to sacrifice so, indicating weak dramaturgy ... or that the true cause of Hunk's concern couldn't, in the restrictive 1950s, be fully portrayed. Homosexual relations between inmates, particularly older cons who take younger, "pretty" arrivals under their wing, dominate most contemporary prison films. Though this could not be included in 1957, that hardly means such situations didn't exist — only that commercial motion pictures dared not openly portray them. Filmmakers, however, have always subverted such taboos through implications which often do not appear obvious until years later. That this was the case here is verified by Marty Lacker, best man at Elvis' wedding; in 1995, while insisting that rumors about a sexual relationship between himself and Elvis were false, Lacker blurted out, "*Jailhouse Rock* might have had an underlying homosexual theme."[8] Temporarily at least, that's set aside as Vince is released.

Act One depicted a transformation from guileless (if dangerous) country boy to cynical capitalist. In Act Two, Vince's altered personality achieves the American Dream through natural talent, calculated intelligence and a notable absence of heart and/or soul. Vince has been in stir for three years and a different world awaits him. It is now is 1957, the film's "reality" catching up to the actuality of its audience. The deep recession has begun. A job as entertainer isn't available since entertainment money has dried up. This increases Vince's sense of an abiding unfairness; the deck appears stacked not only against him, but also against those of his social class. For the self-satisfied white-collar strata, who now owned most of what they'd always wanted, "Naked ambition and the lust for success had gone underground."[9] More correctly, it had been banished to the trailer park, there embraced by blue-collar types, mostly those all at once out of work.

This paved the way for Elvis' emergent image: Poor White Trash, seeing success all around him, desperately coveting it — openly, agonizingly. Previously providing a screen signifier for the disenfranchised young, Presley was about to emerge as a popular icon that allowed a fantasy fulfillment for Americans who fell short of snatching the brass ring as they rode about in maddening circles on our capitalist carousel. Thirty-three years later, a New Jersey policeman expressed his admiration for what Elvis, like alter ego Vince, achieved: "that American Dream come true."[10] Through Elvis' upcoming movies, yet another element of marginalized American, the redneck (rural or urban) could vicariously live out intense longings and unfulfilled dreams for fame and fortune. A sea change was about to occur, if not in the Presley persona, then in how he was perceived by his audience — or, more correctly, audiences.

As Hunk (temporarily) disappears from the drama, he is replaced by Peggy, a pretty go-getter working at a mid-level job in the music industry. Young, smart and success-oriented, Peggy has been pushing the kind of act that didn't exist before Vince began his jail term, the emergent rockabilly singers. With Peggy returns the film's proto-feminist vision: Educated, intelligent, liberated for the times, Peggy holds down a job — more accurately, career — while maintaining her femininity. "I'm an exploitation *man* in the record business," she tells Vince. If he offers an early screen incarnation of the emergent new American male, Peggy symbolizes the iceberg tip of the new woman who would come into her own during the transitional years of the late 1950s and early 1960s. Neither a reactionary (remaining housebound) or radical (putting career above all else), Peggy — aggressive though not arrogant, persuasive but never pushy — manages to have most everything both ways. Her old-fashioned values and desire to build a family (preferably with Vince) temper razor-sharp business instincts.

Deftly manipulating all around her, Peggy does so in a moral manner. She maintains a pleasant relationship with one fresh-faced disc jockey, Eddy

Talbot (Dean Jones, standing in for Dick Clark). On occasion, she dates him, without allowing either the friendship or mild romance to interfere with their business venture. Peggy serves as an inverse to Vince, who tends to tear back and forth between retro-male one moment, contemptuously nihilistic nightmare — man-of-the-future the next. Misogyny, however, has become Vince's shield following his bad experience with the barfly (which he blames on her, in denial that the problem was caused by his hot temper) and subjection to Hunk's anti-female diatribes. Peggy is shocked by Vince's coarseness as she attempts to turn him into a star. We grasp, if hardly sympathize with, him — having witnessed the process by which he was desensitized. The Vince-Peggy relationship becomes a paradigm for a then-emerging social situation: traditional male and contemporary woman, attempting to maintain a relationship despite differing viewpoints.

This is evident from their first meeting. Vince's anger and bitterness surface when, without permission from club owner Sam, he leaps onto the stage, playing and singing. Unfortunately, he does "Young and Beautiful" in the style popular *before* the birth of Big Beat. People pay scant attention — talking, laughing, drinking. In response, Vince turns his act into a wilder show than intended, concluding by breaking his guitar, much to the shock and delight of everyone. The rock 'n' roll ritual of a star destroying his instrument during performance (eventually to be enshrined on-screen by The Yardbirds in Michelangelo Antonioni's *Blow-Up*, 1966) began with Elvis.

Vince is further led down the path of rock 'n' roll when Peggy brings him to a studio for a recording session. He sings "Don't Leave Me Now" *without* the spontaneous gospel beat — i.e., soul — that caused his prison performance to click. Elvis was, in actuality, all about feeling. "Sing it how you *feel* it," suggests Peggy (the intuitive, spiritual woman), and "put your own emotions into the song. Make it fit *you*," rather than, as had been the pop-music style until then, fitting oneself to the song. Vince takes her advice, resulting in an early example of rhythm and blues. Peggy stresses this when she brings Vince to meet a record company executive: "You know [kids are] going for the *new sound*, Jack!" This allows for an exposé of the recording industry at its worst: Jack steals their unique (though non-copyrighted) arrangement to a public-domain tune, handing it over to a performer already under contract.

In so doing, he not only wins an expected punch from the still hot-headed Vince, but deepens Vince's resentment toward men in suits who run the system. An interchange shortly before the double-cross makes it clear that Vince (after his tutelage with Hunk) does not resent big money, only regretting that as a rube he's kept closed out. A close-up of Jack's expensive cufflinks, which Vince admires and resents, reveals the truth behind Vince's seemingly revolutionary attitudes. Later, when Vince does achieve wealth, his first act is to purchase an identical set of cufflinks, hardly what we would expect from an authentic populist-socialist intent on destroying a corrupt system on principle. All Vince hates is his own exclusion; a rugged individualist, he wants just such success for himself.

The film features a more significant symbol for achieving the American Dream through hard work and good luck: A Cadillac. A running gag conveys Vince's desire to own as soon as possible *the* American-made car representing success achieved by working hard to make money. Vince continuously changes his mind as to what color his Cadillac should be; he will consider no other make. In 1956, while the film was being produced, Cadillac's advertising logo claimed: "Success Breeds Success!" As one critic noted:

> The glamour, luxury, comfort, and prestige of their top-of-the-line car was the visible reward of the American male's own "drive," the fruits of his ambition and hard work...."[11]

In this vein, Vince — despite the attraction he feels for Peggy — tells her, "You know the business, and I want to cash in on some of the *loot*!" Studying Vince, we better understand why in time that era's wild ones eventually aligned themselves first with Richard Nixon and later Ronald Reagan, ultimate examples of the "men in suits."

Southern blue-collar types despised not the system or suits but their own lack of cufflinks and Cadillacs. They expressed anger of a selfish rather than socialist nature at mid-level types who possessed just such goods. Peggy offers to introduce Vince to Mr. Shores (Vaughn Taylor), an older lawyer in a more expensive suit than Jack's. Vince voices no objection: "Sounds like *my* man; interested only in *money*." He admires the big city (i.e., Jewish) lawyer, a man who started with nothing and, in an earlier era, forced the system to admit him, fighting his way up to the top.

The leather-jacketed youth takes one look at Shores and proclaims, "We're kinfolks." We begin to understand the irony of Elvis: "Few young Americans have looked so rebellious and been so polite."[12] The formation of Vince's basic personality — cultural revolutionary, fiscal conservative — took place moments before Vince left jail:

HUNK: Without *money*, you're dead.
VINCE: An animal?
HUNK: An animal in a jungle!
VINCE: I get the message.
HUNK: Do unto others as they would do unto you! Only, do it *first*.
VINCE: Yeah, *first*.
HUNK: And it's just as bad on the *outside*. Only worse. Remember that.
VINCE: I don't aim to forget it.

If Vince briefly forgot, Jack's theft bluntly reminded him. Experience turns Vince into an unconscious follower (though he likely never heard of the philosopher) of Nietzsche: "That which does not kill us makes us strong."[13]

Still alive following the betrayal, Vince becomes strong (i.e., *hard*), insisting that Peggy quit her job to create a small record company, dedicating herself to creating an ever-broadening following for the triumph of Vince's will. She does; yet the more she supports Vince, the more he — a convert to misogyny — resents her. Angry when the successful modern woman paid for a meal Vince can't afford, he became purposefully vulgar. "Vince," Peggy implores, "don't you know the meaning of the word 'courtesy'?" But courtesy is what characters like Jack — the middle-management types in moderately priced suits — project to camouflage insincerity. For those on the bottom (Vince) or top (Shores), courtesy is utterly unnecessary.

PEGGY: Happy?
VINCE: When the *money* starts rolling in, I'll be happy!

Vince now has less in common with Dean as vulnerable, confused Jim Stark than that actor toward the end of *Giant* (1956), an elderly, self-satisfied redneck who made big money. Or Brando — not as the freewheeling rebel of *The Wild One* but the slob-brute Stanley in *A Streetcar Named Desire* (1951), most clearly when Peggy unwisely brings Vince home to meet her family. The house is in a middle-class suburb, representing everything Vince fervently resents. He hails from a trailer park; the lawyer lives in a mansion; Jack would inhabit just such a house! Making matters worse, Peggy's father is a college professor, causing Vince to again assume a working-class, angry young man pose.

FATHER: Scotch? Bourbon?
VINCE: Got any beer?

Had Shores offered Vince Scotch or bourbon, he would have accepted without comment. In this context, he prefers to be Yeats' rough best, slouching toward Nashville to be born.

Now, music — and its altered meaning at this seminal moment in American social history — impacts on them. What most offends Vince is the discussion of popular music by gathered guests. They listen to Dave Brubeck's Anglo-intellectualized jazz, music of choice for the elite, and (according to Elvis' widow Priscilla) the only type of music that Elvis despised.[14] Brubeck's recordings lack the heart and soul Vince-Elvis could readily relate to in black jazz, even if Vince's own soul is temporarily under anesthesia. The guests patronizingly attempt to draw Vince into their conversation:

PARTY GUEST ONE: I think Brubeck has gone as far with discordance as I care to go.

PARTY GUEST TWO: I say atonality is just a passing phase in jazz music.
PARTY GUEST ONE: What do you think, Vince?
VINCE: Lady, I don't know what the hell you're talking about!

"Hell" stands in for a word unthinkable in 1957, if not today. The scene, however slapdash its conception, resonates across five decades, representing a profound change in attitudes toward music — particularly, the co-opting of black music by the white Establishment:

> In the past, whites had picked up on black jazz, but that had largely been done by the elite. [Rock] was different; this was a visceral, democratic response by the masses.[15]

From music, we swiftly return to gender. Vince storms out of the house; when Peggy follows, Vince violently kisses her, an act intended (within the confines of the existing Production Code) to suggest an attempted rape. She again appears the inverse of Vince — politically liberal, socially conventional — by questioning his tactics. Vince sneers while replying: "Ain't tactics, honey. Just the *beast* in me." Though Peggy, knowing nothing of Vince's earlier experiences, appears confused, Vince references his human-as-animal-in-an-asphalt-jungle discussion with Hunk. A mournful instrumental, "Young and Beautiful," plays on the soundtrack, making it clear that the filmmakers place themselves at a distance from their central character. Such a self-initiated removal from the human community will ultimately leave Vince unfulfilled. On some level, Vince senses this, too; "Guess I did get out of line," he admits — at once shy and sullen — the following morning.

A hint that Vince is capable of moving beyond macho posturing, this line sets the stage for what will occur in Act Three. Hunk, now released, returns precisely as Vince is wooed by Hollywood. Hunk wants Vince to honor a contract they scrawled in jail; Vince reminds Hunk of the fan mail that was kept from him. Assuming he's about to be cast aside, Hunk is amazed when Vince does a turnabout, never forgetting Hunk's attempt to buy off those who would whip Vince. Once caught between two worlds, Vince — now having achieved the moneyed strata he wanted — finds himself caught between two modes of behavior. So he attempts to balance sentimental loyalty with cold-blooded self-interest. Vince honors the old contract by giving Hunk a job, though at a smaller (if handsome) rate than their paperwork stipulated.

At this point, Vince performs the title number, recalling his Big House days in a stylized manner for a TV broadcast. During filming, choreographer Alex Romero's original notion was to stage the sequence in the manner of a traditional MGM dance musical for Gene Kelly or Fred Astaire. Elvis' attempts to follow Romero's choreography proved disastrous; everything spontaneous (and best) about his iconoclastic movements was lost. Elvis (like Vince in the film) told Romero, "Man, it's not *me*." Knowing nothing of rock 'n' roll, Romero asked to hear Elvis' records, and requested, "Would you show me what you do on-stage?" Romero explained he would "take what you do and work it into the routine, and it's going to be you, what you normally feel comfortable doing, but I'm going to choreograph it."[16] The result provided a perfect marriage of Old Hollywood dance musicals and the uninhibited rhythms of rock.

Memphis Mafia member Lamar Fike expressed relief that Elvis didn't drop his old act to achieve movie stardom or, on the other hand, firmly cling to his roots, ruling out mainstream success. What Vince does in the film — retaining a patina of his rebel image while partly conforming — Elvis achieved on the set: "Romero translated what Elvis wanted into dance steps.... He showed Elvis what he had in mind, and the two of them tied it all together."[17] Though the collaborators desired nothing more than to make the moment "work," the result constituted something greater: Proving that the new music, as well as its corresponding movements, was not antithetical to middlebrow entertainment. Nor was Elvis himself so different from Kelly or Astaire. Always, though, there would remain a hint of the Elvis that had thrilled, angered and/or shocked his first TV audience.

In this classic sequence, the feminine side of a male sex symbol was obvious, even to those closest to Elvis:

> [Y]ou can see why gay men would be attracted to Elvis. His cousin Gene Smith was looking at him one time, and he said, in that funny way he talks, "Elvis, you know I ain't no damn queer, but you're the prettiest thing I've ever seen." And it was true.[18]

Watching the "Jailhouse Rock" number with such a statement in mind, it's amazing the sequence passed by the censors. Vince's initially macho image grows ever more feminine as he slithers down the pole.

As he intones these sentiments, dancing "cons" pair off, performing the "jailhouse rock" (long a synonym for homosexual behavior behind bars) with one another. The sequence becomes more blatant, lyrics mentioning only those musical instruments that traditionally symbolize fellatio — the saxophone and slide trombone.

Nothing — not even possible freedom — can tear them away from their abandoned dancing. When one prisoner suggests a break, his companion says no. He wants to continue.

It's possible to view such "bending" as one more aspect of the star's subversive nature. If unknowingly, Presley set into motion our society's painstakingly slow acceptance of gender ambiguity in music, reaching fruition in the careers of Alice Cooper, David Bowie and Madonna.

In context, the title production number represents for Vince a point of no return. Off-stage, he now has that once-longed-for line of chorus girls, including starlet-fiancée Sherry Wilson (Jennifer Holden), the cufflinks *and* the Cadillac. Like Elvis, he stars in a string of B-movies; there are hangers-on, resembling the Memphis Mafia, several actually played by members of that group. Clearly, though, Vince looks lost. His *malaise* can be written off as merely a restatement of a timeworn formula, dating back to the silent movie era: "In America, this version of the Fall had long been part of the folklore."[19] But with a significant difference. For while the small-town boy may indeed be changed, the small-town girl — Peggy, when she re-emerges — has not altered one whit. However hurt she may be owing to Vince's dropping her for Sherry, ever-positive Peggy hasn't surrendered to bitterness and/or nihilism. Even Vince, as it turns out, isn't changed "forever." Thanks to Peggy — and, to a degree, Hunk — he will complete his hero's journey by coming full cycle, regaining something of that long-lost country boy's innocence, minus the naiveté.

The film, if not the life that inspired it, offers a redemption saga rather than tragedy. "Wanting to be rich, famous, important or powerful," in the context of such a moralistic movie, "was an invitation to disaster. In Hollywood's anti-success scenarios, good but misguided people see the light at the eleventh hour, learning from"[20] previous experience, leading to catharsis. Vince must walk away from superficial Sherry and embrace Peggy if he is to be "saved." Before this can happen, and insuring that we believe Vince's transformation, he must make clear that macho matters *other* than those applying to gender have been banished. We see Vince and Hunk, talking together in a room in Vince's mansion. This echoes their earlier prison conversation; the cage may be a gilded one but, as Vince has learned, life on the outside can be as rough as in stir.

Freedom is a state of mind, which he can only achieve with a woman of substance. Hunk attempts to goad Vince into a fight. Significantly, Vince refuses to swing back. After a traumatic moment in which all fear that Vince may have permanently lost his voice owing to a punch from Hunk, he recovers the ability to perform — and sings directly to Peggy. For the first time, his singing style radiates humility, not hubris. He has rediscovered the emotions with which he first sang, now tempered by worldly wisdom. So he returns to the first song he tackled, "Forever Young" — perhaps the inspiration for Dylan's eventual number of that name. There's no hint that he and Peggy will forsake fame and fortune, heading for the Ozarks to live on a farm, there attempting a separate peace. They'll remain in Tinseltown, while — like the rich hick family on the soon-to-premiere sitcom *The Beverly Hillbillies*— maintaining traditional values that Vince has rediscovered. Values which Peggy never lost, or even forgot.

CHAPTER 4

Fathers and Sons

✦ *King Creole* (1958) ✦

Even as Elvis began his musical career in Memphis late in 1954, his beloved Southland plunged headlong into a labyrinth of struggle and violence over the issue of Civil Rights. Elvis crystallized and reflected, likely without conscious intent, the central concern that gripped his region, then the nation. A great deal of the Presley appeal for youth, as well as the threat he posed to parents, "can be ascribed to his cross-race stylistics — the ways in which he mixed and blended black and white music and black and white modes of performance into the emergent hybrid of rock and roll."[1] As David Halberstam put it:

> The Supreme Court ruling on Brown v. Board of Education, which occurred in the middle of the decade, was the first important break between the older, more staid America that existed at the start of the era and the new, fast-paced, tumultuous America that saw the decade's end. The second was Elvis Presley.[2]

Elvis offered "country [music] blended with black blues."[3] Sam Phillips perceived the boy's potential to fulfill a prophecy he had made after realizing young white Southern kids ardently listened to race-oriented radio stations when their folks weren't around. "Political boss Ed Crump might keep the streets and schools and public buildings segregated, but at night [Memphis deejay] Dewey Phillips integrated the airwaves."[4] Sam Phillips sighed: "If I could find a white man with a Negro sound I could make a billion dollars."[5] Elvis' near-magical appearance was (as *Jailhouse Rock* had illustrated) a case of ordinary (white) people (as compared to the elite) responding en masse to black music;[6] Presley was to rock 'n' roll for Everyman what Dave Brubeck had been to jazz for the intellectuals and academics.

It's not for nothing that Civil Rights and Elvis Presley are often mentioned in the same breath. Or that the esteemed Leonard Bernstein would eventually assert: "Presley is the greatest cultural force in the twentieth century."[7] Unwittingly, Elvis became "the poor white messenger of poor black sexuality."[8] He was attacked by cultural conservatives everywhere; the most vitriolic reactions were in his own backyard.

> [M]any southerners [claimed] that rock 'n' roll was a plot jointly sponsored by the Kremlin and the NAACP, and that ... it was "nigger music," and as such was designed to tear down the barriers of segregation and bring about sexual promiscuity and a decline in the morals of young whites.[9]

Such a reactionary force required a whipping boy; happening along when he did, Presley was made to order.

In direct answer to such diatribes, Elvis transformed *King Creole* into his unapologetic retort. Director Michael Curtiz opens with a long shot of Bourbon Street in New Orleans at the crack of dawn. Few people are up and around, but several street hawkers have set up shop to offer their humble wares, from huckleberries and crawfish to hot gumbo. Curtiz's camera focuses on three, who represent what we would today call an ethnically diverse group: A Cajun, a Creole and an African-American. Each sings about his or her specialty; at first, the voice — like the product — exists alone. Then their tunes merge into a spontaneous symphony of the street. Along with the pungent scents of their varied foods, the integrated voices drift up and into the air, past the humble apartments located above.

In one window, Danny Fisher (Elvis) gazes down with obvious relish. In an impromptu manner, he sings along, incorporating each of the three separate delicacies — and the cultures they hail from — into a *melange*: "Crawfish, gumbo...." Danny does not, however, provide a simple aural mirror of the voices, songs and ethnicities. First, he absorbs the singular strains, joining all together for the first time. The street singers appear oblivious to one another, but Elvis offers his own unique interpretation and appreciation of the rich possibilities below. We witness

> Elvis's undeniable appropriation of African-American rhythms and sounds, his personal acknowledgment of lessons learned from black musicians (as well as other ethnicities).[10]

Like Danny in the film, Elvis "was what first the region and then the [youth of the] nation wanted: a white boy to explode into the beat, to capture it for whites."[11]

The movie cuts back and forth between close-ups of an African-American girl, singing on the street, and Danny. They find themselves engaged in a virtual duet, while other voices seep in to create a multi-cultural coming together. Rock 'n' roll thus provides an apotheosis for American ethnicity.

Such a notion is forwarded in the language of "pure cinema" — image, editing and sound orchestrated for a single purpose, to strike out in (popular) art against the moral idiocy of racism. In *King Creole* as in his music, Elvis Presley "negotiated the nascent terrain of civil rights to participate in the creation of a more democratic popular culture in mid–1950s America."[12]

Screenwriter Herbert Baker followed the basic plot of Harold Robbins' luridly potent bestseller *A Stone for Danny Fisher*, while eliminating the New York City setting and Jewish orientation. To support his weak, alcoholic, chronically unemployed father (Dean Jagger) in their humble rooms, Danny cleans up jazz clubs early each morning before heading for high school. At The Blue Shade, he protects a prostitute, Ronnie (Carolyn Jones), from low-lifes. Danny suffers repercussions, for hoodlums who witnessed the incident kid him about it. Danny angrily retaliates and, as a result, is told that he won't be allowed to graduate from high school despite good grades. Shark (Vic Morrow, doing a variation on his *Blackboard Jungle* character) draws the now destitute Danny into his street gang; Danny uses his singing talent to distract people in a Charles Street store while the others steal everything in sight. A pretty soda fountain girl, Nellie (Dolores Hart), notices and upbraids Danny, who makes a date with her and tries to impress her with his tough guy swagger. When Nellie fails to respond, Danny realizes that she truly is a "nice" girl.

Nellie is a virtual redux of Susan, Hart's character in *Loving You*: the sweet virgin who offers Elvis' current screen incarnation the chance to live the straight life. Nellie senses in Danny something that separates him from Shark and his thugs. Like the young man playing him, Danny is "the safe rebel," if only because he "never intended to cause trouble."[13] Black leather jacket and sideburns aside, Elvis-Danny is, deep down, that blandest of 1950s possibilities, a *nice* (that term will reoccur often in Elvis films) guy — if one who plays the bad boy role to survive. Nellie's own niceness appeals to the better part of him: "I've got to be home early," she tells Danny when they meet again. "My mother's old-fashioned."

Danny remains so immersed in the sleazy street scene that he cannot grasp Nellie's full worth. He brings her to a cheap hotel for a "party," in striking comparison to his white knight behavior with Ronnie. A predecessor of Travis Bickle in Martin Scorsese's *Taxi Driver* (1976), Danny treats the virgin like a whore, the whore as a virgin. Nellie's shock sets into motion Danny's character arc; he's embarrassed about coming on too strong. Tellingly, they pause before a church, which Danny wants to — but at this point cannot — enter, owing to doubts about his worth. The moment provides a hint of the film's religious subtext.

"I *like* you," Nellie explains. That she is not simply a Sandra Dee super-virgin caricature, unaware of her own sexuality and hoping for a platonic friendship, becomes clear when Danny chooses to politely see her home. At the front steps, *she* initiates a passionate kiss. This allows Danny his first insight into what a male-female couple may, at its best, be — allowing us more insight into Danny, the star playing him, and a screen tradition of the postwar era. The aforementioned comment by Jackie Gleason that Elvis was Brando with a guitar[14] is telling here. Yet in his relationships with Hart in both *Loving You* and *King Creole*, Elvis solidified his image for female fans: "the kind of fantasy lover they want: sensitive, soft, and unthreatening, a retooled male, a romantic ideal."[15]

In this regard, at least, Elvis appears a far cry from Brando as the raging bull Stanley in *A Streetcar Named Desire* (1951) — the violence-prone anti-hero as stud and sadist. Elvis has far more in common with Montgomery Clift, particularly his emotionally wounded roles, book-ended by Clift's first film (*Red River*, 1948) and one of his last (*The Misfits*, 1961). Wearing the western garb Elvis would often affect, Clift's sensitive cowboy proved strong enough to stand up against such traditionally macho antagonists as John Wayne and Clark Gable. But when it came to women, he placed his head in the lap of Joanne Dru or Marilyn Monroe. Likewise, Elvis' other favorite star, James Dean, wore cowboy clothing in *Giant* (1956). Alone with Elizabeth Taylor, Dean's "Jett Rink" rests his head in her lap rather than kiss her; Dean had assumed similar physical situations with Julie Harris in *East of Eden* and Natalie Wood in *Rebel*.

As for Brando, the film that most impacted on Elvis was *The Wild One*. There is never a moment when the decent biker Johnny can place his head in Mary Murphy's lap. We nonetheless get the sense that this is precisely what he wants to do. So it goes with Nellie and Danny. She mothers him, perhaps secretly hoping for something more. He — the seeming macho man — is also relieved, happy to just cuddle, because (in Elvis's case) she (as a "nice girl") has become a substitute for Gladys; cuddling is what *they* used to do.

Freud argued that every boy — having accepting that his mother is off-limits — searches for a suitable substitute.[16] In Elvis's unique case, though, they cannot be penetrated. That would violate what in his view — derived from an intense and chronic rather than normal and mild Oedipal complex — is the oldest taboo. An evanescent innocent, he cannot relate to nice girls "that way." Each is temporally Gladys, also the virgin Mary; so cuddling is okay.

King Creole also connects to altering social values. "By embodying both aggression and vulnerability, by being both tough and tender, Elvis was, in fact, blurring the boundaries of gender difference and sexual identity,"[17] as Clift and Dean had done. Elvis takes this further, with a religiosity those earlier stars did not convey. When the Presley persona chances to meet a Mary Magdalene — Scott in *Loving You*, Jones in *King Creole*— he Jesus-like converts them to chastity through the redemptive powers of his own radical innocence. In both films, Dolores Hart's character impacts on Elvis' successive alter egos. In actuality, the opposite occurred: Shortly after completing her movies with the man who, after his death, would come to be widely perceived as a messianic figure, Hart quit the movie business and became a nun, dedicating herself to God.

King Creole's plot reveals other elements in common with the preceding Elvis films. Danny learns that Ronnie, herself once a nice girl, now serves as mistress to Maxie Fields (Walter Matthau), head of the local underworld as well as The Blue Shade's owner. Jealous when he senses that Ronnie and Danny share a special rapport, Maxie nonetheless wants the talented boy to sing in his club. But Danny has agreed to perform at King Creole, a less extravagant night spot owned by poor but honest Charlie LeGrande (Paul Stewart). Attracted to Danny's older sister Mimi (Jan Shepard), Charlie is soon accepted as a member of Fisher's extended family. Danny betrays that institution when he moves over to Maxie's higher paying club — doing so to finance his dysfunctional father's rehabilitation, yet perceived by those he loves most as selling out to greed.

As Peter Biskind has noted, movies about the troubled youth of the 1930s and '40s tended to put the blame on society itself, most notably William Wellman's *Wild Boys of the Road* (1933); in the prosperous 1950s, the source of the problem was less "bad neighborhoods" than "bad families."[18] Danny feels abandoned by his deceased birth mother. Similarly, Elvis would never adjust following Gladys' death on August 14, 1958. Danny flirts and fights with a succession of substitute mother figures, as future Elvis characters will. First is the (female) teacher who denied Danny his diploma. In a notable Freudian slip, Danny even calls the despised older (and not notably attractive) woman "honey" during their scene together. Ronnie, who eventually becomes his lover, is the film's correlative to Scott in *Loving You*— a conventionally beautiful older woman to whom Elvis finds himself awkwardly attracted.

Similarly, in *King Creole*, when Danny rescues Ronnie from bums in the bar, he acts like a surrogate son as well as white knight. This creates a stigma that stands in the way of a sexual union. "Why won't you kiss me?" she asks, confused, as they hurry away in a taxi. Ronnie represents a duality that confuses Danny. She is an available older woman, causing him to want to respond; yet Ronnie has already become a substitute mother, which she doesn't yet realize, so the kiss involves (for him at least) a dark taboo. Local punks, peering in the window, laugh derisively; tellingly, one remarks that the woman is old enough to be Danny's *mother*.

The demanded kiss threatens Danny on another level, echoing the Vince-Valerie confrontation in *Loving You*. When Danny relents and kisses Ronnie, he does so sweetly rather than passionately. However, he then kisses Ronnie harder, more romantically, less out of a desire to do so than his need to project a proper image to those peers he knows are watching. Perception, for Elvis Presley, is reality.

There's also the other parent, Danny's father. The man emerges as a ringer for Vernon, who likewise had to move his family into a poor neighborhood owing to problems with alcohol that led to his being fired from various jobs.[19] Tellingly, Danny's father is never named. This allows him to signify the pathetic 1950s father figure, lacking the masculine backbone of an earlier era's robust patriarchs. Jagger revives the Jim Backus character from Dean's most iconic film; in *Rebel,* the dad was likewise never named. Both movies address a concern over "the erosion of the authority of the father"[20] in postwar America.

Not surprisingly, Danny will, like Jimbo, search for a proper father figure. This quest begins with the school principal, a well-meaning older man who appears to be the teacher's husband. In the office, the two educators form a stern white-collar version of "American Gothic." After the teacher leaves, Danny warms up to the man, hoping he'll act assertively. The principal instead opts for a compromise (night classes) rather than dare to contradict her decision — one more demasculated male. The principal then hints that his motivation for wanting to help is the lack of a son; the man's own child died at age 13. This lost youth, the vulnerable man admits, would be Danny's age now; the principal appears to be as desperate to find a son as Danny is to find a suitable father figure.

Danny comes in contact with a pair of potent if polar possibilities: Maxie, the devil in the flesh, and Charlie, roughhewn guardian angel of the streets. His role solidifies into the next successive father substitute when Charlie visits the Fisher home and attempts to persuade Mr. Fisher to allow Danny to sing. When Charlie suggests he'll look after Danny as if he were his own, Mr. Fisher replies, "You wouldn't watch out for him like he's your son, because he's *my* son. " Danny refuses to take his biological father's "no" over his newfound father figure's "yes." This allows Elvis to again project an ongoing value-scheme:

CHARLIE: What do you want?
DANNY: A pink convertible!

Doubtless, it would be a Cadillac, the car that Presley's persona dreamed of in *Loving You*— the car that he bought for his mother after making his first million.

"I'm through failing," Danny insists, making clear that he isn't opposed to the capitalist system — only a class-conscious outsider, outraged that the doors appear closed to him. Like Elvis, Danny does not reject the American work ethic; he insists on redefining it. When Danny refused the principal's offer to find an alternative way of completing his education, he did so to spend more time working at odd jobs. "No *money* in school," Danny snarls when his sister suggests he attend night classes. Early on, Elvis was perceived as a metaphor for the Commie scare, but he always (in his life and on-screen) championed a redefined democratic capitalism: Determined to make what Nathaniel West once tagged "a cool million" no matter how humble his origins.

Danny's dream is the universal dream of 1950s youth — rebelling against fathers who slaved at a profession that failed to fulfill them, wanting to make it on their own by doing what they most loved, a heresy to convention at that time. The enemy then was not capitalism *per se* but *raw* capitalism — sustaining the modern consumer lifestyle by selling one's soul to unsatisfying work. The Generation Gap theme re-emerges when Danny's father begs him to remain in school and eventually follow in the older man's line of work, pharmacy — become a white collar working stiff. "You've got to graduate," Pop Fisher insists, "if you're ever going to have a *profession*!" What he can't grasp is that Danny's decision to drop out doesn't imply a rejection of working hard to pursue the American Dream, only the older generation's limited vision of it.

Initially, Danny doesn't have a clue what he really wants to do, explaining his frustration. Until he discovers that, Danny willingly takes blue collar day jobs rather than lock himself into a white collar slot and end up, like the negative role model presented by his father, a drunk. Danny then experiences an epiphany — the singing he does for pleasure could be the basis for a career. As Charlie, one of the few adults who "gets" the younger generation, explains to Mr. Fisher, "Singing's a profession, too!" As the title of an upcoming Elvis film would put it: follow that dream. Danny's premiere as a singer makes it clear that his music combines something borrowed and something new.

Confused after listening to the performance, the resident stand-up comic asks if Danny sings "folk songs." It's clear that Danny himself isn't certain whether that term properly describes his emergent sound. His first number is "Dixieland Rock." Danny-Elvis combines elements of Southern jazz — a white interpretation of black spirituals, offering a soft sweet sound — with the new rhythm 'n' blues beat. This fusion works, satisfying older and younger members of King Creole's audience. One of the early Memphis disc jockeys to play "the new music," Bob Neal of WMPS, came up with his own effective term, "cowboy bop,"[21] emphasizing the Western motif so essential to the Presley persona.

What follows is a pastoral interlude that parallels Elvis' outing with Hart in *Loving You.* Danny takes Nellie for a moonlight cruise on an old riverboat. He points out to her the home that had belonged to his family, until his father fell apart and they were forced to move. Though we don't get a glimpse of the place (whether that was an artistic decision or a cost-saving device is unclear), we hear him talk about his dream to buy it back someday. Thomas Wolfe may have been correct when he insisted "You can't go home again," but that hardly stops the modern hero of film and literature from *trying* to — including Wolfe's own autobiographical figures. Danny at this point represents those many Americans who, in the 1950s, found themselves stuck in urban-suburban situations, dreaming of returning someday to a rural — i.e., Southern or Western — way of life.

Such a growing nostalgia movement "informed much of the new popular culture as well as the critical effort to understand it."[22] To try and achieve this dream, Danny must, like Scott Fitzgerald's equally nostalgic hero in *The Great Gatsby* (1925), reply — answering a realist who insists we can't repeat the past — *of course you can!* Setting out to make his own incarnation of the American Dream come true, Danny must raise the necessary funds to purchase this place. The capitalist theme resurfaces — each Elvis alter ego is a further step away from the pure pole posited by Clint in *Love Me Tender*. If Danny allows himself to fall in with Maxie, he's no better than Ronnie, as much a whore professionally as she is physically. Ronnie here serves as Danny's foil; different as the two initially seem, we realize she is precisely what Danny may become.

Ronnie is the personal property of an arch patriarchal (rather than benign father) figure. While Maxie attempts to seduce Danny into deserting the King Creole for his club, Ronnie stands in the background. Director Curtiz frames her so that Ronnie appears to be a statue — one more beautiful object in Maxie's extensive collection, a living embodiment of the sensuous paintings of attractive women Maxie keeps mounted on his walls. In an intense sequence, Maxie objectifies Ronnie by forcing the shocked woman to raise her skirt and show off her attractive legs to leering men. Ronnie quotes Shakespeare — "to thine own self be true," she earlier confided to Danny — establishing her as an educated person who once aspired to noble things — to teach literature, perhaps even write herself. Ronnie states outright that she despises Maxie, staying with him only because she has surrendered to the money principle.

Danny's weaning her away from a "bird in a gilded cage" status is accomplished, despite his juvenile delinquent activities, by an ever more messianic approach; Elvis is able to help fallen characters arc through his positive presence. This he already accomplished for the Egan and Paget characters in *Love Me Tender* and Corey and Scott in *Loving You*. In *King Creole*, this spiritual aspect fuses with the Oedipal theme. For Jesus, there was the Virgin Mary but also Mary Magdalene, the slut (insofar as the Bible is popularly interpreted) whom Jesus de-sexes — turning her into a true believer and, as such, an alternative for His own absent mother. In an early Elvis film, a "bad girl" invariably assumes the Magdalene role, though she will (like her progenitor) transform under his influence.

Ronnie mothers Danny after he rescues her from whoredom, at which point she is reborn — seen by Danny (and the audience) in the sunlight rather than in The Blue Shade's dark rooms. In shock, Danny happily sighs: "You look like a *kid*!" She is, at least momentarily, the girl she used to be before selling out — if such a redemptive state lasts only a brief transitory moment, Ronnie paying for her transgressions with death at Maxie's hand. She expires, via a reverse *pieta*, in the arms of her son/lover. Virgin and Whore collapse into one figure — apparently, she and Danny have consummated their relationship sexually, an appendage to their already ripe spiritual union.

Ronnie's passing implicitly frees Nellie from the mother role, suggesting that she and Danny may now move toward a healthier male-female relationship. Yet for the first time, Elvis has made love to his mother-substitute. The other side of the Oedipal theme is the murder of the father, which almost occurs here. Owing Shark a favor, Danny is persuaded to take part in the late-night mugging of a pharmacy manager who now employs Danny's dad. Danny justifies this brutal act by reminding himself that the pharmacist has been mean-spirited toward Mr. Fisher. As luck (or fate) would have it, the manager sends Danny's father out into the rainy night to deposit their money.

Danny's involvement thus recalls Oedipus accosting Laius on the road to Thebes, destroying the man he hoped to save. The actual death of Danny's father would have made for a more powerful ending than what we here encounter. But this is, after all, a Hollywood studio movie, not a Greek tragedy. Still, the final scene resolves all tensions in a manner that belies the conventional ending. Danny returns to King Creole. LeGrand sits in the audience with Mimi, the two ready to marry — Danny forgiven for all Sophoclean sins against the family unit. When Nellie approaches him, Danny — now Oedipus, Jesus, James Dean, Wolfe's Eugene Gant and Fitzgerald's Jay Gatsby rolled into one — rejects what ought to be part of the formula, an on-screen depiction of the hero's formal union with "the good girl" after the tainted female sacrifices herself for him.

"Not yet, Nellie," he tells her. "Maybe in a little while, when the time is right."

Following this withdrawal from the apparently perfect mate, he sings a traditional love song, "As Long as I Have You." The number, echoing earlier films in which a romantic song is *not* directed toward the likely female recipient, isn't intended for the presence of Nellie or even the memory of Roxie but the absence of Mr. Fisher. At that point, Danny's father enters the club for the first time, a forgiving look on his face. Danny finally smiles — one of the rare times he does — sensing that reconciliation is at hand. The sequence directly mirrors the final moments of *East of Eden*, when James Dean's unappreciated son finally found acceptance with Raymond Massey's formerly distant father.

At last, then, Elvis got to play the James Dean hero incarnate. Fittingly, he did so in the final film he made before entering the Army. When Elvis arrived home nearly two years later, the James Dean era — the American '50s — were all over. Elvis would have to move on or, like an old soldier, fade away.

CHAPTER 5

You Can't Go Home Again

♦ *G.I. Blues* (1960) ♦
♦ *Blue Hawaii* (1961) ♦

Elvis was classified 1-A by the Memphis draft board on January 8, 1957, received his selection notice on December 19 of that year, and reported for official induction on March 24, 1958. The infamously long hair was sheared the following day. He completed basic training at Ford Hood, Texas, on June 1 and shipped out to Germany on September 19. At once, it became difficult for any Middle American to continue believing that this young man was dangerous. Elvis had not tried to avoid Army duty; more impressively, he refused to accept a cushy job as an entertainer, serving as a member of the Third Armored Division. Thus,

> almost overnight, Elvis the Pelvis became Elvis the G.I.... [His] image as a
> draftee who rose only to the rank of buck sergeant is central to their under-
> standing of Elvis as a working-class American. Many recount that Elvis "served
> his country with honor" and "did his duty."[1]

Not everyone found this appealing. In the minds of purists, here began the end of an era for Elvis and rock. Wholesome Dick Clark had replaced swarthy ethnic Alan Freed as rock's reigning deejay; on ABC's *The Adventures of Ozzie and Harriet*, clean-cut Ricky Nelson performed covers of Fats Domino's originals. With "Mack the Knife," Bobby Darin fused The Big Beat and The Big Bands. Worst of all, The King had become homogenized, all that wonderful raw energy removed. John Lennon, who spoke admiringly of Sun Records' Presley, lamented, "Elvis died the day he went into the Army."[2] Following his discharge, the star would drastically alter his status in popular culture via a pair of Paramount films directed by Norman Taurog.

The Innocents Abroad: *G.I. Blues* (1960)

Debuting nationally on November 15, 1960, *G.I. Blues* opened the family holiday moviegoing season. Its status as the second most popular film of the week[3] made clear that Elvis' appeal now reached a broad audience. A title — "Produced with full cooperation of the U.S. Army and Department of Defense" — established that an Elvis vehicle now rated as a legitimate part of mainstream entertainment. So did the opening, involving tank maneuvers in Europe. The one-time rebel could commit himself to a greater cause; Tulsa McLean functions as part of a crewcut-sporting team.

One of the era's leading diplomats, George Kennan, had articulated our need to conform to a strict standard. All "exhibitions" of "disunity" would lead to an "exhilarating effect on the whole communist movement."[4] Clearly, Elvis accepted this. His "image as a soldier [braced] the image of working-class Americans as virtuous, loyal, and self-sacrificing folk."[5] Though this marks a departure from Elvis' original screen conception as a loner, other themes resurface. "Home, James," Tulsa kiddingly calls out to a fellow soldier, "and through the park!" — raising the issue of lower-class characters who hope to achieve greater status, much like the actor who played them.

But these are the early '60s; alienation was out, *Playboy*-style swinging in. That Tulsa incarnates the new era's fantasy — the free-living ladies man — becomes clear. There are "cute numbers I have to break up with" before transferring to Frankfurt, he informs buddies, and "I can't leave without saying goodbye." Women are now a commodity — easily acquired by financial power, then dismissed even as a young man could toss the previous Playmate of the Month pin-up, replacing it with the latest — and perhaps do so with actual women, if one only had financial means.

SOLDIER: Dames is money in this man's army. Huh, Tulsa?
TULSA: Yeah. And I'm broke.

Tulsa in no way opposes this system, only resents his (current) lowly position in it.

The first number, "What's She Really Like," conveys an ongoing male fear that women can never be comprehended. The song is offered in a conventional rathskeller, yet no conflict results between the rock musicians and an older clientele. What five years earlier was labeled the "new" (and threatening) music now can be assimilated into old-fashioned settings. The next song, "Frankfurt Special," is performed on a train. This song also concerns women — or, more correctly, the American male's fantasy of them. Tulsa waxes rhapsodic not about women he's leaving and has "known," but women he does *not* know other than in dreams: they're special.

First one, then another, finally an entire group of pretty young women appear outside their compartment. But Tulsa is too busy singing to notice, their only "flaw" that they are real. He suffers from tunnelvision, remaining so intent on the romantic ideal that he can't perceive the actual (therefore, to an idealist, inferior) women only a few feet away. Comic sidekick Cooky (Robert Ivers) and several others do spot the females, yet allow them to remain outside — swinging to the sound but separated from the men by a window. Surprised to see the objects of his obsession, Cooky smiles briefly, then turns away.

Instead of making dates, the boys are far more fascinated by the *idea* of attractive women. For all their *braggadocio*, they are not young adult men, only arrested adolescents — forever joking about "girls" in exaggerated terms, yet unable to relate when actually encountered. Their actions after arriving make clear that they are 1950s American boy-men, about to encounter the new international woman of the '60s, more liberated than anything they've experienced.

Such an abiding connection between an unrealistic fantasy vision of women and an unquestioned subscription to the capitalist system further develops when Tulsa and friends come into some money, which they hope will fulfill their own American Dream after returning home. "This is what I want to get my own little nightclub back in America," one states about hard cash. The Three Blazes, as Tulsa's band call themselves, will perform now-acceptable new music on the Oklahoma Turnpike, square in the center of Middle America. But the Sergeant to whom they are in debt takes it all, leaving them in the lurch again — allowing for one more case of the Presley protagonist spending much of the movie finding his own way of "making it."

Before that can occur, though, Elvis has one of his now-expected barroom encounters with a troublemaker who resents this velvet-tongued devil's ability to melt women. The number he sings in the bar is the third in a row to convey the heartache of a man who fears he'll never satisfy an unreasonable woman.

The mean drunk — a variation on the one in *Loving You*, by now a key convention — initiates a fistfight, if with a notable distinction. Considering Tulsa a mere journeyman, the drunk shouts, "I wanna hear the *original*!" He heads for the jukebox and plays Elvis Presley singing "Blue Suede Shoes." In 1960, the audience laughed at what, decades later, would come to be called a deconstruction device.[6] The bit, though written and executed as a simple gag, announced the mainstreaming of Elvis. The star is not so much *playing* Tulsa as he *is* Tulsa — who is not what he once was.

In *Loving You*, the obnoxious fellow objected to early rock 'n' roll. The current incarnation objects to its demise in favor of pop, and the middle-of-the-road status of rockabilly's poster boy. In the inevitable fight, the audience rooted for the Presley persona. Members of the still-solidifying Elvis Nation take the position (or are manipulated to assume the stance) of "my Elvis, right or wrong"—a strategy to keep the fan base loyal, despite Presley's new tune. On November 19, 1959, an RCA executive had announced that "everything about Elvis" would be different after his return home, "including his singing style."[7] Phones began to "ring off the hook back in Memphis with angry protests."[8] Though Col. Parker vehemently denied any such thing, Elvis had already begun to transform himself into a countrified Dean Martin with "(Now and Then) There's a Fool Such as I" (March 1959). The trick was to continue that shift while retaining the first wave of fans. This brief bit in *G.I. Blues* induced viewers to agree to do so.

This occurs as Tulsa attempts to replace "Dynamite" Bixley as the group's lothario. An obnoxious member of another squad, Turk (Jeremy Slate), tried and failed to seduce Lillie (Juliet Prowse), Frankfurt's most beautiful exotic dancer: "Steam heat outside, iceberg underneath." To raise cash, the boys bet that one of their own can spend the night in Lillie's apartment. Such hopes dim when Dynamite is shipped out, so Tulsa must do the job. He approaches Lillie at the upscale club Café Europa, which caters to rich, older German businessmen. Such types are convinced (as a result of successful liaisons with other "dancers") that their money will allow them to "purchase" Lillie. But Lillie is not like her predecessors. When one smug, self-satisfied (rich) man (in a tux, puffing a cigar) tries to touch her, she pours a pitcher of beer over his head.

The befuddled club owner can't decide what to do about Lillie: She is his headline act, so he can't fire her. Yet she refuses to accept the retro vision of women whom older men such as Herr Klugman harbor. Lillie is the first of a new decade's new women. She is *not* liberated in a contemporary sense, born during the early '70s—*from* old-fashioned notions of sexuality—for she loves to strut her stuff. Lillie is not only the object of what Laura Mulvey would eventually label "the male gaze"[9] but actively incites it. Crystallized here is the swingin' '60s limited approach to liberation, which derives from *embracing* her sexual allure. Still, this is accompanied by rejection of the earlier notion that any woman who flaunts herself in public can be immediately typecast as a whore.

Lillie has no price, at least not for anything other than what she advertises: A sensuous show. She cannot be easily pegged as a good (virginal) or bad (experienced) girl, in terms of the dichotomization that dominated during the first half of the twentieth century. Lillie defines herself; much like Elvis, she refuses to be pigeonholed. Ironically, though he fought for just such freedom of expression, Elvis has difficulty accepting this in a woman. A male

American innocent abroad, Tulsa necessarily undergoes a sentimental education before he can grasp her complex personality.

Lillie asserts that she disparages class distinctions, leaving the wealthy tuxedoed businessmen to sit by the bar with poor G.I.s. Cooky makes the mistake of trying to impress Lillie by lying about Tulsa's financial status: "He's sole heir to a thousand acres full of oil wells in Texas." She isn't impressed, and when Tulsa tries to sweet-talk Lillie, she asserts, "I'd prefer if you *didn't* call me 'honey.'" When Tulsa foolishly persists, she observes: "You and Herr Klugman have much in common." What turned her off to the millionaire was not that he was old, fat and bald (had he been respectful, that apparently wouldn't have mattered) but his patriarchal viewpoint.

Conversely, Lillie was attracted to Tulsa less because he's young and handsome than that he seemed likely to treat her as a unique individual rather than a sex symbol. Such hopes dashed, she turns away from Tulsa as she did Herr Klugman. Confused but impressed, Tulsa pursues Lillie and begins his character arc. This culminates during a boat trip up the Rhine. As the young people distance themselves from the city, the film embodies the classic-romantic dichotomy.[10] In Frankfurt, each was defined by a corrupt if civilized (in the worst sense of that term) system that reduces people to societal types. Relocated in a natural setting, near simple people who live close to the earth, they are freed to set roles aside and discover each other as individuals. He can admit he has no money; she can respond: "Come on, you 'poor millionaire'— *I'll* buy *you* a drink, 'honey.'" The liberated woman pays the bill since, roles abandoned, she can afford to. As to *her* use of the word "honey," it exists in quotation marks — humorously used to make the male know what it feels like.

If Tulsa wisely stops using that term, he foolishly opts for another: "Ma'am." The Madonna/Whore dichotomy is not easy for the American male to drop. No sooner has he stopped addressing her as sex object than he treats Lillie as mother. She doesn't care for that, either. Lillie wants to be understood as a unique person. Before Tulsa can treat her so, he must reveal something of himself. Here he sounds suspiciously like the man playing him: "Indian grandmother — Cherokee — smoked a corncob pipe." In his semi-articulate way, Elvis states an anti-racist, anti–role-playing attitude: "If everyone got to know each other better ... they'd ... uh ... *know each other better* ... and then we'd be better all around."

The foil for this deepening relationship occurs when Cooky attempts to seduce Tina (Letitia Roman), a pretty Italian girl. In the room that Tina and Lillie share, Cooky insists he lives on Park Avenue. If he's the retro-male, she's perfect for him, asking, "Are you *rich*?" To seduce Tina, Cooky relies on old 1950s tactics, insisting he "respects" her — implying there's something other than romance going on. The dating game must be played according to strict rules. Tina will sexually surrender only if convinced there's something more than a physical attraction between them. But love as a game is what Tulsa and Lillie gradually distance themselves from. He, though, is still locked into "the bet."

G.I. Blues subscribes to the ancient rules of bedroom farce: A seduction of the impossible-to-achieve beauty not out of love or even desire but as a calculated wager based on raw male ego. The question is: Will this overgrown 1950s boy learn how to be a real man (*not* macho, rather a mensch) as he enters the 1960s? The turning point occurs when Tulsa and Cooky discuss the deal. We realize Tulsa is progressing as a person while Cooky is not:

> TULSA: I'm not enjoying it.
> COOKY: You will. And if your buddies can make a little *money*....
> TULSA: I *guess* there's nothing wrong with it.

Of course there is. Tulsa is halfway "there."

In most Presley pictures produced during the 1960s, a full alteration of the hero's psyche can be achieved only by the intervention of children. During the pastoral interlude, Tulsa and an old German bridged any generation gap, actual or mythic, by musically performing together to please adorable kids. This delighted Lillie, a potential mother. "Wooden Heart" is another heartbreak number, so characteristic of Elvis.

Acknowledging children in his audience (and setting up a recurring motif), Elvis experiences *adult* feelings, rather than (as in '50s films) those of a troubled teenager. Tulsa thereafter relates to Lillie not as a sex object but as a possible mate with whom he might build a family.

At this point, another couple appears to serve as a different kind of foil. Rick (James Douglas) and Maria (Sigrid Maier) project the coming 1960s sexual revolution. They already have a child, out of wedlock. *G.I. Blues* does not, like films from the '50s, imply there's anything sinful in what a few years earlier would have been viewed as a deadly serious situation. As they giddily say:

> RICK: We're going to be married.
> TINA: So we need a babysitter.

One social observer described the change-over that took place in two years as "the Great Divide separating the fifties from the sixties generation."[11] That this should be introduced to popular culture within a Presley vehicle was appropriate, for Elvis was our most visible means and viable "way of getting from the fifties to the sixties."[12]

Tulsa's transition from overgrown boy to young adult is evident in the babysitting scene. The results of sex take the place of sex itself; the two must deal with actual consequences rather than a hedonistic fantasy. Afterwards, the appearance-reality motif occurs. Everyone thinks, when Tulsa stumbles out at dawn, that he's seduced Lillie. He can indeed now have whatever he wants; Lillie, the modern female, will give herself to him once she's convinced he desires a lasting relationship rather than passing romance. Beyond that, she — the '60s female in embryo — can do what no 1950s woman would have dared do: Propose. "Yes, I'll marry you." Marriage does indeed remain her goal in life. Still, it's no longer necessary for a "good" girl to remain a virgin until marriage.

Lillie, aware of the wager, says with a wink, "Perhaps tonight, after the show, you'll win the bet." Romance has been liberated from restrictions of class, cash and simplistic morality. Presenting this alternative paradigm — you *can* marry a woman you've slept with — *G.I. Blues* effectively attacked the long-held reductive view of women. Tulsa expresses this in song. The lyrics speak of her being nice but cold, even as the performer's smile makes clear he now understands her attitude was only the emergent modern woman's necessary protection against the retro-male's outdated assumptions. In a tradition of festive comedy dating back at least to Shakespeare, the film ends with all three couples engaging in simultaneous marriages — any and all progressive attitudes tempered by the most traditional sort of ceremony.

Brave New World: *Blue Hawaii* (1961)

At virtually the same time that Elvis first appeared on the scene, William H. Whyte, Jr., editor of *Fortune* magazine, penned *The Organization Man*. Despite his own lofty status, Whyte railed against widespread subversion of original ideas by "that contemporary body of thought which makes morally legitimate the pressures of society against the individual."[13] Whyte's generalized societal complaints were directed against the very mindset that opposed early Elvis. The mid–'50s were, in Whyte's view, a time of institutionalized conformity in which "the organization threatened to transform American men and women into well-adjusted robots, capable of only 'groupthink,' team spirit, and togetherness."[14] During his time in the service, Elvis had certainly had to conform. Following discharge, would he continue to do so? If he reverted to '50s-style rebel behavior, would Elvis become an anachronism?

In *Blue Hawaii*, those questions are fully answered. One innovation is that this film marked the first time (not counting *Love Me Tender*, with its rewritten folk ballad) an Elvis movie begins with something other than a song composed for him. "Blue Hawaii" (performed over shots of the islands) had been recorded by middle-of-the-road pop star Andy Williams. Elvis performs it without violating the song's appeal as a standard. This furthered his gradual assimilation into the cultural mainstream.

Before we ever see Elvis, we meet the female lead who, like Lillie, is a decidedly 1960s woman. Maile Duval (Joan Blackman)— something of a wild child yet a nice girl all the same — is first glimpsed driving a bright red sports car, the kind of vehicle a bad girl would have owned during the '50s. When Maile tears through a red light, she's stopped by a policeman. Learning that she's rushing to the airport to greet Chad, he offers to escort her, sirens blaring. Returning from Army duty, Chad constitutes one more autobiographical portrait. So the same issue with which fans greeted Elvis is voiced by Maile: "What if he's *changed*?" She spots Chad kissing a pretty stewardess, and the answer is clear: Chad-Elvis remains the same.

Still, his hair *is* shorter. Seemingly contradictory truths are self-evident: Things change; not everything changes. In one respect, Chad Gates appears a departure from the previous Presley persona. He hails from a wealthy family. Yet from the opening scenes, and despite the chasm of class distinction, this film serves as a sequel to *G.I. Blues*. Chad arrives on-screen wearing a uniform identical to Tulsa's. Chad, we assume, knows all that we saw the earlier film's hero learn. Chad realizes the secret to a successful life results from rejecting all polar extremes — mindless conformity *and* hostile rebellion. Accepting elements of each, Chad makes his own way in the world by achieving a delicate balance between the two.

A recurring issue is then raised. "My French blood tells me to be angry with you," Maile jealously confesses, "while my Hawaiian blood tells me not to." Elvis' own mixed heritage was admitted in *Flaming Star* and *G.I. Blues*. Here playing a member of the elite, Elvis's screen persona now confronts a woman whose background is "multicultural." His attitude — the diversity within Maile is essential to her appeal — is offered early during a decade in which long-standing taboos would be challenged. Chad and Maile head for a shack on the beach where they used to "shack up," and where they do so again. Yet Maile's "experience" never infringes on her fitness to be Chad's wife.

"You've got a beautiful *home*," Chad says of her humble dwelling, "and a beautiful *family*!" This will prove basic to the film's implied rejection of everything worst about the '50s. Basic to the postwar lifestyle was not only the move to suburbia but from one suburban sprawl to another. *Life* magazine, then our weekly mirror, reported on "a new American phenomenon, the migration of hundreds of thousands of families" whose men "have found that the way to move up in corporate life is to keep moving around."[15] Whyte despised that ever more permanent jobs linked with ever less permanent homes now constituted a "series of way stations" in an ongoing odyssey of unsatisfying impermanence.[16] Ultimate happiness could not be achieved because any social being's two great goals — "certainty" and "stability"[17] — had been misdirected, identity achieved through attachment to a corporation rather than home and family. This resulted in what sociologist David Riesman at this point in time tagged "the lonely crowd."[18]

Such constant relocation was consciously manipulated by the organization that the family breadwinner worked for. IBM, most visible of all postwar corporation monoliths,

> built relocation into the structure of management training and promotion.... In their philosophy, changing communities reinforced company loyalty (while decreasing an older form of American loyalty to the land). A family who put down roots ceased being an IBM family.[19]

Success breeds imitation; other companies followed suit. The syndrome decimated a traditional American notion that can be traced back to the original celebrity folk hero from Tennessee, Davy Crockett, whose popularity with 1950s audiences directly preceded that of Elvis. Like Walt Disney's TV programs, Elvis' own Westerns emphasized an earlier American belief that a strong, supportive family is impossible without a solid and lasting home.

Elvis, like Whyte, had been a voice crying out in the wilderness, if in the medium of popular music. As Richard Goldstein would note about Bob Dylan, "the rock hero is a liberator in musicians drag."[20] As Chad, Elvis offers an alternative to the then-prevalent paradigm. Though rich, Chad admires Maile's humble home, and regards her loving family (that has lived on their land for generations) with great respect. They provide a perfect foil for his own pseudo-sophisticated parents. Chad puts off going to his palatial home, an immense rococo travesty of big money and bad taste, for more pressing reasons than the temporal pleasure of a fling on the beach. When he eventually does return, we grasp why. The aptly named Sarah Lee (Angela Lansbury) and Fred (Roland Winters) live in pretentious luxury. They are not native islanders but stateside Americans who moved here for corporate reasons. The size of their house doesn't transform it into a home.

What Chad most resents is that they've mapped out his career in the family's pineapple business and hope to marry him to some daughter of privilege. As Chad tells Maile, "Couldn't come back with the rest of my life made up for me." Chad's integration into Maile's extended family began at the beach. The natives pulled this Anglo up into a traditional giant canoe; he sang music of the islands ("a lo-ha-hui") with a rock 'n' roll edge they responded to — rock deriving from ethnic sounds. What goes around comes around as he returns the beat to them, they adapting rock into their style. Chad is determined above all else to avoid becoming what in *The Nation* had been mournfully described as "the careful young men" who were "old beyond their years" and devoid of "gaiety and a sense of life."[21] Elvis offered a corrective. He returned gaiety to youth, suggesting they should do the same as he, even if it meant going against the wishes of their parents.

What had been condemned as wicked during the previous decade would be celebrated during the upcoming one. Chad's talk with "the guys" about his flirtations while abroad (he already told Maile he'd been "*almost* always" faithful) foreshadows the Sexual Revolution of the '60s. What remains unchanged is the preference (as in the *G.I. Blues* train trip) that overgrown adolescent males have for a dream girl over more realistic women. Once more, there's an irony as the male community sings about a lovely fantasy girl, as a real girl — beautiful and topless, as Maile has lost her new bikini in the surf — stands behind them. Styles in sexual attitude and behavior may come and go, but the naïve vision of insecure macho males, blind to the beauty around them, threatens to go on forever.

In time, Chad returns home. When he does, we — like him — see this off-putting "civilized" domain in contrast to the charmingly natural setting he and we have just left. Before Chad arrives, his mother and father talk about money and nothing else. They are the raw capitalists we have met in earlier films. Both are surprised to see Chad, whom they refer to as Chadwick. "Four days ... and [he] didn't even come to his *mother*?" Sarah Lee is a throwback to previous Jocasta figures, clear when she continually asks him for some "sugar": long, lasting, liquid kisses.

Just as earlier films balanced self with society, so does *Blue Hawaii*. "Overprotective," it ought to be noted, "was a word first used to describe our parents"[22] during the 1950s. This was the era during which Dr. Spock ended the long-held notion that children ought to be left to fend for themselves in favor of creative parenting,[23] emphasizing the importance of the *mother* as key influence. Such a "preoccupation with children — their inner lives as well as their social activities and games — was something new and peculiar"[24] to the postwar era. Some rare voices insisted that matriarchal indoctrination might prove harmful. Philip Wylie attacked what he labeled "Momism," fretting that "smother love" would result in an endless parade of Momma's boys, young men who looked back in anger at the lack of strong role-model fathers.[25] "She eats him alive," Jimbo says of his mother and father in *Rebel*, "and he *takes* it." Similarly, Sarah Lee plans a party to introduce Chad to eligible (i.e., upscale Anglo) girls; he recoils at this notion of marriage as a financial bond.

What Chad doesn't do is precisely what his parents most fear: Heading for Waikiki to live as a beach bum. His four-day sojourn was a brief vacation. Chad takes a job as tour guide, humble but fulfilling work he chooses for himself. "Do it yourself capitalism was over and done with," Peter Wicke has written about the superficial new consumer culture of the 1950s; now required was a "host of technical employees who could be deployed at will [to] sit out the day in the office."[26] This is what Presley's protagonist, here and in other films, is not willing to do. Chad lives out the prescription for a happy life that Dale Carnegie described; taking pride and pleasure in work creates "the adventure of his existence."[27]

Such an attitude was also espoused by some highbrows. In 1956, Paul Goodman acknowledged that the wide-open spaces we associate with the wild west and the previous century remained alive and well, if now inside each true American. Goodman lamented, though, that the '50s sensibility threatened to fence us in, via a soft society "lacking in enough man's work."[28] Chad, like Elvis' blue-collar characters, is enthusiastic about doing such man's work, particularly outdoors. First, the film's opening act concludes as Chad heads to the birthday party of Maile's 78-year-old grandmother. "You've got to go home *sometime*," Maile told Chad when he avoided facing his parents for as long as possible. After taking Maile's advice, Chad is more sure than ever before that home is where the heart is.

This event is Chad's turning point. When he deserts Sarah Lee and Fred after a few horrible moments, Chad doesn't run *away* from family but *to* it: Maile's family gathering. Dean, Natalie Wood and Sal Mineo, after running away from their homes (more correctly, houses) and families (using the term lightly) in *Rebel*, found a house they could turn into a home, recasting themselves as an old-fashioned family unit. Chad also represents postwar youth, eager to return to an earlier America in which home and family meant something significant, as it still does to many ethnic minorities — here, those native Hawaiians who enjoy a loud, loving luau on the beach.

The hippies wore granny glasses and peasant clothing, tacit symbols of an earlier lifestyle they hoped to reclaim. Elvis served as the transitional figure. In *Blue Hawaii*, he connects the dots between the first wave of 1950s rebel youth and the '60s youth movement to come.

During the party, he performs "I Can't Help Falling in Love." He sings this not to Joan Blackman but to her grandmother, recalling that *Love Me Tender*'s title tune was performed to elderly Mildred Dunnock. Only at the song's end (again, precisely as in his first film) does Elvis take the younger woman's hand, acknowledging her as the current incarnation of what this elderly woman represents: The tradition that modern youth desperately needs but sadly lacks. At this moment, Chad commits to Maile. Never again will he flirt with other attractive women, though they come on to him.

Here begins his disengagement from the adolescent behavior he earlier displayed. Chad doesn't fear Maile growing old, because he adores the current incarnation of the ethnic person she will in time become. When Chad brings his "nature girl" to the vulgarly expensive party, Chad's father (a decent sort at heart) likes her, but his mother is offended. Fusion between the old music and the new sound is achieved even in this unlikely place, though, as the Nature Boys perform play a traditional hula, while Elvis offers up "Let's Rock." The two songs blend into "Rock-a-hula"—satisfying older *and* younger guests. Sarah Lee is the only one who doesn't "get it":

SARAH LEE (disparagingly): What's that?
FRED (agreeably): Something we may have to get used to. It's called the sound of youth.

This is not lost on Chad. "The difference," he whispers to Maile, "between your family and mine." Her retort is even more important: "We're not our families, Chad. We're what we make of ourselves." This is the movie's key line: The notion of personal (rather than biological) determinism, one area of ideology in which Elvis' vision truly is liberal.[29] Moreover, it rests at the heart of the youth movement that would shortly emerge, as certain old values (those pertaining to miscegenation and class distinctions) would be overturned. Maile inspires Chad to reinvent himself. If that sounds Gatsby-esque, recall that unlike Fitzgerald's hero — literally defining America during the twentieth century's first half— Chad does *not* wish to win a female child of privilege by transforming himself from poor boy to rich man. His own inner odyssey (and that of this era's youth) follows an opposite route: Marry the poor girl by embarking on a downwardly mobile journey.

He refuses to become a second generation version of his dominated father. The problem, though, is not marriage per se, or the fact that Fred has a "straight" job. It derives from the woman he married and her values, coupled with the cold, mercenary way he does his job owing to his wife's influence. Turning away from the Oedipal subtext of earlier films, we here encounter an Elvis who does *not* want to either sleep with or marry his mother. Chad will grow ever more aware of this and set out to marry and work without falling into the previous generation's trap. What occurs next constitutes "act two" not only in the film but in the lives of its audience — then leaving their teen years behind, now at college (Chad graduated before going into the service) or taking their first jobs. The world according to Elvis is the progressive-traditionalism which Whyte considered our last best hope: Embracing the work ethic and family values, rejecting more recent ideology.

However appealing, Chad remains far from perfect. His greatest failing is a tendency to slip into assumptive behavior. When Chad lands a job escorting an educator and her charges around the islands, he scoffs: "Shouldn't have any problem spotting a *schoolteacher*!"— certain she'll be an unattractive old maid. Instead, Abigail (Nancy Walters) proves to be attractive and liberated, anything but the stereotype. Abigail, like Lillie in *G.I. Blues*, embodies those 1960s new women who balance serious careers with a fun-loving spirit, something Chad — and, in the ongoing films, Elvis — must adjust to. The situation sets all the hero has been trying to achieve in an ironic context. He recoils when other people prejudge him on issues like appearance, but he does precisely the same thing to women.

The aging process now slips into play. Abigail mentions that her girls are extremely young:

CHAD: I get along very well with teenagers. I used to be one myself.
ABIGAIL: And not that long ago!

Ceasing to be a symbol for America's youth, Elvis will now serve as a mentor. As a veteran of what has been called the first wave of American teenagers, he has experienced what they must go through. He can now provide guidance for the second wave that was not possible when he and his loyal fans needed it most.

As a mentor, though, he must reject the advances of his lovely young charges, including Ellie (Jenny Maxwell), the group's Lolita. When Ellie kisses Chad, he responsibly pushes her away, even if he understands that she is a product of all that was worst about the 1950s:

ELLIE: I've got two mothers and three fathers.
CHAD: But I don't rob cradles.

Chad alone grasps the base of Ellie's problems: "Why do my parents always send me away?" Ellie rebels (more correctly, *reacts*) owing to the lack of strong grounding in an old-fashioned family. Chad finally takes Ellie over his knee and spanks her; afterwards, she's miraculously "cured." *Blue Hawaii* can be read as a rejection of everything Dr. Spock proposed and, in this sphere, propagandizes an ultra-conservative doctrine. "No one ever cared enough [about me] to do that," Ellie appreciatively admits.

Nor will Chad pursue Abigail. When Maile expresses jealousy, Chad laughs: "Oh, she's all right —*if* you happen to like older women." Has the Presley persona actually overcome the Oedipal complex? So it would seem. Despite the plethora of attractive females on view, Chad concentrates solely on the woman — experienced yet innocent — whom he plans to marry.

What he teaches the girls is his own vision of the American work ethic. They have fun fishing, but at the luau, no one eats unless she helps clean and cook. The once-marginalized bad boy — kept apart from the group — is now the responsible young man, drawing isolated individualists (what he once was) into a healthy community — a far more democratic one than those that excluded him. Yet he has not "gone over" to the narrow adult mentality which once spoke out against him. The liberal side of Chad causes him to encourage the girls to dance wildly on the beach, knowing they (like himself as a teen) are only letting off steam. An arch-conservative of that era could insist dancing "is a subtle instrument of Satan to morally and spiritually destroy youth."[30] To Elvis, it is less an incitement to sexual activity (the ultimate wiggler onstage, he himself was utterly uninterested in penetration) than a means of harmlessly releasing young energies that would otherwise be diverted in more dangerous directions.

The obligatory fight scene in a bar with an obnoxious drunk heightens *Blue Hawaii*'s themes. Chad ends up in jail, where he sings the film's nearest thing to a rockabilly tune ("Beach Boy Blues"), appropriate since the image of Elvis behind bars offers a momentary throwback to earlier incarnations. "My baby's back from the big house," Sarah Lee coos upon Chad's return, returning things to a lighter vein. Then we discover the ultimate irony: Sarah Lee's parents were moonshiners. A B-movie Blanche du Bois, Sarah Lee's pretensions to gentility constitute a desperate device by which she denies her humble origins. Fred, in contrast, always seemed a regular guy who somehow became involved with a "classy" woman. The opposite proves true: Sarah Lee married "up" while Fred is the sort of American his son wants to be: A self-made millionaire.

This explains why Fred can see what his wife, lost in a sea of denial, cannot: Maile is precisely the woman Chad ought to marry. "She's pulling you down to her level," Sarah Lee complains. Fred knows that Maile helps the potentially spoiled boy by raising him up to her level of naturalness and integrity. This becomes clear when Sarah Lee complains about Chad:

SARAH LEE: How did we go wrong?
FRED: We got married.

The film does not reject marriage any more than it does capitalism, only fuzzy attitudes about each. Marriage, to the next generation as embodied by Chad and Maile, will be liberating in a way the institution has never before been: A relationship of equals. This becomes clear when Chad proposes, even as *Blue Hawaii* shifts into its third act: "You're not only pretty but you've got a *brain*." *She* suggests Chad leave the travel company and go into business for himself, she a full partner — precisely what he wants.

Life for them will be the adventure Carnegie called for. What we witness offers a vivid portrait of the first modern (1960s and beyond) marriage and a blueprint for the youth movement. Two years earlier, William Graham Cole, Professor of Religion at Williams College, had been asked why young people were marrying and settling down as soon as they could. His reply, if a tad simplistic, made clear that the reconfigured vision of the work ethic that had evolved during the postwar years was at fault: "Pursuit of success is apt to be called the rat race. Any remaining sense of meaningfulness is in marriage and a home."[31] Marriage and home, however, would not be enough; the New Youth of the 1950s wanted it all.

Blue Hawaii informs this new youth, in the years just before it evolved into a social movement, that they could indeed have it all. When Mr. Gates' partner Jack (whom Abigail loves) attempts to draw Chad into the company, he replies, "I want independence [but] I figured out a way to do *both*." Chad and Maile will, via their own company, take over the travel business for Fred and Jack's pineapple industry. Elvis in the 1960s will have it both ways, working not *for* but *with* the Establishment. Even Chad's mother can't object, though she reveals herself to be the one character incapable of arcing. Attending the fully interracial wedding ceremony (to the tune of "Hawaiian Wedding Song," as the film ends as it began, on a pop tune associated with Andy Williams), Sarah Lee still mouths pretensions: "My daughter in-law is of royal blood." Sadly, there are some parents so mired in what was worst about the '50s that they cannot be "taught well" by the youth of the '60s, as they (the younger set) attempted to make their ideals — an odd but appealing combination of traditional values and progressive alternatives — become real.

CHAPTER 6

Mired in the '50s

• *Flaming Star* (1960) •
• *Wild in the Country* (1961) •

More than half a century after the tumultuous events of the mid–'50s, Elvis — the man, the music, and the movies — serves as centerpiece in an ongoing nostalgia movement. Such an idealized image of the era first evolved in the late sixties and early seventies, as a rapidly expanding drug culture, the disastrous war in Vietnam, the assassinations of beloved political leaders, the Watergate hearings and finally a major oil shortage led to an ever more charming if rather unrealistic memory, enhanced through popular culture, of Presley's era as an preferable time. First came the Broadway play *Grease* (1970) and George Lucas' *American Graffiti* (1973); the *Happy Days* TV series premiered in 1974. The filmed version of *Grease* (1978) solidified the highly questionable conviction that 1950s had been America's last great golden age.

Yet what had attracted '50s youth to Elvis in particular, rock 'n' roll in general, was The Big Beat's slap in the face to what everyday life had actually been like: a "no down payment" approach to joining suburbia and "diving into convention"[1] and, for anyone who cherished rugged individualism, days that were anything but "happy." No wonder then that in retrospect, Norman Mailer recalled the '50s as "the worst decade known to man."[2] This had been the untenable culture of convention and conformity that spawned, as a reaction, the poetry of Allen Ginsberg, the paintings of Jackson Pollock, the novels of Jack Kerouac, the acting of Marlon Brando, the humor of Lenny Bruce and (on a more massive level) the Presley phenomenon. Properly understood it represented a pop-culture rejection, at once reactionary *and* rebellious, against the nouveau pseudo-sophisticated norm.

Several Elvis films of the early '60s play as throwbacks to the dramas he'd been involved in during the previous decade. Vaguely anachronistic when released, they offer attitudes from a period that already seemed to be something of a faded memory. Still, Elvis — though already moving on to different things, as *G.I. Blues* and *Blue Hawaii*— would twice return to the aura of his early hits *Jailhouse Rock* and *King Creole*. We find Elvis addressing issues from that era in which, in the words of Stanley Aronowitz, "'youth' (first) became a class, a historical subject and the vanguard agent of change."[3]

Move Over, Marlon: *Flaming Star* (1960)

Marlon Brando had been director Don Siegel's first choice to play the half–Indian, half–Anglo hero of this intelligent civil rights Western, adapted by Fox studio veteran writers Clair Huffaker and Nunnally Johnson from the former's novel. When Brando dropped out, Elvis jumped at the chance to fill the shoes of the man who had long been a key role model. Yet another hero was Frank Sinatra, who could set his musical reputation aside to appear in dramas. When asked at a Graceland press conference on March 7, 1960, what his own Hollywood schedule included, Elvis admitted:

> I have three pictures in a row to do. I hope they won't be rock and roll pictures 'cause I have made four already and you can only get away with that for so long. I'm thinking in terms of, I'd like to do a little more of a serious role. Because my ambition is to progress as an actor.[4]

Though Elvis denied it at the time, he hoped to directly pattern his career after that of Sinatra.

Things didn't work out that way. Col. Parker persuaded Elvis to sing the title song over the credits, then perform another number. However minor a compromise this may seem, it marked the beginning of the end for Presley's hoped-for "serious" career. Still, *Flaming Star* remains far more ambitious than most of what would follow. Elvis pulled off what he had set out to prove, attested to by strong reviews following a December 20, 1960, release. Typical was Arthur Knight's in *Saturday Review*: "a singularly effective [performance].... It is the depth of feeling he reveals that comes as such a surprise."[5] It was less of a surprise, to those who understood Elvis' ongoing ambition to succeed James Dean, whose own talent had resided in "his ability to show profound vulnerability."[6]

That depth is in evidence from the opening. Pacer (Elvis) and Clint Burton (Steve Forrest), half brothers, ride up to their isolated ranch. Native American on his mother's side, Pacer intuits that something is amiss. The house is too quiet. A key convention of the Western film — most recently embodied in

John Ford's *The Searchers* (1956) — appears about to recur: Hostile Indians have raided the place. The men draw guns and enter. They find to their (and *our*) surprise their Anglo father, Sam (John McIntire), and Pacer's Kiowa mother, Neddy (Dolores Del Rio), along with friends and neighbors, gathered for Clint's birthday. (Clint is the product of Sam's earlier marriage.) The sense of relief is palpable, and director Siegel sets into operation an approach he will play variations on. Clichéd situations will be suggested, only to be undermined.

When the party is in full swing, Pacer grabs a guitar and sings ("A Cane and a High Starched Collar") while everyone else dances. However obligatory Elvis' musical performance, Siegel transforms something added as a commercial consideration into a source of meaning. Pacer is reduced to a catalyst, providing the music necessary for others to dance while never doing so himself — integrated but not assimilated. He appears joyful, yet eventually he will express long-repressed anger at being marginalized — even in the context of people who on some level accept him. Despite the handsomely rendered nineteenth century setting, this establishes Pacer as the embodiment of a decidedly 1950s syndrome: "our dread of deviance: those symptoms or behavior causing an individual to be rejected by the group."[7] In literature, this was true of the heroes and heroines in novels by J.D. Salinger (*Catcher in the Rye*) and Carson McCullers (*The Member of the Wedding*). In popular culture, the concept had been embodied in rock 'n' roll music and the early films of Elvis Presley.

The words to Elvis' song bring up further areas of interest. Pacer initially sings from a *female* point of view, expressing the attitude of a woman who wants to rope and hold her Western male. She will give him her virginity if he will marry her.

For the first time on film, Elvis appears in a scene that acknowledges an element of his persona that added to his initial "disturbing" quality:

> Especially during his 1950s "rebel" years ... Elvis slipped "in and out of gender" in performance style and sartorial display, rupturing notions about masculinity and femininity, encouraging new models of visual pleasure.[8]

Elvis' feminine aspect had been obvious even from his first film, if unenlightened critics of that era saw this as an open invitation for ridicule. *Time's* anonymous reviewer of *Love Me Tender* had, with condescending cruelty, described the experience of gazing at Elvis on-screen:

> Is it a Walt Disney goldfish [Cleo, a female in *Pinocchio*]? It has the same sort of big, soft, beautiful eyes and long, curly lashes, but whoever heard of a goldfish with sideburns?[9]

Camille Paglia would eventually reflect "the face is Elvis is a boy-girl, masculinity shimmering and blurred."[10] Though *Flaming Star* will not allow for further development, Elvis' androgyny would reappear in subsequent projects.

Elvis-Pacer soon switches personas, expressing the male who would like to sample her *cherry* pie — virginity which can be had only if he pays the price of his freedom, which he is not ready or willing to give up.

The parallel of marriage to death takes on significance if we set aside the film's historical setting to consider the audience that received this film. In the '50s, 97 percent of all people who had reached marriageable age had indeed married, and many members of each sex found that the institution did not allow them the "happy ending" that movies like *Father of the Bride* (1950) had led to expect. During the following decade, the divorce rate skyrocketed. *Flaming Star* relocates this modern problem in a period setting. Coming at the dawn of a new decade, the film could thus call into question what had been blithely accepted in the suddenly bygone '50s.

Also, the nineteenth century cowboy hero embodies a male desire to remain sexually promiscuous. Pacer expresses this attitude in the song.

That is a fantasy image Elvis would often embody in the '60s. Meanwhile, though, the Presley persona — still mired in the '50s — must negotiate retro-waters. Like the opening sequence, this song also sets up something quite different from what we assume will occur next. Among the party guests is Roslyn Pierce (Barbara Eden), who has arrived in the company of her father (Karl Swenson) and brother (Richard Jaeckel). Since Elvis plays the lead, we expect pretty Roslyn to embody the "ma'am" of the song, he emerging as the man who hopes to sample her "cherry pie." But Roslyn only has eyes for the *older* brother, echoing the romantic triangle in *Love Me Tender*. While Roslyn's choice may be between two attractive men, it sets into place racial repercussions that will surface later.

Now, though, Pacer's uniqueness is touched on by another guest. Tom Howard (L.Q. Jones), drunk, lets a casual comment slip: "No one would guess that your ma and pa is *different* from anyone else," he chuckles. Though the nearby ranchers accept the Burtons, that doesn't mean they aren't aware of a racial component which makes this family (as Tom puts it) "different." Pacer is half–Indian (in actuality, Elvis's maternal great-great-grandmother was Cherokee, adding an autobiographical element). As always, though, Self is balanced with Society. Philip French has asserted that "from around 1950 the Indian [on film] can stand for the Negro when the implications are social"[11] as "the conflict between cowboys and Indians became a covert commentary on [contemporary] race relations."[12]

The first such film had been Delmer Daves' *Broken Arrow* (1950), which ends with the death of James Stewart's Native American wife (Debra Paget). At the decade's beginning, "[n]o doubt she had to die as punishment for the crime of miscegenation"[13] — that is, to make the film palatable to the racist element that would despise Elvis as he "deeply violated mainstream fears of miscegenation"[14] through music and movement conveying a "blatant assertion of race-mixing which derived from [his] basic refusal to be contained within the limited parameters of 'whiteness' and white culture in mid–1950s America."[15] *Flaming Star*, produced ten years later, followed the first wave of the civil rights movement at mid-decade. If accidentally, the two movies serve as bookends — allowing us to view the degree to which the movement achieved some of its goals (the cause had hardly reached closure).

In *Broken Arrow*, the implied politics were motored by a definitively early '50s consensus mentality. First, there is "the dialectic of the Indian"— good peacemaker Cochise (Jeff Chandler), bad eternal-warrior Geronimo (Jay Silverheels) — resulting in "an allegiance of moderates" from both sides, Anglo and Indian, who stand against the extremists from either race.[16] Something altogether different occurs in *Flaming Star*, in which Sam and Neddy Burton might be read as older equivalents of Stewart and Paget (had her character lived), Elvis playing the offspring of their union. Pacer's peculiar status explains why Roslyn and another young woman, Tom's pretty sister, never cast eyes at Pacer. In the manner in which these pioneers have decided to deal with the Burton family, Pacer is tolerated but never conceived of as marriage material. His good-natured singing will eventually be revealed as a genial Uncle Tom-like guise that covers deep resentment.

All this literally explodes when the Howard family, after arriving home, is attacked by a war party of Kiowas. The Burtons know nothing about this when a young chief, Buffalo Horn (Rudolph Acosta), rides to their cabin. The brave's presence is felt by Pacer before his father or brother are aware. "Sometimes I think you're *more* than half–Indian," Clint says. He means nothing negative, yet his words reveal an abiding prejudice. Even if hostilities break out, the Kiowas will not touch this particular family, though Neddy is referred to at the Kiowa camp — even by her own sister — as "the woman who deserted her people." The only true loyalty for the Burtons is, then, to one another: The individual American family, that very institution Elvis had early on been (wrongly) perceived as a threat to.

As one social critic of the time wrote:

> In a world of chaos ... there remains only the solid structure of the *home* [emphasis added] to form the basis for the re-establishment of the ancient standards of virtue.[17]

Now, with the initial controversy all but forgotten, Elvis embodied a new image as champion of what would in time come to be called "family values." "If we have to be a power unto ourself," Sam insists, "we'll resist whoever and whatever comes against us." The Burtons draw together, trapped between two worlds, belonging completely to neither so long as Neddy and Pacer are around.

Clint discovers this when he and Pacer ride into the nearby town and enter the Pierce store, where they learn about the massacre. A tearful Angus (he had been engaged to the Howard girl) informs Clint he can enter, but threatens to kill Pacer "if that half-breed brother of yours sets foot in this store." Even Roslyn, after reaffirming her love for Clint, turns on Pacer: "*You'll* always be safe from them!" As Pacer and Clint ride home, side by side once again, Pacer realizes that he stands utterly alone.

Again we encounter the '50s youth sensibility, a time when "*alienation* was a word that was falling lightly from [Brando's] own lips and those of his friends."[18] As writer Rod Serling put it:

> There was a postwar mystification of the young, a gradual erosion of confidence in their elders, in the so-called truths, in the whole litany of moral codes. They just didn't believe in them anymore.[19]

Such a vision ended abruptly (albeit briefly) with the election of John F. Kennedy, the youth president, and the advent of a New Frontier mentality. *Flaming Star* might be considered the final 1950s civil rights Western. In such a reading, the aptly named Dred Phillips emerges as the local Joe McCarthy, insisting that the Burtons take a loyalty oath: "If it comes to a real showdown, are you with us — or not?" When the Burtons refuse to answer — on the grounds that, as Americans, they should not be subjected to such a test — they are blacklisted from the community that seemed all-inclusive a day earlier, before a Red Threat (Indian in context, Communist in the 1950s) appeared on the horizon.

Those who are different — refusing to even try to conform to a mythic norm — are soon being harassed. Their cattle are scattered, then killed by neighbors who recently partook of their hospitality — now appearing by night, Klansmen-like. "They're worse than the Indians," Clint says, ironically offering an unintentional slight to his half-brother and adopted mother, both nearby. Actions of the area's "Good Citizens Committee" resemble televised images from a few years earlier when, in Arkansas, the recently created TV network news teams trained live camera eyes on nine black students as they tried to enter Little Rock Central High School and "the whole world could watch America at war with itself."[20] That phrase well describes what we see in *Flaming Star* as the microcosm of this town likewise explodes, like '50s America, owing to bigotry.

More striking still, the film allows us a vision of things yet to come. *Flaming Star* is a relic of an era of hope as to the integrationist dream that had been initiated by President Eisenhower and articulated by Dr. King. In 1962, President Kennedy and Attorney General Bobby Kennedy forced the integration of the Universities of Mississippi and Alabama, standing up to governors Ross Barnett and George Wallace — setting off a new civil war, also predicated on the issue of state's rights vs. federal doctrine. But after first JFK (1963), then Dr. King and finally RFK (both in 1968) were assassinated, many true believers lost all optimism. As one young African-American woman, who had up to then subscribed to non-violent protest against racism, put it, "I knew it was all over, that there was no more reason for hope."[21] She left her work as a Democratic party volunteer to join the Black Panthers — moving from inside the system to an organization that rejected working from within.

As Lou Smith, onetime co-director of CORE, put it, "[W]hen I was in that civil rights movement [of the early '60s], I was still trying to be like white people"; after the burning of the Watts ghetto by frustrated residents, "that's over. Over and done with."[22] "Over" was the dream of achieving civil rights via non-violent voter registration drives that would allow *Negroes* to join the system and achieve power within it. "Begun" was an era in which many *blacks* would reject voting as being co-opted by the system, instead embracing violence as the only solution that works. That social paradigm is frightfully present in *Flaming Star*.

Society is counterbalanced by Self. While Sam and Clint are away, the cabin is threatened by a pair of rowdy buffalo hunters, who assume — realizing the woman of the house is a Kiowa — they can have their way with her. This allows Elvis his obligatory fistfight, chasing them away in defense of Neddy. No sooner has this been accomplished, however, than it becomes clear that Pacer's great loyalty (like that of the actor playing him) is to his *mother*. Portrayed by the still stunning film veteran Del Rio, Neddy takes Pacer's hand and kisses it in thanks. They gaze into one another's eyes and embrace. Significantly, it is the only time in the film that Elvis will hold a woman in his arms.

The Oedipal element has clearly *not* disappeared with his return from the Army. *Flaming Star* is the love story of Pacer and Neddy, which explains why, when the issue of loyalty is raised, Pacer drifts toward the Indian element. "You say you are not our enemy," his Kiowa blood brother Two Moons insists. "Then you must be our friend. Will you ride with us?" As Anglo atrocities to the Kiowas and Pacer's family escalate, he acquiesces, after explaining to tribal leaders that he will never fight Sam or Clint. In its second half, *Flaming Star* anticipates the violent racial clashes of the new decade's latter half.

Up to this point, the ethnic minority has requested nothing more than tolerance. From this juncture on, they opt for a multi-cultural defiance of the mainstream and the notion of conforming to that value system — striking out against any attempt to draw them into a 1950s consensus. Elvis still represents the American rebel-loner, at odds with *all* around him. Such confusion is referenced when Pacer, rejected by Anglos and mistrusted by Indians, admits to his mother about her kin: "*They* ain't my people. To tell you the truth, I don't know *who's* my people."

As so often occurs in Westerns, it is a female — a notably liberated one at that — who stands against the men and does the right thing. When Neddy is wounded, Roslyn overcomes her earlier prejudice in a way the men have not done, following Pacer and Clint to the ranch and aiding the doctor as he attempts to help Neddy. The screen mother's eventual death sequence must have been particularly difficult for Elvis, still overcome with a desperate grief following the death of Gladys a relatively short time before filming began. Intriguingly, Pacer turns his wrath on the now-sympathetic Roslyn: "You were the *worst!*" When she expresses shock, he shouts: "Why not *me?* Why my brother?" Roslyn is stunned to realize that Pacer secretly loved her all these years. Though Roslyn insists she never had an inkling, a thorny issue has been raised. Did Roslyn rule out the equally handsome younger brother because he was half–Indian, if only unconsciously?

As Pacer rides to join the Kiowas, he glances at the grave of his mother — the only woman with whom he was completely comfortable, much like Elvis himself. Soon he dons war paint and is ready to shoot on sight the townspeople he believes have betrayed him. An early '50s liberal-consensus approach to social problems is overturned during the dawn of a radically different decade. Pacer transforms not the area's peace-loving Cochise, but Geronimo — played not as a troublesome blocking character, as in *Broken Arrow*, but a *necessarily* violent hero. In life, the Cochise of the African-American movement, Dr. Martin Luther King, would give way to Malcolm X, a black Geronimo.

When Pacer's father is killed in a skirmish and Clint wounded, family once more asserts precedence over any ethnic alliance. Wounded while returning Clint to the arms of Roslyn, Pacer rides off to join Native American Gladys in the hereafter, glimpsing the flaming star of death. First, though, he makes a plea for an eventual acceptance of people who derive from mixed racial backgrounds: "Maybe someday people will understand." *Flaming Star* leaves its audience with a challenge to make the world a better place — one which would be met by teenagers who saw the film and became, at mid-decade, the 1960s radical college youth.

The Mark of Cain: *Wild in the Country* (1961)

Pacer represented one aspect of the '50s paradigm for an anti-hero: Alone in the world, unable to attract women despite his charisma. Yet he was buoyed by the firm foundation of an old-fashioned family unit that can sustain traditional values even as the surrounding world goes mad. Glenn Tyler in *Wild in the Country* provides a perfect compliment, the film itself representing the flip side of that decade's trap for the alienated individual. Here is a young man who attracts every woman he meets, but cannot develop a solid sense of self owing to the lack of the one thing Pacer had: familial roots. Glenn is a country cousin to Dean in *East of Eden* and *Rebel*, desperate to find a father figure to provide non-abusive discipline and a substitute mother to cuddle and comfort him.

As director Nicholas Ray said of "Jimbo":

At seventeen he is filled with confusion about his role in life. Because of his "nowhere" father, he does not know how to be a man. Because of his wounding mother, he anticipates destruction in all women. And yet he wants to find a girl who will be willing to receive his tenderness.[23]

Dean had been "typecast as the rebel, and like Brando," in his actual life "was rebelling against an unhappy childhood and a father he had grown to hate."[24] Glenn serves as an apotheosis of such 1950s characters. This is clear early on, when the 17-year-old's father legally has the boy put away for fighting with a brother whom the father prefers. This echoes the *East of Eden* plot, Elvis belatedly living out his dream to become "the James Dean of rock 'n' roll."[25] He had just turned down (at Col. Parker's insistence) a biographical film in which Presley would have played Dean[26] because Elvis wouldn't have been able to sing.

While Elvis would gradually transform into an ersatz savior, in *Wild in the Country* the (initial) Biblical reference is to an earlier story. On the family farm — for the first time in Elvis Cinema *not* depicted as a pastoral utopia, rather a stigmata visited upon nature by man — Glenn threatens to kill his brother but runs off before he can. Afterwards, he will carry the mark of Cain, in terms of intent — a point he himself acknowledges. Glenn rushes across a natural body of water and, in the process, is re-baptized. Symbolically, Glenn grows gentler while alone with the animals. Like the sleeping gypsy in Henri Rousseau's painting, the creatures he encounters (a raccoon, a bear) mean no harm, sensing this particular human is more at home here than in civilization. The contrived title aside, never once will Glenn be wild in the country — he is sweet and sensitive while in this extension of the original paradise.

Whenever he is dragged off to the social world of men (and women!),

Glenn rebels against the constraints of conformity. He openly rails against the institutionalized hypocrisy he experiences, becoming "wild" until back where he belongs. A far more appropriate (though less sexy in terms of box office considerations) title would have been that of J.R. Salamanch's novel, *The Peaceful Country*. Or, if we accept the script's name (fashioned from the book by no less lofty a literary light than Clifford Odets, author of such studies of youthful alienation as *Golden Boy*), we ought to listen closely to the title tune, as performed by Elvis over the opening credits, as director Philip Dunne treats us to a pastel rendering of the country. We have trouble telling whether the colorful yet subdued panorama is a romanticized painting or the actual landscape, for it resembles a green world from Shakespeare.

The lyrics offer a more restrained (and, in terms of the film's ideology, accurate) notion of what the term "wild" actually means, in context. Wild is *not* crazy; wild is *natural*, the ultimate arbiter of "the good" in a romantic sensibility. We are not far from nineteenth century poet William Wordsworth in his "Ode: Intimations on Immortality" (1818):

> Though nothing can bring back the hour
> Of splendor in the grass, glory in the flower....

Wordsworth refers to a childlike sense of wonderment at what jaded city folk can still recover in the wilds, the "primal sympathy" that, having once been, must ever be if we rediscover the innocent child within.

Though Glenn knows nothing about romantic philosophy, he represents it well. There is little doubt that his analyst, Irene Sperry (Hope Lange), realizes she signifies the alternative classicist view, also that she (old enough to be the boy's mother) and Glenn (who looks like her deceased husband, a youthful suicide) are the infamous opposites that attract. "How old were you when your *mother* died?" is the first question Irene asks after agreeing to treat Glenn. Now, Society is momentarily set aside so the star can deal with Self. Two years after Gladys' death (dramatized in *Flaming Star*), Elvis still mourns her, on-screen as well as off. Like the man playing him,[27] Glenn subscribed to a strong religious background so long as his mother was alive though this dissolved with her death: "There was never a week when this boy and his mother didn't attend *church*," one witness at Glenn's trial points out. The loss of her life led to the loss of his innocent world-view — the persona's plight mirroring that of Presley.

Now, his on-screen hero transforms from Cain to Christ. "My God, why has thou forsaken me?" Glenn cries out. He will soon deal with a Scriptural trinity of women. First, there's his Magdalene, sluttish Noreen (Tuesday Weld), already a mother owing to what, in the '50s, were called "loose morals." Her mirror opposite is the potential proper mother substitute, the film's virgin and designated "nice" girl, Betty Lee Parsons (Millie Perkins). The former lives in a ramshackle house in town with her own abusive father, who brings Glenn to work there, hoping Glenn will marry Noreen and take her off his hands. The latter lives on a pristine farm, like the nice girl in *Loving You*.

This time, the situation grows considerably more complex. Betty Lee's sympathetic mother, a social liberal, believes Glenn can rise above birth and upbringing. Betty Lee's father (archly conservative) insists Glenn's future is biologically determined; if allowed to remain on their land, he will steal away their daughter's precious virginity. The significance of his fear is rooted in the 1950s value system, still in effect when this film was made. One young woman later recalled the pressure to deny her sexuality:

> "If you go all the way with someone, he'll leave you and marry a 'nice' girl." At the other end of the scale, a reputation of promiscuity was the equivalent of inciting a panic — or wholesale dumping of shares [in] a market psychology that described a woman's sexual favors in terms of "giving it away" or saving it.[28]

Noreen gives it away, Betty Lee saves it. "It's like I've got two girls with two roads to go," Glenn tells Irene. "Have you ever thought there might be a third road?" she asks. Consciously, she means college. Unconsciously...?

In *Jailhouse Rock*, Vince had to reject the superficial and destructive appeal of the loose woman, despite his male desire, slowly learning to love the virginal good girl. *Wild in the Country* offers a twist that deconstructs the seemingly set-in-cement formula. In *Loving You* and *King Creole*, the experienced older woman embodied the slut goddess motif— the debased mother figure who ultimately gives way to the hero's necessary relationship with a proper young mother substitute. This film's older woman is elegant, intelligent and traditional. Present here is the '50s' notably limited paradigm of possibilities for women. Such choices were vividly delineated by a female author — a girl during that decade who came of age while drawing on role models from the silver screen. "We saw ourselves in terms of the movies," she explains:

> From '50s movies, we learned that girls turned into wives. They traded in the ingenue's crinolined skirt, the smart hat of the career woman, the sex kitten's off-the-shoulder blouse for the homemaker's Peter Pan collar.... We would become what we beheld.[29]

Noreen is the sex kitten, Betty Lee the ingénue, Irene the career woman ... and Glenn, the '50s male who, as one such real-life person solemnly put it:

> I felt that if I were sexual with someone, that indicated that I didn't respect them. I could be sexual with someone I didn't care for, but not with someone I did care for.[30]

That could be Glenn talking. He feels guilty whenever he is about to engage in "relations" with Noreen, owing to that '50s stigma: Sex, so desperately desired, implied (if taking the form of action) a total lack of respect.

Glenn *does* respect Noreen for her decent qualities, however few they may be. He can't have sex with Betty Lee, wouldn't consider it since he respects her if for no other reason than she is a virgin. That makes her marriageable material, only there's the blocking character, her father. Finally, Glenn is drawn to the only woman left open to him: the beautiful blonde who is neither slut nor virgin. Irene is already experienced, yet only within the system of marriage prescribed by society. *Wild in the Country* offers a bizarre fulfillment of the Oedipus complex so essential to the three Presley pictures that immediately preceded it.

> For Freud, by the time he has reached the age of 4 or 5, the small boy is sexually interested in his mother, wishes to gain exclusive possession of her, and therefore harbours hostile impulses toward his father. However, the hostility arouses fear that the father will retaliate ... [so] the small boy unconsciously abandons his hopes of sexual union with his mother ... and finally turns his attention towards securing sexual satisfaction from other feminine sources.[31]

As the film's narrative progresses, it becomes clear that Glenn and Irene are steadily moving toward consummation, Elvis about to become, on-screen, a contemporary Oedipus.

But the lure of raw capitalism complicates things: "I could've bought my maw her freedom with money and fame," Glenn (sounding notably Elvis-like) whines to Irene during a therapy session. She employs this as an opportunity to get him talking about the woman whose influence was cut short, causing Glenn's problems.

GLENN: You don't know anything about my mother.
IRENE: Your mother appears to mean a great deal to you.

"She was always my best girl," Elvis once said about Gladys.[32] Irene tries to take that missing woman's place in Glenn's life. Upon learning that his mother wanted Glenn to attend college (echoing Danny's deceased mother in *King Creole*) to become a white collar professional, Irene plans for him to do precisely that. For Irene, to "have" Glenn would be to virtually go back in time, repeat the past and recapture, however fleetingly, the lost moment.

This, as in Fitzgerald's *The Great Gatsby*, represents an impossible dream, leading to a tragic situation that can only have disastrous results. In the novel, Irene — after bedding Glenn — kills herself. When producer Jerry Wald decided this might make the film too depressing, perhaps diminishing box office returns (the film flopped anyway), an alternative ending was devised. Yet in its contrivance, the denouement proves highly significant. Irene has been romanced by a local (married) bigwig, Phil Macy (John Ireland). She broke off their mild flirtation after realizing that Phil had no intention of leaving his wife to marry her. (In the book, Irene had been having an affair with Phil, though film censorship of the time would not allow this to be portrayed unless both were in some way punished at the end for the indiscretion.)

Complicating matters: Phil's spoiled teenage son Cliff (Gary Lockwood) is the obnoxious rich kid whom the Elvis hero must in time fight. Cliff Macy loans Glenn his car (cars a potent symbol since that Cadillac in *Loving You*), then tells the authorities that Glenn stole it. Ironically, the brattish boy has an understanding father; there is a sense throughout that if Glenn and Phil Macy were father and son, they would satisfy one another. But that is not the luck of the draw.

For the first time, the Elvis hero's talent is not for singing but something more elevated. A Thomas Wolfe figure, Glenn is a crude boy who harbors literary aspirations. "Write it all down, in your words," Irene requests. She hopes to free Glenn from the limits of birth and breeding by developing this gift, also her late husband's talent. Other characters support Irene's fervent belief that an education can make all the difference: Rafer Johnson appears as Davis, a black butler who will shortly set aside servitude to whites since he's been studying for the bar exam. He embodies one more positive image of an African-American — on the verge of living out the Eisenhower-era ideal of achieving integration through equal education, then becoming part of what, all good liberals hoped, would become a colorblind society.

This represents yet another ideological holdover from the period during which *Wild in the Country* was produced. Shortly after the election of John F. Kennedy, as Jack Greenberg (NAACP Legal Defense and Educational Fund) noted, the Warren Supreme Court "lifted injunctions against demonstration."[33] Assuming an activist stance in the early '60s, the Court "undertook to do certain things that Congress had declined to do or hasn't wanted to do."[34] According to Chief Justice Earl Warren, most important was the decision on redistricting; i.e., the one-man, one-vote issue. But Dr. King's efforts on behalf of integration would be rejected by key African-American leaders in the decade's later half; as Lou Smith (regional director of CORE) put it, Malcolm X's view was, "Man, stop being Negro and start being black!"[35] This signaled the move from "self-hatred to self-love."[36] *Wild in the Country* conveys an earlier ideology, when poor blacks and whites alike were told that subscription to a then-prevalent middle-class ethic would allow marginalized people to "raise themselves" beyond humble roots. "All you need is discipline," Irene insists, meaning a formal education.

Initially Elvis' blue-collar rebel complains that Irene wants to "take my life and twist it into something *you* want." Yet for the first time he coalesces.

Then comes their moment of truth. They drive to the state university, where an English professor insists Glenn may well be the next William Faulkner. On the way back, fate intervenes. They sing their own tragic chorus, if unknowingly: "Marching off to get *married*." A storm forces the two to stop and they must share a single room in the motel. There, they at last confess their love and kiss — the most potently sensuous screen kiss Elvis will ever have with any female co-star. Owing to restrictions of the time, they do not engage in sex. The couple did in the novel and by implication that is what transpires here. From that point on, Glenn can't grasp whether he ought to call her "ma'am" or "Irene." Intentionally or otherwise, Elvis always pronounces "ma'am" as "Mom!"

Melodramatic plot complications have Glenn standing trial for manslaughter after he punches Cliff, recalling the opening of *Jailhouse Rock*. He eventually is freed by Cliff's father, Glenn's father figure (and Laius-like competition for the woman they both love), who admits in court that his son had a bad heart, the actual cause of Cliff's death. Irene almost, but doesn't quite, commit suicide. In the final shot, it is she, not Betty Lee, who sees Glenn off at the station as he boards a train and heads for college. The implication: In time, Elvis will return and marry his Gladys-like "best girl."

Wild in the Country was not profitable, perhaps (as many people suggested at the time) because, like *Flaming Star*, it contained a limited number of songs. The large profits reaped during the same period by *G.I. Blues* and *Blue Hawaii* made it easy for Col. Parker to convince Elvis that he ought to give up any ambitions for a serious career. Yet another reason for this film's failure has to do with a viewing of "the life of Elvis as a parable."[37] Whatever the parallels to Cain, Christ and/or Oedipus, Elvis became the twentieth century all–American incarnation of Faust, always in danger of selling his soul:

> False to his past, to his region, to himself ... "he lost track of who he was" ... creating the morality tale of the small-town boy and girl, changed forever by the big city.[38]

When Glenn leaves for college, Elvis embodies on-screen precisely what his huge audience of suburban teens did at more or less that same moment in time. Once there, they became intrigued by folk music and foreign films, ever less likely to catch an Elvis flick. That included *Wild in the Country*, which portrayed him as paralleling their own experiences. What Elvis needed to maintain at all costs was his original audience — largely Southern, almost entirely blue collar — and they (at this juncture) had no desire to watch a movie in which Elvis succumbed to "the sugarplum of college" with its vision of "endless vistas of upward mobility" and automatic entrance into the "utopia" that seemed "immanent in the fifties America."[39] For Elvis to do this — even on-screen — amounted to a betrayal of this constituency.

Wild in the Country projects William Whyte's pluralist view from the 1950s — a liberal notion of solving problems like juvenile delinquency by winning over marginal types to the mainstream.[40] During the early '60s, academics who still believed in such an approach did not go to see Presley pictures. Those who did still consider spending their money and time on Elvis' latest movie had little interest in assimilation through education. They wanted to stay true to their selves, remaining in trailer parks; or (better still) to make money through luck or pluck, then (like TV's *The Beverly Hillbillies*) wallow in riches without abandoning their white trash attitudes.

They would attend Elvis films, though only if he embodied that principle. Considering the financial disappointment of *Wild in the Country*, Elvis would be careful to do precisely that from then on — at least in one ongoing and significant subgenre of his future work.

CHAPTER 7

Poor White Trash

♦ *Follow That Dream* (1962) ♦
♦ *Kissin' Cousins* (1964) ♦

The down-home mentality of 50 percent of Elvis' films attests to what he had learned from *Wild in the Country*'s failure: A need, in an ever-altering social, political and cultural landscape, to tailor certain movies for loyal grass-roots fans. "In rock as in [Jean-Jacques] Rousseau," Robert Pattison noted, "energy and wisdom are not fostered by formal education but its abolition."[1] The rock gestalt (even at its most urban) is no different from that of those who inhabit the hill country. Elmore Messer Matthews, in *Neighbor and Kin: Life in a Tennessee Ridge Community* (1966), noted "the native distrust of education and special skill."[2] Elvis, who combined hillbilly with rock (creating rockabilly), projected the anti-intellectual stance of each. Often he told people, "A diploma's not that important, [though] life's experiences are."[3]

Films designed with this audience in mind tacitly reject the direction in which the Republican party had led the country during the final eight years of the '50s, an approach the Democrats would further escalate between 1960 and 1968. From the onset of the postwar era, our national leadership actualized the vision of *Time*'s longtime editor-in-chief, Henry Luce. His "American Century [defined] the new vision of an all-powerful America spreading democracy and riches across the globe."[4] Harry Truman initiated this approach, which led to the debacle in Korea; Kennedy and then Johnson continued it, resulting in the Vietnam disaster. Between Democrats, Eisenhower likewise maintained an internationalist approach to our worldly role. This strategy, which cut across old party loyalties, infuriated large numbers of rock-ribbed Westerners and Southerners who lined heartland highways with hand-scrawled signs stating: "U.S. out of U.N.!"

Most of this protest hailed "from the greater center of the country,"[5] "a vast insular landmass"[6] where people expressed only contempt for Eastern sophistication, remaining "confident that theirs was the more *American* culture."[7] No one more effectively represented their heightened sense of xenophobia than Elvis. He emerged (essentially, in every other film) as folk hero *to*, and on-screen spokesman *for*, such thinking. According to Wendy Steiner, "since the mid–1950s, Elvis' image has been continually renegotiated and remade in order to mesh with individual and institutional preferences."[8] Many middle Americans who, less than a decade earlier, perceived the star as the first great threat to their basic values now came to see him as the final standard bearer of their ideology.

Paradise (Nearly) Lost: *Follow That Dream* (1962)

Follow That Dream begins with an image of what had already become a recurring motif, American car culture. Toby Kwimper, a young vagabond, is first glimpsed singing "What a Wonderful Life," while perched on the dilapidated jalopy his father (Arthur O'Connell) drives. The family, their few worldly goods piled high on this sorry car, represents that American subculture often referred to as Poor White Trash. The Kwimpers recall "Elvis' forbears" whose lives were based on

> restless mobility: settling, then moving on, settling again ... then moving on again, escaping problems or seeking opportunity or both, looking for a fresh start somewhere else.[9]

From first glance, they are clearly hillbillies. Chugging along in their old auto, with rag-tag family members of varying ages gathered around patriarch Pop, it's difficult to tell them apart from the identical family that surrounded Pa Clampett on TV's *The Beverly Hillbillies*.

That series had been preceded by *The Andy Griffith Show* and was followed by such sequels and rip-offs as *Green Acres, Petticoat Junction* and *Mayberry, R.F.D.*, rural comedies displacing the dramatic Western (reigning TV genre of the 1950s) as the dominant genre on television; Elvis had in *Love Me Tender* and *Loving You* collapsed the Western cowboy hero with the Southern hillbilly. "Unable to adapt," Marshall Fishwick has written of this stock character in the twentieth century, "he became ridiculous. Once feared and respected, the hillbilly became the Pathetic Patriarch."[10] This process had begun at the turn of the century, as people hailing from rural climes south and north moved in greater numbers to big cities. Considering themselves cosmopolitan, they took delight in seeing cruel caricatures of friends and family members who remained down on the farm.

In *American Vaudeville as Ritual*, Albert F. McLean studies the creation of a stock character called "Toby," the country fool, a great favorite (and subject of derision) on New York and Chicago stages in the early 1900s[11] and soon after in the first flickers. Here was "the hillbilly as buffoon," in sharp comparison to the tall, dark, handsome cowboy hero of Owen Wister's *The Virginian* or Zane Grey's *Riders of the Purple Sage*; "Uncouth and uncultivated, [the hillbilly] was a parody of the frontier which was suddenly as out-of-date [in popular culture] as the horse and buggy."[12] Toby is, not coincidentally, Elvis' name in *Follow That Dream*. With the death of vaudeville, Toby moved to the Great White Way: Erskine Caldwell's 1932 novel *Tobacco Road* was turned into a Broadway play in the '40s.

Upscale audiences in tuxedoes and gowns were formally ushered into a playhouse to watch decadent Southerners of the lowest level — a veritable geek show dragged out of the Dixie's bleakest backwaters, presented in the hallowed halls of ... well, if not necessarily authentic art, then certainly big-time entertainment. During the postwar years, a leading literary light, Tennessee Williams, took just such a Toby, re-situating him (as was indeed the case now with many such Tobies) in a big city. What he came up with was a more brutish variation on the backwoods buffoon: Stanley Kowalski in *A Streetcar Named Desire*.

Why, though, the sudden incursion of hillbillies during the 1960s — at a time when the Camelot mentality created a parallel sense of sophistication? This was the era during which America polarized — not merely in terms of age (as in the over-hyped notion of the Generation Gap) but viewpoint. Many young people who had been expected to outgrow rock 'n' roll and cultivate a taste for "the finer things in life" clung as adults to the aesthetics of blue denim. Others did move on. Part of the instinctive genius of Presley (or, some might argue, Col. Parker) was to turn out alternating films for these two now divergent audiences. Also, by implication at least, race too is an issue in *Follow That Dream* — despite the fact (or perhaps because of it) there are no blacks on view in this film or its semi-sequel, *Kissin' Cousins*.

That other segment of Presley's following perceived him as a civil rights activist. But many blue collar fans had forgotten his early identification with black culture. Labor historian David Roediger has theorized that the concepts of "work" and "working class" are inseparable (or at least *were* in mid-century America) with an identity based on "whiteness." Indeed, "the very term *worker* often presumes whiteness,"[13] at least for blue collar (and particularly *Southern*) people of that time. "Their" Elvis was a man who worked with his hands, not (as in *Wild in the Country*) his mind. For them, Elvis embodies their values.

Though the attitude of most upscale Americans toward poor white trash is that they are lazy, that isn't how this constituency perceives itself. David Hundley observed a century and a half ago that their only "inheritance [was] the ability and the will to earn an honest livelihood ... by the toilsome sweat of their brows."[14] In *Follow That Dream*, Elvis is often seen laboring — though according to his own definition of work. His credo is stated outright in the film's first song: "I got no *job* to worry me!" It is not work that Toby scoffs at, but a white collar *job*: "No *big boss* to hurry me." Malcolm Forbes, life-long Republican and founder of the money-oriented magazine that still bears his last name, said of such early '60s youth, whom he admired: "The young people introduced a whole new set of values, but that doesn't mean they want to do away with capitalism."[15] *Follow That Dream* illustrates Forbes' thesis: Work was then being re-invented, both by white collar youth (*Blue Hawaii*) and blue collar (this film). Elvis' entire generation rebelled against 1950s consumerism and wanted to enjoy the *process* of getting rich as much as the rewards.

The Presley persona we meet here, like Elvis himself, "inverts the standard of mobility pattern, thus affirming the dignity and worth of those generally ignored or despised in American society."[16] Presley initiated what in time would be tagged as our "white trash nation,"[17] middle- and even upper-middle class people affecting vulgar styles long associated with the poor: motorcycles, tattoos, hooker style clothing for women, blue jeans for businessmen. The greatest irony is that Elvis himself "had a strong aversion to wearing jeans. As a poor boy, he had no choice but to wear them and he never wanted to lay eyes on another pair."[18] Yet he, in aspiring upward, inspired the "other side of the country" to conversely aspire downward as to style.

When we first meet the Kwimpers, they already possess half the equation for white trash happiness: solid family ties, though no roots to the land. Again, they strongly resemble Vernon and Gladys. As rock historian Dave Marsh has noted, the Presleys were at the time of Elvis' birth "rural people in the process of becoming, if not urbanized, at least estranged from the soil."[19] Unlike their real-life counterparts, who never fully recovered, the Kwimpers enjoy a stroke of good fortune (much like TV's Clampetts discovering oil on their property) that allows them to reconnect. For them and Americans, our national identity is as "a form of society determined by the interaction of man and land."[20] In the nineteenth century, as Frederick Jackson Turner noted, we were by some migratory-determinist drawn westward;[21] in the twentieth, with that first frontier settled, we re-directed our inborn energy, instead heading south. The destination matters less than the journey's symbolic dimension. As a people, "From Daniel Boone to Spaceman, we have accepted the word 'frontier' [emphasis mine] for *any* movement of exploration and adventure."[22]

The film (directed by Gordon Douglas) had originally been titled *Pioneers,*

Go Home!— as was Richard Powell's popular novel. The author implied the largely dismissed white trash subculture actually constituted the proud direct descendant of early American pioneers. The Kwimpers, signifiers of this syndrome, have had to move owing to local authorities and federal bureaucrats, a confederacy of despised dunces in suits. As to the Kwimpers' appearance, the car is left over from the 1930s; on all sides, sleek new models pass them by. These are the last of the Okies, as displaced as their antecedents during the Depression. Elvis is a modern incarnation of Woody Guthrie — if notably devoid of any radical-leftist politics. As has been said of Brando's generation, Elvis' "was not so much a political rebellion as a restlessness with the conventions of the American middle class."[23] The Kwimpers represent people bypassed by postwar suburbanite society; they reflect, in broad of portraiture, those who came to see this film.

Then comes their defining moment. Disobeying all laws whenever possible as a matter of principle, Pop pulls onto a stretch of the Highway Betterment Project that's closed to the public. "We *ain't* the public," he scoffs. In a way, Pop is right. In an age of prosperity, he collects relief; Toby receives monthly checks from the federal government, his back (supposedly) disabled while in the Army. They are out of touch with the Kennedy-Johnson era, backwards in everything from dress to attitude. Anachronistic pioneers, they alone perceive the contemporary landscape as if it were the open range of yesteryear and decide to homestead.

As Richard Schickel has noted,

> ... one of the great functions of culture, both high and low in ... the twentieth century, has been to [offer us a] vision of the past, a previous fulfillment, the loss of which we can sorrow for, the recapture of which we can work toward.[24]

That's precisely what occurs here ("low culture") even as it does in "middlebrow" (Booth Tarkington's *The Magnificent Ambersons*) and "high" (Scott Fitzgerald's *The Great Gatsby*); in each we are "drawn back ceaselessly into the past."[25] The Kwimpers find themselves on a stretch of unfinished highway that "the country ain't caught up with yet." Toby wonders if it will ever be completed or if funds have dried up. Pop tosses back his white trash wisdom: "The government don't run out of money; only *people* run out of money." They establish a hobo camp, the modern equivalent of an early frontier settlement.

There, Toby cuddles with Holly (Anne Helm), his adopted, underage sister. Their sensuous relationship is a case of emotional if not biological incest. Helm, like so many Presley co-stars beginning with Debra Paget, looks like Priscilla Beaulieu — or, more correctly, Priscilla looks like Paget, who refused to be romanced by the young star owing to her relationship with more traditional male Howard Hughes. Elvis, Pygmalion-like, picked his woman (at age 12, this Paget lookalike could still be molded into whatever he wanted her to be) on the basis of his film experience. At the time when *Follow That Dream* was made, the eventual wife was his "live in Lolita."[26] Though Elvis and the underage Priscilla engaged in quasi-sexual activity,[27] Elvis constantly insisted that he considered her his "sister"[28]—like Helm in this film.

As to the film's marriage of cousins (a theme more fully explored two years later in *Kissin' Cousins*), Billy Smith, a relative of Elvis, insists that inter-marriage between second (even first) cousins was common in the Presley family.[29] As in earlier films, Holly hankers after such a union ("women are natural nesters") while Toby wants to remain free and footloose for as long as possible ("I'm not the marryin' kind"). We never doubt that they'll end up together. Here, as in most American movies,

> Hollywood saw to it that our fantasy selves led straight from that walk into the sunset to settling down as home-loving, God-fearing, hard-working Americans … just like the solid citizens who reared us.[30]

Their natural enemy is a variation on Whyte's organization man — an agent of widespread bureaucracy that subverts original ideas through a "contemporary body of thought which makes morally legitimate the pressures of society against the individual."[31] Mr. King, state supervisor of highways, takes pride in knowing not a single tin can or gum wrapper has been found along the 30 miles of completed road. His name signifies an antipathy toward truly democratic values; King sees red after noticing the makeshift camp. He insists the family leave before the governor spots this slum. "I'm mighty near out of patience with this kind of government," Pop mutters.

King makes certain their previous legal-resident state knows that the family has homesteaded, so there will be no more relief checks. King employs zoning restrictions to limit their access to water: "I owe to *the people* my best effort to run you off of this land!" King doesn't employ the term in a populist sense — the *common* man — rather the vast nebulous of normalcy. That these "folk" could constitute the true American "people" is beyond him. *Follow That Dream* is about settling down, though not in the assimilation-into-the-mainstream sense King can understand. Here are Boone and Crockett, long hunters who don't wander aimlessly but search for places to put down roots for their families.

Like those living on the nineteenth century frontier, this pioneer family survives by making do and keeping faith. Holly, a redneck Christian, prays to God to allow His flock to stay in what they consider the Promised Land. Toby goes fishing to provide food for his family. His natural (or God-given, depending on how one considers the situation) skill provides their salvation.

A businessman driving by stops and offers money if Toby will help him land "a large one." Before long, the family has set up its own incarnation of the American Dream, Elvis transforming from Li'l Abner into Horatio Alger. "This is what comes from sticking up for your *rights*," Pop says when cash flows in — a notably *Southern* vision of the way of the world.

"We started out in this country with a wilderness," James M. Roche (chairman of the board of General Motors until 1971) claimed, "and we have had to build on that wilderness and develop."[32] *Follow That Dream* presents his paradigm in miniature, reset in modern times. Everything Elvis does here, as in his own life, is honed to a Protestant work ethic that ties the Presley persona to all of America's great folk heroes (fact-based ones from Davy Crockett to Thomas Edison) and their fictional counterparts (Dick Whittington through Jay Gatsby). But if some things remain the same, others change: Pop reacts with horror when Toby suggests they invest the profits. "No banks!" Pop screams. A throwback, he recalls the folksy types who held bankers responsible for what happened after the 1929 crash.

This, though, is the '60s; now, bureaucrats (like King) rather than bankers are the villains. However many values Toby shares with Pop, he emerges as a man of his own time. "Kind of like a *church*, ain't it?" Toby asks as he steps inside a bank. The line conveys the attitude of the ordinary but ambitious redneck in the century's second half: He wants big money as much as old-time religion. Another key change is that, in this new decade, women (even in this humble setting) refuse to remain home cooking and cleaning. Holly is the family member who thinks big, deciding they need a fleet of rowboats to serve potential fishing customers — which they can only achieve via a bank loan. In life, Priscilla proved to be the true genius behind the marketing of Elvis Presley Enterprises.[33]

Nonetheless, Elvis (on-screen and off) remains a patriarchal figure. "He'd remind me that his was the stronger sex, and as a woman, I had my place,"[34] Priscilla said; it also describes Toby speaking to Holly. Though *she* makes plans for the bank loan, *he* steps inside to negotiate. In a telling gag, bank guards initially assume this rube asking for money must be a hold-up man. Toby, almost arrested, is rescued by Endicott, benign head of the bank as well as Toby's customer. Impressed with Toby's (and Holly's) instinctual entrepreneurial sense, Endicott turns over as much money as they need. Such magnanimity will lead to the creation of a new American moneyed class represented by the Kwimpers: *Rich* white trash. The expensively suited Endicott feels a kinship with the family because, like Toby (and the governor), he's a self-made man — an implicitly Republican adherent to and symbol of social Darwinism, as espoused by Herbert Spenser. Such thinking is based on the American strain of political-economic thought called rugged individualism: The government ought not to hinder or help people but let the chips fall where they will.[35]

All the film's positive characters (and the work that sustains them) stand in direct opposition to the liberal Democrat government ushered in with Kennedy, advanced by light years when Lyndon Johnson assumed the presidency. Between 30 and 40 federal grant-in-aid programs were in place when Johnson took office in 1963, close to 500 when he left in 1968. The Great Society — a government that hoped to fix every wrong by spending vast sums of money — was designed to take Kennedy's concept of federal intervention to the limit via "the most sweeping social legislation in America's history."[36] Standing in firm opposition to such an approach are Toby, Endicott and the governor (but not King) — homeboys who made the big time through hard work abetted by the luck of the draw. They are success stories in a land where membership in the elite class (at least when America "works right" in their conception) has nothing to do with birth or breeding, only *money*.

Here is a value system initiated during the country's early years, outlined by Ben Franklin in *Poor Richard's Almanac* (1789) — a vision of America which snowballed during the early twentieth century. Elvis embodied this notion, succeeding through pluck and luck — his diligent work as a singer combined with the good fortune to meet Col. Parker precisely when he did.[37] So it goes in the film. If Toby, Endicott and the governor are Southerners, King conversely appears to be a recent arrival. He symbolizes to "folk" like the Kwimpers what they hate:

> The people back East, they believed, were essentially parasitic — they went around making money, while the good (Southerners and Midwesterners), purer of spirit but dirtier of hand, went around making products.[38]

When the governor does at last arrive, he proves to be far more sympathetic than King, who slowly worked his way up in the bureaucratic system by mean-spirited manipulation. To the contrary, the governor hails from the same simple roots as Toby's family, and so expresses sympathy and admiration for them. He agrees that, in the great American tradition, they have a right to homestead (according to local law, any piece of land can be claimed if people put a roof up and stay on the land for six months). This hardly deters King, who employs another arm of despised Big Government under Kennedy-Johnson, the Welfare Office.

This bastion of established order is run by Alicia Claypoole (Joanna Moore), an attractive, older, unmarried woman, a staple of Elvis Cinema. She works not because she needs the money (she's independently wealthy) but because she enjoys patronizing the lives of people she considers of a lower order. Interfering with such folk, Alicia believes she can improve their lives and morality — the old elitist dream of "raising" humble people up to some "higher level" of existence. She's a control freak, and Elvis in actuality always "detested aggressive women."[39] Not surprisingly, then, he rejects Alicia's sexual advances (she is among other things a hypocrite, lusty when not lecturing poor people on the need to overcome their own sexual appetites).

Follow That Dream was released precisely when many conservatives (in particular Southerners) began the transition from a century-old allegiance to the Democrats (assumed in opposition to Lincoln, in particular his anti-slavery stance) to the Republicans — a move which would be all but complete by decade's end. Likewise, the Kwipper family members were once New Deal Democrats. Now, however, under Mr. Endicott's tutelage, they become Republicans. "Folks can take only such much government," Pop explains. "Then they gotta bust out and go someplace where there ain't none." Though Kennedy-Johnson are never mentioned by name, they are the clear target by implication. "You want to get ahead in life," a family member insists at mid-movie, "never do what people tell you to do" — "people" referring to people in power, not the simple folk.

The other danger also hails from Eastern cities. This is The Mob: Gangsters move in next door, their expensive trailer parked not far from the family's humble one. Where honest capitalism naturally mushrooms, sleazy consumerism follows — here as a gambling operation. This is "The Combination," that alliance of the Italian Mafia with the Jewish Murder Inc.[40] One of the gangsters is Jewish (Jack Kruschen), the other Italian (Simon Oakland). Elvis' magnanimous attitude toward ethnics, so characteristic of his more mainstream movies, has no place in *Follow That Dream* — The *Family's* scenario opposing the *family's*. The Kwippers count on the fact that, when they claim the land after six months, it will become part of the county. The gangsters hope to keep the area a modern Cimarron Strip — a lawless frontier forever, under no one's authority.

It comes as no surprise, then, that the rural folk opt for law and order, even as Elvis' blue collar fans (many of them juvenile delinquents in 1958) would by 1968 become supporters of law-and-order Vice-President Spiro Agnew, constituting his Silent Majority. Elvis becomes the marshal of this relocated wild west; the free pioneer who resented restrictions eventually imposes his own on unwanted ethnics and unworthy Easterners. This is precisely how Henry Fonda in John Ford's *My Darling Clementine* (1946) transformed from cowboy to lawman: "Get outta town, *Indian!*" he insisted — also informing a fancy-suited gambler (the equivalent of the gangsters we meet here) he's not welcome.

So Elvis dons a cowboy hat once again, as

In the world of the Western, a man was assumed to do the right thing when he wore the symbol of authority. The marshal's star or sheriff's badge assured us that law and order would be upheld by physical courage. Before the West was won, leadership still had to be earned; it could not be automatically guaranteed by faraway bureaucrats.[41]

Elvis' makeshift paradise does indeed seem lost when the area becomes overrun with Florida residents drawn to the gambling operation. That's when Toby decides to close down the "red light district," or at least take a Destry-like tact — forcing them to shut down at 11 P.M. This leads to the obligatory fight, in which Elvis beats up the hoods.

Even here, though, there's as much of Li'l Abner to Toby as Wyatt Earp. When the gangsters import hit men, Toby mistakes them for visiting hunters. An American innocent, this Candide of the canebrake unknowingly defeats them while trying to help what he believes to be likable lost fellows. Elvis embodies a notion of the yokel as wise fool that cuts back through Al Capp's comic strips to the first Toby caricature from the twentieth century's early days.

In time, the ethnics are forced out before they can corrupt this white trash Shangri-La. America in miniature is saved by Elvis, our traditional national hero-figure re-imagined for a new era. The Old West remains alive, if in the New South. For a while, Toby does hang on to his rebel ways: "I ain't gonna marry and build a home." But as the narrative progresses, Toby must relive, then reject the Oedipal aspect as Alicia tries to seduce him in the swamps.

During this sequence, she lets her hair down, the symbolic on-screen surrender of long-repressed women in Hollywood films since the days of D. W. Griffith and Lillian Gish. Spurned, Alicia does what Old Money women invariably do in films not only *about* but also *for* the lower classes: Hell hath no fury like a woman scorned; she falsely cries rape.

Her Welfare Department — supposedly good liberals all, motored by civic outrage, though we know Alicia's *real* reason — seize the "abused" children. Pappy objects, with words that convey the then-current changeover of grass-roots types to Goldwater (and in time Reagan) Republicans: "You think the people is one thing and the public is another." Pop refuses to get a lawyer because he "don't believe in" them. However critical of the government's then-current agenda, the film has only positive things to say about the American system itself. In the end, authentic authority figures accept Pop's side of the story.

The Kwimpers represent "the spirit of the pioneer," a sympathetic older (and *Southern*) judge points out, "that made this the greatest country in the world"— a spirit that continues to "function today" in the guise of the last pioneers: white trash entrepreneurs who only want to be left alone to fend for themselves. In the denouement, he allows them to do just that, at which point Toby sets aside his childish wanderlust and marries his ... sister.

Paradise (Barely) Regained: *Kissin' Cousins* (1964)

When *Follow That Dream* disappointed at the box office in mainstream bookings while scoring well on the Southern drive-in circuit,[42] Col. Parker decided that such relatively lofty production values would henceforth be reserved for films set in surfside spots such as Hawaii, released in northern climes during the dead of winter. *Kissin' Cousins* was produced by Sam Katzman, known for his cheaply made but profitable B movies. Though Parker had advised Elvis to turn down the lead in Katzman's film bio of Hank Williams, *Your Cheatin' Heart* (1963), he was impressed enough to bring Katzman on board for Elvis' next venture. *Kissin' Cousins* was directed by Gene Nelson on obvious Hollywood sound stage renderings of the rural South. That it only reached #11 on *Variety*'s weekly box office list didn't interfere with profitability, for they had turned out a cost-effective piece of lowbrow entertainment for what was understood to be a limited viewership. From that point on, Elvis had, as Gerry McLafferty lamented, a "financially rewarding [but] greatly misguided career."[43]

Ideas first introduced in *Follow That Dream* were here updated. Arthur O'Connell plays a variation on his "Pop"; again, Elvis marries an underage relative (Yvonne Craig), this time a biological one. The follow-up film also continues the theme of a symbolic marriage between white trash populists and remaining conservative elements in the federal government — the military taking on that positive aura bankers did in the earlier film.

Kissin' Cousins speaks directly to those mostly older Americans who felt disenfranchised during the Kennedy-Johnson years. Such people preferred a time when it was

> Dwight Eisenhower and the men of his generation who were actually running the country, and the America they governed was the one they remembered from their childhoods, during the turn of the century.[44]

What they most objected to in 1964 was the administration's endorsement of Big Government. When Johnson took office (November 1963) there were 35 federal grant-in-aid programs; when he left six years later, 450+. Johnson's special assistant, Joseph A. Califano, reflected, "There has never been anything like that in the history of this country.... No President had ever sent the Congress a message on the cities"[45] and on air pollution, water pollution, consumer rights and truth in packaging.

Far more offensive to social conservatives was another key element of Johnson's vision. As George Meany, long-term president of the AFL-CIO (and a Johnson supporter), put it:

> [F]ederal aid to education in money terms went from a very small amount, a billion or so, up to twenty or thirty billion dollars. This was the first time where

the federal government accepted the theory that education of America was a federal responsibility.[46]

Elvis was already on the record as being against education as a means of rising beyond one's birthright. He predated such diverse rockers as Pink Floyd ("Another Brick in the Wall," Part 2) and Paul Simon ("Kodachrome") with a firm stance against "book l'arnin'" as a means toward self-betterment. Elvis' first appearance here seems to contradict his retro identity now that he had "moved from being a cultural marker for the middle class (young, rebellious Elvis) to becoming a cultural marker for the middle-aged working class."[47] We first encounter him as Josh Morgan, an educated young man!

Kissin' Cousins opens in Washington, where bureaucrats plan a major missile base for Tennessee's Smoky Mountains. The problem is, the Tatums live atop Big Smoky, where even "in the Atomic Age moonshiners still protect stills."[48] They shoot strangers on sight, particularly representatives of the federal government — this at a time when "History left [the hillbilly] standing on his mountain peak, an outmoded rifle and ideology his only possessions."[49] That ideology remained ingrained and deep: utterly isolationist, not only toward foreigners but even from other Americans — *anyone* outside their ingrown area.

Though the idea of a nuclear power base may seem a mere plot convenience today, it resonated in 1964. The country had never completely recovered from the Gaither Report (November 1957) from the Office of Defense Mobilization, expressing the fear that "we were slipping in our nuclear capacity while the Soviets were becoming stronger."[50] All available evidence, the report claimed, "clearly indicates an increasing threat which may become critical in" the early '60s.[51] The recommendation was for $19,000,000,000 for creation of more nuclear weapons. The movie's base will provide one such strategic position.

Enter Elvis: A member of Salbo's command, F-84 pilot Josh Morgan is himself a Southerner (from North Carolina) and distant relative of the Tatums. Since "anything that looks like it's from the government gets shot," Morgan asks Capt. Salbo (Jack Albertson) if, when he heads South to negotiate, he can wear civilian clothes. Once more, an Elvis character proves Thomas Wolfe wrong by going home again. Returning to his roots, Elvis-Josh meets Jodie Tatum (Elvis), a country cousin and his exact double. Among other things, the movie allows Presley to deal with the haunting memory of his twin brother Jesse Garon. On January 8, 1935, Gladys (then a resident of Tupelo, Mississippi) had given birth first to a stillborn Jesse; Elvis arrived 30 minutes later. Two years later, Vernon was indicted on forgery charges, pled guilty, and was sent to Parchman Farm State Penitentiary, where he served a three-year term.

During his absence, Gladys developed not only her unique relationship with Elvis (sharing a single bed with him) but continued her "relationship" with Jesse's spirit, insisting Elvis do the same.

Gladys "worked actively to keep [Jesse] a member of the family, talking about him almost as if he were alive."[52] Elvis "grew up in his dead brother's shadow, and Gladys made Jesse so real that in later years Elvis was certain he could speak with Jesse."[53] *Kissin' Cousins* is the only film to directly address this haunting element in Elvis' life. Perhaps he did, as some suggest, suffer from "survivor guilt"— feeling unworthy to have been the one to live. Gladys believed that "when one twin died, the one that lived got all the strength of both."[54] Elvis grew up with the self-image of one who has twice the capacity of any normal person. He once asked cousin Billy, "If my twin brother had lived, do you reckon the world could have handled two?"[55] Smith insisted that the question, articulated but a single time, was essential to Elvis' identity issues. The star explored that question here as, like an amoeba, he splits himself in two.

The film's Jodie is a fictionalized Jesse, the sibling Elvis left behind when he abandoned the simple Southland — a realm rediscovered here and found still pure, an American Brigadoon. "The past," L.P. Hartley wrote, "is a foreign country: They do things differently there."[56] Josh-Elvis soon learns that Jodie-Jesse does things differently — and, he comes to see, *preferably*. As Josh, Elvis is the prodigal son who visits a past that's with us still, in a transitional America which in the 1960s was awkwardly balanced "between the corncob and the computer."[57]

Kissin' Cousins may have been a compensation for Parker's decision that Elvis would not star in the movie version of Broadway's *Li'l Abner* five years earlier. The colonel did not want "his boy" sharing the stage with other stars who would also sing. In *Kissin' Cousins*, a group of wild country women who chase after visiting soldiers are called the Kitty Hawks, a reference to "Sadie Hawkins Day." Ma Tatum (Glenda Farrell) is synonymous with Mammy Yokum. The film portrays reactionary elements of the South in a positive way. The Confederate flag, transforming in the minds of Northern liberals from heroic banner of Lee's fighting men to a racist rallying point, remains proudly displayed in the Tatum home. An unclean toilet seat serves as the centerpiece of their living room, though visiting S.A.C. officers don't appear to mind. The only problem occurs when such men speak in bureaucratic terms. "Start talkin' *American*," Pa insists. Once they do, the missile base becomes a reality.

The white trash types are in no way against making money, so long as they don't have to mainstream themselves to do so. This idea surfaces in the first song. Elvis is perched on a haystack, romantically involved with two of his cousins, Selena (Craig) and Azalea (Pam Austin). The chorus of "There's Gold in the Mountains" breaks down any previous barriers between those who like doin' what comes naturally and those who make money.

"This won't be used at all unless someone starts a war against us," an officer insists to Pop. But what settles the deal for a missile base is the generous amount of *cash* the government offers, $1,000 a month — which, as family members acknowledge, is "a *powerful* lot of money." Country folk are not, as outsiders romantically depict them, "pure" in terms of capitalism. These people — Elvis' people —*want* to be corrupted. What appeared to be their pure state only existed because they were not in a position to sell out.

This is particularly true of the girls, who can't wait for cousin Elvis (in uniform) to take then to Knoxville. They come back wearing ultra-skimpy bikinis. When Elvis is with only one of them, she's placed on his left side where a female could come "close to his heart, where she gives him strength through her support."[58] The Tatums are no different than Elvis under Col. Parker's influence, grabbing for the money. By doing so, Elvis did *not* go against the grain of his original constituency, rather living out their wildest dreams. Elvis' early promise had been kept; he stayed the same even when rich.

Kissin' Cousins, like Elvis's entire career, belonged to a trend that would come to full fruition in the early '90s, when Quentin Tarantino's movies and Madonna's videos dominated popular culture. In "White Trash Nation," a *New York* cover story, Tad Friend defined his title as the culturally downward aspirations of most Middle Americans, which "best gives voice to the stifled longing of the well-to-do, who covet what they perceive as the spontaneous authenticity of the poor."[59] This explains the presence of Harley-Davidson motorcycles in suburban neighborhoods and the popularity of drinking beer from the bottle, Stanley Kowalski–style, among Manhattanites. That character, whom Broadway audiences of the late '40s perceived as a modern Caliban, was misinterpreted as the *hero* by many moviegoers when Brando again played him again on film, suggesting that a work's meaning may have less to do with an author's intentions than a viewer's perceptions. The original Toby had been a rube to laugh at; the new Toby — Kowalski, Presley — emerged as a role model to emulate.

Had this not occurred, it's unlikely that Elvis could have been portrayed as groping his pretty female cousins, both underage, while singing the song "One Boy, Two Little Girls." Jodie becomes romantically involved with Midge (Cynthia Pepper), a female member of the military and the nearest thing to a liberated woman on view. When Jodie attempts to grab Midge, she throws him through the air thanks to karate training. Shortly, though, she does decide she'd rather make love than war, giving in to his rustic charm. In this film,

Elvis manages both of the romantic feats of previous pictures: Mainstream Elvis seduces country girls; country Elvis conquers mainstream women.

Finally, members of the armed forces regress — drink rotgut whiskey, make it with country girls, dance under the stars. Peaceful co-existence has been achieved between military and moonshiners, an allegory for the similar union in 1960s America which led to a new conservatism that cuts across class lines and geographical boundaries to stand strong against a then-burgeoning counter-culture. Though this Youth Movement was inspired by early Elvis attitudes, he was already moving in the opposite direction. Presley's eventual White House meeting with Nixon (December 21, 1970) — in which the perceived poles (radical, reactionary) of the mid-'50s accepted that in the then-current climate they were more alike than different — was presaged by the unlikely union between Washington's men in suits and the denizens of hillbilly heaven depicted in this film.

CHAPTER 8

The Sexual Revolution

+ *Girls! Girls! Girls!* (1962) +
+ *Fun in Acapulco* (1963) +

When Dwight D. Eisenhower left the Oval Office, the shift in power represented far more than a diminishing of Republican influence in favor of Democrats. Partisan politics were paralleled by sexual attitudes. David Halberstam noted that in 1960, "John F. Kennedy used the phrase 'New Frontier' to describe the *youthful* daring of his administration [emphasis added]."[1] Essential to the Camelot sensibility was Kennedy's stated ambition to put a man on the Moon; no less an intellectual light than Arthur Schlesinger pointed out that such scientific daring closely related to the "new morality": "penetration of outer space" signified a male desire to (sexually) conquer the (feminine) unknown.[2] Conservative values that had defined the American middle class during the 1950s disappeared from everyday discourse, as the popularity of elements as diverse as go-go dancers and the James Bond films, each then risqué, attested.

In 1960, the Sexual Revolution exploded for numerous and complex reasons, among them: The presence of a young, attractive couple in the White House; the marketing of Enovid, the first legal birth control pill, developed by Gordy Pincus under Margaret Sanger's longtime guidance; the release of Kinsey's second report, focusing on women and forcing the public to face the fact that pre-marital and extra-marital sexual activity, particularly among young people, had quietly increased at an enormous rate. Once again, pop culture reflected the changed moral climate. Federico Fellini's *La Dolce Vita* (1960), an art house hit, introduced moviegoers to European sophistication as to sensuality and "the sweet life." The bikini bathing suit, considered shocking when Gallic sex symbol Brigitte Bardot dared flaunt one in 1957's *And God Created*

103

Woman, could now be donned by such all–American girls as Sandra Dee (*Take Her, She's Mine*, 1963) and Annette Funicello (*Beach Party*, 1963). The swinging (early) 1960s had begun in earnest.

On the musical scene, the mainstreaming of rock continued. The Twist, derived from Elvis' movements though pushing beyond anything he offered, failed to catch on when introduced by Hank Ballard and his Moonliters in 1959. For then, it remained one thing to cheer Presley on, his "sensuality ... almost out of control,"[3] but quite another for fans to take it all further themselves. When Chubby Checker redid the number in 1960, the record took off. As Checker stated, "Before it, [kids] danced close together and wore long skirts. When the Twist first came along, the dresses got shorter and things got cooler."[4] The Twist was not an inexplicable aberration but synergistically related to all that was then occurring in the society. It also served as an expression of an emergent zeitgeist; as Checker said, when people "dance apart ... you do your own thing."[5]

Such a change had been quietly fermenting for some time. "In the fifties — hard as it may be to recall in the era of the organic — natural was a dirty word."[6] Nothing could have appeared more threateningly *natural* than a Presley performance of one of the new rock 'n' roll songs:

> Critics of the 1950s viewed Elvis' body, image, and performances, the bodies and performances of his [youthful] fans, with dread: it all blatantly symbolized the sensual subversion of reason and control.[7]

Hollywood responded to the challenge by

> gradually allowing greater latitude in showing sexual matters on the screen. Marilyn [Monroe]'s sexuality, so overt it might previously have been doomed by the censors (in such scenes as the famous blowing up of her skirt in *The Seven Year Itch*, for example) was now not only permissible, it was desirable.[8]

Nude pictures of Marilyn (taken before she reached the heights of fame) were published in 1954 in a new men's magazine. Half a decade earlier, the ensuing scandal would have destroyed her career. To everyone's surprise, her status as the first Centerfold Girl added to Marilyn's aura.

As to Hugh Hefner's then-revolutionary publication, *Playboy* has (since the emergence of the Women's Movement in the late '60s and early 1970s) been widely portrayed as "exploitive of women." In its defense, one can cite a Pulitzer Prize–winning author who notes that, in its time,

> *Playboy* would play a critical role in the coming sexual revolution; it helped, among other things, to sell the idea that sex was pleasure, to be enjoyed, not something dark to be sought illicitly and clandestinely.[9]

Equal in significance with Monroe and Hefner in terms of instigating in the mid- to late-'50s the oncoming Sexual Revolution was Elvis. One woman who came of age in this era later recalled that before him

> [w]e'd been told that sex was dirty, dangerous, and powerful stuff. That nothing could touch it for pleasure and fun (a completely unknown word as applied to sexual congress in our youth) was the best-kept secret of our coming of age.[10]

Numerous elements added to the changing climate; Monroe, Hefner and Presley reigned supreme. As a result of their impact, things changed so rapidly during the late '50s that to "compare the end of the decade with its beginnings is to see two Americas."[11] Overnight, grown-ups did an about-face. Society matrons like Pamela Mason twisted the night away at New York's Peppermint Lounge. Disparaging youthful energy gave way to emulation. David Obst later recalled that such hungry-to-be-hip adults

> seemed obsessed with the youth culture. For the first time kids were setting fashions for adults. Plastic surgeons made a fortune trying to bring youth back to the grown-ups. The currency of the age was no longer money — it was youth. We were the Now Generation.[12]

As to Presley's film career, the major distinction was no longer between musical and non-musicals but musicals that catered to hick audiences as compared to those that aimed to please a segment of young Americans who emulated the trend-makers by embracing a "first wave" of personal liberation. It made sense then that the films catering to this target audience took place in lush settings. For young people not only now attended college in greater numbers than ever before but also composed "the first generation to be 'exposed' (as the phrase of the period went) to travel and study abroad."[13] Two such colorful "travelogues with music" for Paramount Pictures placed #6 (1962) and #33 (1963) on *Variety*'s annual list of top-grossing films.[14] So it was that "Elvis' mystery train chugged out of the gray '50s (and) into a psychedelic landscape."[15]

The Playboy Philosophy: *Girls! Girls! Girls!* (1962)

Directed by Norman Taurog (who had done the honors with the first musical travelogue, *Blue Hawaii*), working from a script by esteemed scribe Edward Anhalt (*Becket*, 1964), the eleventh Elvis film has been described as a typical "musical romp full of pat production numbers and curvaceous babes intent on wedding and bedding Elvis,"[16] who only wants to maintain his bachelor status. As such, *Girls! Girls! Girls!* offers a virtual screen rendering of "The Playboy Philosophy." Hefner had deserted a conventional marriage to live and promote a "swinging" lifestyle.[17] His publication challenged the dichotomization of women by implying, through the concept of "the girl next door" presented *au naturel*, that there are no nice and/or bad girls, rather complex women with the potential for all sorts of behavior. Such a young woman (her nude shot balanced with everyday images of her at work or with her parents) was not wholesome *or* sensual but *both*. The desire of the American male to marry early, so prevalent in the '50s, was replaced by Hefner's notion of "the playboy":

> A sophisticated, urbane, affluent, promiscuous, mature bachelor ... always dressed in expensive, fashionable clothes, off to enjoy such "in" activities as yachting, skin diving, night clubbing, or racing foreign sports cars. Sexy girls, scantily clad, are always near [but his] eyes remain half-closed in a bored fashion; his mouth turns up slightly at the corners, reflecting a smug self-satisfaction.[18]

That description could serve as a character sketch of Ross Carpenter, Elvis' incarnation in *Girls! Girls! Girls!*— his name also providing a hint of the religiosity to come.

For the time being, Elvis embodies what Barbara Ehrenreich would in time describe as a "new" American male's refusal to commit.[19] From the first view, we are treated to the star's suave 1960s image:

> Minus his sideburns and shaggy mane, Elvis now looked well groomed and grown-up: his dyed black hair slicked back and Bryl Creemed, his whitened teeth capped and gleaming, his adolescent pimples buffed away, his face tanned. Sharply styled in tighter, higher-cut raw-silk jackets, Banlon sports shirts, beltless, no-pocket slacks ... Elvis absolutely personified the swingin' 1960s bachelor.... He was *Playboy* sexy.[20]

Ross lives "the sweet life" full scale. The captain of a fishing boat, he sports the expected cap, as associated with traditional American machismo as the cowboy hat Elvis often wears. On the beach, a long line of beautiful young women — all wearing two-piece suits that would have been too revealing a year earlier — wave and hope to attract him.

True to the spirit of *Playboy*, Ross ogles them all while focusing on none in particular. Elvis sings that he loves *girls*, *not* women, which is abundantly clear. Mrs. Morgan (Ann McCrea), beautiful wife of a charter fisherman, attempts to attract him behind her husband's back. Ross prefers to flirt with (and think about) playmates than engage in a relationship with this highly appealing woman of means and, from what we gather, substance. The lesson Presley's persona had learned in several previous films — that a man's goal ought to be a one-on-one relationship with a mature woman — dissipates in this new cultural climate. Once more, though, he's the patriarchal male as white knight, a contemporary equivalent of the chivalrous macho hero of yore. When two twins in red bikinis, piloting their own boat, race Ross' fishing craft back to harbor, he grins and shrugs, "Let 'em win. They're *girls!*"

Females cannot win (or so the typical early-'60s male believes), but the "charming" man of this exciting new era will allow them to think they can. Viewing the film in retrospect, this can't help but raise the issue of Elvis' relationship to the Women's Movement. A harsh approach to the opening holds that this and similar films "firmly situated Elvis in a landscape of male-centered sexual pleasure."[21] However accurate that assessment may strike many readers, it can (and has) also be argued that

> Elvis Presley, like few before him, touched the emotional G Spot for those of us with vaginas — and we and the world are still reeling from that liberating orgasm.... [He] stimulated the cultural change that forever freed women to express their most primitive feelings in public [and] they transported this emotional freedom into every other aspect of their femininity, [thus qualifying Elvis as] a father of feminism.[22]

Whether Elvis Presley was pro- or anti-feminist depends on how one chooses to read his work.

Several elements from earlier movies soon reappear, providing a through-line that cuts across all subgenres. The issue of capitalism re-emerges:

ROSS: I'd like to live on a boat.
MRS. MORGAN: What's stopping you?
ROSS: *Money!*

Mrs. Morgan suggests a gigolo position is possible. This allows Elvis to articulate his traditional-male attitude: "I like to *work* for what I get," apparently meaning his hands rather than another organ. Here again is that blue-collar ethic from rural films, proving this is an essential theme to Elvis Cinema in general. He rejects her offer as "charity," odious in part because it is offered by a woman. And Ross wants to be the financial master of not only his own destiny but also any female he is involved with — an issue that will become absolutely crucial later.

We are a long way here (and not necessarily moving forward) from the Elvis who learned to let an older woman pay his way in *G.I. Blues.* Though Mrs. Morgan and her husband (Nestor Paiva) aren't long for this film, their scene is necessary to establish the protagonist's mindset before he comes in contact with the film's two primary females. While they contradict the pre-1960 dichotomy of good-virginal women and bad-sexual ones, the female leads establish a new (and, in truth, equally detestable) set of polar opposites which allows us to fully grasp the limits of early 1960s "liberation."

First, though, Ross meets with Mom (Lili Valenty) and Pop (Frank Puglia)

Stavros, for whom he works. Once more we encounter the essential goodness of ethnic Americans with old-fashioned family values. Even in such a slick vehicle, they provide a traditional subtext to the progressive picture. A simple, charming Greek couple, the Stavroses (for whom the Morgans serve as foils) bought the sailboat that Ross and his father completed before the latter's death. Though they allow Ross to live on it, that's not enough. "Into" the idea of ownership, Ross pays them a portion of his income every month to eventually claim it as his own.

The Stavros family must leave the area owing to Pop's ill health. This sets up a parallel between Mr. Stavros (now Ross's father-figure) and Ross' biological father, who "left him" also owing to ill health. Themselves the victims of a cold capitalist system, the Stavros family must sell both the charter boats and Ross' beloved *West Wind* to an obnoxious (and, as his name suggests, ultra–Anglo) raw capitalist, Wesley Johnson (Jeremy Slate). In *G.I. Blues*, Slate had portrayed Elvis' evil would-be nemesis; here, he provides the first of this film's many references to earlier entries in the *oeuvre*.

Now we meet the women who compose the film's 1960s nouveau dichotomy. Both show up at The Pirate's Den, a local nightclub run by another appealing ethnic, the Jewish Sam (Robert Strauss). Working for him is Robin Gattner (Stella Stevens), a blonde blues singer. The casting is in itself significant, for Stevens was often compared to Monroe. Like Marilyn, she appeared nude in *Playboy*; she is then the nearest Elvis ever got to co-starring with Monroe herself. Robin is a mature young woman, in many regards a female equivalent of Elvis — preferring to make her own way in the world by singing rather than by taking "charitable" offers from various men, each of whom would like to make her his mistress — a clear parallel to his persona's situation in the early scene with Mrs. Morgan.

Interchanges between the two quickly establish that Robin and Ross have an ongoing sexual relationship as well as a deep friendship. Yet they never made their arrangement official, '50s style — that is, through the institution of marriage. This, more than any other element, designated the Sexual Revolution's impact. As legendary newspaper columnist Abigail van Buren ("Dear Abby") put it when comparing the new youth to her own:

> Yes, we did do the same thing in parked cars, but [secretly] — we certainly could not have lived openly without marriage but they're doing it now. It's getting more prevalent.[23]

Blue Hawaii suggested that Elvis might enjoy pre-marital sex with his "steady" before they get married; *Girls! Girls! Girls!* goes further, revealing him to be in a sexual relationship with a woman he doesn't intend to marry.

He incorporates The Twist into his act, while performing in a suit and tie, breaking down all the old bridges between a Sinatra-style "class act" and the lowlife roadhouse route to which the earlier Elvis had been delegated. His sideburns have *not* been shaved, as numerous critics have mistakenly reported, but *trimmed*: precisely half their old length, the burns allow for a hint of the Old while introducing the New.

Also in the club is Laurel Dodge (Laurel Goodwin), on a date with the obligatory obnoxious guy Elvis must defeat. Purposefully referencing an earlier movie, her date is acted by the same bit player who gave Elvis a hard time in *Loving You*'s diner sequence. An all but simultaneously released film is referenced when, as Ross sends Laurel's date off and running, a jealous Robin scoffs: "You're Sir Galahad, all right — to *strangers!*" (see following chapter): to new, potential playmates he has not yet bedded. At once, though, there's a hint that this girl may turn out to be something different. When Ross walks Lauren "home," they pass by a church, repeating the situation with Nellie in *King Creole*; Laurel also expresses a desire to step inside. When Ross snarls that he hasn't visited a church in some time, she retorts, "You could sing in the choir." Elvis — as an innocent boy — first sang in a church choir.[24] It's clear in his eyes that the Presley persona wants to come full cycle and do just this, but he is not yet ready to seek redemption. In due time, he will.

Meanwhile, he is *Playboy* incarnate — and none too happy when, after arriving at Laurel's hotel, she says goodnight. "Aren't you going to ask me upstairs?" he huffs. Nonetheless, she — the new liberated (sexually, at least) girl — initiates a sensuous kiss before sending Ross off rather than waiting for him to do it. The hotel is but a beard; Lauren doesn't live here but with her rich father. Having recently been burned by a guy who wanted her only for her money, she plans to keep this secret from Ross so that, if he does get serious, it will be for herself. When he arrives late for a lunch date at an outdoor cafe and sees her with her father, Ross assumes Lauren is just a golddigger, mistress to an older rich guy. Still, that she may instead be the last American virgin (having turned him down the night before) intrigues Ross. For the time being, he returns to the more experienced Robin — the American male still managing to have it both ways.

The nature of their bond is revealed at the club:

ROSS: Robin, you know how it is between you and I.
ROBIN: You're going to come back this time. You always do.

The compleat American '60s guy, Ross accepts that his female equivalent (the honest, open playgirl) is a nice person. Despite that, he has no intention of marrying used goods. Here, then, is the new 1960s dichotomy; he will try and seduce Laurel, but if she "gives in," he will not in the end marry *her* either. She may not be "bad," in a 1950s retro sense (i.e., evil), but neither is she good enough for him — at least when it comes time to make a commitment.

In this, Ross resembles Elvis himself: Priscilla, his virgin bride-to-be, remained princess-like in the Memphis mansion on a hill while he journeyed about, sampling other women he had no serious interest in.[25] He, the American male, knows the Playboy role must eventually be discarded for an old-fashioned relationship; the main distinction between him and the 1950s male is that he doesn't want to marry young in order to enjoy sex. Now he can enjoy sex without commitment, then marry a virgin — a "liberated" attitude (or so it seemed at the time) which, on close consideration, may be perceived as even more offensive to the feminist sensibility than the "conventional" view of most '50s men.

Here, it will be a rich virgin at that. Ross (upon learning of Lauren's father's money) initially resists this, fearing such a situation will economically castrate him. He is a hip-looking modern redux of the retro-male who, despite any trendy tendencies, still wants to provide for his woman. This creates a crisis when Lauren buys The West Wind. She does this to keep the villainous Johnson (a lecher who tries to touch her and gets the expected beating from Ross, who wants her strictly for himself) from selling it on the open market. What threatens Ross is the idea of Lauren dominating him in any way. Even if he gradually paid her back, this would still leave him feeling emasculated.

The couple's problem reaches a crisis point when Ross retreats to an island hideaway. Another of his beloved ethnic families, Asians named Yung live here in a happy, humble setting. Such a large and good-natured group — which inevitably has adopted Elvis as part of their extended family — symbolizes a bastion of old-fashioned sanity in sharp contrast to an ever more flashy yet valueless world. Lauren, eager to resolve their differences, makes the mistake of paying Johnson to take her by boat to the cove. This causes Ross to hurry to the rescue, putting the rich, corrupt Establishment guy in his place. At mid-movie, he takes Lauren to the Yungs; they stay overnight during a hurricane and, presumably, *do* consummate their love!

First, though, the following interchange takes place:

LAUREN: This is really *your* family, isn't it?
ROSS: Only family I've ever known.

He's a free-living playboy, apparently, because he's never had what the average American takes for granted. Still, his placement with the Yungs allows him to glimpse, and to a degree experience, what he would really (despite words to the contrary) like: to stop sowing wild oats and settle down. If Mrs. Yung is the nearest thing to a mother Ross knows, it's significant that — in what has become a staple — the movie's most romantic love song is performed not for Lauren or Robin, but Mama Yung. He sings that he found what he was looking for the night they met: love.

This is a pure form of love that Elvis, and any of his incarnations, can encounter only with his mother, or a reasonable facsimile — Gladys still his "best girl." He wants and needs an old-fashioned mother who teaches the work ethic: Classy Lauren is put to work cleaning shrimp, Mr. Yung must do the dishes after dinner, Ross also helps to clean up — and in so doing *earns* his meal.

Another recurring plot element arises when both women turn against Elvis. Robin becomes enraged when she thinks, despite their solid friendship, that Ross has displaced her at the club for money — though his mercenary leanings are not motivated by greed but owing to a desperate need to connect with his biological family by buying the boat he associates with his father, parallel to the dream to buy the old family home in *King Creole*. Lauren suspects him of going back to Robin for a sex-without-love relationship rather than pursuing a committed one with her. Both women grow more jealous of the boat than each other! Ross can't give up his simple value structure, which likewise defines the machismo morality of the generation that came of age in the '50s: "A man's got to *work!*"

In time, though, he does settle for a middle ground with Lauren that reflects what every young couple of the early '60s hoped to achieve:

LAUREN: Either you marry me or we live together in sin.
ROSS: Couldn't we have a little bit of both?

So here is the degree to which the Presley persona has altered for the '60s sensibility: He *will* marry a non-virgin now, though *only* if *he* is the man who deflowered her — and the *only* man she has ever been with. A re-imagining of marriage, from the sexless 1950s conception to a sexy if still far from enlightened (on the male's part) 1960s one, is the image on which this film closes.

Where the Action Is: *Fun in Acapulco* (1963)

The fact that this film is intended as a semi-sequel to *Girls! Girls! Girls!* is established in the opening shots. The title song is performed as the opening credits roll, once again over a "travelogue view" of a beautiful stretch of beach — in this case, Mexico's Acapulco — on which many attractive young women frolic. The bikinis are notably briefer than those on view only one year earlier. Flesh and fantasy were coming out of the closet; this was the year when the scantily clad Bunnies made their debut at the new *Playboy* clubs and, on the West Coast, a young woman named Carol Doda initiated topless dancing at the Condor Club in San Francisco. "It was a *fad*," she later reflected, "but now it's something"[26] — that "something" a revolutionary freedom in America about one's sexuality. Fashion designer Rudi Gernreich eventually insisted that "the freedom of the body actually started in the '60s. No, it started earlier, but by mid–'60s it was [emphasis mine] *there*."[27]

When we first see the Presley protagonist, Mike Windgren, he is again aboard a boat he pilots for someone else, wearing a sailor suit with captain's cap — identical to his outfit in *Girls! Girls! Girls!* Acapulco had just emerged as a trendy watering spot for the international jet-set; it's clear Elvis is once again at the epicenter of "where the action is," partaking of the area's many lush ladies. An exception is Jamie Harkins (Teri Hope), an underage blonde who emerges from the boat's cabin. Jamie is the Ellie character from *Blue Hawaii*; her presence evokes *Playboy*, since Hope (not as young as she appears here) had been that magazine's Playmate of the Month for September 1958. The Lolita-like girl (that Stanley Kubrick film had premiered the previous year) speaks lines almost identical to the ones we heard in the earlier film while striking identical teen-vamp poses. When Mike refuses to succumb to her jail-bait offers, the girl nastily tells him, "It's my father's boat, and I can get you *fired*."

When he insists she wait until she's grown up, the girl displays her body — in tight T-shirt and ultra-short shorts — and smirkingly replies, "Do you think I'm gonna get any more grown up than *this*?" A sense of *deja vu* descends, as the line comes close to *Blue Hawaii*'s "Ever see anything like *this* in a cradle?"

MIKE: Go back down to your dolls.
THE GIRL: Why, so you can go back to *yours*?

Mike has previously been romancing the varied women who frequent Acapulco, locals and tourists — all mature women. But if audiences of the time believed what they saw and heard, the image is only appearance; the reality, if Red West and others who were "in the loop" are to be believed: Elvis was most interested in the young females that the Presley persona always rejects in the movies.[28]

This realization suggests that on one level, the films exist as a smoke screen to convince the fan base that their beloved star was the opposite of what, in private, he knew himself to be — an arrested adolescent who thanked Heaven for little girls. This explains his ability to comfortably relate to Priscilla when she was a 14-year-old virgin — but not once she had become a 24-year-old woman, even if he (as in *Girls! Girls! Girls!*) was the only man she had known.

Fun in Acapulco is a film of transitions. The multi-cultural aspect, though, proves as strong as ever. Entering a nightclub, Mike sings with several Mexican performers. Here is Elvis the musical integrationist, who absorbs their ethnic style into his own approach while affecting the manner in which they perform, even as they assimilate his own mild rock elements into their traditional song. Then there are the words to the number, "Vino, Dinero y Amore": Mike praises money as an equal to wine and love. Goodbye, Jimmy Dean; hello, Hef! Alienation is out, *La Dolce Vita* in. Elvis now reflects an era during which financial success played a major role in defining a man's status.

Mike shortly comes into contact with one of the era's sexually liberated women. Dolores Gomez (Elsa Cardenas) is a female bullfighter, known for her unique style of teasing and then killing bulls — they, of course, symbolic of the male — in the ring. Slightly older than Mike, she sucks him into a delirious but ultimately deadly Oedipal tryst, which he — the fly drawn to the spider — has no intention of resisting. Mike reveals himself as clueless, bluntly stating in the language of a true retro-male, "I thought all bullfighters were men." He's informed by hapless males who congregate about Dolores that she killed the biggest bull in Acapulco earlier that day. Outside the ring, Dolores enjoys reducing men to virtual eunuchs who, after a brief fling, hopelessly follow her about. She is Circe, he the mythical sailor, home from the sea.

Essentially, Dolores has been doing to men what Mike-Elvis has been doing to women. In the '50s, such women — Lizabeth Scott in *Loving You*, Carolyn Jones in *King Creole* — were depicted as aberrant — in need of (and desiring) reformation. Elvis, then radically innocent, revived the fallen angels via the moral strength of his pure presence. This, however, is a whole new era; strong females are on their way to becoming a new "norm." Dolores will not, during the narrative, alter in attitude. Nor will Elvis turn around this movie's blonde teenager, as he did in *Blue Hawaii*. The current Lolita shows up in the club with girlfriends; when her father arrives, Jamie blames Mike for allowing underage girls to drink. He's summarily fired, and those characters disappear from the story without a trace.

In their place, the obligatory cute child figure appears in the guise of little Raoul (Larry Domasin), a shoeshine boy and hustler. Distantly related to virtually everyone in Acapulco, Raoul can pull strings when he wants. He has none of the innocence we saw in earlier (and many yet-to-come) Elvis-child couplings. Raoul befriends Mike not because he feels naturally drawn to a man who retains what Wordsworth referred to as "primal sympathy," a rare ability to maintain childlike innocence in adulthood. Raoul, like Mike, is an operator, interested in quickly acquiring hard, cold cash. Knowing that the moody singer at a local resort regularly calls in sick, Raoul reckons he can introduce Mike to the general manager (a cousin) and serve as Mike's agent, thus picking up a chunk of the paycheck when Mike is called to fill in. Mike likewise sees the relationship as precisely what it is, a financial arrangement, agreeing to meet Raoul the following morning.

A touch of the previous and future Elvis-as-Savior pattern reappears when the two plan to meet in front of a church. Raoul explains that the stately building has stood here for centuries, a bastion of traditionalism often overlooked today. Expressing the patina of religiosity that always exists (however dormant) in the Presley persona, Mike mentions he'd like to see the manger. Though this single line provides the star's only connection to Jesus here, it does keep that continuity alive in what's otherwise one of his least spiritual films.

Soon, the two are off to a notably different place of worship — the resort where upscale swingers surrender to the newly enthroned ideal of hedonism. Mike plunges into a sudden depression when he sees Moreno (Alejandro Rey), the lifeguard, practicing on the high board for his famed dives from a towering cliff on the Acapulco seashore. Despite this revulsion, Mike only agrees to sub for the nightclub singer in the evenings if he can also work during Moreno's time off, as a pool lifeguard — offering to do so for ridiculously low pay. A flashback allows us to see the reason for Mike's horror at the sight of heights: As a circus performer, engaged in high-wire acrobatics without a net, he failed to catch his partner — his own brother — and the young man fell to his death. This memory haunts Mike, though his family constantly writes, begging him to return to the States. Elvis' previous persona was a man who felt lost owing to the lack of a biological family; here he plays an anguished man who has such a family, but lives in self-imposed exile. If Elvis has any Biblical identity in *Fun in Acapulco*, it is — as in the early portions of *Wild In the Country* — Cain, not Jesus.

Mike can't return until, much like James Stewart in Alfred Hitchcock's 1958 classic, he conquers his vertigo. In the earlier work, the fear of heights that plagues "Scottie Ferguson" is actually an emblem of a deeper psychological sickness.[29] In its unpretentious way, this seemingly escapist piece assumes just such an approach. If each film strikes a delicate balance between social commentary and self-expression, *Fun in Acapulco* at this point sets aside its oblique commentary on the sexual revolution to introduce a theme that will be developed in several films to come: the unwarranted guilt Elvis felt over the death at birth of his own twin brother.[30] When Mike, at the resort's front desk, sends a telegram home, the pretty girl at the counter notices that something is wrong. She "comes on" to Mike, as virtually all attractive women do to Elvis: "You have a problem, senor. Anything I can do?" She means, of course, she would happily provide him with sexual healing. As this is 1963, there's no longer any hint that such a woman is a slut. She seems nice, to us as to Mike. Still, he only smiles and then walks away.

Mike is the current variation on the Presley persona — a figure who always suffers some "problem," here vertigo. Those diverse problems provide dramatic-comedic variations on Elvis' *real* problem. Elvis's relationship with Gladys was sealed when he survived after Jesse Garon, who might have shared in Gladys' excessive love, did not. Gladys' focus on Elvis as the object of a suffocating love that might have better been spread between the two led to a textbook case of the momma's boy. The result was a unique variation on a Peter Pan complex, as Elvis — though obsessed with beautiful women — experienced great difficulty in consummating most of those relationships.[31] An arrested adolescent, he remained torn between his intense need to attract the most physically impressive women as trophy dates and enter into a seemingly sexy relationship, most particularly in the eyes of onlookers.

If Albert Goldman is to be believed, Elvis shared his bed with *but did not penetrate* a different woman every night following his break-up with Priscilla.[32] Such a tendency had been apparent in even the earliest films, beginning with the Debra Paget relationship in *Love Me Tender.* In this light, what occurs on-screen in most movies — he flirting with pretty women, winning them away from other men, then failing to follow through — offers a mirror of Elvis' actual situation. Following boyhood experiences that might have turned some men gay, Elvis instinctually opted for limited heterosexuality. This can be interpreted as ongoing denial of homosexual panic, causing him to feel comfortable only in male bonding relationships — while enthusiastically (perhaps *too* enthusiastically) entering into relationships with women that result in much romance but virtually no sex.

No wonder, then, in this instance, Mike appears happy to receive the offer from such a pretty woman; no wonder too that he gloatingly backs off. The offer, not the act, is what he — Mike, Elvis — needs. The young woman looks confused; once we understand Elvis, we can comprehend. Yes, he has a problem — a deep and pervading one, involving his identity. She has already helped him, by making the offer. This is something she can't grasp, not without what we may divine from relating the films to his life.

Little wonder then that Mike is attracted to the one woman who — despite the sexiness of her presence — is off limits as to the sex act itself. This is Marguerita Dauphin (Ursula Andress), the resort's assistant social director. Though she displays herself in more revealing bikinis than any of the other women, Marguerita makes clear from her earliest dialogue that she is conservative, if not as to her appearance then in her personal morality. The last great virgin, she is sexy but not sexual — a phrase that has been effectively employed to describe Elvis after those early explosive years. Throughout the film, Mike pursues Marguerita — hoping to win her away from Moreno, who truly would like to sleep with her, though she won't allow it. This occurs even as Mike is pursued by Dolores — who would like to sleep with him, though Mike won't allow it.

What at first seems an absurd, overly cutesy means of driving the plot forward appears, when viewed in light of the Presley psychology, a mad, sad game. In it, the male who must, to maintain a macho image, appear to hope for conquest of women consistently singles out the obviously impossible female. He knows that what is believed by everyone else to be his ultimate aim (sexual consummation) will never be achieved, much to his relief. Having everyone *see* him win Marguerita away from Moreno is a necessity. He seems most at ease when singing to neither of these mature women but to a little girl he meets at the cliffs. Here, consummation remains out of the question — and, therefore, she is non-threatening to him.

Ursula Andress replaced Brigitte Bardot as the most immediately recognizable international female sex symbol owing to her appearance in *Dr. No* (1962), first of the James Bond films, and in the pages of *Playboy*. An unintended synergy existed between these various pop-culture artifacts, drawing even more power from the interaction between them. Andress was booked for a *Playboy* spread owing to her appearance in *Dr. No*, then signed for *Fun in Acapulo* owing to the attention surrounding her following the pictorial — leading to yet another pictorial.

At this point, we encounter an Elvis far more cold-blooded than before. Witness one conversation by the pool:

MARGUERITA: Moreno's always been good to me — and he's fun.
MIKE: So's a cocker spaniel.

In previous films, the guy competing with Elvis for the current leading lady is glib and superficial, Elvis honest. Here, that is reversed: Moreno is as sincere in his attempts to befriend Mike as he is in his desire to bed Marguerita. Elvis plays a variation on the male-*villain* role from earlier movies. In retrospect, his posturing appears significant, particularly when we consider that all three members of the central romantic-triangle have names that begin with M — the symbolic first-letter for a sexually distressed character in films by Alfred Hitchcock.

Mike hates Moreno at first sight because Moreno is everything Mike — *Elvis*— would like to be but is not: A self-secure sexual male who, if he ever does go to bed with the female lead, will have no trouble satisfying her. The cliff diving then takes on a metaphoric meaning. When we see the stretch of coastline into which men are expected to jump, the water cuts into the rocky land in such a way that the inlet forms a gigantic V. Combining this with the fact that water has, throughout the history of film (and, long before, in earlier art forms), been employed to symbolize sexuality, the dive is, on a symbolic level, into a giant vagina — something Moreno does not fear, but which Mike believes will swallow him up forever. Mike's "surface" problem — vertigo —

represents his deeper problem: a fear of penetrating the female that hearkens back to guilt over the death of his brother, in real life as in the film.

This explains why Dolores, upon learning that Mike refuses to dive, drops him for Moreno. Dolores claims that she needs "a real man"—as if she alone understands the implications (for her, in bed) of Elvis' inability to "take the plunge." Also understandable is Marguerita's lack of concern whether Mike dives or not. As the final virgin in an age of sexually promiscuous women, Marguerita fears penetration as much as she (like Mike) loves flirtation. Mike is perfect for her, while Moreno — quietly aggressive about sex — is someone she must reject for reasons we (though not he, and on a conscious level not she) can comprehend. Marguerita makes clear more than once that she wants to get married, even as Dolores constantly insists she does not want to (though she demands sex all the time). This frightens Mike as much as it attracts Moreno, who appears headed precisely there in the final sequence.

That makes clear why Elvis performs not one but two musical sequences in which he dons the garb of a matador ("El Toro" and "The Bullfighter Was a Lady"). In both, he mimics the movements not of a male bullfighter *but of Dolores*, implying through transsexual parody the desire of this female-male to be as macho as that machismo female.

Mike fears that Marguerita may want to marry him only to bring her elderly father (Paul Lukas) to the United States. Gradually, he comes to see she's sincere in her concern for him *and* her father. Marguerita is as much Daddy's Little Girl as he is Momma's Boy (Oedipus dates Electra), which explains each person's immediate strong feelings for the other. What follows next is the film's obligatory fistfight between Mike and Moreno. This is the only time, however, in a Presley picture when we are likely to root for the antagonist! Then it is on to the moment of truth, when Mike must dive into the Great Vagina.

Religion is evoked once more. Mike kneels and prays after climbing the cliff. Prominent among those watching him — along with both Marguerite and Dolores — is a little girl, the yet-innocent female who consistently inspires each new Elvis character with sudden confidence. Then he dives ... and survives ... and, as a result, is reborn. Emerging unscathed from initiation into female liquidity, Mike becomes friendly to Moreno, as he no longer feels intimidated by the other fellow's self-assured masculinity. Now Mike can marry Marguerite, rejecting The Playboy Philosophy (all good things must come to an end) to find solace as a traditional male in a conventional coupling.

CHAPTER 9

Up the Establishment!

♦ *Kid Galahad* (1962) ♦
♦ *Roustabout* (1964) ♦

The times, Bob Dylan now noted, are a-changin.' Elvis Presley, however, could not or would not change with them. Though Elvis was "the single person who kick-started it all,"[1] Abbie Hoffman (the leading political-cultural activist of the decade) wrote that despite the great debt which our Youth Movement owed to Elvis, the founding father became more out of touch with each passing year.[2] Presley did appreciate the early '60s, when society imitated his model by rejecting the uptightness of the '50s; briefly, he basked in glory as avatar of everything then happening. But as the world grew ever more complex, he (as cousin Billy Smith said) "felt out of touch with the '60s."[3]

The man who had brought rock to the masses "couldn't stand the psychedelic stuff, like Jimi Hendrix," according to Memphis Mafia member Marty Lacker:

> [A]nd he didn't like the attitude that the Rolling Stones and a lot of these English groups had. So many of them came off as a bunch of arrogant jerks.[4]

Elvis had always been respectful. His significance would not wane; the earliest pop culture offerings were "destined to ring in a new era" in manners and mores as well as music and movies. Elvis was the tip of the iceberg of a new America that would roar past him — an emerging lifestyle that left its initiator in the dust. In the late '60s, Elvis (like his literary counterpart Jack Kerouac) had nothing but negative comments for those who took what they had preached to the next level. "Amidst the conformity of the 1950s," some argue, "Elvis defied society's norms."[5] That only tells part of the story: Amidst the chaos of the coming late-'60s, Elvis *defined* society's norms!

The first of these films was released on August 29, 1962, at the height of Kennedy-era idealism. The second premiered on November 11, 1964, nearly a year after the assassination that plunged the country into confusion and cynicism. Despite the Future Shock swiftness with which one era gave way to another, these movies were not notably different in terms of tone — each ignoring all emergent social issues other than those that directly concerned the star's blue collar fan base. In this, Elvis resembled other (loftier) artists, initially assumed to be dangerous yet seen as something else entirely once the system chose to admit and admire them.

Elia Kazan (who briefly toyed with casting Presley in his 1957 film *A Face in the Crowd*) had, as a poor (urban) teenager like (rural) Elvis, pondered people of "class," concluding: "Every time I saw privilege from then on I wanted to tear it down or possess it."[6] The Presley persona experiences similar anger and envy toward what he initially does not have; such emotions dissipate once the hero, perhaps to his own surprise, actually acquires the trappings of success. Elvis' ongoing fan base admired that he had honorably sweated, achieving "material triumphs" not only through his God given talent but also on "how hard he *worked* [emphasis mine]."[7] His character in films designed to please that overworked, underpaid, ever hopeful receiver is "the man [they] want Elvis to be: a white guy who made it big the 'right' way through talent, ambition, and sheer hard work."[8]

Not for nothing is "work" the final word: Hard manual labor to sustain himself before achieving The Dream; an inborn talent he eventually employs to achieve riches. Suddenly, though, a new paradigm appeared, as "the requirements of work and self-discipline"[9] began to wane as more and more people — essentially, the hippie culture — no longer wanted to achieve identity through what one does and/or produces. The dropouts rejected even the meaningful sort of work Elvis always admired.

The challenge to the work ethic and capitalist system, both championed by Elvis even as he challenged inequities, now seemed out of date. For a considerable and highly vocal portion of the country's youth, in its place appeared an anti-work, anti-system radicalism. Elvis' attitude — reform labor, improve the system, enlighten the Establishment — seem downright reactionary by comparison. Overnight, everything had changed — everything, perhaps, except Elvis. He achieved long-term stardom less by altering with the times than by honing to his essential values and defining an insulated audience that still looked to him as a role model.

Peace in the Valley: *Kid Galahad* (1962)

Presley starred in this remake of Michael (*King Creole*) Curtiz's 1937 message-melodrama about organized crime's infiltration of professional boxing. The film cross-references *Blue Hawaii,* likewise about the challenges faced by a returning soldier. Intriguing — and further suggesting the two films interrelate — is that Elvis' love interest is again played by Joan Blackman. Here, discharged G.I. Walter Gulick is as poor as the earlier one (Chad Gates) had been rich. Instead of arriving home to a pompous family he chooses not to visit, Walter stops at a place he can't quite recall to visit a decent set of deceased parents. Once more, shades of Thomas Wolfe and his abiding theme that Presley embraced while notably reversing: You *can* go home again.

Wearing his uniform, Presley's persona is signified as Establishment (he did his duty) *and* rebel (he thumbs rides rather than pay for travel). This is less a choice than necessity, for it's quickly established that Walter is broke. Throughout *Blue Hawaii,* constructed with the college crowd as potential viewers, Chad's central problem had been how he might divest himself of the money culture which stood in the way of his individualistic dream. Conversely, in this blue-collar film, Walter arrives nearly faint; he hasn't eaten since leaving the Army. Nonetheless, Walter appears as free as Chad was a virtual prisoner. Elvis sings that the man who can claim to have nothing is the king of the world.

Chad "found himself" by picking his career and by marrying a woman his mother considered beneath their station. Once both were accepted, Chad happily joined the Establishment. Here, Walter must "find himself" by achieving the career he wants (automobile mechanic, the perfect blue collar job) while marrying a woman whose family considers *him* beneath *their* status. After he is accepted, Walter settles in as a part of small town society (not, significantly, despised suburbia), hoping the garage he buys into will make money, so he can live the square life. First, though, Walter hops off a truck in New York's Catskill Mountains at a resort area called Cream Valley.

Though this is the Borscht Belt, everything appears identical to the *Southern* forest on view in *Wild in the Country.* Walter's drawl is explained when the young man tells locals he left in childhood and was raised in Kentucky. He always dreamed of returning; this valley qualifies as home because it's where his heart is. To visually signify the character's traditionalism, director Phil Karlson has Walter slip into a deserted barn where he finds an 1890s carriage. "It has *character,*" he says with admiration. Walter restores the ancient object with plans of riding around like the Amish of Pennsylvania. Walter also spiffs up on old Model-T Ford, which he prefers to drive while others opt for the newest convertibles. "You think things were different [in] those days?" he asks, eyes wide with an appreciation for an earlier, better America, one that existed before World War II — if indeed it ever existed in reality or is only an abiding American myth.

For Presley, paradise (other than in hardcore country films like *Follow That Dream*) must be populist, thus all-inclusive. So Walter observes two signs: Grogan's Gaelic Gardens is located directly across from Lieberman's Resort. Though the Irish and Jewish hoteliers compete for guests, friendliness and tolerance abide. The film reflects Elvis; always, he wore a Star of David directly next to the cross that hung about his neck.[10] Later, it's made clear that Mr. Lieberman (Ned Glass) is close friends with the Catholic priest. The father prefers this upstanding man's company to that of Willy Grogan (Gig Young), who fails to be as truly Christian as the Jewish gentleman. While the civil rights theme is muted, the attitude is consistent with earlier projects. Though blacks have little screen time, when African-Americans do briefly appear in *Kid Galahad*—a sparring mate for Walter after he becomes a prizefighter, a full member of a Fourth of July party — they are *accepted*.

At one point, Walter inspires local youth to do The Twist, a few years earlier a youth dance craze, now part of mainstream pop-style. Elvis had been influenced by black performers, which in the '50s qualified him as an "egalitarian" musical crusader "who stormed postwar popular culture with an image that evoked a multiracial America, an integrated America."[11] His once shocking "wiggle,"[12] borrowed from black performers, then influenced African-American Chubby Checker, who in turn impacted on (Italian) Joey Dee as The Twist developed. But if the push to include minority cultures in the American mainstream had moved forward, a continuation of the Cold War (culminating in the near-disastrous Cuban Missile Crisis of November 1962) allowed for the extension of a distinct fear of foreigners that, if anything, had heightened.

Near the end of *Kid Galahad*, then, Walter must fight a challenger brought in by the Mob. A huge muscleman, "Sugar Ray Romero" arrives from Tijuana surrounded by menacing-looking "foreigners" (Americans all, though not *U.S.* citizens) who speak a language the valley folk cannot comprehend. Gangsters accompany the challenger; several hoodlums showed up earlier, slinking around the charming rural (i.e., good) setting in citified (bad) sharkskin suits to make sure shady Willy doesn't "sing" to the Feds. What vividly characterizes the mobsters is that (compared to *Follow That Dream*) they are *not* portrayed as Italian or Jewish; it's as if Elvis regretted that element of the earlier movie and here set out to set the record straight. Otto (David Lewis), the gang boss, speaks with a cultivated voice and appears Anglo-Saxon. If the gangsters represent anything, it's the evil Big City mentality *per se*— the intended idea in *Dream*, though there, Presley realized, it could easily be mistaken for racism.

Like other Presley vehicles, *Kid Galahad* forwards a romantic vision. The world according to Elvis is composed of two distinct *demi-mondes*: The corrupt and corrupting, money-oriented approach of The City, as opposed to the innocent (liberating), simple attitude of The Country and those pure people who live there. Rugged individualists, they — like characters in a John Ford film such as *Drums Along the Mohawk* (1939), set in the same geographical area some 150 years earlier — can come together as a community when threatened from the outside. Lost somewhere between the two worlds is Willy, a raw capitalist who gambled and drank his family's fortune away, leaving the resort in disrepair — a variation on Wendell Corey in *Loving You* and, like him, accompanied by a mature blonde, here Lola Albright as Dolly Fletcher.

Elvis' character serves as Willy's foil and potential redeemer. They even share the same initials: W.G. No sooner does Willy grasp that the newly arrived youth has boxing potential — Walter earns a few dollars by sparring with the "tigers" who train on the grounds for Mr. Zimmerman (Judson Pratt) — than Willy attempts to exploit Walter's natural talent. Wheedling his way into a managerial spot, he creates a false myth in which the youth's Army boxing matches are blown out of proportion, a parallel to Corey's character pulling such stuff with Deke's musical career. The sexy mother figure (the older couple become surrogate parents to Elvis' aging youth-hero) is less Machiavellian than her male partner. Attracted to Elvis as a person, she reveals no interest in him as a male.

This furthers the removal of Elvis from his 1950s outsider role while hastening his character's absorption into the mainstream. Walter has hardly disembarked than he's invited to stay on and work for the elderly garage mechanic. This unpretentious blue-collar fellow becomes as positive a father figure as Willy, slick in suits, serves as a negative one. In short time, a third is introduced: Lew Nyack (Charles Bronson), a coach who doesn't encourage Walter to fight (as money-hungry Grogan does) but offers to mentor the youth once Walter decides to do so. "Waiting for my *fatherly* advice" is how Lew refers to his trainees.

All three father figures are tied together by the film's evocation of the capitalist theme: Walter allows Grogan to set up fights and Lew to train him, so Walter can save money to buy into the garage as a full partner. This creates an intriguing inversion of the usual formula that has Elvis working at a blue collar day job until he hits the big time by developing his natural talent, singing. While Walter is good at fighting, and will exploit that talent to achieve his ends, he is *not* dedicated to boxing in a way early Elvis was to show business. He fights only to earn money, as sparring partner for Joe Shakes (Michael Dante), whom Walter inadvertently knocks out. "Will I still get my five dollars?" he asks. His words don't project greed; Walter doesn't have enough money to buy a meal, and his integrity will not allow him to accept a handout.

When Walter does earn enough to buy into the garage, he will never fight again, no matter how much money may be involved. His is not raw but enlightened capitalism. In the meantime, a fighter needs a nickname, and Dolly provides it. Walter proved himself a gentleman by helping Dolly into her chair the first time the two met. Reel and real are inseparable. Elvis had as a person always been "polite."[13] Likewise, his screen persona was "extremely courteous,"[14] early characters projecting "a deferential manner toward adults."[15] Such gallantry creates a contrast in Dolly's mind between the supposedly highborn gentleman Grogan, who treats her like a tramp, and the unspoiled country boy, a natural gentleman. When a big city "torpedo" puts his hands on Dolly, Walter knocks the man down. "Thanks, Galahad," she quips, likening him to a knight.

The choice of names requires a closer look. Galahad was no ordinary knight, famous like Gawain for an ability to defeat even the seemingly unconquerable green knight or, like Lancelot, sexual conquest of a beautiful if forbidden woman. The Round Table's *Christian* knight, Galahad was a male virgin, a medieval Jesus in a tin suit who brought spiritual uplift to all he encountered. Stories about Elvis' wild sexual escapades aside,[16] he became not only an early example of the born again Christian but a born again virgin; once Presley took up spirituality, as Priscilla has noted, he determined to avoid sex even with her.[17] This film's implied religiosity serves as a prelude to the aura that would gradually surround Elvis as the fan base responded to an "ineffable complexity, his transcendent and mysterious significance."[18]

That such strong feelings would be directed toward a pop star seems strange indeed to those who fail to grasp "the emergence of music in the modernizing West as a substitute for religion."[19] Historian H.G. Koenigsberger points out that we have witnessed "the rise of music to a quasi-religious status and cult, as a psychological compensation for the decline of all forms of traditional religion," accompanied by a "deification of music and the musician."[20] So we see graffiti on the sides of buildings all over the world: "CLAPTON IS GOD!" People don't merely listen to Bob Dylan — they *worship* him. If that syndrome did not begin with Elvis (and likely it did), then certainly he was the person who crystallized it.

While Elvis (like Jesus or Galahad) faces temptation, he (the on-screen persona, at least) always overcomes it, and so is more sweet than sexual. When Walter becomes involved with Willy's younger sister Rose (Blackman), the relationship is delicately balanced between gentle romance and platonic worship. That Elvis now follows rather than breaks rules is evident:

ROSE: What do people do when they feel like this?
WALTER: Usually, they get *married*.

He does not want sex before marriage, even if she might be willing to give him her virginity now; Priscilla admits to having begged Elvis to "take her" on numerous occasions, though he perceived their situation as a religious testing of him and refused to do so before their nuptials.[21]

This posits the Presley persona in this film's context as the antithesis of the Sexual Revolutionary he embodied in *Girls! Girls! Girls!* As one observer of the changing social scene noted, what most characterized the Sexual Revolution was that young people now "lived openly without [the sanctity of] marriage,"[22] the institution Elvis feared and revered. Ironically, Willy and Dolly — the older couple — signify it. This explains why Willy grows furious when the young couple arrive home late. Willy assumes that Walter must have done what he would have: Seduced the girl. When Walter makes clear his intentions are as honorable as one would expect from a man called Galahad, Willy at last sees the light and begin his character arc.

As always, the traditionalist side of Elvis is offset by his progressive strain. The generation (1955–65) that Elvis embodied was one in which, as a person raised in the late '40s and early '50s noted, young people hoped to "change their values rather than to accept the values of their elders, as my generation did."[23] There is a hint here that these youths — best described as progressive-traditionalists — hope to achieve an equality within marriage the older generation cannot even grasp:

WILLY: You decided to get *married?*
WALTER: *We.* It's a two-way arrangement.

Walter and Rose do not rebel against adults locked into the old institution of marriage; they react against grown-ups who do not take marriage seriously *enough.*

In many previous and several later films, the question was whether Elvis, the last American cowboy, would give up his wild ways. In *Kid Galahad*, he initially sings a hymn to the (masculine) freedom of the road, expressing his desire to keep moving. This being an Elvis musical, he must express all feelings in song, bringing up the old wanderlust: "Maybe I'm a rolling stone." One wonders if the young Dylan caught *Kid Galahad*, afterwards writing his similarly titled ballad. Dylan did, after all, call Presley "the deity supreme of rock 'n' roll religion as it exists in today's form," and stated that "hearing him for the first time was like busting out of jail."[24] Yet Walter sings spiritual, not sensual songs to Rose while in the carriage or Model T. What Elvis offers women is old-fashioned romance, fast disappearing from the psychedelic 1960s landscape.

Class is again an issue. Willy harbors conventional hopes his sister will marry a blueblood. Elvis speaks for the emerging White Trash Nation (trailer park–bred and proud of it) by scoffing at such outdated thinking. Only through Walter's messianic presence does Willy come to see that the right thing is to marry Dolly and make "an honest woman" of her. This further challenges the outdated 1950s dichotomization of "nice" and "bad" girls owing to sexual experience. In his own primitive way, Elvis acknowledges that experienced women are marriage material — for others.

Identical to Elvis (and the character he played in *Loving You*), Walter becomes a celebrity via television, here a boxing match broadcast from Albany. Upon his return, the people of Cream Valley — mechanic, cop, banker, etc.— gather round to treat him as a Frank Capra hero: the simple man who arrived seemingly out of nowhere, asserted that he shared their roots, then restored a diminished spiritual sense of community while likewise offering financial hope for the future. What most impresses the valley folk is that Walter identified himself on TV as "*from* Cream Valley," something no other fighter who trained there had done. On a realistic level, he may be (to borrow from Sophocles) their "most recent citizen"; symbolically, he has gone home again to those who were always his people.

Still, selfishness and greed have the potential to corrupt this American Shangri-La. "It'll *cost* you," Willy often says — until "saved" by Elvis. In contrast, Walter at first refused to take money when he repaired Zimmerman's car, though even decent Lew (his John the Baptist figure) believed that was going too far. Elvis visually signifies his Establishment status by donning a highly conventional suit and tie. What we see is a far cry from the hillbilly cat who stunned the nation by offering "a kinetic image in white suede shoes, an over-sized, white-checkered jacket over a jet-black shirt with an upturned collar [and] black zoot-suit pants [emphasis mine] *and no tie*."[25] He even takes Rose to the rectory to speak with the local father about following the precise letter of Catholic law.

There is one final testing of Elvis, the rock 'n' roll messiah: Willy, under pressure from gangsters, attempts to talk Walter into throwing the big fight. "Win, lose or draw," Satan reminds Faust, Walter will take home a purse that will allow him to buy into that garage. When Walter learns that the locals are betting on him, he realizes he must fully become what they believe him to be — must, despite flaws, live up to their ideal image of him, something Elvis always felt a need to do.

The film then ends with a double wedding. In the tradition of festive comedy, the *polis* is replenished. Life goes on, perhaps even improves — owing to Elvis having walked their way, allowing Cream Valley to become a modern land of milk and honey.

Return of "The Wild One": *Roustabout* (1964)

For *Roustabout*, Elvis reached back into Brando-Dean territory one final time. His alter ego, Charlie Rogers, is first glimpsed as an established musical performer, at least in backwater clubs — the last autobiographical character of the type encountered in *Loving You, Jailhouse Rock* and *King Creole*. His initial song makes clear this is a throwback to those 1950s heroes who, like Kerouac's metaphysical cowboys in *On the Road*, moves on whenever he fears contemporary conformist culture may claim him.

The modern hillbilly (his guitar plugged in) sings this at the paradoxically named Mother's Tea House, where drunken college students come to party. The spirit of Gladys is, apparently, very much with Elvis still.

College students visit to escape the strictures of society by listening to a singer who lives out their dreams of a different, better, earlier style:

> [B]ecause of changing social circumstances and economic structures within America and indeed the Western world as a whole, [Elvis] could appeal to a national and international audience equally hungry for rebellion and a fantasy of freedom.[26]

Roustabout connects to early '60s entries when an underage blonde, arriving with several financially well-heeled boys, tells a waitress, "We don't need Cokes; we're over 18." She's played by Teri Hope, who embodied the underage Lolita in *Fun in Acapulco*. In contrast to the earlier film, however, Elvis' venom is *not* directed toward the high school girls. Picking up on a motif introduced by Gary Lockwood's character in *Wild in the Country*, he despises the college boys who brought them.

Earlier, such types would hassle Elvis (owing to jealousy over his effect on their dates); he attempted to avoid a fight. Here, they remain well-behaved until Charlie purposefully baits them with the song "Poison Ivy League."

Attacks on college students in 1960s movies, particularly posh Ivy League types, constituted an attack on those fans who had deserted him the moment they left high school and opted for higher education. Largely upper-middle-class, many of them in the mid-'60s turned against America's capitalist framework; Elvis remained the child of poverty who had fought to win the American Dream and now felt only contempt for those who took it for granted.

As Dominic Cavallo observed, "[S]ome blame the tumult and violence of the second half of the decade on the 'spoiled' children of middle-class affluence."[27] The hippies had derived from a "no problem society — not of the United States (per se) but of the relatively privileged part of American society from which they came."[28] Here was a phenomenon Elvis could not grasp, having clawed his way to some level of social respectability and financial security. For "this group of young people, who had everything their society could give them, found that gift hollow and rejected it."[29] To Elvis, the "gift" was the modern Grail; having achieved it, he would never let go.

When Charlie's current girlfriend, Marge (Joan Staley), asks why he's so nasty, Charlie replies, "If you're not tough in this world, you'll get squashed." Shortly, we learn the real reason for his constant anger when Marge notes, "I didn't have any parents, either." Apparently, they've been intimate emotionally as well as physically. Charlie is a throwback to those 1950s orphan-loners who resent family units mainly because they have never known one. Commitment to an old-fashioned institution is what he needs, as Charlie will eventually realize. That happens here after Elvis is assaulted by the insulted college students before riding away on his cycle.

Intriguingly, it's a Japanese model!

STUDENT #1: Aren't *American* cycles good enough for you?
CHARLIE: Don't you believe in world trade after all the economics [classes] they force into you?

Elvis here espouses the new Republican internationalism of the Eisenhower-Nixon years; these traditional types are throwbacks to the earlier Taft isolationist Republicanism. Clearly, though, *they* have the power. When the police arrive, it is the poor boy who is arrested.

Sexual politics, Elvis style, then assumes center stage. Marge puts up the cash to get him out, certain that Charlie will whisk her up behind him on his bike. She's sorely mistaken. "Just because you bailed me out doesn't mean you *own* me," Charlie informs her, leaving her alone — despite the fact that she's attractive, devoted to him, and nice. There are several reasons why he rejects her only to shortly fall in love with a similar (and similar-looking) girl, Cathy Lean (Joan Freeman). While, as in *Girls! Girls! Girls!*, experienced older women are no longer categorized as evil, even postulated as marriage material, that does not hold true for Elvis, who will marry a virgin.

Another distinction: Cathy has a family, if a dysfunctional one, precisely what Charlie (and the retro–1950s antihero he embodies) searches for, if unknowingly. Charlie and Cathy meet when her alcoholic (and Vernon-like) father, Joe (Leif Erickson), driving the family truck, forces the black-leather clad biker off the road after Charlie makes a mild pass at Cathy. They stop to help the shaken boy; it quickly becomes clear that the head of this family (like Gladys) is the wife, Maggie Morgan (Barbara Stanwyck). Besides being one of the first married women in a Hollywood film to go by her maiden name, Maggie is notably the owner of this humble family carnival, her husband an employee, which may account for his alcoholism or result from it.

"They're good friends," Cathy says about her parents, who recall Glenda

(Scott) and Walter (Corey) in *Loving You*. Yet *this* film's adult couple has remained married despite the ups and downs. Important too is that, in contrast to Glenda and Walter (but like Gladys and Vernon), they are rural people — Elvis' key signifiers of integrity, however flawed they may be. Maggie Morgan and Joe Lean aren't interested in becoming rich, only surviving by putting on honest shows. Charlie begrudgingly accepts a job, hoping to move on to a singing gig as soon as his cycle is repaired. As in *Kid Galahad*, he doesn't care about making money for its own sake, only to achieve what he most wants.

The "nice girl" motif is re-established. When Charlie kisses Cathy in a bad boy manner, she makes clear she's "not that kind of girl." As always, that merely piques Elvis' interest. His characters' tendency to "come on strong" (also true in Presley's life) can be taken as a moral testing of women. By giving in to his charms, the otherwise admirable Marge failed the test; by resisting, despite an attraction, Cathy establishes that in addition to displaying positive personality traits, she's the kind of old-fashioned girl who married dear (if dysfunctional) old dad (Vernon), then (in Gladys' case) slept with her son in quasi-sexual innocence.

Charlie is also intrigued to learn that the carnival people speak their own unique language, a way of communicating privately with one another even when "normals" are around. It's hinted that if he were to join them permanently, this wouldn't indicate conforming to the mainstream. Rather, he would enter a loose confederation of unique individuals, operating more by moral compact than legal contract; each of them has had as tough a time as he. Better yet, Charlie would remain "on the road," thus having the best of both worlds: Community *and* freedom. At first, though, Charlie rejects Maggie's offer to turn carny, put off by the idealistic faith she expresses in her subculture: "You got your religion, I got mine."

His words take on significance if we pause to consider Elvis' posthumous metamorphosis into a spiritual icon. "American religiosity," Erika Doss noted, "is essentially flexible and democratic."[30] Just as these carnies transform what little they have into an alternative religion that lends meaning to their lives, so in time would millions of marginalized Americans do the same with Elvis, who wore both a Star of David *and* a cross. Eugene Carson Blake, head of the World Council of Churches, noticed a "miraculous development of the idea of the unity of the one church of Jesus Christ" in Dubuque, as "the Lutherans and the Presbyterians and the Roman Catholics were (after years of distrust) thick as thieves."[31] One perception of this occurrence is that it constituted a miracle; another, that it's easily explainable: Any enemy of my enemy is my friend.

Among Christian (and in time Jewish) sects that had previously despised one another, there belatedly emerged a realization that the rising tide of atheism/nihilism threatened them all. So they banded together — hence, in time, the notion of a Judeo-Christian heritage that could withstand the challenge to all of them. To those in such spiritual need, Elvis represents what Charlie will here become: "a special, wondrous, virtuous, transcendent, and even miraculous figure."[32] Like most of Elvis' characters, Charlie is (in Kerouac's words) a dharma bum — on a search for some truth that will endow his life with the meaning it currently lacks. Such a spiritual discovery of self can only occur if he finds an alternative to his own temporarily enjoyable but ultimately unsatisfying "faith" — personal survival above commitments to others.

Roustabout's most memorable confrontation takes place between Charlie and Maggie when she invites him to stay on. As she explains the value of a family, he insults her pathetic one:

MAGGIE: What would *you* know about family?
CHARLIE: *Nothing!*

What he must learn is that the perfect family, as enshrined on TV sitcoms, doesn't exist. The best one can hope for is what these people have, however humble — the same kind of hard but loving relationship Vernon and Gladys shared.[33]

The Elvis-Stanwyck relationship projects a shadow of the Oedipal aspect from earlier films when Joe (mistakenly) fears that Maggie and Charlie are romantically linked. When Joe starts a fistfight with Charlie, the younger man refuses to defend himself, recalling Montgomery Clift in his climactic bout with John Wayne in *Red River*. When Charlie like Clift does finally strike back, the battle re-enacts a theme articulated in *Rebel* as Jim's mother screams: "Do you want to *kill* your *father?*" The answer — as Freud would have insisted — can only be a whole-hearted "Yes!" But Joe's perception is not reality. Elvis' mother died in 1958; on-screen, that event, thinly disguised, occurred two years later in *Flaming Star*. Ever since, the Presley persona is interested in young girls — Priscilla in real life, Cathy in the film. Charlie romances Cathy and accepts Maggie as a strong adoptive mother, book-ending a theme introduced through the name of the club in the opening scene.

As Maggie's daughter, Cathy is Charlie's perfect mate — a second Maggie, so to speak; still virginal, an Elvis prerequisite (some might say obsession), on-screen and off-.[34] Things quickly grow complicated, as Maggie's family falls victim to a capitalistic system they subscribe to but which fails to reward them owing to their low status. As in *Follow That Dream*, the local banker is a decent type who would like to help. Yet he can do nothing but inform Maggie of the bad news: Creditors want their money; if she can't pay, the bank must foreclose. Maggie sees her salvation in Charlie, so far working only as a roustabout. Realizing he's a singer, she has Charlie perform. His words make their attitude clear: "Want to hear more? *Buy* a ticket ... spend your *money!*"

Elvis on-screen echoes his mentor, Col. Parker, whose attitude toward Elvis was: "You want to see him? Buy a ticket!"[35] This being a carnival, there is no logical place for Charlie to perform but as part of the girlie show. Strippers (their acts kept modest in those pre–ratings system days) cavort around him. Presley performs in tandem with exotic female dancers, raising an issue that haunted his career. Many early commentators who criticized Elvis' "gyrations" were offended not only by race-mixing but gender-bending. Elvis' "gyrating pelvic motions are best described as a cross between an Apache war dance and a burlesque queen's old-fashioned bumps and grind,"[36] the *Dallas Morning News* complained. In *Life*, the era's national position paper, a similar statement appeared: "a bump and grind routine usually seen only in burlesque."[37] It was by conscious decision on Elvis' part. A few years earlier, he dated Tempest Storm, also involved with JFK, whom Elvis admired and associated with — fearing he too would be assassinated.[38] While the president appears to have been intrigued by her sexual abilities, the King apparently was more fascinated by her profession — what he could learn from her, then incorporate such steps into his act.[39]

The issue of Charlie's masculinity is as constant an issue as was Elvis' throughout his life. Though Charlie like Elvis rides that icon of macho posturing, a big black motorcycle, even this would come into question. Paul Willis insists, "The assertive masculinity of the motor-bike boys also found an answering structure in their preferred music,"[40] that of Elvis. But Kenneth Anger's underground film *Scorpio Rising* (1965) would dare to reveal that beneath the macho posturing, such "Teddy Boys" (even their adapted title derived from an early Elvis tune) were inherently homosexual — strutting macho attitudinizing actually a cover-up for deep anxieties about their gender identity. Could the same then be true for their musical progenitor?

This idea helps to explain a key plot juncture. At one point, the carnival daredevils, who ride their own cycles in gravity-defying stunts around the sides of a giant barrel, taunt this new arrival, asking if he'd like to try it. "I'm a devout coward," Charlie laughs, turning to walk away. "Goodbye, *dear*," one man mockingly calls after him. Charlie spins around and attempts the stunt, almost killing himself but winning the respect of the traditional males. This is a person, though, who lives two lives. As soon as Charlie steps onstage, he's into a bump and grind routine, the feminine aspects of all Burly-Q movements overtly emphasized:

> Elvis was always ... a transgendered sexual fantasy. That isn't to say that Elvis was gay, or even bisexual, but that he adopted mannerisms that said it was OK for men to celebrate the sensuality of their bodies in ways other than sports....

Elvis helped destabilize conventional understandings of masculinity with "connotations of sexual ambiguity."[41]

However transsexual his appeal — Charlie's, to the audience within the film; Elvis,' to the real-life one watching it — the result brings in the needed money. Not surprisingly, the recurring character of the raw capitalist appears, as embodied by Harry Carver (Pat Buttrum, who played a similar role in *Wild in the Country*). Harry owns the big carnival down the road and would like to live up to his nickname, "The Undertaker," by putting this "Mom and Pop" show out of business. Carver is Walter Matthau from *King Creole*; also, he's Col. Parker, who before discovering Elvis did indeed run just such a carnival.[42] As in *King Creole* — and actuality — the Devil sets out to steal the talented young singer's soul, providing a moral test for the hero.

The redemptive act — giving up potential big bucks, after a brief lapse in judgment — re-establishes a quasi-religious aspect to the hero's journey. First, though, he performs in Harry Carver's big, glitzy show — again teamed with exotic dancers, a considerably classier chorus line. The lead performer is Little Egypt (Wilda Taylor); Charlie dances as the yin to her yang, moving left as she moves to the right. Elvis inverts each of her bumps and/or grinds, zigging as she zags, "turning on" the women in the audience even as she does the men. At a certain point, any man-woman distinction disappears. Elvis creates (on-stage/on-screen) a pan-sexual aura that openly acknowledges the bisexual nature of his persona — if not his person. In so doing, he initiates/legitimizes gay posturing, setting the pace for such upcoming pop culture experiences as *The Rocky Horror Picture Show* and David Bowie concerts.[43]

This might seemingly conflict with the notion of Elvis as a symbol of the American working class, hardly the people (particularly in the '50s) who would be expected to accept such gender slippage. Though the issue remains complex, Eric Lott cuts to its essence when he notes that American culture, much like Elvis, is ultimately "a site of conflicting interests, appropriations, impersonations."[44] In any one object, including human beings, different groups can find varied meanings. This became clear when one professor showed an Elvis film to a seminar and found that a

> working class white woman identified with Presley himself and his character as an emblem of upward mobility for her class [while a] radical lesbian viewed Presley as an androgynous image, a heroic subject that was neither completely male nor female.[45]

Different audiences — separate factions of the diverse American tapestry — each saw something unique in Elvis, telling us more about themselves than him. Presley's "longevity as a cultural icon" for Kevin Quain "is largely due to his flexibility — his willingness to take the shape of what we most wanted to see. Whether our fantasies were psychic, sexual, cosmic, financial, or religious, Elvis accommodated all of us."[46]

Charlie eventually returns to his white trash roots at the humbler show. In part, he does this owing to Carver's ultimate statement of raw capitalism: "Around here, there's just one reason why the show must go on — the *gross!*" What occurs is for Presley the fabled road not taken; Charlie does what Elvis, who couldn't bring himself to leave The Colonel, failed to do. Charlie has nothing against making money, yet he senses there must be something more to life than *just* that. This turns out to be Maggie's "religion."

When at mid-movie Charlie condescendingly made fun of the religious manner in which she spoke about carny life, fortune teller Madame Mijanou (Sue Ane Langdon) admitted with touching pathos, "It's all most of us have got." That provided his turning point. The rural carnival, with its own language and devout (in every sense) loyalty, is, he comes to see, what's been missing from his life — as well as an answer to Cathy's early question "What are you so *angry* about?" Returning a wiser man, he can honestly say: "I came back to help ... and 'cause I love Cathy."

The anger is gone from his voice and demeanor as well as his words. The hero has been born again into a selfless existence. True to his original promise, Charlie has not settled for the *faux* values of modern suburbia. Yet he has arced enough to grasp what his hero in *Follow That Dream* (owing to his supportive if déclassé family) knew from the start — the truer, more traditional values of an earlier America must be unearthed and embraced if he (or his audience) is ever to find lasting happiness.

CHAPTER 10

From Marginalization
to Mainstream

♦ *It Happened at the World's Fair* (1963) ♦
♦ *Paradise, Hawaiian Style* (1966) ♦

By the mid–'60s, the once-hysterical hillbilly came off more as a homogenized product for the consumer-oriented society he once stood in opposition to. As for the movies, all but the hardcore blue collar fans "had outgrown them,"[1] as cousin Billy Smith reflected. Which helps explain why both the relatively ambitious items covered in this chapter turned out to be financial disappointments. Here, as with the hick films, the movie was designed to promote the album; the songs, despite Elvis' remarkable delivery, inferior to the once-vibrant Memphis cat numbers. Presley's latest material had been purchased by Col. Parker from lesser sources willing to give up 25 percent of their publishing rights just to claim that Elvis recorded something they'd written.[2] This synergy between the music and movies proved to be as strong economically as it was creatively wrong-headed. The result was "McElvis," a product turned out in much the same way as America's popular hamburger chain had marketed fast food since 1948.

"Our whole concept was based on speed, lower prices, and volume,"[3] Dick McDonald said; Parker might have employed the same phrase to describe his "boy," who had by now become part and parcel of the "homogenization of American culture then being wrought by the combination of increasing affluence and mass-production technology."[4] Elia Kazan, who had expressed interest in working with Elvis, might have been speaking of him when he wrote about creative young people in general:

They're like fighters on their way up. It's a life or death struggle ... and they give their utmost…. That quality disappears later. They become civilized and normal.[5]

Kazan's final word hardly describes Elvis in life: a man who slept with several underage girls wrapped around him in Vegas hotel suites, carried a virtual arsenal of weapons on his person at all times, shot out TV sets if he happened to catch sight of a singer he didn't like, and was now hopelessly addicted to prescription drugs even as he ranted and raved about young people who smoke pot. "He made a great distinction between himself and a junkie," Lamar Fike claims. "A junkie did heroin. Not Dilaudid [synthetic heroin, and 2.5 times stronger than the real thing]. As long as things were prescription, it was okay."[6] In addition to living in denial, "Elvis lost touch with the feelings of other people," according to Smith, who noticed the gradated darkening of a once shy, sincere person. "He changed from humble to hard."[7]

Biographer Albert Goldman insists Elvis had always been two people, one good and the other bad—a result of trauma following the death of twin Jesse. That may be pop psychologizing, though Fike does note that "Elvis had a lot of personalities."[8] The great irony—and Elvis is nothing if not an endless succession of ironies—is that, while still unspoiled in the 1950s, Elvis projected a movie image of an arrogant, cruel character; once he started to become just such a person, he wanted, Jekyll and Hyde–like, to play the sort of sweet personality he was, step by step, leaving behind in real life. So the public experienced his "mutation" from rock 'n' roll rebel to "B-movie star."[9]

A Friend In Need…: *It Happened at the World's Fair* (1963)

Almost all the movies begin with a focus on some sort of travel, the very act a ritualized way of defining the Presley persona on-screen. Here, Mike Edwards is first glimpsed flying a plane—a far cry from the beat-up jalopy in *Follow That Dream*, the truck on which he hitched a ride in *Kid Galahad*, or the motorcycle in *Roustabout*. Yet some recurring signifiers are employed; though Elvis is airborne, his vehicle is anything but modern and/or classy. Tying him to traditions of the past, Mike and his callow partner Danny Burke (Gary Lockwood) pilot a 30-year-old biplane. They call her "Betsy," an allusion to the famed long rifle of legendary Tennessean Davy Crockett, likewise associated with a romanticized past.

To indicate this is not a hardcore blue-collar film, Elvis wears the jaunty pilot's cap he donned in *Blue Hawaii* and *Girls! Girls! Girls!* while singing the first song, "Beyond the Bend." The number establishes his latest alter ego's unique position at this moment in time. The boys are crop-dusting in Washington State as Elvis sings that he has no cares because he is on his way to anywhere.

These words remind us of the rootless individualist-loner. Yet we can't help but notice Danny's presence next to Mike. Mostly, Danny remains silent, though occasionally he hums along. Mike openly implies Danny's function in the film's context during the next stanza, even as he reaffirms the continuing theme of the proud pauper.

The concept of friendship will literally motor this movie, as it did in such early works as *Loving You.*

A parallel is established to the star's life. For 1963 — the year when *It Happened At the World's Fair* was released — has been described as the "Year of Change" by aficionados.[10] Elvis divided his time driving around Memphis between his hot Harley and a chauffeured Rolls. That indicated a schizophrenic situation for a man who harbored hillbilly leanings though now was perceived as part of the moneyed Establishment. This latest film was a glossy MGM "family" musical. He ended his relationship with girlfriend Anita Wood as Priscilla officially moved into Graceland. Thereafter, he had to balance the notion of male-bonding with Red West and the Memphis Mafia with an ongoing male-female coupling. Norman Taurog's film roughly parallels that inner journey, beginning with the set-up of friendship as an important part of any man's life.

We could not be further here from Elvis' attitude in *Fun in Acapulco*, in which he refused the offers of various men to be friends to better pursue success in terms of finance, fame and the female lead. For the time being, Mike and Danny remain overgrown boys rather than men, nearly crashing Betsy when Mike flies dangerously low — first for the sheer visceral thrill of it, then to wave at pretty girls in a convertible. Linking this film to ones we have seen before, the boys make no attempt to date the young women. "Pretty *scenery* around here," Mike drawls. They talk about the women as if they were vegetables of the sort that grow below ("You don't know a *sweet* potato when you see one"), no better or worse than comparisons of pretty women to meat in past pictures. Another early theme has resurfaced: Elvis' love of flirtation giving way to his fear of consummation. Apparently, with good reason. One early bedmate, actress Natalie Wood, confided to her sister that "Elvis can sing, but he can't do much else."[11] Linda Thompson, the King's favorite companion after the divorce from Priscilla, "didn't think he was all that hot a lover."[12] Better for one's ego to keep the image alive and well than try and live up to it and fail.

Arrested adolescents — suffering from what has since been tagged The Peter Pan Syndrome[13] in more ways than one — Mike and Danny turn down a steady job with a local farmer to remain "on the road," though they desperately need the money, reasserting the capitalist imperative. Childish behavior becomes a more acute problem after Danny, a compulsive gambler, blows everything they've earned in a fixed card game. When this leads to the inevitable fistfight between Elvis and his adversaries, we witness a major distinction between the current and earlier bouts. Here, Mike has Danny fighting alongside him, re-establishing the once potent but more recently muted theme of friendship.

An "evolved Elvis" is enhanced by costuming choices. Other than in the opening, Elvis wears a suit, often with accompanying tie, not only on occasion (as in *Kid Galahad*) but in *every* sequence. Important, too: He is the more mature member of the duo (though that isn't saying much). Danny is the "bad boy" whom Mike, a middle-of-the-road mentor figure, watches over. The movie posits a "new" Elvis, the old one now incarnated by Danny — played by an actor who had appeared in *Wild in the Country*. This cross-references the earlier films, Danny essentially the earlier immature Presley persona. Elvis did play a youth named Danny in *King Creole*; at times, Lockwood appears to be dressed in costumes left over from that film. As Mike gradually rejects Danny during the story's course, Elvis disassociates himself with the person (or, more correctly, persona) he once was.

During the first act, Mike does recall the *Playboy*-era Elvis from *Girls! Girls! Girls!* and *Fun in Acapulco*. While Danny gambles their money away, Mike visits an old flame, whose name he can't recall. Mike confuses her with other pretty girls he regularly romances. She's played by Yvonne Craig, a brunette who specialized in teen-teaser roles in youth exploitation flicks (*Gidget, The Gene Krupa Story*) and opposite Elvis in *Kissin' Cousins*. Their single scene together here, which ends as her father chases Mike out of the house with a shotgun, is composed entirely of role- and game-playing: He performs as the retro-male, interested only in a sexual seduction; she pretends to be a demure virgin, uninterested in such stuff though planning on "sweet surrender" at the right moment — until interrupted by her parents. Once, such a scene might have been the first of many such moments. In context, the gambit takes on significance as this is the *only* such sequence.

Afterwards, Mike — again paralleling Presley — tries to leave the art of seduction behind for a relationship with a female that stretches beyond a superficial attraction, one in which respect proves as essential as romance. There must be a bridge between his current state — male bonding with the ne'er-do-well Danny; superficial sexual flirtations with interchangeable women — and a loving friendship with a mature woman. The transition is achieved via Mike's temporal relationship with what has become a key motif, the polymorphously perverse friendship with a girl-child — here, Sue-Lin (Vicky Tiu), to whom Mike is drawn. This parallels Elvis' actual first meeting with Priscilla who, as a ninth grader, was only slightly older than Sue-Lin when she met the man who would be king:[14] "Why, you're just a *baby*," Elvis said. As soon as possible, he squired her up to his room, insisting that she shouldn't worry, since "I'll treat you just like a [little] *sister*."[15] Elvis then proceeded to cuddle her in his arms, though without consummation; he will do that with Sue-Lin several times in the film. This is what Elvis and Gladys shared, the age differences reversed. Elvis told Priscilla that first night together: "'I just wish Mama could have been here to meet you.'"[16] For most men, thinking of their mothers while in bed with a beautiful underage girl would not happen — or, if it did occur, that would ruin the experience. For Elvis, it was basic. He nicknamed Priscilla "Satnin"— his longtime monicker for Gladys, the phrase referring to a ring of fat around a woman's waist. The term could not in any realistic sense be applied to slender Priscilla. Emotions were a different matter. Following Gladys' death, Elvis changes complexes, Oedipus giving way to Electra in the guise of Priscilla.

"I was his little girl, Elvis said,"[17] Priscilla recalls. That is what he tells Sue-Lin here. Their liaison begins when her uncle picks up Mike and Danny, forced to hitchhike (recalling the blue-collar subgenre) after their plane is repossessed. The boys were talking about breaking up the partnership (and friendship) before the beat-up truck stopped. They ride in the open-air rear to Seattle, where Sue-Lin hopes to visit the World's Fair. Mike's loyalty shifts from Danny to her. When Danny dozes off, Mike borrows Sue-Lin's ukulele to musically inform the Asian child about the wonders they'll soon see together.

Removed from context, that line sounds romantic: the kind of love ballads Elvis once sang to older, motherly women are redirected to little girls now — still not to women his own age. The girl-children become his adopted daughters, yet they clearly "date." Priscilla reflects that Elvis "became my father, husband, and very nearly God."[18] This at a time when she (underage) appeared in many pornographic videos directed by Elvis, and performed every imaginable sex act with Elvis just so long as he did not have to actually penetrate her.[19] When Mike hugs and kisses Sue-Lin in the film, it's clear from the look in the child's eyes that he is her father, husband and God.

The result is an "innocent" relationship that conveys a disturbing subtext. Coming at the end of the opening act, the sequence further distances Mike and Danny; the friend-partner is marginalized by the camera. Elvis and the child are isolated in a tight shot even as their love (which they openly discuss often) begins. After arriving, Mike and Sue-Lin take the monorail into the fair while her uncle heads off to find work, and Danny decides to reconnect with gambler-friend Vic in hopes of borrowing money. Elvis is the enlightened capitalist, hoping to run a regional airline. "I want to *earn* some money," Mike insists; unlike Danny, he plans to somehow make his personal American Dream come true.

The *Playboy*-era image is by no means a thing of the past. As Mike and Sue-Lin devour cotton candy between the varied rides, a bizarre balance is achieved — Elvis holding hands with a child while ogling beautifully built women who pass by. The situation is satisfyingly masochistic for the apparent stud who fears real women. We grasp why Mike, who deeply needed to elicit waves from those pretty girls in the film's opening, did not choose to pursue the available young women; that would have left him entirely vulnerable. As a responsible chaperone, he cannot desert the child to date pretty women — freeing him to enjoy their presence without risking the trial and error of an actual encounter. Until, that is, Sue-Lin consumes too much junk food and Mike must take her to the nurse's station. There, he meets Diane Warren (Joan O'Brien), older than he and a throwback to mature women whom Elvis encountered in early Oedipal films.

A highly professional nurse, serious-minded Diane is first glimpsed reading a copy of *Space*, a book about the New Frontier. She's a woman of the present with an eye on the future. Owing to previous roles opposite John Wayne (*The Alamo*, 1960; *The Comancheros*, 1961), O'Brien also invokes images of earlier frontiers. Elvis' own ongoing desire to become such a Western movie icon is expressed in one of Mike's later lines to Diane: "Guess you could call me one of the last *pioneers*," explaining his interest in aviation. Whether a frontier is new or old becomes less significant than the very *idea* of a frontier.

Immediately, Elvis-Mike goes into his act, the game of seduction he played with the opening's "girl." The story's second movement glides into his "flirtation" with a grown-up, as such a harbinger of things to come, notably the Ann-Margret character in *Viva Las Vegas*. The old game-playing routines don't work with someone who has no interest in an irresponsible male, though his willingness to care for a child does intrigue her. In truth, that "child" is jealous of what appears to be a developing relationship. Sue-Lin eases Mike out the door as swiftly as possible while casting Diane a "He's mine!" look. Shortly, the no-longer-all-that-young man and the small girl ride the monorail back. As Sue-Lin falls asleep on Mike's shoulder, he — recalling the underage girl's polar opposite, "Miss Warren" — cuddles Sue-Lin while singing a love song. The emotions that the man who has given up on teenage females now feels for a mature woman are physically expressed to a child. In a bizarre bit, the two females become confused in his mind. Mike dreams (how Freud, who insisted that dreams reveal our selves, would have loved this!) about the off-screen Diane, as he nuzzles Sue-Lin. Eventually, Elvis strokes the sleeping child's hair, then kisses her. Sight ("innocently" kissing a child) and sound (desire for the woman he sings about) combine to create a perverse effect from everyday elements.

Mike and Sue-Lin will play out roles for one another. Priscilla recalled of her early days with Elvis:

> We dressed up and undressed … acted out our fantasies, and invented scenes. Whether it was dressing up in my school uniform and playing at being a sweet, innocent schoolgirl … or a teacher seducing her student, we were always inventing new stories….[20]

The film presents their played-out pornographic fantasies as family entertainment. In context, this scene serves as a turning point. Danny continues gambling at the trailer park they call home; Mike is torn between the presence of Sue-Lin (whose uncle mysteriously disappeared, causing her to now sleep in Mike's bed, much as young Priscilla did) and lingering memories of Diane.

Mike remains his own worst enemy. You can't win a woman via child's play so every come-on backfires. When Mike returns to the fair and pays a small boy (Kurt Russell, eventually to play Elvis in a TV film) to kick him so Mike can report to the nurse's office, Diane learns this is a ploy and grows furious. In time, though, she does relent and allows Mike to take her to dinner. They dine at the Space Needle, symbol for Kennedy's promise to land a man on the Moon before the decade ended. The race for space had begun in earnest during Elvis' early era when, on October 7, 1957, the Russians launched Sputnik ("fellow traveler"), a 184-lb., 22.8-inch (in diameter) satellite which circled Earth every 90 minutes. Edward Teller referred to this as "a technological Pearl Harbor."[21] America then launched a missile but (embarrassingly) it blew up. Wernher von Braun and 100 other German scientists, now U.S. citizens, were our first "rocket engineers." Admiral Hyman Rickover criticized our school system; overnight, greater emphasis was placed on science. The U.S. surged ahead.

When on July 20, 1969, Neil Armstrong made his famous "small step," von Braun insisted that it was "as significant to the history of life on earth as aquatic life [first] crawling [onto the] land."[22] In the early 1960s, an optimism about our upcoming conquest of space informed young people. Here, Diane wants her fair share of this New Frontier, revealing that she signed up to be a nurse in the space program. This inspires Mike, who decides his love of flying can best be served by becoming an astronaut.

Though an aura of light romance continues, the desire he initially felt appears to have dissipated in favor of a mutually supportive friendship. It is after all Sue-Lin whom Mike kisses and cuddles. Another such sequence — quite grotesque, closely considered — portrays man and child dancing together in his trailer, at first innocently though in time they slip into a provocative Twist. In an elaborate episode, Mike prepares Sue-Lin for bed; while Mike offers to leave even as she changes into pajamas, Sue-Lin makes it clear that she'd be happy to have him stay. Their goodnight kiss is more prolonged than any between Mike and Diane, at least until the final fadeout with its oblig- atory (and self-satirizing) happy ending: A marching band seemingly borrowed from *The Music Man* trails behind the couple as they head off to the space program. Old-fashioned Americana is balanced with a contemporary dream for the future.

During Mike's second-act relationship with Sue-Lin, the old friendship with Danny (who on one occasion becomes obnoxiously drunk and verbally abusive) is tested. That escalates in the third movement, when the intensity of Elvis' need for a friend passes from an outworn bond with an immature man to a sweetly impossible flirtation with an underage female, then to a workable one with a mature woman who helps the Presley protagonist discover his proper way. Game playing must come to an end if he is to win Diane.

Danny, who once seemed a charming loser, seals his own fate when he speaks of Diane in the same terms both men once employed for females. "What, you lose your wolf's whistle?" Danny cackles when Mike takes offense at Danny's sexist comments. One has arced from overgrown boy to man, the other has not. That Mike must choose between two similarly named people — Diane and Danny — heightens the conflict. Shortly, Danny heads into a bar and slaps a waitress on her rear end, then admits to Vince he can't remember her name. Mike had been just such a retro male, but the scene with Yvonne Craig served as a foil to his more grown-up relationship. One little boy has the potential to possibly grow up. So Establishment adults are no longer posited as obnoxious meddlers. When Miss Ettinger arrives from the Office of Social Services to claim Sue-Lin, she is not the caricature of the dominat- ing woman with power present in *Follow That Dream* but a dedicated career woman who does the right thing.

This is obvious even to Mike, however much he regrets Sue-Lin's absence. Yet they are reunited when she runs away, leading to a lame chase around the fair by uniformed guards. And a denouement at the local airport, where Vince the gangster tries to force Mike and Danny to fly in a load of hot furs to Canada. For the second time, Elvis must engage in fisticuffs, if with a difference: His partner is disabled and can't help. That sets the bout off from the earlier one, leaving little question that the once-strong bond between Mike and Danny is severed.

Mike will have no part in an illegal operation (the troubled teen of *King Creole* who did such things now objectified as the *other* half of the team) and turns the furs over to authorities. When Sue-Lin's uncle finally reappears, Mike is free to shift his attentions toward Diane. Though they may become lovers, it is the sense of friendship that dominates, as the two go off to try and forge a future, combining the best of the old (advancement through hard work) with the new (the Space Program).

Third Star to the Right: *Paradise, Hawaiian Style* (1966)

A plane lands in Hawaii; inside, neatly uniformed Rick Richards (Elvis) makes small talk with a stewardess. At first, the sequence appears a redux of *Blue Hawaii*'s opening: The playboy hero, an ex-serviceman, disengaged himself from a stewardess as she kissed him; on the ground, another beautiful girl awaited his return. What unfolds here, though, turns out *not* to be a repetition but an alternative. This time, there will be no beautiful female awaiting Elvis' arrival. He isn't an honorably discharged soldier but an airline pilot, fired from his company. Camelot is over; in the late '60s, things turn sour.

Significantly, the stewardess does *not* pursue Elvis. A different breed of female than Elvis encountered five years earlier, she declines his offer for a date, showing him her engagement ring. Her words reveal that she once dated Rick, but he remains the early '60s playboy incarnate, and she has no intention of going that route again. "I got over you, *long* ago," she tells him; there is no hint in her voice that this is a self-defense mechanism. She — like the world in general, its women specifically — has moved on, while the Presley persona has stayed the same. "Going home to get away from trouble" is how Rick describes his situation, making clear his problems all stem from "girls" — not, in his words, women.

The attitude toward a harum, applauded behavior in *Girls! Girls! Girls!*, is rendered ridiculous here — the man who persists in pursuing "the Playboy Philosophy" all at once a cautionary figure rather than a role model. Instead of a bevy of beauties welcoming Rick, there are only the native beach boys, who again treat him as one of their own. The integration element is furthered, the hero invariably associating with people of color rather than the Anglo element, as in *Blue Hawaii*. In an altered social (if geographically identical) landscape, however, they are now woman-less, suggesting a possible gay subtext to the scene.

> Today, Elvis is still imaged on erotic terms because of his sexual liquidity, and because many contemporary Americans seem to have largely rejected essentialist ideas about what it means to be a boy or a girl, a man or a woman. Not surprisingly, Elvis' contemporary cultural popularity is largely linked to the different ways that women and men, straights and queers, see him.[23]

Heterosexuality, however, in the most conventional manner is what Rick encounters when he joins his adopted brother (James Shigeta) at his humble home. Though this character is (as in *It Happened...*) named Danny, the situation is reversed. Since Rick's departure, Danny — Rick's onetime woman-izing companion — has settled down and married Betty (Jan Shepard, who played Elvis' sister in *King Creole*), an Anglo woman — making it clear that the stewardess' situation wasn't merely a narrative device but also a thematic element.

Danny Kohana's marital status is heartily approved of by Rick. Direc-tor D. Michael Moore allows us to see Elvis convey a complex progressive-traditionalist attitude: He heartily supports the conventional formal structure of a marriage; he defends the modern notion of a mixed marriage. Danny and Betty have five children — the kind of solid family that early Elvis longed for. Even the kids seem more mature than Rick. When they ask how he happened to arrive, he relates a silly story about flying in on his own. "Only angels have wings," the oldest, most precocious child, Jan (Donna Butterworth), reminds Rick, "and you're no angel. I heard Momma say so!" Jan is Wordsworth's child-as-swain, that poet long ago noting "the Child is father to the Man."

In this case, a diminutive earth mother, solidifying the connection between very little girls and much older women in Elvis Cinema. Also, Presley's own confusion of Gladys and Priscilla, including his similar quasi-sexual relation-ships with each. Jan is the instinctually wise child who proves through depth of understanding to be the moral conscience of a rudderless adult in search of an anchor — true of Elvis as well as Rick. "I think he was attracted by the fact that I had a normal, stable childhood, and that I was very responsible,"[24] Priscilla wrote.

Each of Jan's parents likewise boast what the poet called "a knowing heart, an understanding mind." Rick kiddingly mentions there are a great many children around:

RICK: Must be hard to keep track of them.
BETTY: *You'll* find out, one of these days.
DANNY: Marriage is for the *old* squares, like us.

Significantly, Rick and Danny are the same age. A key bit of business has Rick singing, dancing and playing with Jan and the other Kohana chil-dren. In contrast to similar scenes in earlier films celebrating his desire to remain forever young, there's a melancholic sensibility here. The director positions his camera so that we view Elvis' antics through the eyes of Danny and Betty; the star comes off as an overgrown child who refuses to grasp that he's long overdue for marriage and family.

Pop culture critic George Melly complained that Elvis had been cas-trated, resulting in a harmless rather than appealingly threatening "mastur-bation fantasy-object for adolescent girls."[25] To a degree, true — though Melly misses the larger point. *Paradise, Hawaiian Style* does not mindlessly situate

Presley as such a figure as it posits the sad state that he, like the character he plays, degenerated into. The following narrative is by implication about the institution of marriage — enshrined in the late 1950s, scoffed at in the early '60s, about to again be embraced by born-again traditionalists as a necessary end to the American male's flirtation with the playboy philosophy.[26]

Some 90 minutes later, *Paradise* leaves us with the impression that Rick (like the conventional men he represents) may be unable to grasp this fundamental truth. Rick and Danny create a partnership: a commercial airline to fly tourists between the islands, not very different from what Elvis and that other Danny hoped to achieve in *It Happened....* The reference to a similar situation provides a frame of reference by which we note the greater change. Three years later, Elvis has *regressed.* An early customer is Mr. Cubberson (Grady Sutton), a businessman who manufactures and distributes alligator shoes, which are "a symbol of prestige, wealth and importance." These are the items that Elvis' hero wanted to avoid in *Blue Hawaii,* yet which he now desires. When Cubberson suggests that the new company ought to include helicopters and initiate a sightseeing service, Rick's exchange with Danny is noteworthy:

RICK: Beautiful [the coptors], aren't they?
DANNY: Yeah. So are Mr. Cubberson's alligator shoes.

Mr. Cubberson insists, "If you give people something special, they'll pay for it." He is the latest incarnation of the colonel, and by "give," he means "offer" for *sale.* Instead of rejecting the man's attitude, Rick embraces it. Elvis' persona has been co-opted by the status-symbol system he once rejected. Elvis himself had just stopped fighting Parker as to the issue of higher quality in projects, now willing to do anything that would make money. In earlier films, he wanted to engage in a relationship with a woman that would be untarnished by the clink of cold coins. Here, that is precisely what's on Rick's mind.

At the first island they visit, he approaches Lehua (Linda Wong), one of many playmates Rick enjoyed in past years. Then, he showed up for "dates" (i.e., sex), soon hurrying off to the next girl. His interest now is not merely sensual, like hers for him. Rick, with profits in mind, insists he'll make this island — and Lehua — part of his itinerary *if* she'll use her position at the resort to talk up his service. "You scratch my back," he tells her, "and I'll scratch yours." He'll trade sexual favors for business. Elvis has become precisely what, in *Girls! Girls! Girls!,* he insisted he'd never become: a gigolo.

Part of his outdated playboy's philosophy is to let a series of women each believe that she and she alone is involved in such a business proposition. An island hop brings him to Pua (Lisa Lu), who becomes part of the same bargain. "Tell me you came back to see me, Rick," one paramour sighs. "Lie a little." Apparently, the only female he can truly love is Jan, who at 12 is too young to seduce despite all their suggestive dancing, singing, hugging and kissing. "Uncle Rick," she calls him whenever they embrace — which is often. Priscilla was not much older than Jan during the Christmas 1962 season she spent at Graceland. Elvis visited her bedroom and "Gently, he took off ... my clothes. Then he kissed me and kissed me over and over."[27] Had this film been made two years later, after the establishment of a ratings system, we might have seen some of that on-screen.

Here, fully grown females are regarded as sex objects for one-night stands with no emotional commitment; pretty little girl children are loved, worshipped, embraced but not penetrated — and allowed a deep emotional inroad into his heart. Like the female lead in James Barrie's *Peter and Wendy* (1896), Priscilla made the unforgivable mistake of growing up, at which point she became irrelevant. This film ends before that can happen. Elvis doesn't need to fly off to the third star to the right, then continue straight on 'til morning. That the islands compose Rick's Never Never Land is made clear by the final extravagant number, "This Is My Heaven," in which he happily dances with *all* of his old girlfriends. A tune from the famed stage version of *Peter Pan* might have been incorporated to emphasize that he won't grow up. In *It Happened*, Elvis paused to consider doing so; between that film and *Paradise*, he apparently changed his mind.

The foil for all this is the film's only true single *woman* (rather than *girl*), Judy Hudson (Suzanna Leigh). When it comes time to hire a "Girl Friday" for the successful new company, Rick will only interview sexy bimbos, devoid of secretarial skills. He leaves the bright and talented (if less attractive) women to his married partner. One of Danny's lines perfectly captures the mentality of Presley's regressed persona at this juncture. Danny demands: "Where did you put the ad [for a secretary] — in *Playboy*?" The look on Rick's face makes it clear that Danny isn't far off.

The era's new female wants to achieve an identity not through the man in her life, but on her own — whether or not she happened to commit to a man. Judy is just such a person, someone whose career will provide her with self-fulfillment and who plays down that she is beautiful as well as bright. An attractive blonde, she's hired by Danny owing to her technical talents as a mechanic. What Judy would prefer, however, is to be hired as a flyer — that is, the *equal* of Danny and Rick. "Women can set all kinds of records," she scoffs, "but you men won't give us a *real* job." The film might have caricatured Judy; instead, she's sympathetic. She is right, of course, and we sense this even as the two male "heroes" do not. Then, Danny comes up with a concept that serves as the blocking device to keep Rick and Judy out of each other's arms. Danny slips his wedding ring on Judy's finger; Rick — flitting from one unattached female to the next — will steer clear of Judy and allow her to work.

Elvis engages in his obligatory fistfight in a restaurant with a fellow who comes on strong to Judy. Rick mistakenly believes the man to be Judy's abusive husband. The sequence turns into a virtual apotheosis and, by its conclusion, broad burlesque of all earlier fistfights. Rick takes on, one by one, *every* other male waiting his turn in the Polynesian buffet line. In its overthe-top tone, the sequence communicates a sense of end-game. Shortly, he's the playboy male par excellence again, taking cheesecake pictures of a bikiniclad Judy for the firm's advertising — forcing the intelligent woman of the late '60s into the "Playmate of the Month" role. "Single girls sell more tickets," Rick whispers as he slips the ring from Judy's finger — unaware of the truth of her situation, which renders his attitude ridiculous.

As in the fistfight scene, we sense that enough is enough. Yet Rick doesn't attempt to touch the "married" female; standing face to face with a woman rather than a girl always scared off Elvis in actuality.[28] The mature (and deflowered) woman is too much for Elvis-Rick. He has, of course, his alternative: shortly, Rick allows little Jan to crawl all over him. Tellingly, it is *she* who realizes it might be best to end their sensuous habit soon. "I guess I'm getting pretty *old* for that stuff," Jan admits, her first cognition of her own oncoming adolescence stirring. Wendy begins to grow up, so Peter slips into denial. "Ah, you've got a long way to go," Rick assures her; the disturbing quality of what we see quite belies that.

His infatuation with Jan, so long as she remains a child and does not threaten him with the consummation, continues when Rick takes her on a trip to Moonlight Cove — his favorite haunt for seducing big girls (if not quite women) he's *romanced* in the past! Jan ruins his dream of innocent infatuation, however, when — Lolita-like — she suggests that now, something might actually happen:

> JAN: (getting excited) It'll be like a *real* date!
> RICK: (growing concerned) Gets more and more complicated.

When they do fly off together in the helicopter (this Peter lacks Tinker Bell to shower Jan with pixie dust), they sing a duet — as Jan, not Rick, "directs" their performance, hardly the kind of innocent number that in earlier movies Elvis performed with little girls. "Datin'" allows them to confront the diverse joys and difficulties of a serious relationship. They vividly mimic (including embraces and telling kisses) a romantic couple. Like those Shirley Temple-Bill Robinson dance routines of the 1930s, this number can be viewed in either of two ways: Sweet and charming, at face value; deeply disturbing, if we consider the implications of the maturing child whose parodic performance of adult mating habits threaten to engulf a frightened if fascinated Elvis.

This reaches a crisis point when Rick finds himself stranded on an island with a grown-up girl, Lani (Marianna Hill), *and* pint-sized Jan. Jealous of the child who receives more attention from Rick than she does, Lani throws the helicopter's keys into the sand. When Danny arrives to rescue them, he's furious; the last time Rick slipped off to this place with Lani, he didn't return for three days. As to Rick's explanation about the lost keys, Danny insists, "That story was old when you started using it ten years ago." Rick is the little boy who cried wolf; now he's telling the truth but no one will believe him. This begs a question never openly addressed, but which underlines Danny's anger: Did he fear that Rick brought Jan along to initiate her into full femininity via a ménage a trois?

Hamlet-like, all circumstances conspire against Rick. He has not only failed to arrive home in time to pick up passengers (thereby losing money), but is grounded by the F.A.A. inspector, who (unfairly) blames Rick for performing dangerous stunts. When Rick finally dates Judy (now aware she's single), all his other playmates show up at the club. This allows for an offbeat musical number — "Stop Where You Are" — in which Rick attempts to dance (literally) his way around female reminders of his playboy past.

Every time the lyrics have him sing the first word of the title, the image freezes for a split second. Though this is ultimately overdone, it does invoke the kinds of effects that, following the success of *Tom Jones* (1963), emerged as the 1960s cinematic sensibility. This was not your father's Elvis musical, even if he is still your father's Elvis. If the medium is the message, then style *is* substance: Like his alter ego Rick, Elvis is frozen in time owing to an inability to grow further and change with an emergent late–1960s world.

Eventually, Rick redeems himself by rescuing Danny and Jan from a helicopter crash. He promises that all his girls will be financially rewarded for their contributions. Rick wins back his right to fly by persuading Mr. Belden (John Doucette) that he (Rick) isn't irresponsible in the air like Mike in *It Happened....* Earlier, while transporting dogs that roamed free all over the cabin, Rick flew close to the ground, forcing Belden and his wife (Mary Treen), driving on the road, into the brush. If that was the only way in which Mike remained immature, it is the only avenue where Rick displays maturity. Mrs. Belden isn't well enough yet to attend the island festival, though her husband hardly holds that against Rick.

"This is the first time I've been able to get out without my wife in years," Belden admits. "I think I *like* it!" The Beldens, foils to Danny and his happy family, represent the nightmare vision of marriage at its absolute worst. Perhaps influenced by this, Rick at the movie's end still seems unwilling to give up the bachelor's existence. Though he can now date single and available Judy, if he dares to approach so formidable a woman, he is last seen dancing alone — the eternal child-man — while the others form a huge pageant around him.

As one song, mentioned earlier, notes, this (for Elvis as for Rick) is his "heaven on earth." If such an ending once struck the viewer as a pleasant case of fun and fancy free, this image now reveals that while we may have grown, the star has not. What was once taken as a traditional man's individual freedom, with Elvis' oncoming age at last beginning to show, appears sad — even pathetic.

CHAPTER 11

A Mid–'60s Masterpiece

◆ *Viva Las Vegas* (1964) ◆

In the brutal *demi-monde* of organized crime — a nation within the nation that stretched the American success Dream to its cruelest perimeters — Benjamin Siegel rated as a visionary. According to tawdry legend, during the postwar era, Bugsy perceived in Nevada's unbeautiful desert the potential to create a red-light district for an entire country. For tens of thousands of returning G.I.s, what had occurred following World War I would prove stronger still after 1945: "How you gonna keep 'em down on the farm after they've seen Paris?" For better or worse, "the old puritanism was dramatically weakened: Expectations and attitudes"[1] were rapidly changing. So Bugsy built the Flamingo Hotel and waited for customers to come. And waited, and waited.... When they didn't show, torpedoes contracted by mob bosses who had advanced their colleague the considerable sums necessary to open this seemingly failed venture shot Siegel dead in his Los Angeles home. Succeed and you win our undying admiration; fail and you ... *die*. Bugsy had been right on the money, but — like geniuses of a more conventional order — he was also way ahead of his time.

A Da Vinci of contemporary vulgarity, Siegel created the tip of an iceberg before our generation's body was ready to break from the main. The public remained in utter confusion as to the fraying of the old morality, the late '40s and early 1950s characterized by a growing schizophrenia as to "our national craving for identity and definition."[2] America found itself torn between polar opposites — the huge homogenized suburban mass and a small but vocal live-for-the-moment Beat Movement. Despite an economic upturn, most citizens didn't have money to throw around, nor had they yet navigated the excitingly icy new waters of spending rather than saving. The wealthy, though, had found a destination to direct their as-yet-unspeakable energies: the Cuba of Fulgencio Batista, a vicious dictator who ran an ugly and decadent place, a playland for rich Americans who wanted to escape the puritanical atmosphere of their home country, where they could gamble legally and buy whatever they wanted in terms of sexual gratification. It was a place of gambling, drinking, sex shows, prostitution ... [C]asinos were run by the American mob.[3]

No wonder crime bosses looked askance at Siegel's dream project; Las Vegas would force them to compete with themselves for the same potential profits, at an estimated double the cost. Then, on the night of January 8, 1959, Fidel Castro's guerrilla movement streamed into Havana, putting an end to the fascistic regime while promising to return all power to the people. Rebels shouted Communist rather than democratic slogans, causing them to be perceived as a threat by America at large, organized crime in particular. "Respectable" corporate interests, like sleazy vice dens, could no longer function without restriction. Now the mob looked at Vegas in an entirely different light. Viva the city where suddenly bygone Cuban casinos could be rebuilt! Bugsy's body might be a-molderin' in the grave, but the crime syndicate could claim that Siegel's truth goes marching on.

Vegas developed not in the style of any normal city: organically. Rather, its neon nightscape was imposed on a pre-existing wasteland for the sole purpose of making vast sums of money through a hard, narrow, new definition of entertainment. Life flourished in an utterly *faux* alternative world, a demented Disneyland for grown-ups who left the kids behind when they came here. If Walt's Magic Kingdom appealed to the benign side of our American spirit — a respect for the past (Frontierland) coupled with a reverence for the future (Tomorrowland), melded together by family values (Main Street, U.S.A.) — Las Vegas emerged as its dark doppelganger, a decadent playland of mainstream pornography in an era when the public caught up to Bennie's potent perception of things to come. What didn't work in 1949 seemed just right for 1959; the Rat Pack performed in casinos by night, filming *Ocean's 11* during daylight hours. When that movie was released nationally a year later, it served as a cinematic recruiting poster for Sin City as *Playboy*'s era of accepted hedonism (including the private life of our new president, who represented the sensuous early–1960s male sensibility along with Sinatra, Hefner and Elvis) officially opened.

The precipitous perfection of advanced airplane engines led to a "jet set"; what earlier had been a laborious trip could be completed in several hours. Simultaneously, the birth control pill hit the market, its sudden legality altering mainstream America's views on sex. Gone were the days when its creator, Gordy Pincus, could be dismissed as "a sinister character bent on hatching humans in bottles"[4] by (incredibly!) our country's most progressive paper, *The New York Times*. Alfred Kinsey's second book about modern mores — *Sexual*

Behavior in the Human Female (1953) — had been absorbed. Gradually, everyone became aware that Kinsey's earlier claim of a great chasm between stated moral values and our actual activities carried the weight of truth. While movies with subtitles were generally attended only by academic types, many suburbanites — hoping to catch a quick peek at Europe's *nouveau* decadence, awash in casual/kinky sex — drifted over to the arthouse to catch *La Dolce Vita* (1960).

Still, this remained an America split down the middle: Until 1965, any doctor who dared discuss contraception with a patient (including married women) risked being arrested, tried and jailed under still-existing laws seemingly set in cement by anti-sex activist Anthony Comstock during the late nineteenth century. Meanwhile, the first wave of Elvis fans had grown into young adults. Though they could not resist getting older, they — listening to him or Bob Dylan — chose to remain "forever young," inspired by the performer who had provided the first known mass media example of "sensuality out of control."[5] At last, they were ready to stop observing Elvis in action and to try it themselves, as ever more radical dance crazes — the Watusi, the Frug — made clear. Everything changed as what had begun in the '50s now exploded: "Each year seemed to take the country further from its old puritan restraints; each year, [sex] was a little easier to sell than in the past."[6]

Similarly, Hunter S. Thompson wrote of a town that filled our first gonzo journalist with fear and loathing:

> A week in Vegas is like stumbling into a Time Warp, a regression to the late fifties. Which is wholly understandable when you see the people who come here ... National Elks Club conventions ... and the All-West Volunteer Sheepherders' Rally. These are people who go absolutely crazy at the sight of an old hooker.[7]

It only made sense that Elvis would conquer this synthetic Shangri-la, built on moves he introduced by doing what for him came naturally. But like Siegel, Elvis had initially been ahead of his time — or, more correctly, had initiated the changes. Not surprisingly, then, Presley's one great failure during the early years had been a brief Vegas engagement beginning on April 23, 1956. Scheduled for two weeks, the gig was cut short by the management, owing to scant response from people who wanted to see and hear Sinatra or some reasonable facsimile. Like an ancient warrior with his eye on Rome, Elvis eventually returned triumphant. For the man who longed to be as loved as the first king of Vegas Frank Sinatra, the city represented an ultimate challenge ... his final reward ... some might say punishment! Elvis returned in the mid-'60s to get married (May 1, 1967), but before that he went there to shoot his best film of the decade.

Viva Las Vegas opens as the hillbilly hero arrives and fights for full acceptance. Here called Lucky Jordan, he's halved his infamous sideburns. The Presley persona we meet in *Viva* is not (yet) about to shave away all connection to his country roots. But he diminishes them to achieve respectability.

The essential theme remains basic: a poor boy who wants to become rich, if on his own terms. His nickname signifies the approach; Lucky will/must win the Grand Prix. First, he has to win enough at the slots and gaming tables so that his mechanic, Shorty Farnsworth (Nicky Blair), can get their car's motor out of hock in L.A. and ship it in time for the big race. The opening is light-hearted, compared to the serious attitude toward insufficient funds in earlier projects. However altered the style, the substance — capitalism and its consequences — continues. And, in the massing preponderance of variations on this theme, it takes on ever more weight. Moreso if we consider the changing world around Elvis.

Such influential academics as William A. Williams and C. Wright Mills were even then telling young turks of The New Left that they must break away from "the doctrines according to which the working class was anointed with sacred historical powers,"[8] creating in its place an original form of political idealism. Labor — even as reinvented by late–1950s intellectuals and presented to the masses via Elvis Cinema — would no longer hold a position of primary importance. This emergent notion, basic to the late–'60s youth movement, so offended Presley and other "radical" reformers of the '50s that they were forced to, in defiance, become reactionaries — or, more correctly, be posited as reactionaries after they refused to change. Elvis wants to work hard — for himself. This polarizes him as the opposite extreme from an emergent youth that rejected both the traditional American characteristics (hard work and self-reliance) which we as a people had been promised would lead to the fulfillment of the American Dream. A dream which, thanks in large part to Elvis, finally appeared as open to the lower classes as it always had been to the privileged few. Now, some sons and daughters of the elite opted to drop out and try communal living. Blue-collar poets carrying electric guitars, from Elvis to Neil Young, observed this New Left and, horrified, navigated sharp right turns.

Other essential ideas also re-emerge in George Sidney's film, most notably the sense of competition with older adult males, coupled with a xenophobic attitude toward foreigners — as well as resentment of people who inherit rather than earn money. These three ongoing Presley phobias are for the first time collapsed into a single character, Count Elmo Mancini (Cesare Danova). As Lucky threatens to all but murder this competitor on a dangerous road, Mancini implicitly references half of the Oedipal element so ripe in 1950s projects — if not sleeping-with-the-mother, then certainly killing-the-father. Highly cultivated as well as wealthy and "mature," the count symbolizes the outdated sense of class which Elvis, poster boy for white trash on the ascent, must unseat to reign as local "king" in a glitzy comic epic. Mancini plans to win at any cost. At one point, he suggests that Lucky drive for him. Elvis asserts his all–American credo: "I don't work for *anyone!*" Even in this chintzy city, that doesn't imply aversion to hard labor any more than in the countrified world of *Follow That Dream*—only a refusal to be co-opted by all that he hates.

The count makes clear that his brand of capitalism is anything but enlightened. What he hoped for was to have Lucky enter the race, then—for a tidy sum—run interference by blocking other drivers so that the rich European would win. With Lucky's refusal, the narrative reflects an "America for Americans" attitude. *Viva* serves as an "us vs. them" allegory, if played as easy-going *divertissement*. "I pay *in advance*," our hero tells a fellow in charge of the race, forking over his entry fee. Presley remains the old sort of capitalist, preferring cash to plastic—the all–American boy about to turn 30, the age that then-emergent hippies insisted no one above could be trusted. "I like to *win*," he informs the despised highborn count, Lucky making clear that his rejection of Mancini's offer has more to do with personal desire for fame and fortune than conventional morality.

Gone is the lovable loser of the early films; that figure—tragic, roman-tic—is as "over" as the comparatively innocent decade that contained them. In the '60s, the adult (for better or worse) Elvis always wins. The act of watch-ing him achieve success, particularly in movies about car-racing, would in time take on a ritualistic quality as definitive of this decade as his sensitive loser stance had been in the late 1950s. This arcing of Elvis' image can be paralleled to that of another enduring rural American icon, John Wayne. In early A-movie roles like *Stagecoach* (1939), Wayne portrayed a rebellious youth, living on society's edge, in trouble with the law despite his decency. Yet Wayne is best remembered today for his later portrayal of the man who runs the Establishment—i.e., *McLintock!* (1963). Had Elvis lived longer, he might have in time played such patriarchal roles.

Here, the conflict between Lucky and the count intensifies with the intro-duction of the female lead, Rusty Martin (Ann-Margret). She hopes to find a man who will help get her stalled car going. In this, she seems the needy female of traditional Hollywood movies. But there's a key difference, begin-ning with her appearance. A redhead, Rusty wears an ultra-tight shirt and the shortest short-shorts (then) on record. Her "look" can only be described as in-your-face sexuality, suggesting the kind of woman who in Elvis' 1950s films was cast as "the bad girl"—the appealingly sleazy vamp who attracts Elvis, though he ultimately rejects her for a virgin. This figure had most recently (if in a softer and transitional incarnation) been embodied by Stella Stevens in *Girls! Girls! Girls!* In *Viva*, virgin and vamp turn out to be one and the same person. Rusty does come on strong, completely comfortable with her sensuous body, happy to openly display it. That doesn't mean she is sexually experienced, as both Lucky and the count initially (and incorrectly) assume. It's worth noting that many of *Playboy*'s early 1960s Centerfold girls announced in their biographical sketches that they were virgins. Hefner's magazine, like Elvis Cinema, educated the naïve American male to the then-astounding notion that a woman who liked to *appear* sexy could no longer be assumed to necessarily *be* sexually experienced.

That's precisely the case with Rusty. Ann-Margret, who would in time grace the pages of *Playboy* in a pictorial promoting her body-painting session in *The Swinger* (1968, also directed by Sidney), here depicts this early- to mid-1960s syndrome on film as fully as Marilyn had the altering sexual sensibilities of the '50s. Monroe had been found dead in Los Angeles on August 5, 1962; with her disappeared the last vestiges of an era. Needed was a woman who could serve as the upcoming era's female parallel to what Elvis, navigating the difficult transition between the decades as Marilyn could not, embodied as a male. In her first film, Frank Capra's *Pocketful of Miracles* (1961), Ann-Margret played the sweet, virginal daughter of Bette Davis as that legendary denizen of 1930s New York, Apple Annie. Several months later, she appeared to contradict that initial image, performing the title song from *Bachelor in Paradise* on the annual Oscar broadcast, turning a simple pop ballad into a near striptease. When *Bye Bye Birdie* (a popular Broadway musical that satirized the Elvis phenomenon) reached movie screens, Ann-Margret transformed the skinny, shy teen heroine of the stage show into a wild, gyrating New Woman — Elvis' female equal.

Ann-Margret deserves to be credited not only for her often underrated talents as a popular entertainer (in time a Vegas performer) and serious actress (two-time Oscar nominee) but also (like Elvis) a social innovator. "If postwar America was barely able to reconcile Elvis' transgressive sexuality with normative patterns of male behavior, it was completely at odds with girls who attempted to do the same," Erika Doss has noted; "not surprisingly, female rockers ... met with only minimal success and staying power in the 1950s."[9] Ann-Margret changed all that, paving the way for everyone from Janis Joplin through Madonna to Britney Spears. Considering the innovativeness of her impact, it's not surprising that at first critics dissed her as vulgar — the epithet earlier used to decry Elvis and Marilyn.

Employing a heightened bitchiness once mistaken for true sophistication, Pauline Kael laughed out loud:

> Ann-Margret comes through dirty no matter what she plays. She does most of her acting inside her mouth [and] gleams with built-in innuendo. She's like Natalie Wood with sex, a lewd mechanical doll. Men seem to have direct-action

responses to Ann-Margret: they want to give her what she seems to be asking for. (A new variation on "star quality"?)[10]

That's *precisely* what it was: the 1960s variation! Phrases used by Mabel Dodge to describe Margaret Sanger, mother-goddess of the birth control movement during the century's first half, seem apt for this actress: "An ardent propaganist for the joys of the flesh" who "personally set out to rehabilitate sex."[11] Ann-Margret advanced Marilyn's sweetly sexual manner light years ahead while (significantly!) adding self-determinism — the missing ingredient in Monroe's magic.

Anthropologist Margaret Mead had several years earlier noted that in postwar America, a woman was considered to be a man's "personal possession" if she were seen with him on one or two dates;[12] here, Lucky and the count will each initially assume that if he can only hook up several times with Rusty, he will rule out the other from competition. Their eventual race at the Grand Prix will crystallize of each man's earlier rush to claim her as a trophy. Rusty will have none of it — as if an advanced version of Juliet Prowse from *G.I. Blues* now preferred to remain true to her self than ask Elvis (or any man) to marry her. This was appropriate, coming as it did a year after the publication of Betty Friedan's *The Feminine Mystique,* "a handbook for the new feminist movement that was gradually beginning to come together."[13] Drawing to an end was an era in which the public was regularly informed by "experts" that the "independent woman is a contradiction in terms," and feminism "a deep illness"[14] on the part of a woman who adopted it. Ann-Margret emerged as the new era's New Woman, transformed into a screen icon.

Her teaming with Elvis appears inevitable. Of importance too is that she rates as the first woman to receive above-the-title billing (rather than listed beneath the title as co-star) alongside Elvis. This rightly implied she would prove his equal in more ways than one. The film's subtext suggests women have, in the mid–'60s, caught up with men as to the sexual revolution; Elvis — the era's representative American male — must contend with that in the formidable presence of a female whose pelvic movements are as frantic as anything he dared offer in the late '50s. Indeed, she actually outdoes him; one reviewer of the time marveled that she "gyrates with a stem-to-stern fury that makes Presley's pelvic r.p.m.s seem powered by a flashlight battery."[15] If he is to win her, Lucky must overcome the kind of assumptive male behavior criticized in earlier films. Both Lucky and the count *assume* from her appearance that Rusty must be one of the showgirls who provide decorative female décolletage at glitzy clubs and garish casinos. Each sets out in search of her; when the men meet at the Flamingo, they continue the quest together — a peculiar if intriguing example of male bonding.

The friendly enemies are united by an outmoded vision of the female. Throughout, Rusty will confound them by refusing to conform to their outdated visions. One will adjust to the new woman; one will not. Elvis eventually makes the difficult arc to New Male. Some things about him, however, will always remain traditionalist. At one club, he and Mancini happen to encounter a convention of Texans. This allows Elvis to sing a pair of Western songs, "The Yellow Rose of Texas" and "The Eyes of Texas." They reassert Elvis' connection to the cowboy image that Dean displayed in *Giant,* and to John Wayne himself. The latter song had recently been included in Wayne's big, broad salute to Texas, *The Alamo* (1960). Solidifying the Wayne connection, Elvis dons a Stetson. Gone without a trace is the anti-hero in a black leather jacket. Elvis emerges as a current incarnation of the nineteenth century American male. Here is the "competitive individualist,"[16] with a "self-propelling conscience"[17] of the traditional hero in fact and fiction; all "the good stuff [that] cowboys are made of ... the kind of heroism that makes it possible for a man to live alone and at peace with himself, or to do what seems right whether it comes easy or hard, to stand up for what he believes in."[18] As such, Elvis is a retro-alternative to the despised (by those right-of-center) foreign movie heroes such as Marcello Mastrioanni in Fellini's *La Dolce Vita.* It's not for nothing that Elvis' rival is, this time around, a foreigner, an Italian at that and a dead ringer for Mastrioanni. Rusty, thanks to this sequence, is being asked to choose between the new morality of a jaded European jet set and the old-fashioned values of a fellow from the last frontier; she will choose the latter only after he at last acknowledges (as John Wayne did with Linda Cristal's notably independent female in *The Alamo*) the modern woman must be treated as a partner, not patronized.

Eventually, Lucky and the count give up trying to find Rusty among the city's showgirls. Despite her obvious charms, Lucky relies on talent and brains to earn a living. They (and we) discover her teaching swimming to children at a hotel. A brief scene makes clear that Rusty is highly efficient at what she does. More important still, she doesn't merely work there but is *in charge*— the pool manager. Rusty initially prefers the count to Lucky because the former helped her get her car going when she needed help. Relying on the oldest of male tactics, Elvis (who ought to have abandoned such stuff after they proved out-of-date in *It Happened at the World's Fair)* tried to keep Rusty around (so as to make a date) by lying, telling her that the car needed serious servicing. His learning process apparently doesn't carry over from one film to the next, constituting a ritual; in each movie, the Presley persona must learn the same lesson over again. When he finally acts "modern," treating Rusty in a more honest manner, she mellows. Along the way, Lucky learns to discriminate between appearance and reality. To borrow from McLuhan, Rusty may *look* "hot" but *is* "cool." Essentially a homebody, she lives with her father (William Demarest) rather than in a nest of swingers.

Something of a man-eater, Rusty represents the two women from *Fun in Acapulco* collapsed into a single character — in time revealed as both lurid dominatrix and loving daughter. Trying to make sense of his conflicting glimpses of Rusty, Lucky realizes that his initial impression, based on outmoded values, was wrong — or *is* wrong in this new era. There is no need, then, for Elvis to here make the usual choice between two women because Rusty is *all* women, good and bad girl from past movies, merged into a single character. When Lucky regresses — reverting to his old behavior, treating Rusty as a sex object owing to her appearance — she pushes him in the pool, the first time that a female humiliated Elvis on the screen. The casino money falls out of his pants pocket and is sucked into the vacuum, providing a necessary plot device to make Lucky desperate for funds, perhaps desperate enough to compromise his integrity — the moral "testing" of the King.

Before that can happen, he displays another attitude that reveals Lucky to be decidedly unenlightened. "Ah, it's only money," he laughs, adding: "I won it." This offends Rusty. "I'm a *working* girl," she says in her most serious tone. She *earns* every penny through hard if enjoyable work, planning to spend it not on herself but her father, so that he can have a boat of his own rather than piloting those of others. An intriguing new motif has been steadily developing since *G.I. Blues* that crystallizes here: A *woman* now embodies the work ethic that Presley himself signified in the earliest movies. When Lucky and Shorty take jobs as waiters at the hotel, this does not diminish him in Rusty's eyes; it increases her respect for him. No golddigger (though she looks like earlier movie incarnations of such women), Rusty admires a buck that has been earned the hard way and the man who sweats with either brain *or* brawn to earn it.

Everything about Rusty is unexpected. Lucky asks her to go dancing; she agrees, but invites him to the University of Nevada, where Rusty is a member of an experimental modern-dance group. She teaches Lucky a highbrow form of Terpsichore he never knew existed. Though initially put-off by what he deems to be pretentiousness (recall Elvis's anti-jazz statements), he's thrilled to discover his lowbrow stylings can fit in, as the extremes of American culture — fine and folk — collapse into one another in the emerging arena of '60s pop. The film's value as a piece of unconscious art, mid–'60s style, becomes more obvious when Rusty and Lucky (for the first time in the genre, it feels right to list the female first) engage in outings that include motorcycling (a revival of Elvis' blue collar background and referencing of earlier films). Lucky performs some impressive stunt, only to be outdone by her.

When they take a helicopter tour of Hoover Dam, she rattles off so much information about the construction that he half-kiddingly calls her "professor." This recalls Lili's "educational" comments on Germany during the *G.I. Blues* pastoral interlude. This doesn't categorize her as a woman too smart for her own good. The hero does not respond sarcastically but is *positively* impressed. He gradually realizes that a talented and bright woman, completely comfortable with her sexuality if not necessarily sexually active, is the woman he — attempting to be modern in attitude while maintaining traditional values — wants. In previous (and many later) musicals, women compete with one another to get Elvis to marry them. Rusty provides a perfect foil to them and a true feminist prototype. Lucky proposes midway through; she, though attracted to him, casually says, "I'm not much interested in it."

Rusty is hardly a radical feminist, railing against marriage or a conventional wedding. When and if the time (and the man) is right, she'll likely opt for it. She's a mainstream feminist, perceiving marriage as a probable (and positive) part of her life, if hardly the be-all and end-all. Marriage, *if* (more likely *when*) she does agree, will be old-fashioned, making her — like Presley — a progressive-traditionalist. "When I *do* get married," Rusty explains, "I want a little white house with a tree in front." This retro dream hardly consumes her, as it did the pre–'60s woman. Nor does the concept of marital bliss alienate her, as it would early–'70s women. Rusty is the most vivid on-screen actualization (including far more "ambitious" projects) of the emergent mid–'60s woman who hones her difficult but straight path between the way we were and the shape of things to come.

Previously, Elvis would introduce uptight women to the latest dance steps. Here, Rusty does that for him. At a club — the first true disco ('60s, *not* 1970s style) to appear in an Elvis movie — she teaches him to dance "The Dog" — presented in a positive manner as women as well as men surrender to their natural sides without any permanent damage. Elvis appears as anxious (at first) as she is comfortable with such stuff. A decade earlier, young Elvis taught women to lighten up; now, young Ann-Margret teaches uptight grown men to do that. Her youth adds to the mystique, and also to the autobiographical element, Elvis always preferring younger women.

In a notable sequence involving a putdown of the elegant European, Lucky — serving as a waiter at Mancini's expensive suite — purposefully engages in a series of supposedly accidental mishaps that ruin the count's initially suave, ultimately embarrassing attempt to seduce Rusty. She is dressed in high style for the occasion. Here again, the class-consciousness motif reveals a heightened if often unnoticed ambition: Elvis is the poor white boy who (not unlike the subtle slave of African-American folk literature) wisely employs his servile position to cleverly outwit the upper-class "master" via a seemingly sincere clumsiness that expresses a social anarchism. The film contains implications that are truly political. This owes to the democratic aspect of Elvis' undermining the charming but retro corruption inherent in the very *idea* of sophisticated seduction by a wealthy man of a woman without resources, who harbors upwardly mobile aspirations and, in a tradition that dates back at least to Defoe's *Moll Flanders* (1722), enters into such a situation in the naïve hope of becoming not his temporary mistress but a lifelong wife via her own "smart" handling of the situation. If that sounds like a contemporary replaying of a now archaic socio-political pattern, the modernity of Rusty redeems what we see. What even Lucky remains unaware of (though we sense director Sidney winking at the audience, letting us in on her little joke) is that Rusty needed no such help!

She was *not* susceptible to the count's supposed "charms" for a moment. Rusty didn't plan to give in to his seduction for personal gain, instead accepting his dinner invitation at face value and planning on leaving with what Midge Decter might refer to as "the new chastity"[19] of the post-feminist woman intact. For once, Elvis wasn't called on to save the princess from the dragon, for we here encounter what was then a true cinematic rarity: A princess who can fend for herself. That virtually all on-screen princesses of today can do precisely that ought to be credited to this seemingly escapist but in truth ideologically influential film. A female viewer may have come to enjoy Elvis, yet she discovered in Ann-Margret a new role model, one who legitimized her own longings to compete with a man on an equal basis without in any way diminishing her sex appeal.

All this suggests mainstream feminism was not necessarily at odds with older ideas of femininity, or that a choice between the two was necessitated. "Don't call me 'baby,'" Rusty informs Lucky, much like Lili telling Tulsa not to call her "honey" four years earlier. To earn money and finance their parallel dreams — a boat for her dad, a motor for his car — each enters a talent contest. They do so as equals. Rusty's song-and-dance number further reveals through what emerges as an early example of "performance art" (expressing her values rather than merely putting on an impersonal show) her absolute refusal to be dichotomized. She sings a ditty that insists her mother raised her to be a good girl while performing a modified striptease. Showing another of her many sides, Rusty drops her glamourous guise to collaborate with Lucky, Shorty and her father to prepare Lucky's car for competition. The generation gap is not a problem for Mr. Martin and Lucky; Elvis — nearing 30, defending the old American work ethic, carrying on the John Wayne tradition — is hardly the kind of youth who would threaten the Silent Majority. Rusty herself is all things to all men; party animal, demure date, trusted friend. Elvis discovers in her the three different elements embodied by Tuesday Weld, Hope Lange and Millie Perkins in *Wild in the Country*. At long last, he no longer has to choose between those types of women as they pursue him, but must pursue one total woman and hope she'll agree to share her life with him.

In the sports car competition, the expected occurs to pay off the loyal Elvis audience: He beats everyone, including the count, whose car explodes in a ball of flames. "For a loser," Hunter S. Thompson noted, "Vegas is the meanest town on earth."[20] In the final shot, Lucky and Rusty are married in Vegas, even as Elvis and Priscilla will be — though that event almost did occur between Elvis and Ann-Margret.[21] That might have offered an even more dazzling example of life imitating art, Aristotle's ancient dictum reversed in our own era. Even Mancini (who survived the crash) is in attendance. Though the European has to be humiliated, he need not be killed off— so long as he grasps his inferiority to the all–American boy, seemingly on his way to becoming a man. Basic to that maturation process is less the overly conventional winning of the race than the innovative acceptance of a remarkable woman, unlike anyone Elvis has ever met.

At the film's midpoint, Lucky and Rusty faced off in (as the mildly realistic approach abruptly halted) a series of ultra-modern movie spoofs — an approach that would reach full fruition in several Elvis films the following year (see Chapter 13). The episodes become ever more fantastical, violating any sense of continuity much in the manner of the innovative *nouvelle vogue* films, most notably Godard's *Breathless*, then popping up on the arthouse circuit. "Space and time, as [Gottfried Benn] claimed in his poem 'Verlorenes Ich,' once held man together. What happened when they unraveled?"[22] Vegas is a modernist-absurdist answer to humankind's earlier vision of sense and sensibility; this film reflects its fractured zeitgeist.

Lucky and Rusty act out a series of over-the-top romantic fantasies. All are played as extreme exaggerations of the types of formula films then disappearing from movie screens, the kinds of films young Elvis dreamed of going to Hollywood to star in. Soon, *Bonnie and Clyde* and *The Graduate* (both released in 1967) would kill off what little was left of Old Hollywood. Then it seemed impossible to mount timeworn Tinseltown concoctions with a straight face. They could be camped up in the self-consciously tongue-in-cheek style (*Batman*, played for laughs, would shortly premiere on TV) that defined our pop culture at mid-decade.

Viva Las Vegas shifts toward the surreal, allowing the characters to change costume and setting at will. Elvis and Ann-Margret grin and bear it; they live out the audience's desire to escape the disturbing no-man's-land that the once-potent '60s degenerated into (following JFK's assassination) by deliriously dancing their way through nostalgic fantasies from what seemed a preferable era in American lives and American movies. Foremost among these set pieces is one in which they appear in mock cowboy garb, broadly burlesquing the once-potent myths of the American frontier but with a notably modern touch. The female will, in defiance of the "man's man" cliché of the Old West, shortly prove to be the stronger of the two. That same year, the comedy–Western *Cat Ballou* (starring Jane Fonda, looking like an upscale Ann-Margret) took precisely that approach — feminist revisionism via genre satire — only extending it to the length of an entire film.

Though that movie was considered the more important at the time (winning an Oscar), it is rarely revived today. Yet the more modest middlebrow musical *Viva Las Vegas* has passed the test of time and entered into the shared mythology of American popular culture. Rusty and Lucky march down a dusty street toward one another, grim-faced though barely repressing giggles, ready to draw their guns. Not since the finale of *Duel in the Sun* (1946) has the concept of the pistol as violent surrogate for sexual activity between a man and a woman been so potently conveyed; each clearly bristles with sexual desire, though they "shoot" at one another with toy "guns" instead of moving toward consummation. Beautiful adults, afraid of their own sexuality if not the mutual sexiness, dress up like children — a reversal of little kids dressing up like adults and playing grown-up. Priscilla recalled that she and Elvis continually donned costumes to act out movie-inspired scenarios of a sexual nature, always stopping just short of the sex act,[23] which vividly describes what we see on-screen. Significant too is that here *Rusty* wins. Elvis-Lucky staggers off after losing the "duel," to perform a mock death on the *faux* prairie — an early female victory in the battle of the sexes.

At the time of its release (April 20, 1964), *Viva* grossed $4,700,000, approximately twice what a typical Presley vehicle could be expected to bring in. Partly, this can be credited to cutting across the two subgenres, playing well with middlebrow Northern fans who attended films like *Fun in Acapulco* while also scoring big on the Southern drive-in circuit where *Kissin' Cousins* had been a hit. Another reason is that *Viva* received far more decent reviews than any Presley film since *Blue Hawaii*. Glib as ever, *Time* claimed that this "has the wholesome, mindless spontaneity it takes to create a successful Elvis Presley movie."[24]

More recently, *Viva* has been recognized by highbrow-serious film critics as "a visionary artifact."[25] A fully realized example of the early- to mid-'60s pop art movement, in its cinematic specifics it signifies "every American fantasy of innocence and lust, flawless beauty and easy money, good times and charmed lives."[26] Marshall Fishwick defined pop as an "unflinching look at the real world of today," growing out of "a fascination with and acceptance of our mechanized, trivialized, urbanized environment; a mirror held up to life, full of motion and madness."[27] Andy Warhol painted Elvis, Marilyn and

Campbell's soup cans instead of presidents, saints or traditional landscapes, doing so in commercial art techniques (silk screen processes previously used to put illustrations on T-shirts), then presenting those vulgar images within Manhattan's toney museum scene. In so doing, he enshrined low-life icons in the once-sacrosanct *demi-monde* of haute culture, destroying the always artificial but long-existent wall between the two.

Susan Sontag was among the first of New York's intellectuals to be "as comfortable writing about pop culture as she was about politics and philosophy."[28] In 1964, her writings were controversial, for she suggested that rock 'n' roll ought to be taken as seriously as symphonic music, thereby upending "cultural values"[29] at a time when the still-potent prejudice held that there are two cultures, high and low. Shortly, rock 'n' roll, the contemporary cinema and pulp fiction (and, in due time, comic books and sitcoms) would come to be appreciated as the most American (therefore most significant) art — "the un-self-conscious efforts of common people to create satisfying patterns, not inspired by ancient tradition, but imposed by the driving energies of an unprecedented social structure."[30]

As Fishwick asserted, a true and viable work of pop culture is all about "the gorgeous, erotic, glossy embrace of cornflake materialism."[31] Thus, kitsch culture — from Disneyland to Vegas to Graceland — possesses more artistic integrity (though each is denounced by elitists) than a cultural collective of artists and poets putting their more delicate work on display. Sontag understood this, insisting that "the sensibility of an era is not only its most decisive, but also its most perishable aspect."[32] The works which most effectively preserve that sensibility are, according to the dictates of this aesthetic, the era's greatest works. *Viva Las Vegas* then rates as the Best Film of the Year for 1964, though of course no one would at the time of its release have considered putting it on a critic's list of the year's top movies. Many of them, including *Becket* with Richard Burton and Peter O'Toole (which producer Hal B. Wallis liked to brag was financed on profits from his Presley pictures) are (quality notwithstanding, on an upper-middlebrow level) forgotten today. However déclassé, *Viva Las Vegas* lives on as a cultural artifact, a genuine reflection of both its central performers and gaudy refraction of the national sensibility — all its fears, frustrations and fantasies crystallized into what Warhol might have tagged a mid–'60s "trashterpiece."

CHAPTER 12

Out of It

♦ *Girl Happy* (1965) ♦
♦ *Tickle Me* (1965) ♦

"All [modern] problems," Republican Congressman Dick Armey would reflect in 1995, "began in the '60s." The opening salvo occurred with the assassination of President Kennedy, which shattered the optimism of the New Frontier mentality and left all Americans, particularly the young devotees of what had seemed to be a glorious new era, desperate to find some sense of national identity. If we were too confused and fragmented to discover or invent one for ourselves, it would be provided from the outside: On February 9, 1964, the Beatles made their first appearance on TV's *The Ed Sullivan Show* and the British Invasion began. A sense of *déjà vu* pervaded as the latest generation of teens screamed to "I Want to Hold Your Hand," reacting as people who were now adults had to Elvis in 1956. Many of the oldsters were unable to grasp the current youth's reaction to John, Paul, George and Ringo. They now felt as "out of it" as their parents had upon hearing Presley perform "Heartbreak Hotel."

There was one key difference, however: Unlike Elvis, the Beatles were taken seriously by the Critical Establishment. Initially, this had less to do with the music than the movie *A Hard Day's Night*, released in the summer of 1964. Richard Lester directed in the flippant manner of the French New Wave; Truffaut's *The 400 Blows* had recently opened on the art house circuit to great acclaim as contemporary cinema finally came to be considered a legitimate art form. Lester cast the British musicians as a modernist variation on the Marx Brothers, now revered owing to the sudden respectability of popular culture. Ecstatic reviews, even from discriminating critics (including *The New York Times*), transformed a rock 'n' roll exploitation flick into a *cause celebre*. Reaction to the film embodied a then-emergent tendency of elitist art and popular culture to collapse into one another in mid–'60s society, a watershed moment in our letters and life.

As musician Jerry Garcia later recalled:

> I think the movie had more impact on me and everybody I knew than [early Beatle] music did.... The style of it.... Suddenly a good flash, a happy flash. Post-Kennedy assassination. Like the first good news.... All of a sudden it seemed [that the] musical possibilities opened way up.[1]

Clearly, yet another sea change was occurring. Early in the decade, the burgeoning Youth Movement, embracing pro–Civil Rights and anti-war causes, had scorned the commerciality of rock 'n' roll. Such music, after early Elvis but before the Beatles, degenerated into mundane pop, performed by middle-of-the-roaders like Bobby Vinton. Serious-minded youth turned instead to the "pure" folk sound. Joan Baez revived protest music of the 1930s; then Bob Dylan joined her, adding a new repertoire of songs that updated the old Woody Guthrie sensibility for the '60s. This alternative music for college students only added to the long-standing distinction between elitist and mass culture. These *nouveau* folkies took earlier musical forms and removed them from the original situation from which they organically had sprung.

Offering such songs to "hip" people, they transformed what had been at the time of its inception an unconscious folk art into an utterly conscious genre of precious rather than popular art. The embrace of the Beatles by virtually *everyone* changed the negative stigma against rock 'n' roll. As did Dylan when, the following summer, he dared (on July 25, 1965, at the Newport Folk Festival) plug in his guitar. Until then, Dylan had been hailed as King of Folk, viewed by purists as the artist who offered an alternative to the "corruptive" influence of rock. Hearing him perform with a rock guitar for the first time, folkie Pete Seeger angrily swore, "If I had an axe I'd [have] cut the cable." Many agreed and felt betrayed. From their point of view, they were right: The '60s folk movement formed as a reaction against the vulgar electronics of rock-pop.

From another perspective, they were wrong. The 1960s folkies failed to take into account that the bygone folk artist, whose simple, supposedly pure art they attempted to keep alive and well, had adapted earlier forms in the emergent world he had inhabited. Musical instruments now considered authentically archaic were in the 1840s — American folk then in the process of being created — nothing less than state-of-the-art.[2] In the early '30s, Woody Guthrie performed with the most modern guitar he could find; had electric instruments been available, he likely would have employed one. Sociologist Howard Odum has implied that, by clinging to what we incorrectly perceive as pure forms, we turn them into something phony; if we are to truly follow in the line of what actual folk singers of earlier eras had been all about, we like him should embrace all contemporary possibilities, replacing "folkways" with "technicways."[3] And admit that Dylan was right going electric. To rigidly cling to a past tradition, in the process of trying to keep it pure automatically falsifies the material, owing to the anachronistic context in which it is now presented.

The folk movement provided a necessary and valuable bridge between an actual rural culture that created folk music in America and the rock 'n' roll that, in due time, would come to be understood as an authentic form of folk music for the latter half of the twentieth century — a true urban folk (as compared to a once-authentic, now affected rural folk). "Popular culture," Marshall Fishwick noted, is "rooted in folk culture"[4] — it is folk culture experienced in the present, before anyone has had time to reflect on it.

This concept had its germination in *King Creole* when an uncomprehending character asks Elvis if his rockabilly music is or is not folk; Danny — not certain but on some level aware this is so — hesitates, then nods "yes." A decade later, Dylan — inventing folk-rock — likewise did what needed to be done, actualizing a form patiently waiting to come into being. The new music by hippie troubadours proved highly political in intent and impact — a necessary reaction to ever more volatile times, as Vietnam escalated and the civil rights movement turned increasingly violent. Initially referred to as Underground music (mainstream radio stations feared to play it), the sound caught on first at Frisco's Fillmore and Chicago's Kinetic Playground, then found air time (and an expanding audience) via newly popular FM stations.

Ralph Gleason, who helped launch *Rolling Stone* in 1967, claimed that the New Music constituted "the most potent social force for change"[5] in the country. Conversely, Elvis "had no political interests at all."[6] Further, in sharp contrast "with rock pioneers like Elvis," Dylan, Lennon and their imitators "did not think of themselves solely, or even mainly, as entertainers," rather "elevating their function as *artists* [emphasis mine]."[7] This was the era of the singer-songwriter; hearing any of them perform amounted to listening to a poet read from his or her own work. As rock critics (now suddenly respectable) insisted, "[T]he records meant a lot more to them than Dean Martin's ever meant to him."[8] Or to Presley, who in 1956 had been perceived — or misperceived — as an alternative to "Dino." Martin was in fact Elvis' idol.

Lennon, Dylan and their ilk were initially inspired by Elvis. Now, though, they constituted a different breed:

> For the first time in the history of rock 'n' roll, the music attracted a sophisticated audience, including huge numbers of college students.... They saw it as a medium for self-expression and personal authenticity ... [Dylan] was the avatar

of the composer-performer, the artist-artitsan who controlled his labor. And he was seen by fans, distinguished literary figures ... as a major poet who more than any other figure transformed rock 'n' roll into an art form.[9]

Heavy statements, be they personal and/or political, for the moment took precedence over commercial success. As Rock Scully, manager of the Grateful Dead, put it, "[W]e won't make bad music for bread."[10] That, in the minds of many, was precisely what Elvis had done since leaving Sun Records for RCA. Likewise, his films seemed silly in comparison to the second Beatles vehicle, *Help!* (1965), which embraced the next wave of youth, psychedelia. Elvis was relegated to the junk heap of pop culture icons that briefly flamed though now only exuded the thin smoke of irrelevance.

If this vision of him held true for long-haired youth who poured blood on government records at draft boards, seized control of college campuses, and marched into the Deep South to campaign for equal voting rights, Elvis at least maintained his hardcore blue collar fans. They bought albums and attended films that, in comparison to social statements ranging from *The Graduate* to *Bonnie and Clyde* (both 1967), appeared downright conservative. His mid-decade movies provide a paradoxical portrait of a man who had all but created contemporary youth culture, yet now appeared utterly (as they said in the '60s) "out of it."

Mo(u)rning Becomes Electra: *Girl Happy* (1965)

The opening of *Girl Happy* features a virtual redo of the first scene in *Where the Boys Are* (1960): long distance tableaux of the favorite Florida spring break spot and the announcement: "Soon, the beach will be jammed with girl-happy boys." The *Playboy* model's pluperfect measurements are stated — "36-24-36"— as we see a pretty girl enjoying surf and sand. Then, a cut takes us, as did the earlier (non–Elvis) film, to a snowy northern clime, where young college women prepare to leave a frosty campus for the sunny haven. The college students we see here are, like Elvis at this time, utterly anachronistic. Though their fashions and cars are true to the year when the film was shot, their mindset is 1960-ish — before Dallas, November 23, 1963.

On the campus, we also discover Elvis (as Rusty Wells) singing the title song, the first of 11 in the movie. He lets us know that all the girls he sees appeal to him. The film that follows will reject that *Playboy*-era view, even as many Elvis musicals of the '60s already have. By this point, though, the perpetual presentation of a narrative in which the Presley character undergoes virtually the same arc had become not only ritualistic but tiresome. He appears doomed to live out a *Twilight Zone*-type fantasy in which he escapes from such arrested adolescence at the end of a movie only to relive the same experience with a shift in location during the next, on and on ... and as that occurs, Elvis Cinema threatens to stiffen into a formulaic experience. Again, Elvis embodies his now-outmoded early–'60s incarnation, wearing a suit and tie and, at last, without any trace of sideburns. The original longhair, to show his displeasures with a new youth that had taken longhair further than Elvis ever intended, has gone the other way entirely.

There is one bone thrown to a post–Beatles zeitgeist: Rusty (his name borrowed from the Ann-Margret character in *Viva Las Vegas*) fronts a fab group of four, a post–British Invasion move necessity for an American star of the '50s who hoped to survive. Their audience is not compromised of screaming underage girls or jealous preppie boys but young adults. All are nicely dressed, yet moving to the original rock 'n' roll beat, hardly controversial after the Rolling Stones have arrived. A glass chandelier hangs above them; this is clearly an Establishment club, the kind of place where rock wouldn't have been allowed ten years earlier. Now, such retro-rock rates as part of the Establishment, what older people (young in the '50s, now early-middle-age) arrive to hear.

The owner, Big Frank (Harold J. Stone, a veteran of gangster roles on TV's *The Untouchables*), may be intended as a reference to Sinatra. Frank is so pleased with Rusty's success that he offers them four more weeks, though the band plans on heading for Fort Lauderdale. Elvis and his band members are college graduates themselves — the star no longer the redneck holdout from academia. Though this might appear to conflict with the formula, it didn't interfere with Elvis' connection to his fan base. Community colleges had spread during the early-to-mid 1960s owing to LBJ's belief in universal education. As his one-time special assistant recalled:

> Most of the Great Society programs were directed toward putting people in a position where they could stand on their own two feet and pull off their own piece of the economic pie ... education ... that kind of thing.[11]

However headily the blue-collar constituency had resisted the push for greater education, they had by this point in time succumbed — and would now accept Elvis as a grad.

That sexual liberation had not yet been fully achieved for women becomes clear in a conversation between Frank and his college-age daughter, Valerie (Shelley Fabares):

VALERIE: I want so much to be *on my own*.
BIG FRANK: If I had a *son*, that would be great. But let someone else's father do the worrying.

A young woman who longs for equality again smashes into the thick wall of a double standard, allowing for the recurring raw capitalist theme. Not wanting to anger Frank by leaving the band, Rusty suggests heading for Florida to chaperone Valerie, without her knowing it — for a fat fee. Once the sexual target of young women on the loose, Elvis is about to become not merely an older-brother mentor (as in *Blue Hawaii*) but a father figure, if for a price. He becomes one of those despised false fathers he once railed against.

First, though, during the long car trip south, "Spring Fever," Elvis' next obligatory song continues to suggest this film is not only sexy but sexist. In truth the film is *anti*-sexist. The focus does not remain on Rusty's male band as they drive and sing, instead cross-cutting to a car in which Valerie's girl-friends sing the same song. As directed by Boris Sagal, and despite its innocuous tone, *Girl Happy* does not mindlessly celebrate such an attitude on the part of men; its central theme is that women must have the same rights. If these females want nothing more than the same superficial things boys have always wanted, at least they are depicted as having an equal right to it.

"We're down here on a babysitting job," Rusty reminds the boys, once they've checked into the same motel where the girls stay. That he's a father figure is re-established when Valerie is typed as an intellectual simply because she wears glasses. The resident brainy guy, Brentwood (Peter Brooks), is attracted to Valerie when he spots her reading; Rusty turns away from her to other girls for that reason. One of Valerie's friends actually dares to say, "I think a guy likes a girl who's intelligent." The others gasp at her gross naiveté; the boys pick Valerie as a "loser"— until she (a beauty) strips down to her swimsuit.

In the long-standing tradition of conventional comedy, Valerie appears willing to use Brentwood to get Rusty's attention. Valerie's major competition is introduced at the club where the boys perform. This is Deena Shepherd (Mary Ann Mobley), the local "untouchable" in the tradition of Juliet Prowse's Lili in *G.I. Blues*. Still locked into the retro male mentality, Rusty pursues Deena as a challenge. Since no other guy "scored"— not even the local Latin lothario, Romano (Fabrizio Mioni), still another despised Italian in the style of *Viva's* Mancini — Rusty's male ego pushes him to be the first to do so. Though Romano remains a blocking character, a significant difference develops this time around: The home boy and the despised foreigner fight not over the worthwhile woman (bright, personable Valerie) but a female whose only notable qualities are her impressive physicality and fortress-like stance toward the opposite sex. Elvis' alter ego must learn to discriminate between seduction and love.

In the meantime, he's happy to see Val show up at the club with Brent. "She's with the brain" and so "couldn't be safer." But the brain makes the mistake of introducing Val to the seductive foreign student. In a virtual paradigm of the double standard, the all–American male wants the girl next door to be safe from a predator so he can pursue a "different kind of girl," chauvinism and xenophobia tied together. By the denouement, such male behavior will be mercilessly satirized, even ridiculed. "Shallow," Brent says of Romano. "All he thinks of is sex. You know those *Latins*." This from the supposed brain of the contingent. The intellectual suffers from the same lingering prejudices as his redneck counterpart, Rusty; the film — presenting them as equally laughable — displays an ironic attitude toward both. Here then is a caustic comment on the moral blindness and self-important attitudes of the time.

If the Valerie-Romano romantic relationship serves as a blocking situation, keeping Rusty (responsible to Big Frank) from Deena, he in turn is the blocking character who keeps Valerie and Romano apart — first on a boat, later in the bedroom. Rusty must constantly insure that sex doesn't occur between Val and Romano whenever he isn't attempting to make sex happen between himself and Deena. The Elvis of *Loving You* and *King Creole* is gone; he here resembles the despised Wendell Corey and Walter Matthau characters. The boy who swore to make the world a better place has been co-opted by the system he set out to change, now serving as a cynical centerpiece of all he opposed in his idealistic youth. Watching over Val for Frank, Rusty becomes her substitute father and, as such, the new Big Frank, even as Presley himself would become the biggest Vegas draw since Sinatra.

A hint of homosexuality is included when Rusty returns to his hotel room and hops into bed, expecting Deena to be waiting for him; instead, the body turns out to be Brent. Throughout *Girl Crazy*, Rusty prefers to be with "the boys in the band" than Deena *or* Valerie. As to real life:

> In the 1970s, rumors abounded that Elvis was gay and that the real reason his marriage failed (Priscilla left him in 1972 and they divorced a year later) wasn't his (or her) infidelity, but his preference for the all-male company of his Memphis Mafia.[12]

Elvis was not homosexual in his activities, withdrawing from friendships if he felt a man might be interested in him "that way."[13] Such extreme reactions might be viewed as homosexual panic. Clearly there's a hint of homoeroticism in Elvis' preference for the male group over one woman. As to his clothing choices: "He wore ruffled pink shirts and black pants with pink stripes, deliberately claiming 'girl' colors (pink being *the* female color of the 1950s) for himself."[14] No wonder a homosexual fan said, "I love the fact that here's this gorgeous guy passing for straight but wearing mascara and gold lame."[15]

Even the film's focus on gross heterosexual activity is so intense as to appear questionable. The next morning, when Andy (Gary Crosby) literally throws himself down on a bikini-clad blonde stretched out on a beach blanket, the action seems less an attempt to strike up a relationship (however superficial) than a mad performance intended to convince the other young men he's the proverbial red-blooded American boy; over-compensating, the gentleman doth protest too much. When Rusty finally manages to manipulate Deena into the woods to begin a calculated seduction, Elvis appears relieved when Doc (Jimmy Hawkins) ambles by. The overgrown boys seem most comfortable when, reviving the recurring theme of ocular involvement, they view Valerie and other women through binoculars: At once magnifying the female's attractive features while creating the sense of voyeuristic distance that alleviates any threat that an actual in-the-flesh woman might pose to bellowing braggadocio — an example of what critic Laura Mulvey labels "the male gaze."[16]

Seeing is believing in Elvis Cinema; vision takes precedence over actual experience for the unenlightened male. Understandably, Rusty finally falls for Val when she becomes a part of his act and performs a vamp routine to his latest tune, "The Meanest Girl in Town," for him to *watch* as well as listen to. Val mockingly caricatures the concept of woman as evil; he appears blissfully unaware of her understanding of his own lack of comprehension about actual women. He has been programmed by Hollywood's dichotomized portrayals of the female. The movie itself appears "aware" of male infantilism in a way that its central character is not. So women who make a living by playing off male fantasies are not mocked here. When Val and Romano visit a strip club, the headline performer, Sunny Daze (Nita Talbot), is portrayed as decent and knowing, helping Val to understand the arrested adolescent male.

Moving ever further in a Christ-like direction, Elvis as Rusty decides to practice celibacy. He takes Val dancing on the beach, motorcycling, water skiing — non-sexual fun as the camera cross-cuts to reveal Andy, Doc and Wilbur (Joby Baker), their bodies interlocked with attractive women. Elvis (once referred to as Galahad) is re-directed on a religious journey, toward a higher level of existence, spirituality replacing sexuality as one form of passion substitutes for another. In actuality, when precisely this occurred, Priscilla wrote in her diary: "I am beginning to doubt my own sexuality as a woman."[17] In the song Rusty offers Valerie his heart and asks her to be careful with it. When they finally do kiss, there is no lust in the image; reel life mirrors real life. The boys try and get Deena to take Rusty back, failing to realize he's moved on — less from Deena to Valerie than to another plane of existence.

The capitalist theme must be resolved. Rusty's early insensitivity comes back to haunt him when Val speaks with her father on the phone.

VALERIE: Daddy, I've met the most wonderful boy in the whole world. I think

even *you* would approve of him. [She reveals that it's Rusty, who has treated her with total respect.]
BIG FRANK: "Nice" to you? That's what I sent him down there for.
VALERIE: You're ... *pay*ing him to be with me?

Valerie does a total about-face, deciding to live out *la dolce vita* with (who else?) the Italian. She calls Romano: "*Anything* is fine with me — as long as it's *wild*." When Rusty tells Andy that he wants to rescue Val from Romano's clutches but not to touch her himself, the band member answers, "The king is dead!" Indeed, he is. Not Elvis in body (that was still a dozen years off) but certainly Elvis in image — everything the "old" Elvis signified.

Girl Happy must, like all films of the beach genre, end with a late-night surf party. Rusty's band performs as young people wildly frug. As the first rays of sunlight appear, morning becomes electra; the male who has so often perversely found himself a modern Oedipus in the arms of an older woman now must deal with his complex feelings for adopted daughter Val. Though they end up in each other's arms, his fatherly feelings toward her have not abated; she is the little child Elvis "innocently romanced" in earlier films (and others yet to come), now a few years older. She is Priscilla, transformed into a screen character; had he not been so threatened by the idea of his wife fulfilling her ambition to act, Elvis might have effectively cast her in this role. As they begin to kiss in his room, her father calls on the phone; in an image of transference, abetted by the editing, Val appears to be kissing her own father.

At last, Elvis admits something we sensed building in earlier films — the hoped-for seduction was something he secretly dreaded. "I'm afraid you're going to have to face the fact that you are very *nice*," Val says. As Rusty, Elvis smiles, in a way he was afraid to in earlier films, while still attempting to imitate tough guys like Robert Mitchum. In time, Elvis discovered that he was in fact something else entirely, a countrified Montgomery Clift, the *new* male hero. For Peter Biskind, the "feminization of American men"[18] in postwar cinema (reflecting changes in our social history) began when Howard Hawks offered Clift as a "new" cowboy — "soft," more butch than macho — as an alternative to Wayne's traditional male in *Red River* (1948). Robert Sklar went so far as to argue that Clift's character in *Red River* appeared "androgynous,"[19] a term often applied to Elvis' "sexual ambiguity."[20] Though the name "Rusty" may not mean anything within this individual film's context, it takes on considerable significance when we consider the whole oeuvre. Ann-Margret, tagged as "the female Elvis," had been called "Rusty" in *Viva*; the character's name in this film then posits him as the male Ann-Margret.

That homosexual subtext dominates during the final sequence. "Elvis as drag queen" is incarnated as, after tunneling into the cell, he leaves the precinct in a dress, passing himself off as one of the girls. Elvis hesitates on the way out to make certain that he can pass as female. "Officer, you would get my purse for me, please?" he asks. The policeman, attracted to this "pretty" person, smilingly does as requested. In addition to the macho Dean Martin, Elvis' other early role model had been Liberace. In high school, Elvis confided to close friends: "Boys, if I could ever get anybody talking about me the way they are talking about Liberace — man! I'd have it made."[21] The two met in 1956, inspiring Elvis to wear a gold lame suit that he had asked N. Cohen, Liberace's designer, to create for him. When Elvis donned his white jump suit for Vegas, Priscilla grasped that he was "beginning to look more like a Liberace act."[22] Presley had "appropriated Liberace's truly outre drag sensibility — and turned his brand of transvestism into admissable popular culture stylistics."[23]

Girl Happy contains the most notable example of cross-dressing for a male star previously associated with sex-symbol roles since Tony Curtis donned drag in *Some Like It Hot* (1959) — Curtis yet another of Elvis' idols. Like that Billy Wilder classic, this less ambitious film provided a cathartic experience for its audience. *Girl Happy* allowed moviegoers to subliminally accept while watching that even stars who had been accepted without reservation as role models by males in attendance and as objects of romantic longing by females had feminine sides. Such an approach that dates back to matinee idol Cary Grant slipping into lingerie in Hawks' *Bringing Up Baby* (1938), openly admitting when confronted by confused visitors: "I've just suddenly gone *gay!*"

Meanwhile, Back at the Ranch: *Tickle Me* (1965)

The motif of movement is immediately present: Lonnie Beal is first seen on the road, aboard a sleek Greyhound heading west. Elvis sports a cowboy hat, making clear that he's heartland America, not one of those beads-and-flowers types then preaching free love. Lonnie is the forgotten man in more ways than one. The initial song tells us that he lives a lonely life traveling alone on the road to nowhere. When Lonnie disembarks in a southwestern town, he learns that the old friend who was supposed to meet him and provide a job isn't there. Individual people as well as society have forgotten this American icon, the man of the west.

Elvis' initial appearance references two of his idols and a single film. He appears to be a combination of *both* Frank Sinatra and Dean Martin in *Some Came Running* (1958), the first Sinatra-Martin teaming. Sinatra played a returning serviceman (a role Elvis often incarnated) and was first glimpsed disembarking from a bus in just such a small town; Martin was memorably seen wearing a cowboy hat while taking a bath. Sinatra and Martin collapse into Elvis, he playing both of his heroes simultaneously. Also, he incarnates Dean Martin from the Martin-Lewis comedies, with Jack Mullaney (as Stanley Potter) taking Jerry's part. *Tickle Me* recalls that duo's final outing, *Pardners*, a comedy set in the Old West.

In many regards, this film is a throwback to the kind of B movies (or more correctly "studio programmers") that flourished in the '50s but, other than for Elvis, were now no longer being produced. Director Norman Taurog was a holdover from that era; screenwriters Elwood Ullman and Edward Bernds once wrote gags for the Three Stooges (and Bernds directed the Stooges). Even the cast members suggest middle-level filmmaking from a bygone era: Julie Adams, as the owner of a fat farm, had appeared in such legendary B-movies as *Creature from the Black Lagoon* (1954); two of her "clients" are played by Merry Anders and Allison Hayes, also female leftovers from the fifties. The local sheriff references old B Westerns: he's Bill Williams, a '50s cowboy in minor movies and the lead in TV's long-running *Kit Carson* series.

The Oedipal theme, which seemed to have been laid to rest long ago, roars back — making clear that, as Norman Bates would have it, a boy's best friend is *still* his mother. To make money while waiting for the rodeo season to begin, Lonnie performs in a bar. Though there are numerous women present, he ignores the youngest one and sings directly to the sexy-motherly types, something he'll do again after arriving at Vera Radford's "ranch." Immediately, there's a fistfight with the jealous boyfriend of a bar girl; the man is played by Red West, a member of Elvis' Memphis Mafia. Another fight breaks out at the fat farm-ranch with Brad, a big, brawny lifeguard who has designs on Miss Radford, even as she directs her interest toward Lonnie, any "motherly" concern shifting to something far more sensual. This sets Vera in conflict with Pam Merritt (Jocelyn Lane), the young woman who runs the exercise program and with whom Elvis becomes involved in a love-hate relationship.

Pam is played by Jocelyn Lane, whose mouth is made-up to resemble Juliet Prowse's *G.I. Blues* pout; her normally brunette hair has been dyed red-blonde to make her resemble Ann-Margret in *Viva Las Vegas* — as several previous women conjoin into a single character. This, and the expected fistfights with brutes — their masculinity threatened by androgynous Elvis singing (though nothing more) to their girlfriends — leads to the notion of recurrent patterns turning into tired formulas, the put-down of Presley's pictures. Alternately, they can be interpreted as actions that have occurred so many times that they become rituals — not unlike the fistfights in those B Western films Elvis enjoyed and which *Tickle Me* alludes to. Brad refers to Lonnie as a "saddle tramp," heightening an association to the fast-disappearing conventional Westerns.

Running throughout is a humorously played gag about how hungry the ranch's "guests" (all married to or the mistresses of millionaires who want their women slimmed down) are, owing to a near-starvation diet. Any and all will gladly prostitute themselves for "a piece of meat." They offer themselves not only to hunky Lon and Brad but also skinny, goofy Stanley. The irony is that women are all, in true retro-male fashion, perceived as "meat" by the men on-screen as well as those husbands and sugar-daddies who remain unseen; these women exist to be "devoured" during the satisfaction of male appetites. The only female who won't sell herself—who isn't, in a traditional moralistic sense, a whore—is Pam. "Strictly business," she informs Lon as to their relationship. Pam is convinced that he's a corrupt capitalist (on the premises only to win one of the older women away from her husband, then marry the rich divorcee) even as he insists he's a more enlightened person (working at the ranch to earn enough to cover his rodeo-competition entrance fees). When this issue is resolved, another quickly develops as Pam rushes into Vera's office and finds Lonnie in the boss' arms.

A suspense element is introduced as several masked villains try to kidnap Pam, who has been searching the nearby hills for a treasure buried by her grandfather in "the old days." She heads for a ghost town, with the romantically inclined Lon (and pursuing villains) trailing her. As Lon and Pam walk the deserted streets, the *Viva* sequence in which Elvis and Ann-Margret headed for just such a place is revived. To make it clear that this repetition is anything but accidental, *Viva*'s dream sequence (in which the leads briefly acted out an Old West movie fantasy) is repeated and extended, with a significant variation. In the earlier film, Elvis—appearing to accommodate himself to the changing role of women in the world—allowed himself to be defeated by the feminist-feminine Ann-Margret. That baby step forward is here countered here by a giant step backwards. In *Tickle Me*'s Western fantasy, we are back to the cliché delineation of men's and women's roles: Elvis, the black-clad gunfighter who must protect sultry saloon girl Lane from local villains. If Presley briefly appeared to be adjusting to the future, he's since changed his mind.

Likewise, in the relatively realistic sequences, Pam proves to be the antithesis of can-do Rusty Martin. Lon is twice attacked by villains; when Pam attempts to help, she hits the hero by mistake. "Do me a favor? *Don't* help next time!" he instructs (orders!) her. Pam, then, despite her initial appearance as a career woman who can fend for herself, turns out to be anything but—always needing to be saved, playing "cute" romantic games with Lon (hanging up the phone when she's really glad to hear from him), and consistently posited as virtually helpless until The Men arrive. She's the beautiful bimbo that Prowse, Barbara Eden, Hope Lange, Joan Blackman, Anne Helm, Laurel Goodwin, Joan O'Brien, Ursula Andress and Ann-Margret were *not* in their respective films. All had suggested a slow but steadily growing advanced-consciousness on the part of the American male, idealized by Elvis. The other alternative — women portrayed as ornamental and useless other than for beauty and/or sexual prowess — had been kept alive in the more rural movies. *Tickle Me* implies that, having attempted to adjust to an evolving paradigm, Elvis bolted backward in an all-out last ditch effort (shared by millions of mainstream men threatened by the changes) to go home again — or at least try.

Elvis actually kisses his female lead at a relatively early point in the plot, followed by a fadeout suggesting that, for once, they may actually engage in normal relations of a sort the Presley persona usually avoids. Such kisses became a part of the story and, without much difficulty, Lon even tells Pam "I love you!" — a phrase we did *not* hear Elvis utter to the woman in a half-dozen previous movies. They kiss again at a luau. He performs Western numbers with a Hawaiian beat, allowing for *another* collapsing — this time, the cowboy-themed movies with those set in the South Seas. Elvis-Lon makes the sort of remarks then coming to be considered sexist and which, in early '60s films, he had distanced himself from. Regarding one of the fat farm success stories, he snidely states, "Now, she looks just as good walking away from you as toward you!"

Most offensive of all, at least by today's standards, Lon takes Pam over his shoulder, caveman-style, and spanks her — even as Chad did to the Lolita-like brat in *Blue Hawaii*. Here he administers such corporal punishment to a *grown* woman, even if she has been portrayed as having the mind of a girl-child, which appears as basic to Elvis' attraction to her as her developed body. He reduces a grown woman he's already promised to marry, and who has done nothing wrong other than refuse to follow orders without question, to the level of a child — much to the delight, no doubt, of the audience that remained loyal to Elvis, even as those who continued to grow (and outgrow such films) fell away from the fold. "JUST MARRIED!" announces the sign on the car that Lon and Pam drive away in after they find their cache of cash — making it clear that Elvis, at least in his current incarnation, is as traditional as apple pie. There's a hint, though, that Elvis (on-screen as in life) can never leave the lure of male bonding behind for a one-on-one relationship (sexual or otherwise) with a woman — as he inadvertently takes male "bunkmate" Stanley along on the honeymoon!

CHAPTER 13

Everything New Is Old Again

◆ *Harum Scarum* (1965) ◆
◆ *Frankie and Johnny* (1966) ◆

The great paradox of Elvis' screen career is that the man who forever altered what Hollywood produced had wanted nothing more than to become a part of all he inadvertently helped to destroy. Growing up in the rural South during the early 1950s, Elvis, like other young people of that time, watched the same films that their parents attended: the final examples of a long-standing studio system. Genre films were churned out assembly-line fashion to satisfy the public's hunger for new entertainment *and* the Hollywood studios' need to keep contract employees earning their weekly salaries. Along with each studio's prestigious "A" items, there were "programmers": Westerns, comedies, horror films and minor-league screen musicals.

In 1955, television became affordable for the masses and everything changed. Many middle-aged people stayed home to watch for free, causing Hollywood to rethink its approach. The studios started making fewer if bigger (and in some cases better) films, in widescreen (as well as color, not yet available on TV) and stereo sound, with all-star casts: *The Ten Commandments* (1956), *The Bridge on the River Kwai* (1958), *Ben-Hur* (1959), etc. Musicals remained significant though, like most dramatic projects, they became gargantuan undertakings, mostly based on well-known Broadway plays, pre-selling the film version: *West Side Story* (1961), *My Fair Lady* (1964), *The Sound of Music* (1965) and *Funny Girl* (1968). The ever rarer original musicals (Disney's *Mary Poppins* and Warners' *Robin and the 7 Hoods* with Sinatra, Martin and the Rat Pack, both 1964) were "event" films — one-of-a-kind productions. There was but one exception, the Elvis musical — filmed on tight budgets, by mid-decade usually filmed on timeworn studio sets that were about to be eliminated.

Presley was a major reason why routine musicals were no longer mass-produced. He created (in the minds of some pop-culture historians) the youth culture, more correctly crystallizing a syndrome already occurring. His movies, in the mid- to late 1950s, were marketed to a new generation of youth that didn't want to see films (or listen to music) their parents liked — if those parents even went to the movies any more. TV became the entertainment medium of adults; desperate to get out of the house, the kids flocked to drive-ins to see low-budget items like Roger Corman's *The Little Shop of Horrors* (1960) or the latest Elvis Presley musical. But after the advent of the Beatles, Elvis no longer spoke to and for the young — and stopped making movies for that audience.

A nostalgia movement emerged among those who had been young in the 1950s and, like Elvis, felt utterly bypassed by post–Beatles youth. Elvis fans began to miss pre–Presley movies of their childhood. Two films from 1965 play as anachronistic throwbacks to a bygone genre that his own early work had ironically helped to kill off.

Deconstructing Elvis: *Harum Scarum* (1965)

Harum Scarum deconstructs the very concept of an Old Hollywood giving way to the New with its first sequence. Two men in Arabian dress duel with swords; a beautiful woman — clad in a scanty yet modest harum outfit, hands provocatively bound above her head — gazes on, hoping the handsome hero (Elvis) will win. We apparently have come in during the middle of a program picture like those churned out a decade earlier by producer Sam Katzman, who filled that role here. Everything about the scene, save only that Presley portrays the hero, appears vaguely familiar and out-of-date. This is the sort of silly project that Tony Curtis, in his pre-superstar days, appeared in (for instance, *The Prince Who Was a Thief*, 1951) — winning the admiration of young Elvis, who dyed his hair black to resemble Curtis.[1] The obvious back lot setting seems quaint as the public had experienced such on-location movies as *Lawrence of Arabia* (1962), which rendered such a studio-bound approach irrelevant.

Then it becomes clear that the filmmakers are themselves fully aware of this. Director Gene Nelson's camera pulls back to deconstruct what has been the on-screen image by rendering it as an image within an image. What we've been watching has not been the movie we came to see but a movie contained within that movie. The unnamed on-screen hero was not played by Elvis but by "Johnny Tyronne" (played by Elvis), a popular mainstream movie star. Still, Johnny is clearly modeled on Elvis or, at least, Elvis' image. Like Elvis, Johnny is an international star whose films — including *Sands of the Desert*, the one we've been watching — exist as excuses to introduce songs which could be sold on "singles" and LP albums. Johnny is a broad burlesque of the product whom Col. Parker transformed Elvis into, while throwing his star the bone of allowing him to model himself on the image Curtis had left behind. Like Elvis, Johnny is now an artistically unsatisfied "money machine."

He is also, like mid–'60s Elvis, a symbol of the Establishment. The audience within the film is composed entirely of Middle Easterners, watching a Hollywood fantasy image of their homeland in, irony of ironies, their homeland. An agent of American commercial-imperialism, Johnny is on a goodwill tour for the State Department. A patriot as well as a capitalist, he serves as ambassador to Babustann, an Arabic Ruritania, hosting the event in white tux and black tie, semi-youthful spokesman of the United States military-industrial complex. So he provides Arabic people (played by Hollywood actors, the "real" country created on a set as *faux* as the one in *Sands of the Desert*) with an American misconception of their country, to be released worldwide. The movie will disseminate misinformation about foreign lands as only arrogant Hollywood can.

Elvis had become such a consistent on-screen image that his remaining fans had no idea where the "reel" Elvis ended and the "real" began. That situation is vividly realized in *Harum Scarum*: Arabs in the audience assume the adventurer they've just watched on-screen is one and the same with the person-star who stands before them now. Beautiful Aishah (Fran Jeffries), accompanying arch Prince Dragna (Michael Ansara), invites Johnny to travel with them to an even more remote kingdom; they hope — after watching his character's talents (seeing is believing) at killing — to persuade him to assassinate Dragna's brother King Toranshah (Philip Reed) so that Dragna can rule. Here is a deconstruction of a deconstruction: Elvis, whose image and reality were now so intermingled even *he* couldn't tell where one ended and the other began, playing Johnny, who has such identity problems.

Oblivious to their scheme, Johnny — in the company of seemingly friendly hosts — crosses the Mountains of the Moon, "stepping back 2,000 years." The Sexual Revolution attitude toward women resurfaces as playboy Johnny attempts to seduce Aishah, after the others are asleep, for no other reason than that she's gorgeous and available. Or so she seems: Aishah is the film's retro femme fatale, as wicked as she is attractive, easily identifiable as the bad girl because she is sexually promiscuous. Elvis Cinema, which during the early 1960s attempted to adjust to our ever-changing society, has abandoned that ambition, retreating to a fast-fading value system. Abandoned here is the enlightened attitude Elvis appeared to achieve in mid–'60s films. We are in the métier of *Goldfinger* (1964), *Thunderball* (1965) and other James Bond films, in which the cynical hero seduced then abandoned (and often casually killed) bad girls, afterwards falling for the virginal princess.

In *Harum Scarum*, that is Shalimar (Mary Ann Mobley), daughter of the very man Johnny is expected to kill during the Feast of Ramadan. As Dragna lies to this princess and her father, Johnny wakes in a harum. In his now tiresome early '60s style, Elvis attempts to sample the residents until the guards arrive. Johnny's skills are *not* merely part of his movie performances, we now learn, for he fights all of the black-robed soldiers with surprising finesse. Like Johnny, Elvis was fascinated by martial arts and studied Asian self-defense, which became part of his screen persona.[2] He escapes with the help of Zacha (Jay Novello), a comedy-relief servant who will do anything for money, evoking the raw capitalism theme. This allows Elvis to appear in drag, which would become an ever more common element in his late 1960s films.

Hiding in a fountain, Johnny dons a huge Carmen Miranda hat, with flowers instead of fruit, though the implication is clear. Elvis "violated the familiar ... appropriating the woman's world of cosmetics for his own look [and creating] inflections that suggested sexual ambiguity."[3] The term *gender slippage* was not yet a part of the popular lexicon; it has since become basic to the academic pursuit referred to as "queer theory," Elvis an unconscious initiator. After all, "Elvis's regal dandyism" promulgated "a new male fascination with color and finery" as his "outlandish get-ups represent[ed] feelings of personal liberation and pleasure."[4] Disguising himself as a woman had, by this time, become one more staple of Elvis Cinema; significant too is that "the word 'impersonator,' in contemporary popular culture, can be modified by either 'female' or 'Elvis'"[5]—creating a correlation, however accidental, between Elvis Presley and the female of the species. In *Harum Scarum*, the escape works because Elvis looks so pretty that none of the guards would ever suspect that the fleeing person is actually a male.

For now, though, heterosexual text takes precedence over gay subtext as Johnny meets and falls in love with the princess. Elvis leaps over the wall, landing in the water next to a pagoda where Shalimar relaxes. "I'm Johnny Thorpe," he says, "an *American*." He might have said *the* American; Elvis had come to represent the ordinary American on-screen, however unlikely — even impossible — that might have seemed ten years earlier. It makes sense, then, that his romance with Shalimar unfolds in a uniquely *American* guise, the runaway heiress screwball comedy approach. Such films often starred Carole Lombard in the 1930s and reached perfection in Frank Capra's *It Happened One Night* (1934) with Clark Gable and Claudette Colbert. That it has not entirely worn out its welcome is attested to by the success of Disney's animated *Aladdin* (1992). The princess pretends to be a slave girl; the hero falls in love with her, not knowing that she's rich and "important," a populist ploy. The raw capitalism of Zacha rises from the level of comic relief to necessary foil by which we better appreciate their true, selfless love. "A loaf of bread, a jug of wine, and thou beside me," Johnny tells Shalimar, quoting Omar Khayyam as translated by Sir Richard Burton, "singing in the wilderness." This allows for another song, as he performs "Kismet" to her — referencing another Old Hollywood staple, *Kismet*, filmed in 1920, 1944, and 1956.

Meanwhile, Shalimar makes clear this land is anti–American, particularly its consumer culture: "The king does *not* allow *Western influences* to enter our civilization," she explains. This helps Johnny understand his mission: Change all that and, in the numbingly limited vision of this film and the era in which it was produced (an attitude which, though challenged in the late twentieth century, has resurfaced early in the twenty-first), open the "backward" land up to all the "advantages" of our full-throttle consumer culture. In the marketplace, Johnny joins an acting troupe to lead a proletariat insurrection of artists and outsiders — *not* against the benign dictatorship of Toranshah but in protest of the corrupt forces aligned behind his brother. When they are caught and thrown in prison, it's clear to all that Johnny's own brand of capitalism may save the day. As one on-screen sage notes, "He is an American, which means *nothing*; but he's filthy *rich*, which most assuredly means something!"

The imprisonment allows for one of the most bizarre yet telling sequences in the entire oeuvre. While enjoying the company of the dancing slave girls, Johnny assures them he will find a way to spirit them all off to America. He'll also rescue the child Sari (Vicki Malkin) — in fact, not only will she escape, but she won't have to work as an exotic dancer (as the older three likely will). Up to this point, Sari has been played as low-key, a plain child in comparison to the charming, bubbly little girls Elvis sang and danced with in so many "innocent" sequences. No sooner has Johnny related this supposed good news than Sari leaps up, insisting that's precisely what she hopes to do! The homely, clumsy girl slips into a highly erotic dance. As she does, her appearance transforms. She's a conventionally beautiful — and notably provocative — child now.

Sensing this, Elvis rises (in every sense of that term) to join her. "Hey, Little Girl" takes the eroticism always implicit in his earlier duos with female children and makes it painfully obvious. Elvis pursues her like a testosterone charged male animal, while she coyly slips away, only to hurry back the moment he seems ready to give up the chase. Their bump-and-grind (no other term describes what unfolds) is not only bizarre in context but sheds an other light on all such previous numbers. His movements precisely repeat ones he performed in *Roustabout*'s "Little Egypt" sequence. There, though, he danced with a mature woman, suggesting a desire to become a mature man, able to relate sexually (and perhaps in other ways as well) to a grown woman; here, he throws all caution to the wind, abandoning himself to openly erotic Terpsichore with a little girl.

Midway through, Johnny and Sari exchange personas. At one moment, he appears to be the big bad wolf, she Little Red-cap; he leers knowingly while she affects a *faux* image of frightened innocence. He alters his appearance, smiling (actually, smirking) to suggest his menacing approach was an act, part of a perversely twisted vision of good clean fun. The moment he does, she alters too; feigned innocence gone, a knowing woman's look appears on her child's face. In reaction — as if he'd been duped into believing in her innocence and backed off accordingly, now angry to have been naïve enough to believe that a female (even a female *child*) could be *innocent*— he changes back to what he was. Then, so does she ... again and again. The two passionately embrace, cuddling close in a way Elvis will never do with the femme fatale or the full-grown virgin.

This is precisely the sort of game-playing between a (physically) mature man and underage woman that Priscilla describes at length in her autobiography:

> Whether it was dressing up in my school uniform and playing at being a sweet, innocent schoolgirl ... in the privacy of her own bedroom, or a teacher seducing her student, we were always inventing new stories, and eventually, I learned what stimulated Elvis the most.[6]

Always, the fantasy-play between Elvis and 15-year-old Priscilla was sexual if *never* leading to full consummation:

> Gently, he took off the rest of my clothes. Then he kissed me and kissed me over and over. This night we almost went too far.... Then, before I knew what happened, he withdrew saying, "No. Not like this." It had to be special....[7]

This may satisfy the (emotionally) immature male but not the objectified female. Her dreams and/or desires mean nothing; she exists solely for his satisfaction, her own fantasies sublimated by a ritualistic role-playing substitute for actual sex. As to virginal (but, like young Priscilla, eager-to-experiment) Shalimar or dominating, "experienced woman" Aishah, Elvis appears relieved when every tryst with either is interrupted. Only with Sari does he appear at ease. He sings to her, his eyes popping out as she dances wildly, and tells her she looks hot. The kiddie-porn subtext was not recognized as such owing to the "family film" text; people saw what they believed they were supposed to see (harmless wholesome fun), not what actually appeared.

Johnny soon moves on to the central moral issue: Will he kill the good king to save all these poor people from execution at the hands of the assassins? Meanwhile, the princess undergoes a moral crisis of her own: Will she unmask the man she loves to save her father? Johnny, proud to speak for

American moneyed interests, negotiates a deal that leads to the expected happy solution by suggesting that this nation lease its oil fields to a major U.S. company; what's good for Bashir Oil is good for the country, theirs and ours. The old king realizes the error of his ways and agrees to allow American influences — cultural social, and economic — in for the first time. The finale shows Johnny — having protected American financial interests in the world — returning home to perform in Las Vegas. Here, Elvis sets the pace for his own sequin-jumpsuit image that soon would emerge on-stage. Like Elvis himself, *Harum Scarum* begins with Hollywood and ends in Vegas — an autobiographical correlative to Presley's own changing fortunes.

Presley Reflexivity: *Frankie and Johnny* (1966)

This film features an elaborate (at least by the standards of Presley pictures) recreation of life along the Mississippi in the latter half of the nineteenth century. Such period trappings are augmented by stock footage of an oldtime paddle wheeler rollin' down the river; long shots feature hazy cinematography that suggests the ambience of a daguerreotype. Also impressive is the title sequence, a surreal rendering of the old blues-folk ballad which Elvis will perform with a rock beat — again referencing that pop is not something other than folk but folk adapted to contemporary times (a concept posited from Elvis' onset, the folk song "Aura Lee" transmogrified via a rock beat into "Love Me Tender"), updated as the truly authentic folk music of our era. Additionally,

> [b]oth folk and popular culture are often contrasted with private (high, elite) culture, produced by talented individuals who follow rules (say, for the sonnet or sonata) which both they and their audience know and respect.[8]

High culture is "private" in that it appeals to an elevated viewer-receiver, qualifying it as non-commercial. Pop culture, on the other hand, includes "works and events (both artistic and commercial) designed for mass consumption and majority tastes. Entertainment is the key, and money is the spur."[9] According to that definition, nothing in the mid–'60s more qualified as popular culture than the Presley films, just as in the 1840s, there could be no more striking example of then-contemporary popular culture than the gaudy Southern riverboat shows like the one depicted here. Likely, the term *folklore* was coined by William Thomas in the 1840s, a period that feels like folklore to us but was perceived as cosmopolitan by those living then — who hearkened back to an earlier, pre–1800 America they thought to be fast-fading. Music from the 1840s riverboat shows — to us, a significant part of folklore — would have then been considered the era's popular culture — commercial and condemned by "purist" fans of that era owing to a then-contemporary attitude about the music, as well as the then state-of-the-art instruments.

Even before it had been given a name, what we call popular culture was first taken seriously in 1948 when a Prof. McDowell formulated a "first law of American Studies." He noted that there existed a deeper meaning than any-one had noticed (indeed, deeper than anyone had *intended*) in the products we daily, often obliviously consume.[10] Until recently (after Elvis), Americans who wanted to appear "tasteful" in the eyes of sophisticated Europeans aspired to a naïve notion of class by importing "high culture" concert music and opera from Europe. These musical forms were patronized by the rich as a plaything,[11] demarcating them from ordinary Americans who enjoyed crass, indigenous "popular" diversions. Regional music — white hillbilly out of Appalachia, black gospel by way of bayou tracts, etc. — was something no "respectable" person wanted to listen to. This narrow view went unchallenged, at least until the advent of ragtime at the turn of the century and then the jazz craze of the 1920s, but not significantly contested until the cultural revolution of the '60s.

Then, no longer was a line drawn between the false poles of what was artistic *or* commercial. Andy Warhol soup cans, Robert Rauschenberg ham-burgers and Roy Lichenstein comic-strip panels enshrined icons from the everyday in the no longer sacrosanct halls of haute galleries and formidable museums; notables in attendance were suddenly as likely to show up in sneak-ers, jeans, T-shirts and black leather jackets as tuxes and gowns. No single person (save perhaps Monroe) came to signify this changeover so well as Elvis: Two silk-screen/acrylic pieces, Elvis I and Elvis II, were unveiled by Warhol in 1964. These pop-art works were among "the first clues that Elvis' status had gone beyond the temporal world of entertainment"[12] composed of B-movies and pop music. Now, icons of Elvis had invaded the no longer off-limits realm of "serious" art and "fine" culture.

There's little doubt that "The Ballad of Frankie and Johnny" was per-formed in its entirety during the opening credits for the benefit of younger audience members, who may have never heard the tale and needed a quick preview of what was to come. The number is heard while we visually consider the kind of pop artifacts so popular in the mid-'60s, adding an element of camp, defined a year earlier by Susan Sontag. Related to but distinct from the pop art movement, camp enshrined as most worthy all those "bad taste" *objets d'art* from the past that cultured people shunned, from statues of pink flamin-gos in front of a Florida bungalow to Tiffany lampshades hanging in the foyer. A leading intellectual, Sontag shocked the elitist artistic Establishment by praising "the democratic esprit of camp" which "appreciates vulgarity" and heralds "the coarsest, commonest pleasures in the arts of the masses."[13] Sontag identified the keys to camp: "androgyne"[14] and a "sentimental"[15] feeling for what, when introduced, was dismissed as being in bad taste.

How appropriate, then, that this film is inebriated with a camp sensibility, since ideas that constituted camp could be traced back to Elvis. Johnny is the entertainer aboard a showboat owned and run by mustachioed entrepreneur Clint Braden (Anthony Eisley). Johnny's co-star and love is Frankie (Donna Douglas), a blonde who — like so many previous "good girls"— hopes to formalize their relationship via marriage. Neither wants to settle down just yet, for they dream of heading to Broadway and achieving a fuller level of fame. The major obstacle thwarting this talented twosome has always been Johnny's penchant for gambling; no sooner do they receive a sizable paycheck than all the money is lost at Clint's tables. "She's crazy about the wrong guy," Johnny tells his partner, the piano player and musical composer Cully (Henry Morgan), "*me!*" The situation has reached a point of crisis, Frankie delivering an ultimatum: Johnny must choose between the cards and her.

The "other woman" is introduced: To break Johnny's losing streak, he and Cully slip ashore to visit a fortuneteller, who insists that Johnny's luck will change when a new woman — a redhead — drifts into his life. Presley, breaking with his Playboy image as a man who always has an eye for the women at the *beginning* of a film, insists to Cully: "We'll just *use* her to make a bundle." When the redhead, Nellie Bly (Nancy Kovack), does appear, we realize he meant precisely what he said; despite the fact that Nellie is a stunner, Johnny pursues her for the pay-off. Unfortunately, Johnny never thinks to tell Frankie of this arrangement, so she becomes jealous. This deepening situation enriches the long-standing capitalist theme, the dangerous potential of money to corrupt when it becomes central to one's life. In *Love Me Tender*, Elvis was the naif who saw money's potential to destroy his brother. As the films progressed, he would often face temptation himself.

Here, in a total turnabout from the formula, Johnny has met and committed to — in all ways but marriage — the nice (if experienced) girl. When Elvis sets out to seduce Nellie, we cannot forgive him as operating strictly out of passion, Oedipal or otherwise. Johnny is cold and calculating; he comes on strong with no thought other than, as he callously put it, to "*use* her." This might have led to a work conveying sexist attitudes were it not for a twist provided by screenwriter Alex Gottlieb. While seeming to fall for the attractive Johnny, Nellie Bly is actually using *him* for *her* own purpose — as calculatedly as Johnny uses (or thinks he is using) Nellie, providing at least a roughhewn equality between the sexes. Nellie is Clint's former girlfriend; she left the riverboat because he hoped to continue the master-mistress relationship. Commitment to marriage is not only an issue for the leads; here it extends to supporting characters — a theme that sets Elvis off further from then-current youth's fascination with "free love," defiant of social institutions. "We're not starting up where we left off," Nellie tells him, though it's also clear she does want to "start up" again, if in a more serious vein. When Nellie arrives, she discovers Clint in the arms of the likably sluttish Mitzi (Sue Ane Langdon). When Clint tries to tell Nellie he only grappled with Mitzi because he was lonely, she curtly answers, "Lonely enough to get *married*?"

This Nellie is something other than the bad girl who loves 'em and leaves 'em, or even the femme fatale of the old ballad — once folk, now pop, in truth camp. In the original, Nellie sets her sites on Frankie's man for no better reason than that *he's there*. The film's Nellie Bly — whether or not she has any inkling that Johnny's come-on is anything other than sincere — does what she does out of an ambition to win back her man by making him jealous enough to marry her. We encounter seemingly tempestuous characters who treat one another in an amoral manner, if paradoxically for a moral reason: success with the one person each loves. The movie offers a unique if strange blend of old-fashioned values and libertine behavior.

At this point, Frankie and Johnny takes on a modern (and, before it's finished, post-modernist) approach. Rather than merely retell the Frankie and Johnny legend, the film offers a recounting of the manner in which a myth is made. This occurs when Cully observes the strained relationship between all key characters (though the film we watch remains light-hearted in tone) and employs it as an inspiration. He composes "The Ballad of Frankie and Johnny" in context based not on what has happened but what *might* happen. In a nightmare scenario of what could result from the jealousy, Cully creates (if the film is to be believed, which of course it isn't) what has come down through the decades as a bluesy narrative of a scorned woman who kills her lover.

The film further veers into bizarre self-reflexivity when Cully convinces Frankie, Johnny and Nellie Bly to play themselves in a musical sketch based on his imaginings — leading to the classic confrontation in which Frankie kills Johnny while Nellie Bly, initially in Johnny's arms, throws herself against a wall and weeps. In previous film, stage and TV incarnations, this occurred as the conclusion to the love triangle. Here, it happens precisely at the movie's midpoint and is not actual but theatrical. Or, more correctly, cinematic. The stylized approach is further heightened by director Fred de Cordova's choice *not* to shoot the event in the same manner (itself stylized, since this is after all a movie musical) as the film in which it's contained.

The song 'n' dance sequence is played as a over-the-top mini-musical (high camp) within an on-the-edge feature (low camp) — performed by created characters, circumscribed by the fiction we watch as they embody fictional versions of themselves. Also unique: From this point, all characters continue with their established individual agendas — Johnny and Nellie Bly "performing" a passion for one another that does not actually exist (they act within the work's context of acting) while others fight for what they want; Frankie, to continue her relationship with Johnny only in a marital situation, and Clint to carry on his long-term relationship with Nellie Bly, hoping to do so outside marriage. While the film proper is brightly lit, the "Ballad of Frankie and Johnny" sequence is dark and arch — serving as a foil for the work that encloses it. They go through the motions of what may actually in time happen every night before an audience.

The figure of the enlightened capitalist now appears. Producer Joe Wilbur (Jerome Cowan) offers Frankie, Johnny and Cully the chance to perform on the Great White Way. The Catch-22: They must get to New York on their own, which means *money* — the *absence* of which has always been the root of all evil for Elvis. The only way Johnny can win the necessary funds is to return to the tables, where he will win only if he has Nellie Bly as a good luck charm — in addition to the one he wears around his neck. This is precisely what Frankie won't tolerate, owing to jealousy, however unfounded. Johnny finds himself in a lose-lose situation. Attempting to decide what he should do, Johnny relaxes in his room. We view his fantasy of a perfect ending. He and Frankie are filthy rich Southerners, portrayed in highly caricatured form, as Elvis sings "Angel in My Arms." His dream vision of the happiness that could occur if they achieve their financial goal is rendered as a variation on Graceland. After all, what was Presley's mansion on the hill if not a dirt-poor Southerner's dream of achieving respectability through money?

The on-screen alter ego longs for what Elvis achieved: Remain true to his roots while making the transition from poor white trash to rolling in dough. This doesn't violate the vision of his humblest fan, Elvis realizing on-screen their fantasies of excess following dreamed-of financial success. Their roots were not poverty (that a despised condition) but Southern. How perfect, then, that Presley's co-star for this film was the young female lead on TV's *The Beverly Hillbillies*, which throughout the 1960s presented such a mind-set. Elvis appears in a cowboy costume, continuing his theme of the New South as final vestige of the Old West.

In another bizarre interlude, Frankie and Nellie Bly change places and identities for a Mardi Gras sequence that has them (along with Mitzi) masked, in similar costumes and blonde wigs, Johnny confused as to which he's relating to and what the nature of relationships are. The obligatory fistfight follows, this time with Clint, as well as the movie's moral, delivered to the now money-obsessed Johnny by pure Frankie. "You know what I think of this money," she asks, throwing his winnings overboard, "or *any* gambling money?" Frankie recalls what the Presley persona knew ten films earlier but appears to have forgotten along the way: Money is only meaningful when it derives from hard *work.* As always, a good woman reminds him. In Johnny's case, his work is his music. So he throws himself into performances.

This allows for a return to the civil rights theme. When Johnny sings and dances on the streets of New Orleans, he's joined by a poor black child. Despite his overly ornate and obviously expensive costumes — hinting at the Vegas Elvis he was morphing into — he's at one with this child. The two perform blues together, a reference to the parallel moment in *Lovin' You.* While they sing, the two meld together, black and white, their open relationship able to cocoon both from the still-segregated Deep South world around them. More than ten years had passed since the May 17, 1954, Supreme Court decision on Brown v. the Board of Education, which ushered in the modern Movement; less than three weeks after that landmark moment, Elvis provided the first pop culture expression of this new attitude with "That's All Right, Mama" at Memphis's Sun Records. His humble work of American Hot Wax has come to be perceived as "an act of musical integration"; and "he knew what he was doing. He said, 'The colored folks been singing it and playing it just like I'm doin' now, man.'"[16]

The film closes with Frankie, Johnny and Nellie Bly again performing the act we witnessed at mid-movie. In fact, the actors — Presley, Douglas and Kovack — do not re-perform the number; we watch as the earlier footage is repeated. Doubtless, this was done to keep the budget down by employing a single musical sequence twice within a single film. Context, however, redeems recycled material. This time, we know something the characters don't. Blackie (Robert Strauss), Clint's dimwitted assistant, has slipped a real bullet into Frankie's gun, in place of the blanks used in the show. This will eliminate Clint's competition for Nellie Bly without Clint being implicated. As it turns out, Clint isn't such a bad fellow after all. When he learns what Blackie has done, he hurries to the stage in hopes of preventing the catastrophe. Recycled footage is intercut with images of Clint hurrying to save Johnny's life, creating an entirely other context. As we witness precisely the same number rather than a similar one, the experience takes on a ritualistic aspect. A redo of the number would have left us feeling Clint may arrive to save the day; the precise dance number lends a sense of inexorability. We sense early on that the tragic outcome cannot be avoided. History repeats itself as pop culture asserts its power, the characters now about to meet the fate they performed many times, life and theater inseparable.

Yet it *is* avoided, not by Clint but a *deus ex machina.* The good luck charm Johnny always wears pays off, stopping the bullet. As in Shakespearean comedy, near-death is averted and we witness an oncoming double wedding. In the story, conventional life can now continue; as to the film, traditional musicals can still be made, if adjusted to the state of the art. Folk becomes pop,

pop transforms into camp, and — in large part, at least, thanks to Elvis — Americans come to see that the long devalued theater, music (and, today, films) that they love best do not condemn us as hopeless vulgarians, but pass the test of time that defines all true art in a way that many more pretensions (and in their time acclaimed) undertakings do not.

CHAPTER 14

Hot Wheels and Wild Women

◆ *Spinout* (1966) ◆
◆ *Speedway* (1968) ◆

The germination of American car culture occurred at the twentieth century's onset, as mass production of Henry Ford's creation opened up the industry to the public at large. A.S. Eddington was among the first to grasp that the car would profoundly change the world we lived in while altering man's self-conception. The "fast-moving traveler" achieved something on the edge of immortality, eliminating wasted time, thereby increasing the number of meaningful experiences he could enjoy.[1] "Travelers addicted to motion," according to Peter Conrad, "wanted more than merely to reach their destinations," demanding "the thrill of acceleration."[2] F. R. Marinetti published his *Futurist Manifesto* in 1909; machines and motion, linked by speed, were the way of the future. As such, they would prove essential to any art or entertainment if it were to accurately reflect the evolving modernist lifestyle. Shortly, culture — high, middlebrow and low, elitist and pop — reflected a sea change. The beat of contemporary music increased overnight, "catering to a fickle modern attention-span" engendered by the auto.[3] Gertrude Stein admitted that, after acquiring her first car in 1917, she had to adjust her prose stylings to imitate "the movement of automobiles."[4] After all, "distances," Marcel Proust argued in *Remembrance of Things Past* (1927), "are only the relation of space to time"[5] rather than fixed realities — our perspective on spaces changing once the car allows the New Man to propel himself across vast terrains as if they were, in the driver's window, speeded-up motion picture images.

No wonder films — like the automobile, an element of modernity, quite impossible before the industrial revolution — displayed an affinity to cars. Automobiles viewed as speeding projectiles — a man inside the bullet he fired — has been a screen staple at least since Charlie Chaplin wrote, directed and starred in *Kid Auto Races in Venice* (1914). Chaplin's mentor, Mack Sennett, had built an entire career on sending Ben Turpin, Chester Conklin and diverse humoresques spinning around the modern metropolis of Los Angeles, across elegantly thin shadows of this new century's Babel-like buildings. The first wave of Sexual Revolution occurred during this period as a direct result of affluent young people able to distance themselves from adults. Still, car culture as we know it today must be considered one more outgrowth of the postwar era. Clearly the leading international power, America demanded automobiles that in appearance as well as performance (the former suddenly more significant than the latter) incarnated our new role. "Design became the critical decision," engineering "steadily less important."[6] In Detroit, designer Harley Earl's chrome-lined cars "were longer, lower, even sleeker, ever more rounded, and even when they were standing still, they were to give the impression of power and motion"[7]; Charles Kettering's invention of the high-compression engine employing high octane gas "helped tip the balance away from small cars."[8] Above all else were the "fins, the most famous automotive detail of the era ... solely a design element whose purpose was to make the cars seem sleeker, bigger, and more powerful"[9]— the operative word here being "seem."

As to Earl, "Some critics thought his cars reflected the postwar excesses of American Society: They were too large and flashy without being better."[10] Chief among such naysayers was industrial designer Raymond Loewy. In a 1955 speech before the Society of Automobile Engineers, he dared attack "the entire philosophy behind Earl's cars, which he said (the first official cognition that the era's cars were somehow linked to its music) had become like jukeboxes on wheels: 'Is it responsible to camouflage one of America's most remarkable machines as a piece of gaudy merchandise?'"[11] Early Elvis seemingly sided with Loewy: In *Kid Galahad*, the Presley persona scoffs at all the fast, flashy cars on the road, preferring to fix up an old classic from the golden age of Ford. That was then (1962); this was now (1966). No longer the hungry up-and-comer, actual Elvis as well as the Presley persona had undergone a metamorphosis of style if not necessarily substance. He looked less edgy, far more slick; the retooled surface implied that here was an American male who had achieved The Dream, now reflecting this in his choice of automobiles. "A demigod on wheels"[12] is how B. A. Botkin described the automobile; he might have been talking about Elvis who, following his death, was recalled for "the perpetual motion of his memory."[13] Similarly, the motor car plays a "key role of mobility and motion in American life."[14]

The car (as advertisements make clear by fusing images of new models with lovely women) rates as a "supericon"[15] of our society; so does Elvis, more recognizable worldwide than any other image except Mickey Mouse. Icons, as pop-culture studies inform us, "tie in with myth, legend, values, idols, aspirations"[16] of the society that produces them. Sleek as a contemporary car, likewise photographed with beautiful women hanging on him, Presley "has become inseparable from many of the defining myths of U.S. culture."[17] His initial surly image connected with the "anti-social revolution of automobilism, reaching its peak in the hedonism and anomie of the beat revolution [as seen in Jack Kerouac's *On the Road*, 1955]."[18] Elvis and American car culture are, as signifiers of energy in movement, inseparable — he identified with a means of transportation at the beginning of each film: horses in the Old West, planes during the jet set, boats when near a beach, and, in all other cases, a car.

The Female Gaze: *Spinout* (1966)

The title aside, this had not originally been intended as a racing movie. Writer George Kirgo delivered the script to Col. Parker, who told him (perhaps recalling the success of *Viva Las Vegas*) to go back and fit in a racing car. The scribe changed the title from *Always at Midnight* to *Never Say Yes* and, finally, *Spinout*. This was originally to have been the name of a race film that Kirby wrote for Howard Hawks, which was released as *Red Line 7000* instead.[19] However arbitrary this sounds, the autobiographical element remains strong: Mike McCoy loves cars so much, he sings less out of a dedication to his music than to support his "habit"— speed. *Actual* speed, not the drug ... though Waldo Frank had early on identified the automobile as an addictive, providing the narcotic of endless "self-motion."[20] Elvis had succumbed to Parker's strategy to turn "his boy" into a product via middle-of-the-road music and formula films, compensating by becoming one of those contemporary consumers he once scoffed at by acquiring an ever larger fleet of flashy vehicles.[21] Ownership of mass-produced commercial objects now substituted for actually owning his self, soul and singing talent.

When we first encounter the Presley persona, he's already behind the wheel. The 1950s sideburns are gone, any vestiges of a hillbilly rebel removed. When Cynthia Foxhugh (Shelley Fabares) passes Mike on a narrow road, they are soon locked into a duel — not only between the two young people specifically, but a battle of the sexes bout, set in the rapidly changing no man's (and no *woman*'s) land of the mid–'60s. The male, significantly, remains in control, at least initially; in the conventional Hollywood style, Cynthia — the female who challenges the man's power and loses —finally veers out of control and crashes, her expensive car landing in the water. True to Hollywood convention, they "meet cute." Rescued, Cynthia makes clear she's the New Woman, willing to go after a man in the way Elvis has always pursued females. Cynthia caught Mike's act at the Crazy Club, now admitting it was

> all I could do to keep from jumping up on stage. You're cute, Mike. I really *go* for you.

Though Cynthia is independent, Mike wants to re-characterize her as something more manageable. He assumes his old pose (if in the current context it appears patronizing), acting as he did with the spoiled nymphettes of *Blue Hawaii* and *Girls! Girls! Girls!*

We are aware of the self-importance of such male behavior in a way the film's "hero" is not. For the "four years between the Class of Sixty-one and Sixty-five were the Big Divide"[22]: The former composed of the last graduates of Eisenhower's era; the latter, first foundlings of a Woodstock Nation. Between, there existed a twilight zone in American arts and letters, as well as popular entertainment — embodied by this film, which posits New Woman opposite Retro Male. Mike relies on an old line that once (in *Blue Hawaii*) caused receivers in the audience to grin, here more likely to elicit a groan:

> I'm going to put you over my knee.

In *Spinout*, though, he never does spank her. Elvis' initial attitude may remain unchanged, but the world has altered. The beautiful-wealthy spoiled brat of earlier films now emerges as a candidate for marriage.

The age gap between protagonists (antagonists?) — the Younger Girl more or less the same age as in earlier films, Elvis four to five years older — has widened. Like so many (unenlightened) males in the new America then taking shape, Presley's persona, now early-middle-aged, prefers a relationship with that very younger woman he earlier considered off-limits. It is time for the Older Woman to emerge as The Girl's competition. This is Diane St. Clair (Diane McBain), observing the opening incident from a distance, through field glasses. Voyeurism is now introduced as a key theme. As Harry M. Benshoff (University of North Texas) and Sean Griffin (Southern Methodist University) explain in *America on Film*, the term implies "a visual pleasure that arises from looking at others in a sexualized way."[23] More important still is the secretive manner in which Diane does this, as part of that visual pleasure "comes from watching people who are not aware that they are being watched (thus giving the watcher a sense of power or control)."[24] The on-screen voyeur serves as symbol for the audience:

> [F]ilm is fundamentally based on watching, [so the very act of attending the commercial] cinema falls easily into the realm of voyeurism [for the attending audience, each of us automatically becoming something of a "Peeping Tom"].[25]

Importantly, in *Spinout* the voyeur is a female — compared to, say, James

Stewart in Alfred Hitchcock's *Vertigo* (1958), a quintessential example of commercial cinema. The typical Hollywood approach consists of a young woman observed by an older man, though their age difference does not rule out a romantic relationship. Here, Diane the female voyeur is older — the same age as Abigail in *Blue Hawaii* and Alicia in *Follow That Dream*. Nonetheless, Elvis will not here couple with the latest substitute mother, as he did in *Wild in the Country*. Between that film and this, we have borne witness to a plethora of underage or fully developed nymphettes he refused to touch and as many underage or undeveloped female children that he *did*. The two subgenres of nymphette merge into Cynthia, overpowered by her Electra-like desire for Mike.

In the meantime, Diane visits the Crazy Club to again *observe* Mike; in *Watching Elvis: The Male Rock Star as Object of the Gaze*,[26] David R. Shumway commented on the manner in which what Laura Mulvey terms "the male gaze" (a Hollywood editing paradigm consisting of an objective shot of the male looking, then a subjective shot of the gorgeous female he looks at)[27] is reversed. Though this hardly eliminates such a compliment/insult, it does allow women to return it, providing a semblance of equality. She and we notice his movements are minimal, a slight sway to the rhythm. The dancers outdo anything young Elvis offered, with post-twist discotheque gyrations. While seated, they "frug" and/or "monkey" to his songs. An irony exists in the contrast between the now sedate performer and the ecstatic mid-'60s youth: Elvis appears old-fashioned in comparison. Signifying this altered situation is Les (Deborah Walley), a female musician who sports a Beatle hairstyle, making her appear so androgynous that the boys in the band pay no attention to her.

The combo has been belatedly integrated to include a female, who — a pioneer of sorts — feels the need, like Shakespeare's Viola, to pass as a boy in hope of acceptance. Despite this, Les (even her name avoids gender-specificity), like other members of this film's female triad, is motored by attitudes no screen woman could have expressed five years earlier, before the first inkling of feminism. *Spinout* looks forward to the next wave of liberation as women seize for themselves all that was once restricted to men. For as Diane again observes Mike, the male bias (and thus male controlled "visual pleasure in narrative cinema") is countered, the gaze now acceptable for female as well as male audience members — and gay as well as straight viewers.

As the argument goes,

> [I]n most Hollywood films, the narcissistic pleasure of identification usually involves identifying with the male characters looking at the female characters on-screen ... men are positioned as the ones in control of the gaze while women are positioned as the objects of that controlling gaze.[28]

Spinout— its humble origins aside — rates as a revolutionary work, for that is *not* the case here. Like the Younger Girl Cynthia, Diane is not (as was the female, whatever her age, of the 1950s) demure — willing to passively let the man gaze at her, trained to never look back.

That these are the mid–'60s is clear from the Op/Pop paintings on the walls, as well as the integration of the audience: A beatnik with goatee and a black with a mild Afro sit among conventional Anglos, their presence causing no disturbance. Elvis appears blithely unaware of the major cultural changes that have taken place, singing "Adam and Evil." A performer who will following his death be compared to Christ conveys the patriarchal–Biblical view of woman as corrupter of man: she isn't the angel from his dreams, but the devil, yet he can't live without her. Such joyous masochism, nothing new for Elvis, portrays man as victim, prey to the female tarantula. Three women wink at Mike, who insists on remaining the uncommitted male we've seen countless times before.

Some things never change. The corruptive influence of hard cash as employed by an instrument of power is here represented by Santa Barbara's Howard Foxhugh (Carl Betz), Cynthia's rich father. When Howard offers Mike a considerable sum if the band will cancel a Los Angeles gig to play at his daughter's birthday party, Elvis references himself: "Why don't you get her a *Teddy bear*?" Howard too is a car fancier; telling indeed is that Mike's favorite among the impressive fleet is a Model J Duesenberg, oldest in the lot, reasserting Elvis' old-fashioned attitude toward automotive possibilities. "Sure don't make 'em like *that* any more," Mike sighs, dreaming of owning just such a car someday. Robert H. Boyle has written at length about the subgenres of car culture, noting that it "embraces a number of cults given over to the veneration of a particular type of vehicle."[29] These include the antique, the Cadillac, the motorcycle, the sports car, the pick-up truck, the racing car and the hot rod — each present in at least one Elvis vehicle (pun intended), in some cases more than one car on view.

Soon the band is on the road again, evoking the old wanderlust theme, their own humble transportation serving as

> a fulfillment of man's universal dream of conquering time and distance and of the American dream of the open road as the road to freedom of activity and movement, to opportunity and success, and related goals in the American credo.[30]

If there is an accommodation to changing times, it is that Elvis now travels with a committed community rather than as rugged individualist. Enjoying a late evening picnic in the woods, they fantasize about the possibility of long-dreamed of success:

BAND MEMBER ONE: We'll be on *The Ed Sullivan Show*.

MIKE: Ah, stars have responsibilities. Have to sign papers, live in a house ...
stay put.
BAND MEMBER TWO: But we'll make *millions*!
MIKE: And you'll get *married*. Not me. I'd rather stay single.

On-screen, Mike embodies the road not taken by the star himself. Mike
is the person Elvis might have been had he resisted the colonel's promise to
make him a millionaire overnight. In the past, such a statement on the part
of Presley's persona represented male *braggadocio* while setting up his eventual reversal. Not here; *Spinout* depicts the last pathetic gasp of the *Playboy*
generation male, the only Elvis film that allows him to remain stubbornly true
to a code that had already worn thin.

The woods provide the pastoral interlude, a Green World between the
up-side city setting of Santa Barbara and the downscale sprawl of Santa Fe —
connected, of course, owing to "the automobile's and the highway's breaking
down of the separation between city and country."[31] This is a notion that early
Elvis (who via TV brought the old country sound to contemporary suburbia)
also embodied. Les serves a gourmet dinner on fine china, with a formal can-
delabra worthy of Liberace, bridging the gap between romantic and classicist
poles, *haute cuisine* presented wild in the country. Elvis soon again references
his 1950s image; when a canine appears on the scene, he reminds all present
it's a "hound dog." He must learn to deal, though, with an emerging gender-
free society. "I'm *not* a guy," Les reminds Mike. "I'm a *girl*!" (*Not*, notably, a
woman!) She repeats this until it becomes a refrain, though her words fall flat
when Diane appears, as impossibly glamourous as ever.

As always, Diane's presence is heralded by ocular imagery; Diane stares
directly through glasses, into Elvis' face. When he tries to kiss her, she doesn't
let him, reminding Mike of her namesake: "The goddess of the hunt," who
in Greek mythology destroyed any man that dared assail her virginity or, for
that matter, even cast a male gaze in her direction.[32] How appropriate that,
toward the end of its run, the oeuvre would consciously address the issue of
mythology. Elvis himself had long since passed beyond star (even superstar)
and emerged, more through his movies than the music, as a modern myth.
"Like a hero of Greek mythology," James Miller wrote, Elvis "belonged to a
world apart."[33] If Elvis is indeed a mythic being, *Spinout* is the film that evokes
the myth concept in its context.

The intellectual-professional woman, Diane — on a quest (again, the
mythological element, re-established by her name) for the perfect American
male — has set her sights (in every sense of that term) on Elvis. Impulsively
Diane kisses Mike; in a reordered world she can initiate a kiss, he can't. She
refuses to do so again, controlling the situation in a way no earlier woman
dared with the Presley persona. While their party frolics in the woods, mem-

bers of the moneyed class congregate in a mansion on the hill. "Told me to go to Hell," Howard muses about Mike, though he is impressed: "Quite a boy!" Corrupting Mike into doing his bidding (helming Howard's race car in an upcoming meet, a variation on the *Viva Las Vegas* theme) becomes an obsession. Howard confides to Cynthia, "First he'll sing for you, then he'll drive for me." In time, Mike will do both. For the present, Elvis and his cronies cling to a fast-dying coda. As they rehearse the song "Never Say Yes," the words sound suspiciously like bits and pieces of leftover thinking: settling down would put an end to their freedom.

Such dreams of freedom, as well as success on one's own terms, are dashed when Mike learns that the powerful Foxhugh has managed to get the band's upcoming gigs cancelled. This leaves them with no alternative but to play the party. Mike doesn't yet know the female he raced with earlier is Foxhugh's daughter. When he speaks about the birthday girl, he remains locked into the male gaze as primary means of appreciating any woman: "I'd like to see what she *looks* like."

First, Mike must fend off the overt Oedipal efforts of Diane to domesticate him: "Always wanted a big church wedding ... as soon as I get you housebroken ... you'll be the best husband a girl ever had ... Mike, I'm going to *marry* you!" By this time, the once cool-as-ice glamour girl has come to represent a nightmare scenario for the retro male. But when this mythic hero hurries away from Jocasta, he rushes directly into Electra's arms. We witness his life-as-theater romance with Cynthia at her party when he sings "Am I Ready?" As the song ends, Mike (seemingly enraptured) nearly kisses her. Yet the number is over, so his sexiness dissipates. The seduction was all show; a musical gigolo, he turns away, his moneyed obligation met. Continued here is a theme that first surfaced with *Loving You*: The Elvis performance as sexual aggressor is a sham.

Cynthia remains convinced that no one is beyond the reach of greed: "Anything goes because Daddy can *pay* for it." Cynthia makes clear that she, however different from Diane, is also a purveyor of the female gaze: "I just wanted to *see* you again." Affronted by her insistence on acquiring him through corrupt capitalism, Elvis angrily retorts, "So you had Daddy *buy* me?" Being reduced to a purchasable thing to look at is a legitimate feminist complaint about women's status in patriarchal society. Here, the *man* suffers that situation, a star more often described as "beautiful" than "handsome," allowing the film's viewer, male or female, straight or gay, to sympathize with a *person* subject to "the gaze," all gender considerations aside. Elvis objects to becoming a trophy spouse; as he insists to Diane, "I'm not marrying you. I'm not marrying her. I'm not marrying *anybody*. I'm staying single, single, *single!*" The big surprise is that at film's end, he does precisely that.

Meanwhile, class consciousness raises its ugly head. "I want him to drive the Fox 5 for me," Howard tells his daughter, "but he's *not* my idea of a son-in-law." Mike feels the same way, telling Howard, "I'll agree to drive your car — but *not* to marry Cynthia." White trash and proud of it, with no plans to "marry up" — or marry at all! Grasping Mike's redneck, anti-authoritarian spirit, the wealthy father and daughter conspire to have the police throw Mike's band off their land, assuming this will make him so angry he'll fall into their trap and insist on staying. When Officer Richards (Will Hutchins) arrives, the situation briefly appears to hold a mirror up to life as the cop kicks hippies off a rich man's private land. However true to the anti-police attitudes of the era's youth, this would conflict with Elvis' own attitudes. He insisted we should "Support Your Local Police" long before it became a pat phrase for Spiro Agnew's Silent Majority. So Richards turns out to be a decent sort. "You've got to leave town," he tells them, whispering that they can take their own sweet time. More surprising, he turns out to be a gourmet chef — a unique feminization of the ordinarily stereotyped macho cop character.

Mike distances himself from his own macho stance when he visits an elderly millionaire couple in their mansion, becoming spiritual saviour of their marriage. To achieve this, he invokes the film's ocular theme: "You haven't really *looked* at each other in a long time." The problem, he assures them, is not marriage per se, but what it does to people locked into conventional lifestyles:

MIKE: When was the last time you had some *fun?*
ELDERLY LADY: On our honeymoon!

They soon head off for a belated second honeymoon. This allows Mike and his quasi-hippies to move into the mansion and throw a pool party next door to the Foxhughs. Mike does not want to act classy, any more than Elvis himself did after moving into Graceland. There, he devoured peanut butter and hot grease sandwiches off fine china; here, his alter ego has the butler serve hamburgers on a silver platter. True to his roots, Elvis has not in any essential way changed.

Desperate for marriage, Cynthia and Diane propose to Mike as the wedding march plays. He only wants the freedom of the speedway, even if he must use someone else's car to achieve it. Mike is willing to drive the Duesenberg, trying to win the title of future champion in the present by aligning himself with a long past golden age. Cynthia dreams of transforming Mike into a conformist: "When we get *married,* [the driving and singing are] all *over,*" she tells Howard. "He'll come to live [in the mansion], work for the *company.*" To give in to that would be to finally surrender to an offer extended ever since *Blue Hawaii.*

Mike has promised each of the three women that he will marry after the race and is true to his word, if ironically so. Becoming a makeshift clergyman, he marries each to some *other* man. Now he meets Susan (Dodie Marshall), who shares his retro early–'60s swinging inclinations:

MIKE: How'd you like to get married, Susan?
SUSAN: Not until I'm 50.
MIKE: I'm with *you!*

His next song is "Smorgasbord," suggesting he — the last playboy — perceives women as food, recalling the "sweet potato" line from *It Happened at the World's Fair*. In previous films, the *Playboy* coda had been raised only to be dismissed as he in time entered into a full relationship with one woman; now, Elvis opts to go on forever as an arrested adolescent. As was the case with those millions of American women who had a crush on Elvis in their youth, then moved on, Cynthia, Diana and Les (now transformed into a conventional beauty, winning a beau as soon as she conforms to a more traditional model) all realize that Mike — i.e., Elvis — was always an impossible dream that had to be experienced, then relegated to a mental memory book. *When I became a woman, I put aside childish things....* Happy to settle for less perfect, more realistic male partners, they now perceive Presley as an ideal to be worshipped in one's youth — though they are growing up.

Like Wendy with her Peter in James Barrie's classic, he was the object of a naïve adolescent crush. Now it's time to move on to the real world; they accept with sweet sadness that that's something he can never be part of. "Elvis," Priscilla has written, "created his own world and lived in it."[34] So she left him (though still loving him) to pursue relationships with less mythic men. And so, in the film, Cynthia, Diana and Les marry ordinary fellows. Like Priscilla in actuality, each still loves Mike, and always will — as did each of Elvis' devoted fans. Still, each is able to finally accept the bittersweet truth that her lingering emotion is but a holdover from a fading girlhood, an endearing if not enduring crush on a teen angel-idol. Faithful in their fashion, they will love him from afar forever. On some level, each grasps at last that to possess him would be to crush what they loved best — always more fantasy than reality, a status that eventually proved as destructive to him as it was to ancient heroes of legend.

One of the Boys: *Speedway* (1968)

[C]onvinced that aping Frank Sinatra was the key to lasting popular success ... Elvis modeled himself after Frank all through the 1960s ... copying his casually sophisticated, Edwardian cool clothing style, dating his girlfriends (like Sinatra's fiancée Juliet Prowse), forming his own Rat pack (the Memphis Mafia).[35]

What was there left to do but date and co-star with Nancy Sinatra, who had already been married to Tommy Sands — the ersatz Elvis, playing a carbon copy of the King in *The Singin' Idol* (1957), an early TV attempt to dramatize the Presley phenomenon, and in the 1958 film version *Sing, Boy, Sing*. In the movie, Sands' *faux* Elvis is befriended by a young man played by Nick Adams, one of Elvis' actual best friends in Hollywood.[36] Though Elvis and Nancy had gone out together often, *Speedway* united them in the public eye for the first time since Papa Frank hosted the "welcome home" special in 1960.

The autobiographical element is present. Once more, Elvis (called Steve Grayson) is cast as a race car driver, allowing him to live out on-screen one of his favorite fantasies.[37] Making that fantasy appear real is the presence of real-life stock car racers playing themselves, including Richard Petty, Buddy Baker, Cale Yarborough, Dick Hutcherson, Tiny Lund, G.C. Spencer and Roy Mayne. During *Speedway*'s trackside sequences, Elvis-Steve melds in with them, becoming one of the boys — a theme that will in more than one sense serve as this light-hearted musical's serious subtext. That this is about more than is initially apparent becomes clear when, after winning yet another race, Steve returns to the trailer he shares with his old friend and business manager, Kenny Donford (Bill Bixby). The place has been furnished to look like a miniature Playboy Mansion; a striking brunette has arrived and waits for Steve, who likes her. But Steve finds the young woman in the arms of Kenny who, despite protestations, tries every trick in the early 1960s book to seduce her. Elvis' alter ego will ruin various ruses Kenny pulls on women who show up to meet Steve.

If we accept racing stardom as a correlative for Presley's status, it's clear that Kenny serves as a one-man symbol for the long-standing Memphis Mafia. In simplified fashion, he represents the coterie of old friends, distant relatives and hangers-on who served in various capacities such as business managers, enjoying the spoils of stardom — including countless women attracted like magnets to Elvis but often ending up in the beds of one of the other "boys."[38] Also, that expository sequence in which Steve rescues the brunette from Kenny's attempted date rape (at least in contemporary terms), re-establishes (following his momentary return to that value system in *Spinout*) Elvis' own gradual distancing of himself from the image he embodied during the decade's early years. Though he will be surrounded by pretty girls throughout *Speedway*, never once will he attempt to corner and seduce any in the way he regularly did in films from the 1960s' first half. If anything, he is now the white-knight, saint-like Galahad, showing up in the nick of time to rescue another woman from Kenny.

Those who dismiss the Presley musicals invariably see *Spinout* and *Speedway*, owing to similar titles, as the films that are easiest to confuse — the ultimate proof that, by this point, all were produced cookie-cutter fashion, the same script endlessly recycled. When closely considered, though, *Speedway* is the *antithesis* of *Spinout*, they the two most *different* films in the oeuvre. Until *Spinout*, the Presley persona had arced with each successive 1960s picture away from the "good life" that defined male behavior during the early 1960s. In *Spinout*, he experienced a panic attack at the thought that he was transforming into something more mature. Elvis in *Speedway* embodies the opposite of what he'd become in that film. Here, the *Playboy* image is embodied by Kenny; Steve-Elvis finds it offensive. The great irony is that Steve never considers dumping Kenny, despite many slights, any more than Elvis himself could (at least until the bitter end) bring himself to dismiss his numerous hangers-on.[39]

In the film as in actuality, this can be perceived two ways: The hero's decency and long-standing loyalty to male companions who have been with him since the beginning; or, alternately, as a pathetic, perhaps tragic personality flaw deriving from an insecure man's compulsive need for the company of men. Such friendships interfered with his relationship to Priscilla (and other women) in real life, and the latest actress in each film. Not surprisingly, then, *Speedway* recapitulates and apotheosizes a theme introduced in *Loving You*: The star's need to appear to be a stud for the public even though he can't live up to the reputation. The brunette he saved from Kenny turns out to be Miss Charlotte, who will hand the winner of the Charlotte 100 his trophy. Kenny tries to kiss her (symbolic substitute in pre-ratings Hollywood films for attempting to bed her) though Steve puts a stop to this every time.

When Steve is alone with Miss Charlotte, he makes no attempt to "kiss" her himself. He doesn't view Steve as competition, but as a man with an alternative agenda to his own — which is to keep Miss Charlotte at a distance, a beautiful friend rather than a lover for himself *or anyone else*. He will avoid every opportunity to kiss her, except one. He wins the race and *wants* to kiss her "for the *newspapers*." When he notices press people in the crowd, Steve's demeanor changes; as the camera points his way, he alters from nonchalant guy, apparently uninterested in the lovely woman's charms other than as a trophy — a flesh-and-blood incarnation of the silver statuette he holds — to a surly stud. Steve kisses her wildly, passionately, *madly* — until the pictures are taken. Once assured his legend as a lover will be furthered, Steve turns away from Miss Charlotte, who is anxious to carry on their relationship. He returns alone to his trailer, where he talks with Kenny about this staged conquest in lieu of following through. Longtime friend Red West recalls similar real-life situations in *Elvis! What Happened?*[40]

This incident sets the pattern for the remainder of the movie. Steve wins the next race and returns to his trailer only to find yet another attractive young woman, Susan Jacks (Nancy Sinatra), waiting — apparently a self-appointed spoil of war for the victor. As always, there is competition as to who will be alone with the latest lovely. Steve wins, slamming the door on longtime companion Kenny, and has every opportunity to now enjoy the willing flesh-and-blood prize. Again, though, Steve's pleasure at winning the girl at Kenny's expense is unmasked as a semblance rather than the real deal. Upon realizing he is truly alone with a mature young woman — a post–*Viva Las Vegas* woman who may well harbor sexual designs on *him*— Steve panics. He darts about the trailer, while she remains calm. Susan is not threatened — if anything, genuinely surprised by his obvious state of abject horror. Though played by a different actress, the Susan of *Speedway* is the Susan of *Spinout* all over again, if in an entirely different context.

Once she has gone (and become the impossible dream, the girl that got away), Steve appears intrigued, even obsessed in a way he wasn't while Susan remained a tangible possibility — thereby threatening him with the potential for consummation. This pattern is reflected in the set design for the film's nightspot, as well as the obligatory Presley performance there. "Speedway" (the club) offers a charming "fantasy recreation" of American car culture, in which every booth represents, in gaudy plastic *faux* form, a hot car. In each, couples dine on burgers and shakes before heading off to the dance floor, as go-go girls shimmy (*de rigeuer* a mere three years earlier, antiquated in '68) and bop in cages and on elevated platforms, perhaps inspiring the retro dance club in Quentin Tarantino's *Pulp Fiction* (1995). The young people are all white, surprising since during the decade's early years, Elvis' films (far ahead of their time) always appeared integrated. His films were by 1968 box office successes only in the Deep South, attended by people who continued to emblazon stars-and-bars flag decals on car windows—*not* as a reminder of bygone Confederate soldiers. *Speedway* (despite the presence of Nancy Sinatra, then as hot a property owing to hit singles like "Boots" as Ann-Margret had been four years earlier) only managed to rate #40 in *Box Office*'s list of the year's top-grossing films;[41] *Viva* had been #11.[42] Even as most movies were becoming ever more integrated (this was, after all, the year of *Guess Who's Coming to Dinner?*), Elvis Cinema appears ever more vanilla in its flavoring.

The choreographed number reveals a great deal. Steve breaks into song, performing "Let Yourself Go," one more tune that implies freedom and the fun of sensuality, at least when confined to the dance floor. An attitude expressed in Elvis' body language contradicts the words of his song. First, Steve approaches several of the gorgeous go-go girls who prance about him, each casting longing eyes from either side of his own locomotive-like gyrations.

He glances back and forth, from one to the other, grinning lasciviously. As they inch ever closer, Steve-Elvis coyly slips away. He approaches a particularly gorgeous female — one of those "untouchable" women encountered in his earlier films. When she removes herself from a somnambulist-like state of narcissism (dancing more to please herself than any of the gawking men she appears not to notice) and responds, he smiles, then abruptly leaves her. Victory for Elvis, reel or real, does not reside in the conquest but the knowledge he *could* have "had" her if he wanted to. So he moves on to the plastic cars, far more comfortable serenading couples as a musical mentor. His words instruct them to enjoy themselves while young. They — symbolic of the ongoing Elvis audience — nod in agreement. As the sequence ends, he appears a lonely figure, the catalyst who unleashed youth's energies but ends up all by himself once the show comes to an end.

Until this point, he has not (except as a publicity stunt) "kissed" one woman. Now he will meet a female whom he will *constantly* kiss; not surprisingly, it is a beautiful *child*. Steve notices blonde Ellie (Victoria Meyerink) stealing hot dogs from the snack bar. He pays for the food once she slips away, then follows her out to the back where her destitute father (William Schallert) and her four sisters camp out in a dilapidated car. Steve immediately hands them money; Elvis defines his arc away from the Hefner-like Playboy of the early 1960s to Elvis as Saviour of the decade's final years, giving to the poor, Jesus-like in reality and on screen.[43] Abel Esterlake insists on handing him a promissory note for everything, which idealizes the poor white trash audience attending the film, they associating with this decent if down-and-out man. Steve shares kisses with little Ellie before leaving, as eager to embrace the child as he was reluctant with grown women.

With her, Elvis repeats the peekaboo sequence from *Harum Scarum*, in which another child similarly peered seductively at him — the *female* gaze, from a pre-pubescent female at that. When underage Ellie makes clear she wants Steve for her man someday, he performs, as his defense mechanism, "Your Time Hasn't Come Yet, Baby"— tantalizingly dancing for her, his sensuous rhythmic style in full gyration (the child wears a brief mini-skirt modeled on the ones sported by grown females in the film). All the while, he insists she'll be his so long as she remains underage, thus non-threatening; Ellie will be abandoned as soon as she matures and joins the ranks of grown women, all of whom hope for a one-on-one with Elvis though this is denied them. Then, he actually *marries* Ellie in a "cute" mock ceremony — though of course it's implied that Steve has no intention of touching her (any more than Elvis did Priscilla) until it is "her time." Likely, if that were to happen, he would make love to Ellie once, then lose all interest.

Most notable among the grown women is Susan, whom Steve *does* come on to inside the club. Significantly, he only feels comfortable doing so after joining Susan in her plastic car. Though the film's dialogue (by Philip Shuken) is notably unrealistic, the lines that pass between Presley and Sinatra are further heightened in lowbrow theatricality. He makes a pass; she rejects it. Both clearly play a game, which makes sense since they are in a *toy* car. This proves fitting as we shortly learn that Susan is Steve's counterpart in at least one sense. Even as he plays at being something he is not (the secretive saviour showing off for crowds and cameras as a stud), her projection of a hot babe (particularly during her own choreographed number, "Don't Talk to Strangers") is all *performance*. Susan works for the IRS and has arrived as an undercover agent (again, acting). Her assignment is to seduce either Steve or Kenny (or both) to discover what has happened to racing money never properly reported on tax forms.

Again the film turns autobiographical, as Steve learns that the money he handed to Kenny for charitable causes (helping distraught people out of trouble, as Elvis did) has been gambled away by his old "friend." The capitalist theme returns, if in a new guise; unlike the early Presley persona, this current one does not need to achieve the dream of achieving success through amassing money as he has done so before the story begins. Once, the question was whether or not he would "make it" and, if he did, whether the big time (and big money) would corrupt him. Such problems seem quaint, from a dimly remembered era when the belligerent boy in blue jeans faced rejection by slick types in sharkskin suits. Times have changed. When Steve and Kenny are called in before IRS agent R.W. Hepworth (Gale Gordon), both wear suits and ties; Elvis, who once appeared ill at ease wearing such a get-up, looks completely comfortable. He scolds Kenny when the sidekick momentarily undoes his tie, insisting he re-tighten it.

There can be no doubt about Presley's patriotism. As a half-dozen other businessmen begin to sweat, Elvis' alter ego launches into a red, white and blue song and dance number ("He's Your Uncle," meaning "Sam"), calming them, insisting our government is not persecuting them; all will be treated fairly. A one-time poster boy for anti-bureaucratic rebellion has gradually become the young adult apologist for everything he used to scorn. As other suits form a chorus, he blends in perfectly. His current association with the auto industry adds to his this, since "General Motors was Republican, not Eastern sophisticated Republican but heartland conservative Republican — insular, suspicious of anything different."[44] Political implications reach further: Ralph Nader's *Unsafe at Any Speed*, a frontal attack on the dangers inherent in our reliance on the automobile, had appeared in 1965.[45]

Most of the false tax deductions Kenny took are disallowed. The boys are put on a strict allowance, Susan assigned to insure that they maintain it.

This allows for a growing romance between the two who (as so often occurs in romantic comedy) did not initially hit it off. Like many women before her (particularly the self-sufficient women of the later films), Susan is less impressed with the hero's good looks and sports success than with the fact that (unlike Kenny, forever lavishing money on himself and the women he'd like to seduce) Steve has slipped into financial trouble by aiding the less fortunate, particularly people who share his humble beginnings but did not get life's lucky breaks. Steve allows Ellie and her entire family to sleep in his trailer when the new car he bought them (Elvis really did buy cars for strangers) is repossessed. The "final girl" in a Presley film appreciates his Christ-like decency and will love him from a distance. There are no intense romantic scenes between Steve and Susan; Steve, like Elvis, has moved beyond that.

When the obligatory fistfight occurs between Steve and his competition, it is played in an over-the-top manner, as if director Norman Taurog, his star and everyone else involved understood no one believed in this kind of stuff any more, if indeed anyone ever had. A sense of community dominates the third and final act; Susan, Kenny and other members of their crew scurry about, like characters in a Frank Capra social comedy, borrowing parts from other drivers so that Steve's damaged car can be reassembled in time for him to enter the 600 the following day and win enough money to save the poor people. As they all labor over the stock car, the camera cuts from one to the other so quickly that, as in a Soviet montage from the 1920s, all meld into a single personality. The group's great mission incorporates individual endeavor into communal identity. Like those who support James Stewart in Capra's *It's a Wonderful Life* (1946), they are "the people."

Once the race begins, though, Elvis is the rugged individualist again. He dresses the part perfectly, appropriate since each sub-cult of Automania has its own "uniform," be it "the black-leather jacket of the demon motorcyclist" or the "hot rodder's 'Weirdo shirt'"[46]; Elvis sported the latter in *Loving You*, the former in *Roustabout*, and the tight-fitting racer's uniform here, each fashion statement from the world of Automania allowing the owner to "indulge in a craving to show off."[47] It's clear from cross-cuts to the crowd that Susan and the other Elvis apostles believe in him as the source of spiritual as well as financial salvation; this ever-enlarging aspect of the cult for Elvis likewise fits in neatly with car culture, since this can and has been defined as "a quasi religion, what with its concept of the car as power, its special set of doctrines and the extraordinary behavior patterns exhibited by its devotees."[48] If Elvis took on aspects of the demi-god, then first the hot rod, later the motorcycle and finally the sports car served as his chariots of fire.

He is the epic hero, he who wins just enough to save his destitute dependents. If there is nothing left for him, that's not such a bad thing. Back in the club, where they can afford nothing more for their victory celebration than all–American franks and beans, he dances with Susan and sings "There Ain't Nothing Like a Song," insisting that if you keep music in your heart, the future will work itself out.

Steve and Susan are not finally framed in the expected clinch. Though they dance together, each appears to do so separately. Kenny (like the Memphis Mafia) hasn't been banished, despite his many transgressions. Steve appears to be drifting away from Susan, back toward Kenny and the back-up boys in the band — still more comfortable as a member of the male group than committed to pursuing a relationship with the most outwardly striking and inwardly substantial woman he has met.

To sum up Elvis' relationship to car culture, Botkin argues that the two "way-out" cults are those for the sports car and the hot rod and that "there are striking contrasts in decoration and costume. Each has its mystique, fetishes, and gambits."[49] The shiny chrome, hot oil and loud motor of the "rod" signify the blue collar owner-rebel's revenge on the ordinary, everyday, homogenized society around him — early Elvis roaring up in just such a car in *Loving You*. The sports car serves as "a special kind of exurbanite status symbol which has its roots in the leisure-class exclusiveness of the wealthy"[50]; by the late '60s, that was the case with Elvis in real life and the Presley persona on-screen. Though at first the hot rod and the sports car might seem polar opposites, they — in actuality and here — form a fascinating continuum: The American Everyman owns one in his youth, the other in middle age. The switch does not suggest some fundamental change in attitude, only a rise in status. The hot rod *was* the poor boy's sports car, if one he would gladly exchange for the real thing if only his life experiences allowed him to. That was precisely the case with the heroes of these films — and the star of them in actuality.

CHAPTER 15

The Summer of Love

◆ *Easy Come, Easy Go* (1967) ◆
◆ *Double Trouble* (1967) ◆

By late 1967–early 1968, Students for a Democratic Society (SDS) and other protest organizations (SNCC, the Northern Student Movement, Berkeley's Free Speech society) busily spread an anti–Vietnam war, pro–Civil Rights agenda across the nation's campuses. Radical political ideas emanated from SDS's inception point in Michigan, where *The Port Huron Statement* had been drafted in the Spring of 1962 by Tom Hayden and Al Haber. Peace demonstrations and sit-ins at administration buildings were soon part of the college scene. Such experiments in "direct action" (individual citizens involving themselves in a "movement") challenged the older, more traditional notion of "participatory democracy" (voting for candidates who were supposed to, but often did not, represent the wishes of the citizenry). This was one aspect of the revolutionary fervor that motivated the country's youth in a land that had never gotten over the shock waves created by the Kennedy assassination, for cultural revolution also filled the air.

One of the biggest misconceptions of the late '60s is that the two "movements" were essentially mirror reflections of one another. Despite some overlap (Dylan's "Like a Rolling Stone" did become an anthem of the peace movement, while a line from another song provided the monicker of the ultra-violent Weathermen), those who actively campaigned to end racism at home and imperialism abroad expressed outright contempt for those who followed hippie guru Timothy Leary's advice to take drugs and turn their backs on the social scene. Such lifestyle-oriented radicals developed their own counter-cultural enclaves, cocooning rather than trying to change an abiding structure they believed too far gone to save. The attitude of one group toward the other might best be described as tolerant contempt. As Stanley Aronowitz later recalled:

> There were really two counter-cultures in the '60s.... [These] cultural radicals believed the struggle within the state and its institutions hopeless and beside the point. For them the important question was freedom to be different ... building art and cultural communities ... where poetry and stories were recited.[1]

Such activity first gained national attention when numerous "hippies," as the post–Beatnik youth culture came to be called, drifted toward the West Coast during the summer of 1967. There they participated in "happenings"— some spontaneous, others staged, involving free sex and costly drugs. Shortly, a popular song, "If You're Going to San Francisco (Be Sure to Wear Some Flowers in Your Hair)," conveyed to a nationwide audience a romanticized notion of this youth-migration. Hollywood immediately attempted to capitalize on the syndrome via films ranging from inexpensive exploitation flicks (*Riot on Sunset Strip*, 1967) to glossy if misguided big-budget productions (*The Happening*, 1968).

The Presley persona never involves himself with the political wing of the Youth Movement, as their attack on the "labor metaphysic" of C. Wright Mills and their anti-military stance was antithetical to all he stood for.[2] Elvis did star, however, in two films that posit him as a youngish if no longer youthful retro-male, he attempting to deal with the non-political "scene" and, in each film, *another* example of the "new woman."

Nowhere Man: *Easy Come, Easy Go* (1967)

The film opens with a reference to an earlier movie, *Kid Galahad*. Elvis (here called Ted Jackson) is again a serviceman on the eve of retirement, this time from the Navy. One difference is apparent: Rather than an enlisted man, he's an officer. We watch as Elvis and four friends leave their ship, anchored near the mainland, and head for Fisherman's Wharf. Breaking with *G.I. Blues*, all are lieutenants, part of the once-feared officer class. While older and enjoying more status than the boys in Elvis' first post-service musical, they appear no less shallow. As they approach the dock in a transport, the men speak (and sing) about girls they hope to meet and (in the old macho sense) conquer. Once ashore, they pass by ordinary servicemen — the fellows Elvis and his own immediate group portrayed in the earlier picture — who salute them, even as the Elvis clique saluted superior officers then. In *Blue Hawaii*, the on-screen military iconography made clear that Elvis was co-opted by the Establishment. Now, he's not only a part of the system but *in charge*— an officer who thinks in terms no more enlightened than those of the humblest sailor; status aside, the mindset remains unchanged.

The Presley persona has come full cycle, distancing himself from the emotional and intellectual rewards of his long on-screen journey — the learning process apparently for naught. No longer is he the naïve, unspoiled redneck but a college graduate. No wonder this was the first failure with his target audience since *Wild in the Country*. *Frankie and Johnny* had brought in an impressive $4.5 million (mostly in rural Southern bookings) at the box office one year earlier; *Easy Come, Easy Go* netted a shabby $1.5 million — notably weak when compared to *Paradise, Hawaiian Style*, also from the previous year, with $2.5 million.[3] As one critic complained,

> [W]hen Elvis became inaccessible to ordinary people, when he lost physical touch with "his own kind" — the fans who lived in mobile homes and listened to him in honkytonk road-houses — Elvis was a dead man.[4]

Here, he truly is the Nowhere Man the Beatles sang about.

When the foursome arrives at the Easy Go-Go, a mid–'60s disco that appears embarrassingly anachronistic in this late–'60s setting, the boys spin a wheel of fortune, covered with pictures of pretty girls. Owner Judd Whitman (Pat Harrington, Jr.) keeps this on display to determine which customer will date which local beauty. The photograph of each girl looks suspiciously like a *Playboy* Centerfold, her measurements brazenly listed. The guys are willing to let fate or fortune decide which of the lovelies — each valued for no other reason than her looks, all treated as pieces of meat — they will spend time with. All each wants is a Playmate of the Month. In sharp contrast, there's Jo Symington (Dodie Marshall, Susan in *Spinout*), a *real* girl in a revealing two-piece outfit, dancing with the band as musicians rehearse. The boys eye Jo (the male gaze presented without the irony present in earlier movies) as her movements exude sensuality, in the manner of popular dance crazes of the disco era that had already passed.

As soon as the song is done, each lieutenant leaps forward to make a play, Ted explaining he's a barnacle scraper. His actual job is to search underwater for live mines and defuse them; life as theater returns as a theme. Even before each male makes his big move, Judd warns them Jo is not what she seems. However sexy, Jo (her name like Les in *Spinout* is gender non-specific) signifies something other than the readily available women who opted for liberation through sexuality via birth control pills. Jo dances here during the day because she likes the music and finds it a perfect place to exercise and even get paid for self-expression so long as male gazers are allowed to watch. Though sexy, Jo has no intention of becoming a temporary sex object. She believes in the power of free *love*, though not interested in engaging in free *sex*.

This totally confounds Ted and his friends, who have finally adjusted to the early–1960s attitudes and can't believe they are already expected to transform once more. Jo is one of the first screen depictions of the then-emerging late-'60s women, an early Hollywood incarnation of the female hippie, other examples including Leigh Taylor-Young in *I Love You, Alice B. Toklas* (1968). Jo represents a departure from the early–'60s woman: "She *doesn't* 'swing,'" Judd (clearly confused himself) insists, referring to the decade's early years and the go-go mentality his club still (embarrassingly) features. Yet Jo certainly *does* swing, in other senses of the term. For the time being, Ted and the boys put the confounding Jo out of their minds and go out on dates, which prove disastrous. Though we don't see the encounters, we hear about them as the boys head back toward their ship the next morning. Their language is by today's standards overtly sexist. One's physical measurements added up to her age; another was, in a lieutenant's words, "a dog." The sequence might rate as unbearably offensive were it not that the film implies a rejection of the attitudes Elvis-Ted and the others profess.

Ted and company will encounter other vestiges of the swinging female. Back aboard, they watch as a small craft comes alongside. Peering down, they — like ordinary enlisted men on-board — watch as, one after another, three bikini-clad blondes step out of the cabin and on deck, giddily displaying themselves for the sailors. Though they are conventionally beautiful, their action recalls clowns coming out of a car in a circus, rendering them laughable — if not to the naval men, at least to the judicious viewer. Enlisted men whistle and catcall as expected. Officers silently gaze down from an elevated position, then whisper sexist comments. The females are interchangeable, as bland as they are blond — pretty, none in any way a unique personality, like Jo. Then a male companion, Gil Carey (Skip Ward, playing the role once embodied by Jeremy Slate) joins the playmates. Like the master of a harem, he herds them back into the cabin. Waving in a flirtatious manner left over from the early '60s, the girls whirl away. Ted will soon come into contact with one, Dana Bishop (Pat Priest).

In full gear, Ted dives down in search of a dangerous mine, discovering a sunken galleon with a treasure chest aboard. The boatful of playgirls (Gil, also blonde, looks like a male version of the women) anchors nearby. Gil is not the "male master," rather as recessive in personality as he is rugged in appearance. Dana, the early–'60s playgirl incarnate, proves a dominatrix, insisting she wants a photo of attractive Ted, reviving the "female gaze" theme. When Gil hesitates, she insults his masculinity; the macho appearance, as so often is the case, turns out to be a pose from an inwardly insecure man. To recoup a little of his self-esteem, Gil slips into gear and dives, taking an underwater photo not only of Ted but also the ancient ship, *Port of Call*.

Once all are out of the water again, the following sequence offers a parallel to one of the great films released that same year. For reasons of national security as well as his desire to eventually return and recoup the treasure for himself, Ted demands that Gil hand over the film. After a momentary argument, Gil appears to do so, though we learn that he kept the incriminating film and handed Ted a bogus roll — precisely what occurs toward the end of Act One in Michelangelo Antonioni's *Blow-Up*, the Italian director's London-based thriller. Set against the backdrop of a city surrendering to psychedelia, *Blow-Up* concerned a hip photographer (David Hemmings) who shoots film of something he was not supposed to see and lives to regret it. With such a comparison made, it's impossible not to be all the more aware of the degree to which this minor musical offers a glimpse, through the eyes of an uncomprehending male, of the revolutionary late '60s.

Enter old Capt. Jack (Frank McHugh), a sailor who is afraid of the water. His experience took place in front of a camera when, years earlier, he hosted a Saturday morning children's TV show. Jack is the latest signifier of a recurring theme: The distinction between the powerful image that celebrities (Elvis included) project and the disappointing reality we encounter after realizing they are only "performers" on the stage of life. From Jack, Ted learns that the local expert on *Port of Call*, Symington, is a descendant of *its* captain. Ted drives into the hills, in search of this person's home, only to discover the "fellow" he believes to be "Joe Symington" is Jo, the utterly untouchable Elvis woman (here necessarily re-imagined as a "hippie chick") he met at Judd's club. Her house is a hippie commune. Most (though not all) of the residents are young women; they are *not* lorded over (like the blondes) by a man. Their happy little coven is overseen by a mature if eccentric woman, Madame Neherina (Elsa Lanchester).

When Ted enters, this benign matriarch conducts a Yoga class, Jo and the others in attendance. When Ted freezes by the door, he's ordered by one woman: "Make the scene or split!" Others employ the term "man" in every sentence, an idiomatic practice of the era that would reach its apex in the dialogue in Dennis Hopper's *Easy Rider* (1969). A comedy bit makes it clear that Elvis, one-time pioneer of liberated body language, has become an old fuddy duddy. He joins in the exercises (highly characteristic of the hippie scene), only to realize he can't compete with the young women and men in terms of pelvic ability. As they follow the instructions of elderly Madame Neherina and demonstrate "the spinal thrust," Ted — the only early-middle-aged person present — finds himself knotted up like a human pretzel. Times have changed, Elvis comically outdated — reduced to a clown-like foil for this new generation.

"Yoga is as yoga does," they all sing; Ted — interested in learning about the sunken ship — guides Jo into an adjoining room. Before they can talk, he must deal with more aspects of the era. A boy and girl kiss; another youth drops pasta down on them as other youths applaud. Confused, Ted looks to Jo; she explains that this is "a happening." That term was first employed by Allan Kaprow as early as 1959 to describe "a spontaneous, unrehearsed, and often unconnected cluster of events"[5] occurring in small, isolated circles of bohemia like the one encountered here. For Daniel Boorstin, the happening consisted of a "pseudo-event,"[6] in that it appeared organic and spontaneous though was in fact planned in advance. As the counter-culture spread to the mainstream during the next several years, such an occurrence would grow ever more popular. When Elvis glibly puts all this down, she explains, "We're part of a bunch of people who like to live free," devoid of old restraints. She is the Ann-Margret character from *Viva Las Vegas*, taken a giant step (to accurately reflect the rapidly changing scene) further a mere three years later.

But if Elvis had begrudgingly adjusted in *Viva*, he can no longer do so. Several young women, bodies covered with paint, enter and brush up against a wall-sized canvas, creating an avant-garde work of art, precisely as Ann-Margret would do that year in her own starring vehicle, *The Swinger*. Though here Ted laughs with contempt, the filmmakers appear to side with Jo when without pretension she explains, "People always laugh at things they don't understand" — a complaint Elvis fans were quick to toss at middle-aged suburban adults (the same age Elvis is here) who failed to understand (or even try) what he had offered ten years earlier. Jo's friends are attempting to break free of convention, a desire initially sparked a decade earlier by the man playing Ted. Now, he shakes his head condescendingly. The film will chronicle his acceptance, then support, of the commune and its edgy values.

Meanwhile, he remains a diehard conservative, happy only when he and Jo are alone. This occurs when they enter the house's most traditional room, the office of Jo's now-deceased sea captain father. Old charts line the wall; models of wooden ships are on display. "*This* is more what I *expected*," Ted sighs at the sight of traditional items. Jo reveals a manifest of the ship, which she refused to show to any of the numerous fortune hunters who came around. Naively Jo believes Ted a selfless individual who for the good of the Navy in particular, and the country at large, wants to write a manual about *Port of Call*. He, sensing that she's anti-materialistic (what the early Presley persona had been), withholds the truth: He's interested only in the treasure. In early films, Elvis played the representative of a New Youth who stood up to early-middle-aged men corrupted by raw capitalism. During the intervening years, he has transformed into precisely what he found most offensive. Here, Elvis is just such a middle-aged man, willing to do anything for the almighty dollar.

Jo symbolizes a *newer* New Youth. Now that her slightly older counterpart has succumbed and, with age, become no better than the adults he once stood against, it is Jo's duty to morally instruct him. Before this can happen, Ted must encounter and then reject an early–'60s style of self-serving (by implication promiscuous) woman, symbolic of a waning era. First, Ted — now discharged from the Navy — needs to raise money for a treasure-hunting expedition. Jud agrees to help finance on one condition: Should they come up empty-handed, Ted must return to his pre-service job at the club. Earlier, Ted made clear while visiting Judd that he wanted no part of his old musical career.

> TED: Maybe I should go back to *singing* for you?
> JUDD: Yeah!
> TED: Thanks, but *no* thanks!

The lack of interest in music suggests — for Elvis as for Ted — a sense of corruption. Initially, the music defined him. Now, he has little interest in it since he can make more *money* elsewhere. Old friends of Elvis recall that he at this point lost interest in recording, since the colonel — believing anything recorded by Elvis would sell — negotiated deals with minor companies and saved money by providing his "boy" with third-rate songs (top songwriters demanding better deals for their work).[7] Elvis-Ted's (begrudging) agreement at mid-movie to perform again implies he's about to recover his soul — the music that once motored him.

The film works like a Faustian morality play with no clear-cut Mephistopheles — the "villain" that side of Ted that thinks only of the profits he can make. Then he begins to reconnect with his roots. Jud fears that promises aside, Ted may have become so corrupt that he can no longer connect with the audience that once loved him — the audience in the club signifying Elvis' own Memphis-based following. To prove Jud wrong, the protagonist performs with the band; in a truly memorable musical sequence, he grabs a guitar and jams, recalling his rockabilly roots while also offering the harder guitar riffs characteristic of the "new music" superstars, most notably Jimi Hendrix. As Elvis bridges past and present, he appears reborn, and the crowd goes wild with this realization: The King is back! No wonder, then, that when he must choose to leave the club with either the superficial early–'60s go-go girl Dina or the more in-depth hippie-era princess Jo, he chooses the latter. He can't yet grasp, though, that free love does not necessarily include loose sex.

So Ted takes Jo home, certain he'll be invited to spend the night. Still conventional, he's uncomfortable that she, clearly wealthy, doesn't choose to wear shoes. Significantly, he points out that in the rural South where he (Ted and Elvis) hails from, he went without shoes because he couldn't afford them.

What Ted appears unable to grasp is that members of the American mainstream now purposefully affect artifacts of white-trash culture their parents hoped to remove them from — a cultural movement that began on that day when young people of the mid–'50s embraced Elvis. Yet he, a self-conscious poor boy, wanted to move up. Whether he intentionally instigated change or unconsciously crystallized an existing undercurrent is not possible to determine. Clearly, as so often happens in culture (popular or otherwise), the instigator was left standing in the dust by those he inspired.

Here, the greaser encounters the hippie. Jo's pad features a waterbed, musical instruments mounted on the wall, hanging beads in place of doors, Tiffany lampshades, and rugs on which she likes to practice Yoga. This is the only "night action" she's interested in, assuming a position and indicating that Ted is welcome to join her. Again he's the confused American male, unable to grasp the latest future-shock alteration in women's attitudes. He chooses to leave, though she invites him to become a member of the poetry-reading group.

A retro-male, he mouths all the clichés then going out of fashion. When he rents diving equipment, Judd's suggestion that they take Jo along is countered with, "It's not a job for a *girl*." Circumstances force him to bring Jo, she carrying her hippie-veggie lunch of sliced carrots and prune yogurt. Ted must reveal the true purpose of the mission. Judd convinces him that Jo may not mind that they aren't out to create a navigational text but make quick profits, uttering words oblivious to the evolving female sensibility: "Every *chick* I've ever known loves *money*." That seemingly makes sense, so Ted tells Jo the truth, only to be rebuffed: "You're just a get-rich-quick type like all the rest."

Jo's foil, Dana (the mid–'60s female whom Judd naively believes is still prevalent) shows up on her boat. The other blondes have mysteriously disappeared, as if they were never anything but Dana clones, as the two groups compete for treasure. However pretty Dana may be, Ted loses interest in her (and the generation of women she represents) as he becomes intrigued with communally minded Jo. "My favorite charity is *me*!" Ted (rugged individualist still) grunts when Jo tells him she'll help with the treasure hunt but only if the money is used to finance an artist's colony. His words are echoed, word for word, by Dana on several occasions when she makes clear that her relationship with Gil is superficial; she's using him as her all-around handyman by day and lover (in a strictly physical sense) by night, planning to abandon him as soon as she becomes rich. When Ted briefly dates her back on shore, he is — after being around the positive moral force of Jo — offended when Dana casually admits, "I don't have any principles."

Suddenly, Ted feels guilty about something he casually said to Jo earlier that afternoon: "*I'm* an unprincipled, get-rich-quick creep. Would you like me any better if I grew a beard and didn't care about money?" He realizes now that she would. "Happily broke and full of all kinds of crazy principles," he mutters to Dana about Jo, sensing that however "crazy" her principles may seem to him — and the way his generation of males looks at the world — they are values he admires. And once (in a dimly recalled innocent age in his own life) projected. From then on, Ted is in league with Jo, agreeing that her portion of the riches can go to "the cause." At her apartment, varied hippies carry signs announcing a then-radical agenda: "Conserve water — shower together!" One fellow shouts "Cinderella is a junkie!" Ted notices a woman carrying a sign that reads, "We protest!" When he stops to ask her what, she replies: "Give me a minute; I'll think of something." He smiles. Ted (Elvis) was young once, too. At last he joins in with the Hippies, performing "Sing, you children, sing!" The song suggests, as he steps into the middle of the crowd with Jo on his arm, that he accept his status as progenitor of their current rebellion.

Ted and Jo can't drive into town; a wild-eyed hippie, Zoltan, has transformed Ted's car into an auto-mobile, now hanging in the garage. They borrow Zoltan's "wheels"; soon Elvis is seen riding a psychedelically painted car onto Fisherman's Wharf. Car culture is again in evidence, Elvis adjusting to the "hippie van" as the longhair version of his own hot rod from greaser days. There is the obligatory fight scene in which he punches out Gil, as well as an underwater competition in which they rush to get the treasure, Ted of course winning out. Dana — who viewed the entire thing as an elaborate game — bids them a glib goodbye and sails her ship out to sea, heading for other ports of call, other suckers to "take." Rugged individualism of the most crassly commercial approach may have been temporarily defeated, but it has hardly been dispelled. Ted appears happy to see her go, turning to Jo, now ready to accept her values — he having learned something about the worth of communal ideology.

Though the treasure turns out to be worth considerably less than estimated, Ted convinces both Judd and Capt. Jack to join him in throwing his share of the profits into Jo's common pool, helping her to build that commune for the arts — those contemporary art forms he formerly laughed at. Elvis at last comes back in touch with his roots, taking a musician's job in Judd's club, singing with the band — something which, in his corrupted state, he had vowed never to do again. The lyrics to "I'll Take Love," Elvis' final song, reveal the degree to which his character has arced — to where his on-screen persona began, so many years (and movies) ago. Instead of wealth and material treasures, he will choose love.

His words would be echoed by several dozen tunes of the Woodstock era.

"Never Trust Anyone Over 30": *Double Trouble* (1967)

The new youth loved to proclaim, "Never trust anyone over 30!" Elvis Presley had passed that mark two years previous to this film's release, as had many members of his fan base. However hard they had tried to remain "forever young," that was not easy to accomplish. Elvis's status as an anachronism was enhanced by the May 24, 1967, release of *Double Trouble*, which to hippies seemed hopelessly out of date, despite the fact that the intent was to update his image. Had the film been released several years earlier, it might have signaled a breakthrough for Elvis. Nineteen hundred and sixty-four had been the year in which the British Invasion exploded onto the American pop-culture scene. The public had, during that seminal 12-month period, witnessed the appearance of Peter Sellers as the lovably inept Inspector Clouseau in *The Pink Panther*; *Goldfinger*, the biggest and best of the Brit-lensed James Bond films; and the Beatles in the cinematic confection *Help! Double Trouble* would have provided a witty antidote had it followed hard upon all that, Elvis' movie turning the British Invasion around and upside down.

Sad to say, it turned out to be the right movie at the wrong time. Guy Lambert (Elvis) is an American singer who arrives in London, while the Beatles and their counterparts are in America dominating radio airwaves, record purchases and musical segments on *Ed Sullivan*. American teenage girls were screaming over John, Paul, George and Ringo as their (the girls') counterparts of eight years earlier had over Elvis. The film posits a situation in which every British "bird" is crazy for the American singer who, while their favorite stars are in the United States, has invaded their haunts. But by 1967, that rated as ancient history, Elvis once again undone by the cultural phenomenon called Future Shock.

The script by Joe Heims is patterned on the more lighthearted Hitchcock thrillers, including the British-made *The Lady Vanishes* (1938) and its American counterpart, *North by Northwest* (1959). Suspenseful situations (including one character's grisly death) are mixed with easygoing romance and edgy comedy. In combination, this mélange makes it clear that nothing here is to be taken seriously. Hitchcock was the master of such stuff, though other directors proved themselves adept, including Stanley Donen (*Charade*, 1963) and Mark Robson (*The Prize*, 1964). Not that Norman Taurog was in their league, or that the material he and Presley had to work here with matched those Hitchcock-esque scenarios. Still, the pattern is present: A MacGuffin (the object everyone's after, in this case a cache of jewels) is present during a journey. For the leads, this trip transforms a difficult romance into true love.

Also present is a mystery lady of the type Hitch introduced in his first classic of international intrigue, *The 39 Steps* (1935): Claire Dunham (Yvonne

Romain), a darkly elegant European woman who haunts the clubs where Guy performs, focusing her female gaze on an ever more androgynous Elvis. Though Claire insists that her reason for arriving on the premises each night is an attraction to the singer, she seems surprisingly willing to watch Guy shower his attentions on Jill Conway (Annette Day). A prim and proper English girl, Jill whisks in and out of Guy's life, causing him to become enamored — even obsessed. In the title song, Elvis laments falling for two women instead of just one like other guys would. This is the extent of the "doubles" that lend the film its title, unless one counts cute twins who perform in the club's back-up band.

Owing to this seemingly inappropriate title, *Double Trouble* might be confused with *Kissin' Cousins*. Actually, the title derives from the doubling theme various critics have noted in Hitchcock films. Every on-screen element — from the women whom the hero becomes involved with, to objects with which he comes in contact — prove twofold.[8] In Hitchcock, this literal doubling suggests a more profound subject, the duality of life, appearance and reality often far apart. On a considerably less ambitious level, *Double Trouble* popularizes for the late 1960s such a theme in a divertissement, such films less frequent now that the master (Hitch) had moved on to darker work like *Psycho*.

Within this altered context, various ideas from earlier Elvis movies are introduced. Observing that Claire is clearly older than Guy, a friend notes he, Oedipus-like, brings out a strong "maternal instinct" in such women. The notion of marriage as a dangerous situation for any man who values his freedom surfaces. Elvis' friend and manager cannot pursue women, as Guy reminds him, since "you're *married*." With a shrug, the companion notes, "That's the problem." Guy must try to choose between a *la dolce vita*-type relationship with Claire and a more committed one, leading to marriage, with mini-skirted but morally conventional Jill. She eventually appears ready to surrender: "I suppose if anything's to come of us," Jill sighs, "it'll have to be tonight," adding in a moment: "I want to go with you to your flat." Shortly, they are in his "pad," as it is called here, where Guy tidies up and prepares tea, then plays his own records.

This being a Presley film — which, by 1967, dictated that the work can flirt with sexuality but not openly embrace it — his moves are all rejected. Every time Guy attempts to kiss Jill, she slips away, though such activity had (from what she herself said) been her reason for joining him. Guy — modeled on the star playing him — sings along with his recording during his planned seduction. This augments the doubling theme, Elvis doubling himself — though there already were two Presleys, the leading character serving as a doppelganger for the performer playing him. Singing a duet with himself references his own work while deconstructing the viewing experience, reminding us of the ripples that occur in all popular culture: a star portrays a star mimicking his stardom.

The difficulty of admitting to each other that they are in love — each is locked into the mid–'60s dating scene, though neither particularly likes it — causes Jill to flee the apartment while Guy changes in an adjoining room. When he emerges, a red herring shows up in the guise of one of those huge enemies who at this time regularly appeared out of nowhere to menace Sean Connery as 007. He brings Guy down with a single punch, then — realizing he's arrived at the wrong address — apologizes while noting that "you probably deserved it anyway." Shortly, John Williams, one of Hitchcock's favorite actors — best recalled as the detectives in *Dial M for Murder* (1954) and *To Catch a Thief* (1955) — introduces himself over the phone as Jill's uncle, insisting that it's time they met. Guy is ushered into a mansion, where he learns about Jill's huge inheritance. "Did you have it in mind to marry my niece?" Uncle Gerard asks, the implication being that Guy would marry for money — something the Presley persona has steadfastly refused to do. In this film's pop-op art context (trendy in 1964; passé in 1967), the recurrent capitalist idea takes on a new guise.

Moments later, another key issue reoccurs. Jill enters the room to visit her "uncle," utterly unaware Guy is there. The hero is stunned, for Jill — adding to the doubling theme — appears in her true (rather than assumed) guise. Instead of the stunning young mini-skirted "swinger" who haunted the club scene by night, she is by day an underage schoolgirl, dressed now in childish uniform. She had been playing at being a playgirl, though she's a virgin — and, her well-developed physique aside, a child. Having romanced (and almost seduced) her, Guy nearly suffers a stroke. But what appear to be simple emotions (revulsion upon realizing that Jill is legally a minor) grow more complex. While Guy does rush off as quickly as possible on his trip to Brussels for a gig, he hasn't forgotten Jill. She is Elvis' latest (and last) on-screen Lolita; one wishes she had been played by Sue Lyon from Stanley Kubrick's 1962 film (or perhaps Hayley Mills, of *Pollyanna* fame) rather than the listless Annette Day.

As in previous films, Elvis finds himself caught between a mother figure and a virtual child. Incredibly, he can dream only of being in bed with the little girl — despite Claire and other would-be companions. We notice them everywhere: in the club, on the street, etc. The great irony is an extension of the ocular theme: *we* see them; Guy-Elvis doesn't. He believes he's become trapped in this impossible two-way stretch, while we intuit that the situation doesn't derive from destiny but his character — Guy's and, invariably, Elvis'. This is a trap of his own making, though he cannot acknowledge this.

The Lolita character — part innocent child, part studied seductress — will haunt Guy, even as Priscilla did Elvis after he first met her in Germany, though there were plentiful frauleins about.[9] He's stunned to notice her aboard ship while crossing the Channel. Gen. Waverly decided that, to keep Jill away from the crass American, he'd send her off to a boarding school on the continent. Elvis appears shocked and relieved to see her; this is an attraction-repulsion reaction to the one piece of forbidden fruit. Legal-age swingin' women dart about, vying for his attention, as he sings "Long-Legged Girl (with a Short Dress on)."

The narrative plot, in striking comparison to the bizarre subtext, is routine: A team of diamond smugglers (the Wiere Brothers), each disguised as a Clouseau-like detective, must find a way to get their stolen goods past customs. They plant the jewels in the unsuspecting Jill's suitcase. After disembarking, the team pursues her across the Continent to retrieve their ill-gotten goods. Jill is gently romanced on-board (before meeting Guy again) by a clean-cut American college boy — the type Elvis, in his early–'60s films, found himself in competition with. At the Brussels nightclub, Guy again lands in double trouble as Claire and Jill simultaneously arrive to watch him perform. They serve as foils, the Presley persona here at least vaguely aware that, by film's end, he will be in the arms of (to marry and consummate his relationship with) either his mother (as in the good ol' days) or (in his new guise) his daughter.

Jill is the one he brings back to his latest flat, fully aware he could face a jail term: "Seventeen will get me 20," Guy notes as he nonetheless hops on the bed with Jill. With the older woman, he would not need to feel silly about her being more experienced than himself and could allow her to teach him about love. With the child, he — no matter how insecure about his sexual prowess — could still be the teacher and mentor, the case here as in his relationship with underage Priscilla. We ought not to be surprised when Guy realizes that Claire is not as much older as he had thought, closer to him in years and (in the limited thinking of the time) more "suitable" for a wife; immediately, Guy becomes uncomfortable when around her. On every occasion that would allow them to be alone and near (in?) a bed, he takes great pains to make certain this will not happen. He relishes being alone with Jill, even while decrying that he cannot "do" anything with her. (If Priscilla's memories are to be believed, he in fact could do absolutely "anything" with her except "it," which he wants to avoid, the girl's underage status allowing him to do so without his ego suffering damage.) The result is a masochistic situation, perversely satisfying by being so totally frustrating.

The irony derives from Jill, when we finally come to grasp that she has less in common with Mills in *Pollyanna* than Lyon in *Lolita*. However much

Elvis may believe himself "safe" with the younger woman, so long as he controls any aggressive behavior, this is a new era — one in which the hippie child-woman asserts her own sexuality, choosing to give away her virginity to whomever she considers the right man. Like Jill with Guy, Priscilla tried to get Elvis to take her, he refusing and insisting: "Don't get carried away, Baby. Let me decide when it should happen. It's a very *sacred* thing to me [emphasis mine]."[10] Jill pushes Guy down on the pillows. He — symbolically, a male virgin if perceived as a sex symbol — can, in his sexual panic, surrender only to a child who is at once virginal and instinctually "knowing."

Elvis now hungers for marriage to the younger woman, perhaps because he legally can't have it. In four days, Jill will be "of age"; if they can hold out that long, there would be no way for anyone to stop them from coupling. After waiting so long, they can legally consummate the grotesque relationship and, like Elvis with Priscilla, make it "sacred." There remains, however, a blocking character: Jill's uncle-guardian, whose permission must be secured if they are to marry anywhere except Sweden. So they hurry off to that land known for its relaxed standards. Meanwhile, they engage in what emerges as an earnest if awkward allegory for abstinence. The bizarre nature of their liaison — innocent *and* sexual, fraught with frustration for both, though they appear to adore this aspect — is transformed into a singing sequence. A farmer picks up the hitchhikers, they riding in the back of his truck with the animals. The two sing the childhood ditty "Old MacDonald's Farm," the words altered to make clear that they have fallen in love.

The little group stops in Antwerp where an elaborate sequence involves them in a street carnival. Everyone is in costume and mask, making it difficult to tell who is trying to apprehend them — the jewel thieves or agents paid by Jill's possessive uncle. In a bizarre turn, Guy forsakes Jill for a moment to sing and dance with an *actual* child — one of those little girls he so lovingly performs to in varied films while ignoring the willing nymphette — as Claire emerges from out of nowhere to (female) gaze on. The reject-mother scrutinizes the scene as the ever more confused hero turns away from his chosen child-bride-to-be even as she approaches legal age (and becomes threatening). At this point he seeks out a younger (thus, safer) female companion who will not in several days demand the sexual consummation Elvis always avoids.

While Guy "innocently" romances the child, Jill — a child on the verge of womanhood — finds herself abandoned and menaced. The American boy she met on the boat turns out to be a killer assigned to do her in. Jill's uncle has siphoned off Jill's inheritance for years; now that she's reached the age where she might actually claim the money, Gen. Waverly must arrange for her to meet with an "accident," deconstructing John Williams' stalwart screen image. Guy pulls himself away from the child he's performed for on a carousel (echoing *G.I. Blues*) and arrives on the scene to kill the assassin with a karate chop, martial arts now a trademark of the Presley persona as well as a fascination for Elvis in life.

In the final fade-out, he's relieved to know that the capitalist pressure (marrying a rich girl) has been relieved, since Jill's money is gone. On the other hand, he does appear concerned: He is soon to marry the child companion as she becomes a young woman — something he seems less than comfortable about than the previous "innocent" flirtation.

CHAPTER 16

The Cowboy Way

◆ *Stay Away, Joe* (1968) ◆
◆ *Charro!* (1969) ◆

One of the many major motion pictures Elvis had been considered for was *How the West Was Won* (1962), in which he would have played the role that eventually went to George Peppard: A man whose entire life is played against changing vistas of the nineteenth century frontier. For each era, a legendary star of Western films appears in an archetypal(less charitable observers said stereotypical) role: James Stewart as an early mountain man, John Wayne as a Civil War general, Henry Fonda as an Army scout in the far West. Such parts are essentially cameos; the male lead, the character Presley hoped to play, was the single figure who at various points in his life journey comes in contact with all those larger-than-life Westerners. In the final act, he emerges as the last and greatest frontier hero, a *fin-de-siecle* lawman who defeats a train robber (Eli Wallach) and his gang. Then the West finally is truly "won." Had Elvis played the part (whether he was passed over for then up-and-coming Peppard or convinced by the colonel to again turn down a non-singing role remains unclear), he would have lived out his greatest ambition: to become a cowboy star of the type he grew up admiring at the movies as a little boy, this typical of the entire generation he eventually came to represent.

In truth, though, even if Elvis had been in the movie, the sort of silver screen Westerner he admired and wanted to become was fast disappearing. If *How the West Was Won* rates as the biggest (if hardly the best) of the old-fashioned Hollywood blockbuster oaters (shot in the ultra-widescreen Cinerama process), it marked the end of an era by offering an apotheosis of timeworn formulas that had finally lost their luster. America entered the post–JFK world — the dream of a New Frontier which combined the best of modernity with warm

220

memories of the way we were shattered in the streets of Dallas by a gunman who forever altered the nation's (and the world's) notion of violence American style. And that the assassination occurred in the original cowboy state caused many of the president's supporters to at last question our long-standing six-gun society; "I wish that goddamn State of Texas had never been invented," Ted Sorensen exclaimed upon hearing what had happened.[1]

He spontaneously expressed an attitude that would take on greater weight as the decade wore on: The loss of JFK (and other assassinations yet to come) was not the result of one person or even a vast conspiracy. Rather, it represented the end-product of a pervasive national sensibility forged by our violent confrontation with the very frontier that, as Frederick Jackson Turner once argued, initially defined our American Character.[2] Now, like some evil spirit that cannot be left behind, our propensity toward violence haunted all our attempts to achieve a more sophisticated society. Writers like Norman Mailer suggested that our disastrous Vietnam experience represented a subconscious need on the part of Americans to play ("good") cowboys with ("bad") Indians in other parts of the world now that our own wild west had (supposedly) been "won."[3] As war in Southeast Asia, as well as escalating violence over Civil Rights in our own South, set ever more polarized angry Americans against one another, the patriotic tone and proud sensibility of old-fashioned Westerns seemed hopelessly out of date.

If the genre was to survive, it had to change with the times. The same year that *How the West Was Won* bid a fond farewell to now anachronistic styles, Sergio Leone shot *A Fistful of Dollars* in Italy. That film introduced a hard-bitten, serape-wrapped, cigar-smoking Western anti-hero (Clint Eastwood). Like Alan Ladd in the classic *Shane* (1953), this man with no name never commits himself to the right side in a good fight; realizing there is no right side and that the fight isn't good or bad (it simply *is*), he amorally manipulates both (equally corrupt) sides in a range war with the cool calculation of Toshiro Mifune's self-serving samurai in Akira Kurosawa's *Yojimbo* (1961), on which this (if not the first then certainly the first *significant*) spaghetti Western was based. With that film's success, a new international style in Westerns emerged, culminating in Sam Peckinpah's *The Wild Bunch* (1969). Its bloodthirsty outlaw gang, despite their wanton brutality, appear notably less horrific than the "decent" townspeople (including children) they come into contact with.

A reinvented Western called for a revised image of the Indian. Arthur Penn's *Little Big Man* (1970) transformed the once-lauded U.S. cavalry from films of a more sentimental era into neo–Nazis, led by a crazed Custer who in this version unleashes an American holocaust. The film's vivid depictions of the Seventh massacring Indians obliquely commented on our then-current

Vietnam activities, most obviously the incident at My-Lai. At such a point in time (and popular culture), Elvis needed to star in Western-themed vehicles that would reflect an altered American landscape. Unfortunately, both attempts were disappointments.

Cowboys Are Indians: *Stay Away, Joe* (1968)

A striking Arizona landscape appears as the initial shot of Peter Tewksbury's film, followed by a montage of traveling shots which suggest that what we are about to see might be on the order of a John Ford classic. This is augmented by the voice of Elvis singing a contemporary variation of the folk ballad "Greensleaves." Many earlier Westerns began with music that firmly placed the tale in a mythologized vision of American history; also, this continues the Elvis Cinema theme of collapsing folk and rock into modern pop. Four years earlier, the Ford Westerns had drawn to a close with *Cheyenne Autumn*, an epic footnote to the director's long career in which he had ennobled the U.S. Cavalry, Native Americans mostly cast as threatening antagonists. His final film shifted focus, dealing with the tragic plight of Indians newly placed on a reservation. In offering such a correction to his considerable canon, Ford provided the transition piece between "old" Westerns (which he didn't actually invent but certainly did perfect) and their "new" counterpart — films which, with varying degrees of success, ennobled the Native American: *A Man Called Horse* (1970), *Soldier Blue* (1970) and, most memorably, the aforementioned *Little Big Man* among them.

The opening here, in the neo–Western style, references earlier on-screen imagery only to undermine it. Elvis plays Joe Lightcloud, a cowboy who is three-quarters Navajo. His father Charley (Burgess Meredith) is a pureblood tribal member while Joe's mother Annie (Katy Jurado) is half–Navajo, half–Mexican. From this auspicious beginning, we might assume *Stay Away, Joe* will be a film of heightened consciousness, one that takes a serious approach to the sensitive issue of Native American issues, so effectively raised at the decade's beginning by *Flaming Star*. If that had been the case, the two films would exist as effective bookends to a key subgenre of Presley's career that deals with ethnicity in general, Indian rights specifically. If this had been the case, Elvis would have stood at the vanguard of popular culture for the first time since 1955.

Surprisingly, this contemporary Western (written by Michael A. Hoey) does precisely the opposite of that. While *Little Big Man* and films of its ilk attempted to destroy old clichés, in *Stay Away, Joe* every negative stereotype is included, particularly those that *Flaming Star* effectively helped diminish.

Elvis and company appear to have set out to imitate *Cat Ballou* (1965), a self-consciously cornball parody of old oaters that included numerous disparaging jokes about Indians, even the old chestnut about Native Americans being the lost tribe of Israel. That film had scored at the box office three years earlier, a humorous postscript to *How the West Was Won*. But as some sage once said, a joke is an epitaph on an emotion; the emotions (and ideas) of old Westerns all at once seemed dead or, at the very least, absurdly anachronistic. However popular in its time, *Cat Ballou* had already dated embarrassingly; mounting a belated redo added fuel to the fire of opinion that Elvis was now hopelessly out of touch with the vanguard.

From the outset, Charley, his father, grandfather (Thomas Gomez) and Charley's best friend Bronc (L.Q. Jones) embody the most offensive clichés about Indians. They are portrayed as lazy, shiftless, dishonest, dirty, alcoholic, brutal, dumb, ignorant, foolish, untrustworthy and as dangerous sexual predators. The element that reveals Elvis' self provides even more of a shock than the film's social sensibility. He countermands every value the Presley persona stood for in previous motion pictures, most notably *Flaming Star*. This shift is facilitated by the transition from the title sequence to the narrative proper. Reversing an audience's expectations, the segue sets us up for a film that will diminish Elvis' image. As a herd of cattle cross green and brown mesquite-laden ground, set against a soft pastel background of the purple hills, we are lured into believing that Elvis will at last live out his desire to be a B-Western movie star. A swish pan to the left, always a most disorienting camera movement,[4] makes clear this is not the case. A Cadillac convertible roars up, driven by Joe, so we must adjust to this being a *modern* Western.

Still, we can hope for the best. The 1960s had — as more traditional Westerns dealing with the early days had begun to fade from sight — offered up contemporary cowboy stories. Respectively, *Lonely Are the Brave* (1962) and *Hud* (1963) presented Kirk Douglas as the last of the optimistic oldtimers and Paul Newman as the first of a new breed of cynical Western men. Soon to follow were other ambitious films including Abe Polonsky's *Tell Them Willie Boy Is Here!* (1970), based on the real-life story of an Indian who jumps the reservation only to be tracked down and killed during the early twentieth century. That is not the case here. As the camera quickly cuts to a close-up of the lead, he appears an anomaly. In heavy reddish makeup, Elvis is obviously portraying an Indian. Yet he wears a cowboy hat and corresponding clothes; all the other Navajos in view, herding heifers toward the ramshackle Lightfoot home, are attired in Southwestern Indian garb.

Alone among them, Joe has mainstreamed himself, and clearly not in a positive way. He has plenty of money, all won by fleecing innocent Anglos — and other Indians. This might not constitute a problem if what we encountered was that early Presley paradigm in which his character comes to see the light and arcs from rugged individualism toward social commitment. But his smarmy protagonist doesn't reform, owing to the guidance of a good girl or for any other reason. Throughout, he remains as obnoxiously self-serving as at the opening. In the context, this reflects negatively on Native Americans. Worse, the film appears to applaud his superficiality. There is no hint here (as there had been in *Hud*) that the audience ought to reject this charming but morally reprehensible character. This might yet work if the film were intended for the era's anarchic youth. But they did not choose to attend Presley's movies, while his blue-collar fan base could hardly be expected to show up for a film that ran against the grain of all they believed, and all that he had come to signify for them.

One by one, sacred cows we have come to expect from diverse examples of the oeuvre are overturned. This occurs with the movie's approach toward postwar car culture. Elvis is immediately associated with the Cadillac convertible his once-marginalized anti-hero could only dream about at the beginning of a film like *Loving You*, likewise set in the modern Southwest. There, such a status symbol initially seemed an impossible dream to the poor, decent, honest boy who lived by a strict code if on the edge of mainstream society. When he did in time attain such a car — key symbol in that film and most movies to follow — he treated it with love and care. The car embodied his vision of the American Dream, eventual success through hard work that results in earned money; we saw in his loving appreciation of the vehicle a dramatization of Elvis' abiding respect for the country and its values. That concept was further developed in *Kid Galahad, Viva Las Vegas, Speedway* and *Spinout*, among others — foreign sports cars eventually replacing the all–American Cadillac as the object of his dreams while the created world existing within his films, reflecting the real world around them, became more internationalized.

Stay Away reverses that. Contrarily, Joe recklessly drives his car across the plains, endangering both the Native American cowboys and the animals, as well as the automobile which this blasé, corrupted character owns — without having in any way *earned* the car. The cowboy coda has honed to merit and work, most obviously embodied in Howard Hawks' seminal *Red River* when Tom Dunson (John Wayne), after making adopted son Matthew Garth (Montgomery Clift) wait 15 years to see his first initial added to their ranch's brand, finally does this — smiling with respect as he admits, "You *earned* it!" If this film offered to overturn that conventional morality — if it presented its amoral hero in a thoughtful rejection of traditional values — it might rate as a truly subversive alternative. But nothing that follows suggests such a point of view — or, for that matter, *any* point of view.

Charley lands the car in a creek, casually deserting it. He (dishonestly) picks up a flashier red convertible, then sets about destroying that vehicle too — a nonchalant attitude replacing the sincere love we earlier noted for that great American icon. If this suggested that Elvis had come to disparage the American consumerism which the Cadillac symbolizes in a film that dared announce a radical new agenda, such a reversal might be accepted as a heightening of his consciousness — a coming-out of the closet of commerciality he previously championed. This would indicate that he was now in touch with the values of the late–'60s youth culture, which did indeed assume such an attitude. But the tone and style of *Stay Away, Joe* fails to validate such a political reading.

In one sense alone, *Stay Away, Joe* might be read as a reflection of its times. Nineteen hundred and sixty-eight was a year that had begun hopefully (the war finally called into question following the Tet Offensive) yet ended in disaster, after Dr. King and Senator Kennedy, two rare adults who had offered a sense of hope, were assassinated. Numerous Americans, notably the affluent young and socially disenfranchised, gave up on peaceful forms of direct action (sit-ins, etc.) as their means of changing imperialism abroad and racial inequality at home. At a time when hope died and positive approaches seemed absurd, working to better things no longer appeared a valid approach to achieve a better world — such a dream, the essence of the early 1960s, now seeming naïve. The only logical reaction to an illogical zeitgeist was to turn nihilistic, leading to violence, apathy or cynicism, witnessed in the streets of Chicago during that summer's Democratic Convention.

The final possible choice — outright cynicism — forms this movie's essence. The storyline concerns the 20 cows we see in the opening. A con man at heart, Joe has approached a suited agent of the Establishment, Hy Sager (Henry Jones). Hy hopes to get an equally super-straight Anglo friend, now a Congressman, elected as the state's next governor. Both men are aware that a newly assembled government program (a result of Johnson's Great Society approach to legislate for a more equitable America toward long-deprived ethnic peoples) encourages the support of local political and professional endeavors on the part of Native residents. Both are eager to get started, less out of any sincere desire to do the right thing by helping impoverished Indians than owing to the strong PR they can get for the upcoming campaign by displaying themselves as champions of the underdogs. Aware of both the available funds and the politicos' desire to move quickly, Joe has talked them into providing a herd of cattle and a bull so his family can establish themselves as ranchers, disproving the theory that Indians are lazy and/or dishonest.

No sooner do they acquire the herd than Charlie fails to take care of the animals on his property — a rural slum that blights the otherwise beautiful land — while Joe sells the heifers to make fast money which could land him and his family in prison for illegal sale of government property. In earlier films, notably *Follow That Dream*, the Presley persona incarnated the seeming white trash man on the move who wants to become an honest worker, willing to perform hard labor to achieve the American Dream. In *Stay Away*, the suits who again surround him may be bad as ever but Elvis' alter ego proves worse still. This might have resulted in a revolutionary statement, he no longer the rebel who claws his way into the mainstream but a true anti-hero with no respect for the Establishment. To legitimize such a view (that is, the Woodstock-era attitude), a simultaneous rejection of any and all ethnic stereotyping, in particular any disparaging portrait of Native Americans, was required. The Navajo we see are odious, getting drunk and fighting one another at the slightest provocation, unwilling to work unless it proves unavoidable. Every time there is a celebration, it degenerates into an alcoholic brawl.

During such moments, tribal members appear more stupid and ignorant than when they are sober. At one late-night event, Joe realizes there is nothing to eat and instructs Bronc to kill a heifer, then roast it. In the morning, all realize that Bronc slaughtered their bull, leaving them with no way to enlarge the ranch, reneging on their promise. Joe views this as one more problem to be solved in the most dishonest way possible; he earns money to pay for another bull in trickster fashion. But if he were intended as an American Loki, the mythological mischief maker, such an interesting idea is cancelled out by the Presley persona. Elvis' star image was too rock-solid by this point in time to allow him the maneuverability to play a puckish figure.

This incident does lead to the most interesting plot element. When Joe arrives with a new bull, everyone cheers. The camera frames them closely, suggesting a relationship between man and beast. *Stay Away, Joe* offers yet another variation on an old theme via a vivid new symbol: The stud, it turns out, is anything but what he appears. Though a striking physical example of the male, this bull refuses to approach the females, at least when expected to impregnate them. The stud bull, like the stud star playing Joe, is all sizzle, no fire — precisely what the Elvis hero turned out to be from the earliest films and, as many of those women who were his bedmates claim, what Presley was in life. At one point, Joe faces off with the bull, trying to reason with the beast, encourage him to transform his appearance of total masculinity into a viable reality. The bull stares at him; as Elvis stares back, he seems to be looking into a mirror, encountering a perfect reflection of his own self.

Augmenting this is the sequence in which Joe sneaks off into the wilds with not one but two Native American women, supposedly for sexual activity. Again he encounters "double trouble." Like Elvis' alter ego in *Kissin' Cousins*, Joe discovers that it's impossible to embrace both women at the same time. Yet he arranged this situation rather than slipping away with either of the appealing females. Purposefully if unconsciously, he created the sexual frustration he then suffers. This allows him to be sexy without sexual, appearing to prove his masculinity. He only offers an exaggerated performance of the lover-boy for everyone while providing himself with a seemingly valid excuse to *not* act. Instead of a double dose of sex, he ends the day without consummating either relationship — and, as so often has been the case, he appears relieved rather than disappointed, singing not as a prelude to but as a substitute for sex.

Even here, though, *Stay Away* features a reversal of the moral value system so basic to Presley's film work. Those two women are the girlfriends of members of Joe's tribe, men who have always trusted him, treating him as a brother. Joe is entirely aware of their deep feelings for the women while frolicking with them, however innocent (in deed if not in desire) that pastoral interlude (now corrupt rather than the innocent sojourn of early films) turns out to be. Early Elvis would never violate a bond of friendship for a woman, even a female he happened to be in love with. More than one previous Presley persona anguished over such a situation. Here, there is no anguish, only crass behavior as he grinningly puts his hands on women he has no true interest in, despite strong, sincere feelings for them on the part of the fellows these women are engaged to. Such a violation — of his own marginalized people, not members of the mainstream — reverses everything most admirable about his own earlier traditionalism.

Everything Elvis once stood for dissolves before the viewer's eyes — not that there were large audiences for this film. His casual deconstruction of previous attitudes toward women does not end there. If there were two basic rules as to his approach to females, they were his refusal to date a married woman under any circumstances (a distaste for sex with any woman who had given birth most prevalent, paralleling Elvis in real life)[5] and refusal to ever consummate relations (even after flirting) with underage virgins — even when they approached him, Lolita-like. In *Double Trouble*, which commented on his relationship with Priscilla, Elvis — though engaged to an underage virgin — refused (despite her pleas) to consummate the bond until she reached legal age and they were married, providing the "sacred" aspect he always dreamed of. Here, though, an outright violation of this personal coda occurs when Joe visits the isolated Callahan desert store.

First, he encounters Glenda (Joan Blondell), an older woman who brings to the film the Oedipal theme Elvis had seemingly distanced himself from long ago. Before Joe left the area, he and Glenda were involved, and not merely on an emotional level. As they engage in conversation, we gather they were sleeping together — which they appear ready to do once again. Once, such potential proved provocative owing to the beauty of the slightly older women

(Lizabeth Scott, Carolyn Jones, Hope Lange); here it appears repulsive for most viewers as the beat-up, blowsy Blondell looks old enough to be Elvis' *grand-mother*. Though such a theme can lead to a wonderfully offbeat romance, as in Hal Ashby's *Harold and Maude* (1972), that occurs when such a situation is presented with a winning mixture of warmth and irony, definitely *not* the case here.

Any possible continuation of the relationship halts the moment Joe gets a look (male gaze) at Gloria's daughter Mamie (Quentin Dean, who had embodied the Southern white trash nymphette the previous year in Norman Jewison's *In the Heat of the Night*). While Gloria is out of the room, Mamie displays herself to Joe in an abbreviated mini-skirt, evoking Sue "Lolita" Lyon enticing James Mason in a bikini — she in that film also the daughter of a blowsy mother (Shelley Winters, Blondell appearing to be a Southwestern equivalent of that character). Reversing himself on this (as on every other issue), Elvis now tries to bed the very underage girl (this one younger than any previous one while he is now notably older). The old Elvis — or at least his popular image — has truly reached the end of the trail.

End of the Trail: *Charro!* (1969)

Charro! has been written off as a late, lame entry in the spaghetti Western genre featuring Elvis as a grizzled, serape-draped figure grimly riding across a ghostly range. In part, this misconception owes to its musical score, composed and conducted by Hugo Montenegro. A few years earlier, he had adapted Ennio Morricone's main theme from *The Good, the Bad, and the Ugly* (1966) for a popular record release in the U.S. Correctly understood, *Charro!* actually rates as a throwback to the American films that inspired Sergio Leone and dozens of lesser artisans who labored in the spaghetti Western genre during the 1960s — that is, the films Elvis had watched at local theaters while a teenager during the '50s, dreaming about starring in one someday. These were the B Westerns that set the pace for all those low-budget, high-intensity action items reconceived (and in some cases, particularly with Leone, sharply caricatured) by Italian and Spanish directors.

Charles Marquis Warren more or less defined the earlier genre, working steadily at Republic throughout the 1940s where he produced, wrote and directed B Westerns until the studio finally closed its doors in the late '50s. Then Warren turned to television, where the form had gone to briefly flourish, then ignominiously die. Warren labored in such series as *Gunsmoke* and *Rawhide*. *Charro!* was written, produced and directed by him and shot in Hollywood, on standing Western sets, as well as on locations in Arizona. Warren purposefully populated the film with numerous character actors who had appeared in now bygone Western shows, some of which he had been associated with: Tony Young (*Gunslinger*), John Pickard (*Boots and Saddles*), Paul Brinegar (*Rawhide*) and Charles H. Gray (*Gunsmoke*).

Elvis' character is called Jesse Wade, apparently a combination of two legendary Western outlaws, both of whom had been the subjects of numerous old movies: Jesse James and Jake Wade. Hardly the spaghetti Western it's invariably described as, *Charro!* is (arguably) the last old-fashioned minor-studio-style B-Western to be lensed in the U.S. Actor and auteur pursued the old-fashioned project with a dogged seriousness. The narrative is as formulaic as one might expect. Jesse, referred to as "Charro" by the Mexicans whom he befriends, finds himself cornered in a bar in a small border town. He is taken prisoner by a band of outlaws he once rode with. They are led by Vince (Victor French), a surly bully with reason to resent Jesse, who took away Vince's girl, Tracey Winters (Ina Balin) — only to himself lose her when Jesse failed to go straight, which Tracey insisted on.

To get even, Vince sets up Jesse for a crime he and his followers committed: the theft of a national treasure of Mexico, the golden cannon which fired the final shot in the war for freedom against Maximilian. Vince has sent a series of false wanted posters around the Southwest that implicate a man with a scarred neck as the culprit. To make everyone — particularly lawmen and bounty hunters — believe Jesse is their man, Vince and his gang members hold Vince down and brand him with an iron. Then they allow Jesse to wander away. In time, he stumbles into the very town where Tracey owns a high-style saloon, replete with can-can girls (including a blonde played by Lynn Kellogg, a modestly popular folk singer who received her greatest exposure on CBS's *The Glen Campbell Show*).

However negligible *Charro!* may be as a program Western of the type still circulating on the drive-in circuit (such oaters shortly to be replaced by the new sexploitation flicks and karate films imported from Asia), the film does serve as an effective if entirely unconscious allegory for Elvis' career. Like Jesse, the man playing him is a good ol' Southern boy mistakenly perceived as an outlaw in his youth. Actually, he did little to earn such a reputation, and is always well-mannered. Leading townsmen in Rio Seco (where the story unfolds), self-proclaimed "decent" folk in suits and ties, quickly if wrongly assume that this lumbering hillbilly represents a clear and present danger to their way of life. Jesse is defended by Sheriff Ramsey (James Almanzar), he sensing the youth's goodness; similarly, various adult leaders of the 1950s entertainment business (i.e., Ed Sullivan following his "conversion") made others of their ilk see that their initial response to Elvis had been incorrect.

In the film, when Ramsey is incapacitated, he hands his gun and star over to Jesse, insisting that the misunderstood youth take charge of ending the current crime wave by Vince's young henchmen, including the younger Hackett brother, long-haired Billy Roy (Solomon Sturges). Not long after *Charro!* was released (March 3, 1968), Elvis met at the White House with President Nixon (December 21, 1970), who had 15 years earlier damned him. During this meeting, the singer-actor asked the leader of the American Establishment for a badge so that he might "clean up" the dangerous, drug-addicted, long-hair youth then menacing the streets.[6] In real life, Presley did indeed receive the badge; the film can then, despite its grim tone and grimy settings, be interpreted as a roughhewn allegory of actuality.

He proves to be the town's saviour, a Jesus in blue jeans. And a right-wing one at that: Jesse arms previously non-violent townsmen. As owners of a general store, a bank, a livery stable and a hotel, they form a microcosm for America, then (1868) and/or now (1968). As to Elvis' own political agenda, long-time friend David Stanley wrote:

> He was a true conservative who loved his country. He didn't care too much for the Jane Fondas, the Angela Davises and the John Lennon types. He was wholeheartedly concerned about the influence these kinds of people had....[7]

For those who insist on perceiving Presley, at least in his earlier stages, as a liberal crusader for revolutionary causes, such a statement shocks and angers. It is, of course, correct. Those disappointed in his position might rationalize the situation by insisting that Elvis changed over the years, when in fact he did not — the reactionary bent was there from the beginning.

Rock — hailed as the most revolutionary musical style ever known to mankind — can, like Elvis Presley, the man who first popularized it, offer a reactionary view: calling for a return to the basic pulse of our American spirit. If rock does indeed rage against "the machine," it is just as likely to be the liberal Democratic machine, not the rugged individualism that is much at the heart of rock, from Elvis to Neil Young (a Reagan supporter, as Elvis likely would have been had he lived long enough to see him run for president) and beyond, as it is to the Republican party. Reagan on the campaign trail, posing in a Stetson in front of the Alamo, would claim the cowboy motif in 1980; Elvis embodies the attitude of the Western as much as he does rock. In truth they are one and the same, legitimizing that largely forgotten but highly accurate name for "the new music" that evolved during the mid–'50s: cowboy bebop.

CHAPTER 17

The Last Temptation(s) of Elvis

◆ *Clambake* (1967) ◆
◆ *Live a Little, Love a Little* (1968) ◆

In the watershed period of 1957 and 1958, the conservative attack on Jack Kerouac and the Beats, as well as Presley and other early rockers, focused on what their fans found most appealing: an "emotional intensity" and "primitive" dislike of civilization, as well as their enshrinement of "spontaneity"[1]—everything then missing from mainstream society. Yet in the equally impactful transitional decade of the '60s, Jack and Elvis had nothing but negative comments for those hippies who, at first glance, simply took what they preached to the next level. However paradoxical a turnabout that seems, some had predicted it. As early as 1956 (that remarkable moment when *On the Road* broke all the rules of polite literature and "Heartbreak Hotel" did the same for popular music), John Sharnik suggested that in two decades, Elvis would likely become a "middle-aged statesman" who "speaks for his generation [and] against whatever new musical menace has arisen among its baffling young."[2] Indeed, Presley did just that.

The initial desire of a vocal minority of youth to "teach the world to sing" a different tune began during the early 1960s, when a small, truly radical group of college students that included Tom Hayden composed "The Port Huron Statement" on a Michigan campus. Thereafter, a protest broke out at California's Berkeley, California, campus over student rights to free speech, Mario Savio a key spokesman for the organizers. Things did not (and might not have) reached a wider, broader level were it not for our involvement in Southeast Asia. Our postwar commitment to contain Communism — the "domino theory" holding that if one country fell, so would they all — had initially remained subdued. In 1964, Lyndon Johnson won re-election over

Republican nominee Barry Goldwater in large part by insisting that "American boys will not die doing the job Vietnam boys should be doing." Within months of the swearing-in ceremony (January 1965), he — pressured when North Vietnam threatened to invade South Vietnam — escalated the war. In response, draft boards pulled students out of college and ghetto youth off the streets. By mid–1967, 17,000 Americans were dead in Vietnam, Congress had just approved an additional $70 billion for the increased effort, 230,000 men were called up for the draft — and the Peace Movement caught fire.

Many members of the nation's youth had no desire to die in an undeclared (and perhaps illegal) war. Vietnam provided "the engine of the '60s," as Terry Anderson noted, for without a unifying event, "the decade would have remained a liberal reform era, not a radical decade, not 'the '60s.'"[3] The greatest bone of contention, then, for Presley had less to do with young people now openly surrendering to the hedonism he had championed than the *political* implications. Elvis had taken great pride in serving in the military when called upon, though that had not been too difficult at a time when the country was at peace; the next generation of young people (or more correctly a highly vocal minority among them) loudly decried not only our governmental policy but the military (even the common G.I., often greeted with derision upon return home), an untenable idea to Presley.

More significant still is that Elvis (again like Kerouac) had been a Beat hero incarnate — "the self-propelled, competitive *individualist*" (emphasis mine).[4] That concept had more to do with Republican thinking than Democratic values, which (at least since FDR and the New Deal) emphasized the communal aspect of our American way of life. Relatively recently, JFK had requested in his inaugural address: "Ask not what your country can do for you but what you can do for your country," a *we* rather than *me* approach. Such a sense of community is precisely what the Beats opposed; "The [despised] organization man [spends] his existence not as an individual but as a member of a *group*" (emphasis mine).[5] While hippies are portrayed as an outgrowth of the Beats, their values were antithetical; the counter-culture constituted a "melange of communal bonding and 'do your own thing' individualism."[6] If this indeed truly was individualism at all (most often, hippies did things *together* and more correctly could have claimed to "do *our* own thing"), it wasn't an individualism that made sense to an aging Elvis. He had more in common with an intellect of his era, C. Wright Mills, who insisted: "I have never known what others call 'fraternity' with any group ... academic nor political."[7] Here was the issue that defined virtually everything, forcing people to cross a political line in the sand.

The Prince and the Pauper: *Clambake* (1967)

The film opens with a cross-reference to *Spinout*: A red sports car roars along an Interstate highway down the Eastern coast. As the film cuts to a close-up on Elvis — alone rather than part of any group — we spot a significant departure: He's wearing a large, clean (right off the rack) cowboy hat and dude-style rhinestone Western clothing. This is the kind of costume the gritty *real* cowboy rejected in *Loving You* ten years earlier; also, the image provides a sharp contrast to "authentic" cowboy garb worn by the star in both *Stay Away, Joe* and *Charro!* Faux Western duds signify a confession: Presley has become the very thing he once hated. Not that he's completely lost touch with the common folk; though rich, he waves while passing humble people in a warm way. Like Elvis himself, Scott Heywood is rich, if wishing perhaps he still lived a simpler life. Shortly, the King will become a commoner once more.

As an oldtimer fills Scott's gas tank Elvis' onscreen alter ego grabs a sandwich and chances to meet his on-screen character's alter ego: Tom Wilson (Will Hutchins, one-time star of ABC's *Sugarfoot,* in which his character was also named Tom), an itinerant cowboy of the type Elvis once played. Tom has accepted the job of water ski instructor at a Miami resort. Frustrated that he can't pick up the cute waitress because she resents his motorcycle (a vehicle previously associated with Elvis in *Roustabout*), Tom would like to be Scott as much as Scott wishes he could be Tom. That waitress throws herself at Scott less owing to appeal (Tom is also boyishly handsome and might have been played by Presley, a concept that would have heightened the ongoing doubling theme) than his car and fancy clothes. Tom comments that Scott has it made. He's surprised to learn that Scott flees an unhappy life.

Reviving the marriage theme, Scott is a runaway bridegroom, rejecting a loveless wedding. He deserted his fiancée at the altar after realizing she wanted to wed into the family fortune of Scott's oil magnate father, Duster Heywood (James Gregory); Duster wanted Scott to take a corporate job. A first generation millionaire, Duster made it on his own; Scott resents the idea of living off cowboy capitalism not of his own making, a theme introduced in *Blue Hawaii.* "There's more to it than that, Dad," Scott explains via phone to the Texas compound. "I want to be able to do something *on my own.*" If his statement seems apolitical, we ought to recall that "some blame the tumult and violence of the decade on the 'spoiled' children of middle-class affluence."[8] That "some" included Elvis Presley.

Clambake offers a complex variation on the already entrenched themes of rugged individualism and acceptance of one's identity. As Scott and Tom continue on to Miami's Shore Hotel, Scott sings about the greatest things in life being free and asking who needs money, claiming he does not.

In earlier films, Elvis (despite show business success) could yet embody the poor boy, traveling by his wits, living off the land. That early image is here deconstructed. Scott represents an Elvis who can no longer convince us (or himself) that he's anything but a superstar. Still, *playing* at being a poor boy is what he has done for a considerable time off-screen and now on- as well. The scene cuts to his new friend, who warbles an alternative that it only takes a million or two and he does need the money. Tom (a reference to Col. Parker?) is the person Presley might have become had he not achieved his dream.

Assumptive behavior is in evidence from the moment the two arrive — simultaneously if hardly together — at the Shores. Tom (now calling himself Scott, adding to the role-playing motif) is ushered inside with great fanfare. Scott (identifying himself as Tom) is rudely told to move his cycle away from the entranceway and head for the servants' quarters. At that moment the female lead is introduced: Dianne Carter (Shelley Fabares), who initially appears to be another wealthy young woman. In keeping with the theme, Fabares plays the role of a person who is playing a role. Dianne is a poor girl who sets her sights on marrying a rich man (*any* rich man) to move "up." Her calculated tactic was to save enough money to stay at such a hotel, coldly target a likely prospect, then wed him before he learns the truth about her lowly status: marriage as a game.

Like many other girls on the scene, Dianne has her sights set on James Jameson III (Bill Bixby), wealthy playboy and yet another alter ego for Elvis (how fascinating it would have been had he played all three roles!). If James represents one extreme pole of the Presley persona (the early 1960s Playboy), Tom the other (marginalized cowboy-drifter), Scott is actual Elvis at this time: rejecting his most recent incarnation, trying to reach back to an earlier, preferable version of himself, trapped by the extremes. James has arrived for the upcoming boat race, which he plans to win with his state-of-the-art craft, the *Scarlet Lady*— as red in color as the sports car driven first by Scott/'Tom' and later Tom/'Scott'— rather than green, the color of money.

The story structure and relationships contained therein (if not the dialogue) prove as intricate as those in a French bedroom farce, as attractive young people attempt to win what they want in life (or have been taught to believe they want) by pretending to be something other than what they are. Jameson opts to take a tall blonde (Angelique Pettyjohn) for a boat ride rather than demure brunette Dianne. Here is the "blondes have more fun!" mentality, endlessly reinforced by TV Clairol commercials. ("We learn by imitation," Wordsworth wrote two centuries ago, the Romantic poet condemning civilization and its corruption of decent individuals.) By virtue of sticking with her own hair color, Dianne remains a natural woman, despite the corrupt ambitions she's picked up from a society in which she is immersed. Jameson's source of income adds to the film's topicality: He became rich marketing "jamies," pre–Victoria's Secret lingerie that become popular with the newly "liberated" (in the sexual sense) women who wanted to market themselves to men as Playmates of the Month, hoping to eventually become companions for life — at least until the costly divorce.

The relationship between the two leads reflects the manner in which role-playing to win a societal goal thwarts any spontaneous discovery of true love. Dianne enlists the apparently penniless Presley to give her water-skiing instructions (though she's an expert) and to catch Jameson's eye — bringing up "the gaze." During the second such session, Dianne's bikini top falls off, yet another reference to *Blue Hawaii*. The arc that Dianne follows suggests the canon's retro ideology. Following the Sexual Revolution, the essentially nice but poor girl must "unlearn" all the early–1960s false values. In a traditional romantic roundelay, Dianne pursues Jameson as Scott pursues her. Apparently, he sees something special in Dianne, despite her hoping to do to Jameson precisely what that girl back in Texas tried to do to Scott.

The obvious irony is that Scott is actually wealthier than Jameson. Though attracted to Scott, Dianne immediately assumes he must have taken the ski instructor job to latch onto a rich woman, and decides that they ought to conspire to aid one another in achieving their dubious ends. They become friends, Dianne even joking that once she lands Jameson, she'll check as to whether he has a rich sister for Scott. This conversation takes place at night, after Jameson rejects Dianne in favor of *another* showy blonde; though the young woman is not nearly so beautiful as Dianne, she remains a brunette — and blondes rate as trophy dates. Then Tom shows up with a pair of interchangeable bimbos. Scott asks Dianne out; though disappointed about not connecting with the wealthy man she targeted, Dianne heads off into the night with the "poor boy" she cares about — though considers off-limits for romance.

They ride on "his" motorcycle, associated with the ruggedly individualistic hero ever since *The Wild One*. A pastoral interlude follows: They stop and build a fire at a secluded spot, away from the corrupting influences of civilization. Other than the tropical foliage, this recalls diverse previous symbols of the romantic spirit. The sequence — one of the two times in *Clambake* when we are removed from the glitzy hotel — allows Dianne to reveal her true colors. In nature, she can comfortably be a natural woman:

SCOTT: Why go out with me?
DIANNE: I ... kind of *like* you.

Elvis sings his next number, a projection of what Dianne's life will be like if she continues to follow the route she's taken. She'll live like a queen in a castle and have everything except love. Dianne's facial reactions make clear that he's expressed her own worst fears as to what could soon transpire; this is her turning point.

The search for a proper father figure is revived. Sam Burton (Gary Merrill), though a millionaire, is an enlightened one, able to enjoy the freedom money buys rather than allow money to smother him — the case with Duster, who views money as power. Heightening the parallel, we learn that Duster and Burton once were in business together, though their polar views ruined that. In a previous boat race, which Burton hoped to win, his craft fell apart owing to the lack of a strong coating. He and Scott discuss a deal in which Scott will repair the boat and pilot it, equally sharing the proceeds should they win. This is the kind of deal Scott would have loved to engage in with his biological father; Sam — whose regret in life is not having fathered a son — relishes the experiment, which Duster fails to appreciate. Dramatized here is the call in the '50s and '60s for the male to be more sensitive. The problem for traditional men: "Who [was] resocializing them with the skills needed to realize such relationships — skills in openness to feelings and fantasy, skills in self-disclosure and emotional sharing?"[9] Elvis provides that necessary conduit.

The "primal sympathy" theme reoccurs. Scott discovers a teary-eyed little girl afraid to ride down the slide with other kids. His "Confidence" song allows Scott to slip away from the adult world, crawling all over the monkey bars and other set-ups which children enjoy, proving he's that rare adult who has not lost the innocent sense of play. Other children join in (the girl finds courage under his guidance), playing Indians. Priscilla noted, "Elvis created his own world; only in his own environment did he feel secure, comfortable, and protected."[10] Elvis' happy effect extends to adults as well. The ice cream salesman deserts his post, joining in the fun. The child-man incarnate and (despite his father's money) Rousseau's "natural man," Scott brings out the long-repressed ability to think and act freely in other, more conventional types. He revives in each a remaining spot of childlike wonderment which Wordsworth claimed "having once been, must ever be." An ordinary playground becomes Neverland — Elvis dancing about with underage children in what, long before Michael Jackson, may or may not be so much "innocent fun."

A deconstruction device forces us into an awareness of the project's self-consciousness. Director Arthur Nadel and editor Tom Rolf cut to the famous pursuit of the title object by Apaches from John Ford's semiotic western *Stagecoach* (1939). We are reminded that when people play "cowboys and Indians," their knowledge of "the West" does not derive from reality but movie mythology, the film we currently watch a part of that ongoing tradition as well as an exposé of it. Elvis (first glimpsed here in a cowboy hat) like his loyalists had not turned his back on retro-macho, the ability of a "real man" to win out through the triumph of his will, best embodied by the man who became a star via *Stagecoach*, John Wayne.

Here, Scott will achieve his individualistic American dream by using his *imagination*, the quality that attracted Carl Betz's paternal figure in *Spinout*. Also, his knowledge allows Scott to solve the problem with Sam Burton's boat. Scott is educated, the script making clear he's been to college. This no longer poses a problem for Elvis' target audience, owing to the advent of community colleges during the Great Society: "A college education for all one's children was like a barbecue or a new Chrysler, just another suburban status symbol"[11] at a time when more of the original Elvis fan base found they could now afford the Levittown-like areas from which they had once been excluded.

The key combination of intelligence and imagination is how Scott plans now to win Dianne. The two pursuits — win the race and win the woman — become interlocked. The title clambake serves as a midpoint; each major character has halfway completed his or her necessary transition. Dianne has finally attracted Jameson; now that he's in the realm of possibility, she has second thoughts. Tom has won the company of a comely blonde, Sally (Suzy Kaye), though can't enjoy the affair because he would like to believe she has feelings for him. Elvis, now posited as perfect, does not need to arc, only complete what Joseph Campbell describes as the hero's journey.[12] He performs the title tune; partygoers frolic on a beach that recalls the secluded Green World where Scott earlier took Dianne to escape society and the limiting codes it imposes, the Shore Hotel barely visible in the background. They occupy an acceptable middle-ground between the polar natural and civilized worlds, where each hopes to find a happy compromise that will turn inner dreams to outer reality. As everyone interacts, Elvis picks up on his status at the end of *Spinout*— a demi-god who crystallizes others' relationships without fully partaking in them, slipping in and out of the dancing.

Everyone seems interested in sex except him, though he is the sexiest man on view. For some, this creates "a confusion between the very mortal and corporeal Elvis and the risen savior of Christianity"[13] he was well on the way to signifying. But why should this be a problem? If Jesus was, according to Christian doctrine, 100 percent human and 100 percent spirit, why would Elvis' obvious corporeality interfere with his also being a spiritual-religious figure? At this time, Elvis refused to make love to Priscilla: "Any sexual temptations were against everything he was striving for"[14]— that being a transcendent state. He (Kid Galahad, the *Christian* knight) entered into the fundamentalist's equivalent of a Catholic concept, "passion"— surrender to spirituality equaling in impact (and as Elvis' gyrations attest to, also resembling in appearance) the converse surrender to sensuality.

Dianne becomes aware that she and Jameson are mismatched. Her desire to marry a millionaire is confounded, now that they date, by his living the tired *Playboy* philosophy Elvis once embodied: To conquer without committing. "He's romantic, all right," Dianne sighs to her confidant. "His propositions just don't involve *marriage*." In a sequence that draws on conventions of Edwardian romance, Scott leans forward and undoes Dianne's carefully coiffed hair, allowing it to fall down — natural now — on her shoulders. This sort of liberating action can be considered patriarchal: "freeing" her from one male to enslave her for himself. Like Lawrence's Mellors psychologically drawing Constance Chatterley away from wealth and position by physically escorting her into the woods, he represents the unspoiled natural force who "saves" a sophisticated (in the worst sense) lady from false societal values by returning her to a natural state that he then completely controls.

Scott knows Dianne plans to visit Jameson in his penthouse suite where she'll likely give in to his seduction. Scott serves as (her name evoking the goddess myth) Dianne's conscience, the moral force that wants to keep her chaste; he is more realistic than idealistic, since he wants to do so for his own benefit — to, like Elvis with Priscilla, isolate her in his mansion, if in Texas rather than Tennessee. Actress Fabares — second only to Ann-Margret as Elvis' favorite co-star, the only woman he chose to play opposite him three times — here appears a double for Elvis' then-wife. "Elvis would become as obsessed with Priscilla as he had once been with his mother"[15] — the two long since fused in his peculiarly unique vision of the world. If Presley was attracted to Priscilla as she reminded him of his first co-star Debra Paget (who had rejected him off-screen and on), only younger (able to be molded), later leading ladies are chosen for resemblance to Priscilla ... as art imitates life imitates art imitates....

Throughout the Elvis oeuvre, his characters are victims of identity crisis, reflecting the performer who played them. Alone, he sings the old standard "You don't know me...." The scene takes on deeper resonance, reflecting the greater reality of Elvis' self as opposed to a world that has passed him by. Next, the film introduces a cliché situation only to undermine it, seeming to redo the similar *Viva Las Vegas* sequence. Jameson does corner Dianne with champagne to "put her in the mood." Rather than a one-night stand, however, he offers precisely what she's been wishing for, an engagement ring. With this reversal of expectation, the conflict we witness is no longer the simplistic (and expected) one (between the supposedly poor boy who wants to share his life with her and the rich man who only wants to use her) but between two men who sense her essential worth as a person. That altered situation is significant in terms of our point of view on Dianne's character and our perspective on her inevitable union with Elvis.

This occurs after a series of happy couplings: Tom realizes that Suzy likes him enough to remain with him even if he's poor, while Duster becomes close friends with Sam. And, of course, Elvis defeats Jameson in the Orange Bowl race, a situation which can be viewed as the stereotypical happy ending or a necessary adherence to essential rules of the heroic pattern that date back to ancient codas. Presley's persona has long since taken on mythic dimension, not only for his déclassé audience but in the eyes of some of the era's leading artists. Tennessee Williams had hoped to have Elvis appear as a modernization of an ancient poet-hero in his Broadway play *Orpheus Descending* (1959) and in Sidney Lumet's film version, *The Fugitive Kind* (1960), though the colonel said no.[16]

In the climax, the two "fathers," business associates at last, enjoy the race side by side, Sam with his genteel pipe and Duster with his vulgar cigar; the house of Laius is reaffirmed. A denouement must also occur in the romantic plot. Elvis arrives in the red sports car (which he supposedly borrowed from his "rich" friend) to drive Dianne to the airport. Her arc was completed when she turned down Jameson's invitation to marriage. Dianne emerges as the "new" woman (actually marking a return to old moral values) who will not for money's sake give herself in marriage to someone she knows to be the wrong man. Only then, after admitting she loves (and will marry) "poor" Scott, her best friend and soulmate, can Elvis reveal his true identity. Her "reward" is getting the best of both worlds, money and marriage reconciled within the context of enlightened capitalism.

Tune In/Turn On/Drop Out: *Live a Little, Love a Little* (1968)

In the opening sequence, Greg Nolan speeds his dune buggy across crowded L.A. thoroughfares, Elvis here acting like drag-racing wiseguys of 1950s films: Corey Allen in *Rebel Without a Cause*, John Ashley in *Hot Rod Gang* (1958), himself in *Loving You*'s opening sequence. This re-establishes him as a '50s figure — the rebel of yesteryear now appearing out of place compared to the notably different 1960s youth on the streets:

> Suddenly, everything was popping: empires, ideologies, arts, ghettoes, population, platitudes. Cold wars got hot, kids became cool, and God was said to be dead. Suddenly, a counter-culture, shouting its barbaric yawp from the rooftops of Academia, was turning periods into question marks.[17]

Reclaiming something of his original self, Elvis again sports redneck-style sideburns; incidental people he passes by are the era's long-hairs. The star rejects his many attempts during the '60s to keep up with a changing America that remained one step ahead of him, settling into his final role as a reactionary icon.

Still, there remains in his opening image at least a hint of the '60s Elvis who attempted to "stay in tune": a pseudo-trendy leisure-style suit, as well as "Wonderful World," the song he sings. There's a hippie-era quality to the tune, which transforms into Woodstock's unique form of pantheism when he sings that we can find heaven on earth, as it is in everything around us.

A sense of religiosity pervades, preparing us for the Christ-like image now emerging, though hints of this have been present since the first film's final image of Elvis. Rock historians have noted that "pop icons still embody heroic models for human behavior and represent a striving for transcendence from the everyday world."[18] At a time when many people felt estranged from traditional religion, if still deeply in need of the sense of ongoing meaning religion had previously added to their lives,

> [t]he folk religion of Elvis Presley speaks to something so deep and widespread in the psyche that orthodox religious leaders who ignore it are failing to see how religion works on a gut level.[19]

Ironically, all early religious writing about Elvis questioned whether or not he had been sent by the Devil to corrupt mankind.[20] Toward the end of his career, and particularly after his death, Presley came to be seen as a positive alternative to conventional religion, then inseparable from old-time faiths.

For the time being, it's a beach he's headed to. Greg is a professional photographer planning to capture the late afternoon on film, an artist of the beautiful who wants to immortalize for all time an ephemeral moment. Greg's life changes when Bernice (Michele Carey), a crazy-beautiful-rich hippie princess lounging on the deck of her beach house, spots him through the telescope (the *female* gaze). Bernice sends her Great Dane Albert to keep this attractive man on the premises: "Don't let him get away!"

Identity is again a theme. Bernice constantly changes her name, depending on her mood at the moment. "Today, I feel like Alice," the kooky woman announces to Greg. All but imprisoned by the huge dog, Greg awkwardly makes room on his beach towel for her to join him. Without hesitation, she speaks the words of a flower child to an unknown male she finds attractive: "Would you make love to me?" Bernice is a Jill from *Double Trouble* taken a giant step further, making the middle-aged man, so daring in his own time, feel intimidated by her incarnation of the "free love" dictum he initially preached. Here is a female who dares to do what Elvis did with females in earlier films — sex first, relationship later.

Bernice manages to get Greg up to her house only by having her huge dog force him into the surf, keeping Greg there until he becomes ill and almost dies. She nurses him back to consciousness while keeping him prisoner, Circe to his Odysseus, the mythic element again strong. Her bewitchment includes drugging him (Greg experiences visions like these inspired by LSD) while captive. She does not impose herself on him sexually, diverting this energy to an almost endless string of men who appear at her door. Each addresses Bernice by a different name; each is distinct from the next, including a younger, long-haired delivery boy (Eddie Hodges), an older milkman (Sterling Holloway), even her estranged husband Harry (Dick Sargent). "I just love watching men in the morning," Bernice coos when Greg finally rises to shave.

Greg later heads for his job at an L.A. newspaper. No sooner has he arrived and tracked down the editor to the immense room where presses print the paper than the two are involved in an argument about Greg's disappearance. Borrowing a technique from other late–'60s films, director Norman Taurog allows the din of the machinery to drown out their words. Such an approach may seem conventional (or clichéd) today; appearing here, it furthers the notion of a figure from the past trapped in a re-adjusted cinematic landscape. No sooner has the editor fired Greg than a fight erupts with blue-coated men, traditional masculine types who rush from their stations to take a punch at the floridly dressed photographer. The fight here takes on epic proportions. As Elvis trades punches with one after another of the big, burly men, the sequence references every previous Presley fistfight. His bout with each fellow is modeled on one or another of those he then singly entered into. By implication, we momentarily revisit each movie, including Elvis' internal anger at the world, as expressed through violent (and notably macho) competition.

As the battle moves toward its conclusion — men in overalls piled unconscious everywhere, Elvis unscathed — the scene spills over into satire. An apotheosis of all that's gone before, the ritual fight scene is deconstructed as the canon hurries toward closure. Obvious too is an aura of desperation that causes this sequence to contrast with the Strawberry Fields Forever "flower power" feel of the film's overall style, so distinctively different from anything previously seen in Elvis Cinema. A sense of end-game permeates everything; by doing such a typical routine on a bigger scale than before, Presley at last puts it to rest. Then, nothing that follows in the narrative — nor in the notably few films to follow — will appear to belong to the long-standing genre. Anything can then happen, as *Live a Little* has been freed from genre strictures, leaving it wide open to possibilities.

Momentarily, the film becomes a cross between a Kafkaesque surreal-scenario and a *Twilight Zone* nightmare-by-daylight, as Greg heads to his home and finds other people living there. Using her rich husband's connections (she is a raw capitalist *playing* at being a hippie, both the acting-as-life and corrupting capitalism themes revived), Bernice has paid Greg's back rent and relocated him to her beach house. With no place else to go, he heads there. Arriving, he encounters Harry, who suggests that under what appears to be a nymphomaniacal surface beats the heart of a frigid woman: "Making love never quite works with her. She always stops short." Bernice is unmasked; she turns out to be what Elvis all along has been, in film as in life: All smoke but no fire when it comes to consummation of "the act" which he passed himself off as a master of. Elvis finally encounters his true and ultimate female counterpart, a woman who comes on stronger than any we have seen in a Presley picture but who, when push comes to shove, is uninterested in "the act."

Scrape the surface of a hippie princess, the film tells us, and like the rebel prince preceding her, you'll find a frightened child projecting a brave image. As he sleeps upstairs, under the influence of the magic mushrooms which Bernice likes to add to her stews, Greg hallucinates. This allows Elvis to perform one of the new psychedelic songs, "Edge of Reality." As he sings about her, Bernice dances enticingly. He insists that she almost drives him mad — Elvis a symbol for the middle-aged male experiencing the era's youth culture.

The plot device that motors the second half involves Glen trying to work two jobs. In each, he (the retro man) photographs previous visions of style as the society around them takes on an entirely other zeitgeist. He slips from the offices of a mired-in-the-'40s *Gentleman's Quarterly*-type magazine, run by a nattily dressed older gentleman, Louis Penlow (Rudy Vallee), to a suite in the same building where a mid-'60s *Playboy*-ish publication (here called *Classic Cat*) is lorded over by a fiftyish hedonist, Mr. Lansdown (Don Porter). To collect double salary, Greg has to make sure that neither editor knows about the other's assignment. For the former, he immortalizes women as they were dreamed about a quarter-century earlier, which now looks like ancient history; for the latter, as they were fantasized about a mere *five* years ago. This — in the late-'60s counter cultural context — seems even *further* removed from the current day. After all, the hippie sensibility revived elements from the 1940s; the crass early-'60s had no place.

Greg, however, is far happier in either office than in the flower-power world of the present day, which Bernice appears so comfortable within. He gladly wears a suit and tie for Mr. Penlow and goes casual-conservative for Mr. Lansdown. This allows Elvis to reveal his comfort with slipping into varied lifestyles of the type that existed before and after his own radiant moment of early trendsetting fame. He can now happily go formal with the women posing for the *G.Q.* clone and more overtly seductive with those at *Playboy*'s stand-in. By now, Elvis appears less a representative of any one past period than *the past itself*, perceived by this point in comparison to a complex present that around him metamorphoses into a confusing future, untenable for those locked into old ways.

This is obvious (and odious) when Glen attends a pool party at a reasonable facsimile of the Playboy Mansion. There, he meets a Centerfold girl, Ellen (Celeste Yarnall), compliant and thus non-threatening. She is no more or less attractive than Bernice, yet the hero feels comfortable with Ellen, again in a situation he knows, understands and can *control*. In "A Little Less Conversation," he asks Ellen to satisfy him; clearly, she's willing to do so. The blonde eagerly agrees to go home with him, their one-night stand interrupted by Bernice, who fakes an injury to ruin the tryst. Now it's Greg's turn to care for Bernice. This allows her to finally ask Greg what's been bothering him all along, as — whenever he is isn't fending off her attentions — he hankers after other pretty women. Bernice stands for a generation of women who existed just after the *Playboy* philosophy argued for free sex with the man posited as controller of all action-pleasure but before the Women's Movement of the early '70s insisted on equality for women.

Finally, as Elvis Cinema careens to a close, the Presley persona gets to speak a line that all but defines him:

Look, I'm a *man*. I like to make decisions for myself.

Nothing, apparently, has changed. Though in almost every earlier film he appeared to arc, as we move toward closure he now reveals that the ongoing persona has learned *nothing* over the past 15 years and 27 movies. A cowboyish Candide of contemporary lowbrow cinema, he remains as blithe a spirit as when the celluloid saga began. In each installment, though, the world — the macrocosm of real life, the microcosm viewed as background of the successive movies — inexorably altered around him. Elvis has become a total, even embarrassing anachronism — except of course when he cocoons himself, as in the 1968 "Comeback Special," the upcoming Vegas act and the documentaries that would round out his screen career.

Finally, he opts for the approach of one unique sect of early American puritans: Testing himself by sleeping in bed alongside an attractive young woman but with a sturdy hard-board set up between them. For a while, he appears to revel in the frustration, so near and yet so far, the great American sex symbol revealed to be the last American virgin. Then, in an hysterical mood, he tosses away the board and ravishes Bernice, much as Elvis did with Priscilla[21] when belatedly he realized she was about to walk away from the marriage because of the way he was sexually ignoring her. Flighty as ever, Bernice disappears the next morning. For her — and many women of her generation — a one-night stand is as normal since the 1960s as it has been for men. He, more old-fashioned than even he grasped, sets out to track her down and get her to marry him, precisely what each women wanted in the good ol' days. Fifteen years after Elvis entered the arena of sexual politics and popular culture, the male-female roles are reversed. It is now the man who needs to marry once the relationship has been consummated.

As they meet again by the seashore, the mood grows strangely melancholy, despite a half-hearted attempt to raise our spirits via buoyant music. There is little room for the oeuvre, as we have known it, to continue. Elvis has encountered his last temptation; now, Jesus-like, he necessarily must move on, past the way of all flesh to an entirely spiritual plane of existence.

CHAPTER 18

Pilgrim's Progress

♦ *The Trouble with Girls* (1969) ♦
♦ *Change of Habit* (1969) ♦

Presley's stardom came after 1950, and in a radically altered America from the one he had been born into in 1935. Even in the century's first half, though, writings of Freud, Darwin and Marx — initially known only to an influential elite who spread such modern ideas to their disciples in academia, these concepts trickling down to the masses — led to an era of doubt. As a popular song of the 1940s put it: could we continue to believe in an ordered universe or were we all only lost in the stars? Following World War II, development of nuclear energy and an intensifying space race created a more universalized scientific mindset; Nietzsche's *fin-de-siecle* dictum that "God is dead" gained ground with a post–Hiroshima population. Yet despite all evidence to the contrary, "Today, as in every epoch, men want to make sense out of the universe."[1] Still, ever fewer people believed that their traditional place of worship provided the proper avenue to achieve a resurgence of faith. Where then must the average person look for signs and symbols of a greater consciousness in the cosmos? For Harvey Cox, contemporary people, removed from God's Country and living in some great metropolis, seek God in the mean streets[2] — or the continuous barrage of mass media sights and sounds that shape our collective unconscious. Now, "Our icons are no longer [found] in church but on the tube,"[3] Elvis chief among them. The very concept of an icon, however, is religious in nature; that religiosity carries over to our celluloid equivalents of pagan demi-gods and Christian saints. BBC Religious Reporter Ted Harrison claimed that like earlier spiritual hero-figures, Elvis "reaches through to the eternal spirit in all of us, which yearns for truth, meaning and purpose in a [now] cruel, incomprehensible and uncomprehending world."[4]

This explains why what seemed merely one more cult for a dead celebrity (like the one that briefly surrounded James Dean) actually attests to "worship, adoration and the perpetuation of the memory of Elvis."[5] Anything is acceptable that negates doubt, since

> [t]o isolate, define, and if possible dispel that meaninglessness has been a job with A-1 priority.... In carrying it out, old myths and traditions have been discarded, and new ones have taken their place.[6]

Dropping Jesus for Elvis (or as in the case of *Jesus Christ, Superstar,* re-imagining Jesus *as* Elvis) substituted easily accessible icons for worn-out ones. Such a process allows for relevant re-imaginings of tired old myths that once lent meaning to existence. Early, Elvis came to see himself as "an earthly messenger sent by God."[7] He conscripted the services of one Larry Geller, a self-styled religious scholar he had met in 1964; Geller thereafter instructed the star as to metaphysical issues.[8]

Having discovered (and studied) Buddha, Muhammad and Moses, Elvis wondered if he too had been "chosen by God to serve a purpose."[9] He now viewed each concert as an opportunity to share his gospel with a captive audience. As Sammy Davis, Jr., remarked: "He opens with that [*2001: A*] *Space Odyssey* theme — bummm, bahh, bahhh — you think it's the second coming."[10] And for the untold millions who would never have the opportunity to catch Elvis live, the films — always dismissed as the least significant aspect of Elvis culture — likewise spread the word, leading to Elvis eventually being "canonized by popular acclaim."[11]

The Passion of Elvis: *The Trouble with Girls* (1969)

For the transitional picture that removes Elvis from the secular world, screenwriters Lois and Arnold Peyser created a nostalgic tribute to the Chautauqua traveling tent shows of the early twentieth century. Included was music from that era, performed in realistic context and offered up when the characters (themselves performers) sing and dance for Main Streeters who, to relieve the boredom and heat of heartland summer, pour into local fairgrounds and take in a combination of (dubious) highbrow culture and (broad) popular entertainment. The show's producer, Walter Hale, wasn't originally set to sing, though that changed after Dick Van Dyke, initially set to star, passed on the project. Elvis performs several numbers, including a duet with stage actress Marlyn Mason. The cast also included Joyce Van Patten and Sheree North, plus screen legends Vincent Price and John Carradine. Mason attested to this being Presley's long-sought-after crossover from pop icon (musicals that were designed with him in mind) to a Sinatra-style star of pre-existing projects.

The title addresses a lingering attitude then being rejected: Females over 21 now chose to be referred to as women, something the Presley persona earlier encountered with such self-sufficient types as Juliet Prowse and Ann-Margret. Charlene (Mason) likewise objects when Walter uses such epithets as "girl," "honey" and "babe." Charlene's job in each town they visit is to mount a children's pageant ("Alice in Wonderland"), showcasing local talent, the case with the actual Chautauqua show. Here we do encounter the "trouble with girls." After arriving in Bradford Center, Iowa, Charlene wants to cast Carol (Anissa Jones) in the title role. Elderly owner Johnny (Edward Andrews) prefers to pick the mayor's less-gifted daughter owing to the pressure that such a powerful man can exert. The mayor himself recalls "George Babbitt" in Sinclair Lewis's unsparing satires on Middle American life in the 1920s, signifying the raw capitalism that threatens to overwhelm the Elvis hero.

This is, despite its status as a one-of-a-kind movie, part of the Presley canon. The civil rights theme reoccurs, reviving Elvis' "sociosexual identification with black male performers."[12] In *Loving You* and *Frankie and Johnny*, Presley related to a lone black child in a sea of whitebread fans. Here an African-American child becomes significant, eliciting a smile of recognition from Elvis in a way other children do not. One of the earliest arguments that Presley did the Lord's work on Earth came from an African-American minister, who insisted that Elvis created the concept of a New South as the first pop-culture personality to break down barriers between blacks and whites.[13] That interpretation combines the godly aspect of Elvis with his civil rights sensibility. Fittingly, he has been compared to a national hero, both a religious leader with traditionalist values and civil rights activist of liberal social leanings: "Elvis was a Martin Luther King, Jr., in the music field," as he "did not see music as divided by color."[14] As a tribute to each/both, Fred Stein, a photo-collage artist based in Milwaukee, successfully blended pre-existing images of *the* King and *Dr.* King into a single work.

Significantly, this black child is half-brother to the blonde female child whom Charlene hopes to star as Alice. Though their relationship is never fully explained (likely so that the film could be booked in the south, many theaters there then still refusing to show anything that dared hint at racial mixing), black boy and white girl walk around town hand in hand, followed by their mother, Nita Bix (North). A poor woman, she raises them on her own, though whether a widow or deserted is never clear. Elvis handed out free tickets for expensive shows to just such wide-eyed fans who couldn't afford to buy them.[15] Stepping down from the Chautauqua express, Walter gives free passes to poverty-stricken Mrs. Bix and her children.

A focus on sexual harassment, befitting the emergence of feminism, sur-faces with the Bix subplot. She works in the local drugstore, lorded over by Harrison Wilby (Dabney Coleman), a smug hypocrite who forces himself on a hapless woman in dire need of her job. Though a period piece, the film — in keeping with a longterm Hollywood approach of presenting contemporary issues in historical settings — has the sophisticated Charlene, much like a con-temporary feminist, take up the cause of a "sister" with less social status. Wal-ter aligns himself with the women; Elvis emerges as that rare male who supports an anti-chauvinist agenda.

If Walter is patriarchal, at least he's an enlightened patriarch. He sup-ports Charlene on the issue of casting a poor talented child over a rich man's daughter. For him as for the star playing Walter, the show's the thing; talent must take precedence over all other considerations, including cold hard cash. Still, Walter *is* out to make a buck, even by exploiting Nita's upcoming prob-lems to collect cash, some of which will go to her. Character (and star) par-take of "the American obsession with transformative consumerism ... faith in consumption: collecting (which in Elvis' case) may help fans construct mean-ing in their everyday lives, [if] it mainly keeps them addicted to an ideology of buying things to feel better."[16] In our capitalistic democracy, founded on separation of church and state, there developed a "consumer religion": finances and spirituality combined in a secular shrine such as Chautauqua, at which visitors could pick up ceramic souvenirs, or Graceland, where the faithful can purchase plastic Elvis likenesses.

Love of money for Elvis is not the root of all evil, though an *obsession* with it is. "I'm not anti-union," Walter insists to Charlene, the show's spokesperson for workers' rights. Initially, she conceives of Walter as a younger incarnation of Johnny, who clings to Coolidge-Hoover values and keeps work-ing people "in their place" to achieve maximum profits for those at the top. If Walter is a Republican, he's a liberal one, willing to bridge the gap between the polar extremes of Johnny and Charlene — she a precursor to the next decade's Roosevelt Democrats, dedicated to the good of "the people." Elvis, of a nineteenth century Republican order defined by Fremont and Lincoln, prefers to help people like Nita one on one, making American individualism a little less rugged. If Walter and Charlene aren't identical in approach, the essential decency of each person's values is enough to override any minor differences in attitude.

When Charlene realizes that Walter plans to share the proceeds not only with the troupe but also with destitute Nita, she finally allows herself to fall in love. His brand of capitalism, if enlightened, is surely offbeat. When the show threatens to go bust owing to a fall-off in attendance after Wilby is dis-covered dead, Walter kick-starts the box office by insisting that the killer will confess on stage as a grand climax to the show. Among the songs performed is an earlier folk version ("Aura Lee") of what in Elvis' first film became "Love Me Tender," which he self-referentially sings here, "popular culture [after all] rooted in folk culture."[17] An inebriated Nita must be sobered up enough to admit that she (not a member of the troupe wrongly held for the crime) killed Wilby, if in self-defense. All's well that ends well: Nita is exonerated, unmasked as a victim of male chauvinism, and Charlene is hailed as a feminist hero. Walter splits the money with Nita so that she and her children can move away. The show will financially survive a little longer. After 1929, the popularity of talking pictures, coupled with the economic disaster of the Great Depression, ended the golden era of kitschy traveling tent shows.

Happily, though, their offerings were reborn in the early days of TV, notably on *Ed Sullivan*, in which a pop-rock act like Elvis could precede a British actor offering a recitation of a Shakespearean soliloquy, likely followed by a sequence from some Broadway musical: high, middle and low culture sandwiched in a decidedly democratic, notably American fashion. How fitting then to have Presley play an avatar of the Chautauqua show; he would, in time, complete what these pioneers of modern entertainment began: an end to a viewpoint in which a fine line remained drawn between what that was exalted as "artistic" and everything else that could be scoffed at as merely "commercial." After all, "'High' and 'serious' art imply unwarranted judgments. Who is to say what is 'low' and 'frivolous'? Painters called Wild Beasts (*les Fauves*) in one generation will become the Establishment [of] a later one."[18]

Walter becomes a savior, a point we are prepared for by the inclusion of religious music. In mid-movie, when the gospel performers are to go on, their lead singer fails to arrive. Walter takes his place, Elvis performing "Swing Low, Sweet Chariot." The swaggering 1950s rebel who served as leader of the pack has become a righteous shepherd to his gentle flock. Early on, "He took white gospel, black gospel ... and that was where his music came from."[19] Properly understood, his "Elvis the Pelvis" movements are

> indigenous to certain highly emotional religions in both white and black communities, Pentecostal meetings in particular ... a result of emotional abandon coming from spiritual uplifting.[20]

This is passion in a spiritual, not sexual sense — passion as it exists in a Catholic consciousness, earthly longings re-directed into heavenly aspirations; passion as employed in the titles of sacred cinema from Carl Dreyer's *The Passion of Joan of Arc* (1928) to Mel Gibson's *The Passion of the Christ* (2004). And, in Elvis Cinema, a long-standing theme that would reach full fruition in his final musical drama.

If I Were a Carpenter: *Change of Habit* (1969)

Early on in Presley's career, moralistic

critics of the 1950s viewed Elvis' body, image and performances, the bodies and performances of his fans, with dread: It all blatantly symbolized the sensual subversion of reason and control.[21]

He appeared to offer up the Devil's music. As Elvis sang hymns, the perception changed. He learned "the use of elaborate melismmata, a typical gospel technique [in which] rational control is ... threatened by hints of ecstasy, physical or spiritual, and therefore by a touch of the irrational."[22] This impacted on youth, hungry to *believe* after traditional faith was smashed by modern science. The King offered followers the sort of spiritual solace they failed to find in conventional venues. J. B. Priestley complained about "the stammering helplessness of the contemporary church"[23] — the theme of *Change of Habit*.

The film opens as three novitiates — Sister Michelle Gallagher (Mary Tyler Moore), Sister Irene Hawkins (Barbara McNair) and Sister Barbara Bennett (Jane Elliot) — pray, each hoping that God will provide her with a "continuing source of dedication and inspiration." Finishing, they rise and, without warning, begin a striptease — teasingly slipping out of their habits, into hip street clothes. Then-trendy slo-mo photography focuses on each attractive woman's hair, flying upward as they dance about like high-fashion models. The audience (male *and* female) gazes on, embarrassed if aroused by director William Graham's sensuous imagery as gorgeous novitiates sensuously pull stockings up over toes, legs, knees, thighs ... while still wearing their habits. Early Presley films argued against the dichotomization of women into good or bad girls; *Change of Habit* takes that idea to its extreme.

Looking even "hotter" than the "hippie chicks" they pass on the street, the nuns head into the ghetto — and are mistaken for streetwalkers. A jump-cut takes us to Dr. John Carpenter (Elvis). He sings "Rubberneckin'" (one of only four songs he performs) to an assortment of late-'60s Youth types, black, white and Hispanic; ebony, ivory and others all move in perfect harmony thanks to their overseer, *the* Carpenter. Back on the street, Sister Michelle insists, "If we're going to reach these people, we've got to be accepted first as *women*, *then* as nuns" — the strong woman with us again, more formidable than ever. Street guys, attracted by the sleazy get-ups, close in, salvation hardly on their minds. The street, incidentally, is obviously a *real* street — moreso than any to appear in a Presley picture since *King Creole*. In fact, some studio sets were employed. In every instance, though, the intent (and effect) was to disguise this, allowing for a semblance of reality, bringing the by-now stock Presley persona out of his solipsistic existence and into an accurate rendering of the real world not unlike the one viewers observed in examples of "the new American cinema" such as *Midnight Cowboy.* "We'd better stop calling each other *sister,*" Michelle says as they arrive at Carpenter's street clinic. Though we know these "hot chicks" are novitiates, others — Carpenter included — remain oblivious.

The theme of perception and reality cuts both ways: Reporting for nursing duty, they are amazed to learn the hipster-hillbilly who rocks and rolls with the brothers and sisters is in charge. Again, Elvis becomes the subject of the *female* gaze: "You don't *look* like a doctor," Sister Michelle says. This echoes a prejudicial view Elvis himself had to overcome; in *Blue Hawaii,* he assumed a teacher must be a prissy older woman and couldn't fathom lovely Abigail. Here *women* must overcome stereotypical ideas as to what a professional male looks like. He too can still slip into assumptive behavior: "Which one of you is in trouble?" Carpenter asks, assuming from appearances that one of these sluttily dressed women needs an abortion. A progressive-traditionalist, Elvis-Carpenter makes it clear that while he won't morally condemn a non-married pregnant woman, neither will he perform the operation.

Carpenter assumes they are spoiled rich girls, an end-of-decade re-imagining of the blonde brat in *Girls! Girls! Girls!* He receives a comeuppance from Irene, a sister in more ways than one: She's black. "Which end of Park Avenue do you think *I'm* from, doctor?" Whatever his limitations, Carpenter's approach appears enlightened compared to that of Father Gibbons (Regis Toomey), the parish's elderly religious leader. As the nuns report to begin their two-month tour of duty, they encounter an older woman:

ELDERLY WOMAN: Tell [Father Gibbons] one of them's *black.*
MICHELLE: I think our neighbors are Catholics.
IRENE: Too bad they're not *Christians.*

The church disappoints them. The place is dirty and maintains "banker's hours" rather than relating to people who need help around the clock. Gibbons resents not only the youth who come to him for aid ("I keep the doors locked!") but also what he refers to as "underground" nurse-nuns with "bobbed hair ... silk stockings." His resentment borders on sociopathic anger; Gibbons has a bunker mentality, his church a last bastion of outmoded, uptight religious form that no longer functions for those "out there." He cannot grasp that the Now Generation will accept traditional values only if presented to them in a progressive form, spoken in the language they speak — the language of the streets; i.e., rock 'n' roll.

Simultaneous with the release of *Change of Habit,* Christian rock (following the success of the stage plays *Jesus Christ, Superstar* and *Godspell*) came into existence. Father Gibbons embodies know-nothing conservatism; Carpenter (who sings "Let us pray" with a gentle rock beat) fills the vacuum. Still, it would be a mistake to take Gibbons as an implied put-down of Christian values or, more specifically, Catholicism. The film never challenges the church's viability. Offered is a paradigm for how it can reclaim a central position in the lives of people. Gibbons signifies an uncomprehending, irrelevant hierarchy, barking out such insults as "I warn you, sister, none of your *radical* lip!" They aren't radical but *progressive*; like Carpenter (and the man playing him), revolutionaries as to style, not substance.

Despite all the changes — in life, as reflected on screen — this remains a Presley picture. Just as he had to ward off underage women in earlier films, so must he here, if in grim surroundings. A 17-year-old Spanish girl (a streetwise, realistic rendering of Anglo-Lolitas from breezy musicals) tries to undress Carpenter as he performs a check-up on her. Reversed now is the class consciousness. In the past, upscale females flirted with the poor, uneducated boy. Here, the girl is poor and uneducated, he holding a medical school education. Yet Elvis' long sideburns make it clear that he hasn't been "changed none." If he stumbled along the way, shaving them during his cinematic saga, he's at the oeuvre's end a born-again good ol' boy.

What remains constant is his embodiment of the great white hope for poor blacks. This neighborhood is exploited by a white man as corrupt as Carpenter is idealistic. The Banker (Robert Emhardt) serves as the film's devil in the flesh, a fitting foil to Elvis-Jesus. The Banker oversees drug-dealing and prostitution. He resents the sisters whom he mistakes for independent whores who won't surrender a portion of their take. When not saving children, Carpenter and the sisters attempt to diminish the Banker's influence. First, though, come their charges. This allows Elvis one final relationship with an adorable child. Despite seedy surroundings, a plot device resurfaces from *It Happened at the World's Fair,* in which Elvis fell for the adult female nurse who cured a little girl he unofficially adopted, even as she fell less for his looks and charm than his love of children. Here that occurs when a girl, considered deaf, reveals that she's autistic by responding to his music. This provides the path for Michelle to help the child; Michelle comes to love the caring man who can break through to children, he at last admitting that he's in love with her less owing to good looks than Michelle's mind and spirit.

He's "groovy," one nun says of Carpenter. When he and some of the guys from the 'hood show up to help the nurses paint their apartment, Barbara asks the young doctor what he thinks of this era's youth. The question is addressed to his character, if by implication asked of Presley himself. His curt answer makes clear that he disapproves of their attitudes and actions; Barbara — herself the age of the typical hippie — stands with Woodstock-era youth.

BARBARA: Don't we all have to storm the barricades?
CARPENTER (*sarcastically*): At the Ajax Market?

Significantly, his glib retort — one of those put-downs of self-important, pretentious people we've heard from Elvis' many alter egos — is in this film's context *disproved*. It is *precisely* here — at the Ajax Market in every late-'60s ghetto, where people of color are treated differently than Anglo customers — that protest must take place, the revolution begin. Carpenter will in time come to see this.

Even the nuns are less than unanimous. Surprisingly, perhaps, the Anglos want to turn activist while their black companion sighs, "I think we're here to do a job, *not* get involved." Irene signifies an outmoded early–1960s view, oblivious to the fact that people of color now prefer to be referred to as black (rather than Negro), only a few years earlier considered a derogatory term. The phrase "black is beautiful" had just become a part of the national lexicon; the next generation of African-Americans do not (like her) want to be accepted by whites. Rather, they prefer to forge an ethnic identity all their own.

After King's assassination, leadership was passed to Stokely Carmichael to Rap Brown to Huey Newton, ever younger and more violence-prone leaders. They did not (like King, Kennedy and Earl Warren) support a Voter's Rights Bill. "Participatory democracy" came to be seen as one more means by which the Establishment could control a naïve if hopeful population, "direct action" the alternative. As activist-author Ken Kesey concluded, all that happened during the late '60s led to people now "demanding the right to [determine] their own destinies instead of having it legislated" by elected politicians.[24] Now "we don't hate ourselves any more," Lou Smith (the Congress of Racial Equity) said, and by "not hating ourselves [for not being white] we don't have to aspire to be like somebody else."[25] Following King's death, "hatred, bitterness, revenge"[26] caused many African-Americans to perceive themselves as a people apart from all others in the country, including the white-poor and other ethnics. So the concept of a "black community" within a multi-cultural America was born.

Such an approach led to the epithet *African-American*. Politician Julian Bond continued in the tradition of King, working within the Democratic party, carrying the torch of participatory democracy. Even he noted that for many others, "The shift was [ever further] away from the integrationist ethic,"[27] King's murder followed by another, Robert Kennedy, perceived by many as the last white politician in the JFK tradition. One young black woman concluded:

> I knew it was all over, that there was no more reason for hope.... My attitudes
> changed so much and so rapidly, from going to peaceful things, like marching

and praying, to really being able to relate to [the ghetto burnings] in Watts. You know, "Burn, Baby, Burn"! Integration? There's no such thing now.[28]

Sister Irene negotiates this arc. She sees too many beatings of street people to continue believing that she can do a simple medical job without getting involved on every other level. Irene is particularly distraught when street blacks inform her that, other than the color of her skin, she isn't black at all, having sold out to the white establishment. She embodies the dated Dr. King approach; they are the next generation, Bobby Seal and the Panthers. Huey Newton's group fought for "a kind of justice"[29] which, as Barbara Walters observed, demanded separatism, including "control over their neighborhood schools" as part of "a society of separate pockets"; post–King blacks "want very much to have their own culture," opposed to "the integrated society [dreamed of] ten years ago," a land of diversity now allowing for people to live "block by block" so that people can maintain their own identity."[30]

Throughout *Change of Habit*, the society surrounding our characters — a typical, even allegorical "inner city" — proves complex in make-up. The whites who once lived here mostly deserted "downtown" in a mass flight to the suburbs. The few whites who remain (financially unable or unwilling to leave) feel they live in enemy territory. Old (Anglo) ladies try to escape from what they perceive as chaos in the streets by visiting a theater, only to be grossed out:

> Disgusting movie. When you see pictures like this, you realize what a great force for "good" Irene Dunne was.

They seemingly form a Greek tragic chorus, expressing the conventional wisdom of society at large — or, more correctly, one segment of it as America shattered into a kaleidoscope. When Elvis and the nurse-nuns play guitar inside the street clinic, the ladies on the porch agree, "It's got to be an orgy!" The session reflects Elvis' personal predilections at this time: platonic. So the Old Guard is employed as the *inverse* of a Greek chorus, getting it all wrong.

Like Jesus, Elvis is 100 percent God and 100 percent man. As a man, Carpenter asks Michelle out on a date. She says no.

CARPENTER: Is there somebody else?
MICHELLE: You *could* say that.

Michelle combines science with spirituality. She draws the autistic child out of her invisible cocoon by insisting, "I *love* you!" As this film (and the canon) draws to a close, it becomes clear where the emergent vision is heading: Unconditional love is the only answer, as Presley (the ongoing persona; the character Carpenter) will soon grasp.

The religiosity that came to surround Elvis was not imposed on Elvis by his fans after the star's death. He had, during the last decade of his life, perceived himself as "an earthly messenger sent by God."[31] "Granted [his] unique position, could he contribute to save a world burdened with hunger, disease, and poverty?"[32] In *King Creole*, Elvis, confused, pointed to a place of worship, then told Dolores Hart, "I can't enter a church again — until I'm *sure!*" What he needed surety of was his own purity, tempted (like Jesus) by the ways of the world. No wonder that "an image of Elvis a lot of fans cherish" is a vision of him "in pain, Elvis suffering, Elvis crying out to be taken care of."[33] Fans perceive on his face a kind of crucifixion.

Each aspect of Elvis worship has a direct parallel to the development of a traditional faith. Americans have long made a habit of spiritual synthesis and reconfiguration[34] as we "continue to mix and match religious beliefs and practices, creating and claiming [our individual] spiritual convictions out of that amalgamation."[35] One fan always

> looked on Elvis as a modern-day sacrifice ... if you want to see the false gods of success, if you want to see how forgetting who you are and where you came from delivers you into the forces of darkness — Elvis died to prove that to us again.[36]

So it's altogether possible that Presley may "evolve into a major religion some day," says Doug Isaacks, pastor of the First Church of Elvis, founded in Austin in 1991. "Let's face it, it's no sillier than any other religion."[37]

Carpenter finally opens up to Michelle in a park and explains that he lives and works in the ghetto because a black man and close friend died on the "other end of the world"—i.e., Vietnam. He admits:

> Learned more here than I would in the suburbs, giving out vitamin pills and diet shots.

That early hatred for whitebread suburbs remains constant. Other key elements continue in this altered context: As in *G.I. Blues*, he sings (here, "Have a Happy") while riding on a carousel with Michelle, the song's words directed not to this attractive grown-up female but to a small female child — his love for each influenced by feelings for the other.

All three nuns discard their hooker garb for unisex outfits, suggesting the feminist influence rippling into mainstream thinking. Father Gibbons not unexpectedly finds this even more troublesome than the previous sexy clothes: "*not* even dressed like *women.*" Their earlier outfits were liberated in an early-1960s sense from previous constraints for respectable women as to appearing sexy for men. Their current clothing signifies liberation in an oncoming 1970s value system, they now liberated from the need to appear sexy. When Father Gibbons addresses them as "sisters," that term has three layers of meaning: nuns, civil rights (for Irene) and feminism via a new sense of sisterhood.

FATHER GIBBONS: [You] shame other women of the cloth, who know their place.
MICHELLE: How we dress is of no importance.

Openly rebelling against the unenlightened patriarch, the sisters plan a "folk mass," a fitting example for the liberal church that first germinated in the late '60s. After the half-century mark, "the main thrust of theology has turned from dreams of New Jerusalem to the reality of Secular City."[38] For revenge, Father Gibbons attempts to have their street festival cancelled. This is something the villainous Banker — ultimate symbol of corrupt capitalism in an oeuvre filled with such figures — also wants, which sets the conventional religious leader and a drug dealer up not as foils but mirror images for one another.

As their tenure comes to an end, the sisters must once again don their habits. Carpenter finally understands why Michelle resisted his charms — and his sincere love.

MICHELLE: John, please say something.
CARPENTER: I'll be damned.

Meanwhile, Barbara's arc causes her to realize that she can no longer conform to church dicta. She leads a protest march on the Ajax Market, hoping to get arrested in the manner of prominent Catholic radicals (i. e., the Berrigan Brothers).

Now the Panthers, not the police, keep order. When Elvis engages in the last of his ritualistic fistfights with the Banker and his cronies, a policeman makes ready to arrest Carpenter. Street brothers intervene, insisting that "there ain't trouble here," and the cop backs off. Owing to Irene's sea change, the Panthers now accept her, too.

IRENE: I'd like to thank you.
PANTHER: We help our own, *sister*.

At last, that term exists on all three possible levels for Irene. She will continue to wear the habit, though Barbara drops out to bring her crusade to the streets in her own individual way — resembling such diverse screen presences as Sylvia Pinale in Luis Buñuel's controversial Spanish art film *Viridiana* (1961) and Julie Andrews in Robert Wise's Hollywood production *The Sound of Music* (1965). Each chooses secular humanism — doing God's work in the world in their own individualistic ways.

Carpenter hopes he can persuade Michelle to do much the same thing. When he tells her "I come from a long line of people who believe in getting married," he means not only John's antecedents but the Presley persona's earlier incarnations — and Elvis himself. Michelle discusses her trauma with the

Mother Superior, who insists that Michelle must choose between Elvis and Jesus. She isn't necessarily correct as to this, as the movie's final moments make clear. Carpenter performs his beloved rock 'n' roll, now doing so *in the church*—where he has displaced Father Gibbons. If not the first, this is certainly an early example of Christian rock. In 1955, mainstream "preachers across the land thundered against the rock and roll revolution [oblivious that] the instigators of the new sound [Elvis included] gathered around the piano to do another chorus of 'Jesus, Jesus, Jesus.'"[39] Now such religious leaders grasped that what Sol Myron Linowitz, who represented the U.S. in the Organization of American States between 1966 and 1969, said about technology held true for rock music: "[It's] amoral and it's a tool. It's what you do with [the medium] that makes the difference."[40] Here, young churchgoers join with Elvis as he sings "Let Us Pray," inviting everyone to pray and praise the Lord with him.

"Reaction against the 'God is Dead' position has started," Marshall Fishwick noted in the early 1970s after observing "Jesus Freaks," adding that this phenomenon "will grow in the years ahead."[41] It began in pop culture with *Change of Habit*. Finally, even Father Gibbons gives in to the good vibes, admitting: "He works in mysterious ways." There are some holdouts: "Give me the old days," the most reactionary of the elderly ladies sniffs, "when you could go to mass and not [have to] *think* about a thing."

As John performs the new version of the Good Book, Michelle—still trying to make up her mind—glances back and forth, from Carpenter in performance to a statue of the Carpenter in church. Michelle's choice will take place as her life continues, after the film concludes. The ambiguity is preferable to a clear-cut ending for, on one level, she doesn't need to choose. To embrace one is to accept the other. This is "the message of Pop Theology," then: "God is neither *in* hand (sunny assumption of romantic optimists) nor out of hand (gloomy contention of romantic pessimists) but *at* hand."[42] As the film cuts between Jesus on the cross and Elvis in performance, the two collapse into a single image—or, more correctly, *icon*.

Always throughout man's history "the concept of icon [touches] a center near man's essence."[43] Elvis morphs into a human wafer; the body of Christ, fit for consumption by a public sorely tested as to its faith since Nietzsche's dictum yet remains hungry to go on believing, since

> from its "city on the hill" creation myth to the present-day proliferation of New Age spirituality ... religiosity—mainstream and fringe—remains central to American identity and experience.[44]

Whatever changes have occurred in our country, still

> as a profoundly religious people, Americans tend to treat things on religious

terms, apply religious categories, and generally make a religion out of much of what is touched [upon].[45]

In its final moments, the film looks forward to that most remarkable aspect of the Elvis phenomenon: Deification following his death by fans who began to report "sightings" of Elvis, then flocked in ever greater number to Graceland. The notion of spirituality emanating from Elvis, rather than just another (if extreme) example of cult celebrity worship, became clear when observers of visitors to Graceland first realized that they resembled "pilgrims" of the early Renaissance — more interested in spending quiet time in the Meditation Garden where Elvis was buried than in the mansion, in which all the kitsch could be viewed.[46] Respected mainstream publications began to describe Graceland as a true "shrine,"[47] an American Lourdes.[48] And so "[e]ven in death, the King has it all ways. His fans ... come to Graceland to gawk at ... Golgotha with gold drapes."[49]

CHAPTER 19

Nostalgia Ain't What It Used to Be

♦ *Elvis: That's the Way It Is* (1970) ♦
♦ *Elvis on Tour* (1972) ♦

If you want to see him, Col. Parker early on said of Elvis, "you gotta pay." Following the Timex-sponsored homecoming broadcast (May 8, 1960) with Frank Sinatra, Presley did no television, concentrating on feature films. Most brought in a great deal of money; few supported his stated desire to, like Dean Martin, initiate a Hollywood career allowing for serious drama as well as occasional big-scale musicals. With a profound disappointment, he had by 1968 made up his mind to leave Tinseltown and would if necessary force this decision down the colonel's throat.[1] Elvis wanted to go back to his roots, perform in concert once more. First, though, he would test the waters, returning to the medium that brought him early fame along with unexpected controversy: TV. Rehearsals for his NBC "Comeback Special" (that term referring to television, as he had never been absent from theater screens, radio airplay or record sales) took place during early June, with final dress rehearsal on the 21st. The hour-long show taped in Burbank between June 27 and 30, "a grueling and difficult experience but one that [proved] so satisfying [there would be] no turning back."[2] Nervously, Presley stepped out before a live audience for the first time in longer than he cared to recall, performing two one-hour sessions. A post-production team edited the material down to a 50-minute show.

Horrified that he might have failed to recapture the magic, Elvis nonetheless loved the experience. He bided his time until the broadcast four months later when, for once, he would not be disappointed. The show aired December 3 to ecstatic reviews and huge ratings. This time, there was no controversy over his occasional wiggling-giggling, though his sleek body was revealed in a black leather jumpsuit that would have been utterly out of the question a decade and a half earlier. In 1954, a mere jacket made of that material had sent shivers down the spines of suburbanites when worn by Brando in *The Wild One* or, four years later, Elvis in *King Creole*. Compared to the tattered street clothes of late–'60s hippies, however, the glossy item seemed somehow nostalgically charming. And while Elvis dared move his pelvis more provocatively than he had in 1956, such motions now appeared "innocent" — at least in comparison to the outrageous shenanigans of current youth-oriented artists like the Rolling Stones.

In truth, the country was split once again in 1969, more virulently even than a generation earlier when Elvis found himself postulated as the divisive factor. Patricia Jobe Pierce notes that late in 1954 and throughout 1955, pop culture events (Elvis on TV, rock 'n' roll everywhere) and such key issues as the Generation Gap and the Civil Rights Movement first emerged, signaling "a turning point in American history."[3] The next watershed moment occurred late in 1968 and in 1969. Elvis' own transitional moment — his return to television, now welcomed into middle-class living rooms rather than causing mass hysteria — rated as one of many factors that offered proof that America was again undergoing a major upheaval. Two essential stories vied for attention and headlines in 1969: The Moon landing and My Lai.

The former, which occurred in mid-summer, momentarily recreated the sense of community that briefly flourished following the election of JFK. Any resurgence of national pride would shortly be shattered: The massacre of an Asian village in March 1968 by members of the recently created American Division — First Battalion/20th Infantry's Charlie Company, under the command of 24-year-old Second Lt. William L. Calley — finally broke as a major news story, splitting hawks (who lionized Calley) and doves (who demonized him) more strikingly than ever. The previous year, in a close election, Richard Nixon had defeated Hubert Humphrey for the presidency. Tipping the scales in Nixon's favor were demonstrations during the Democratic convention in Chicago by longhairs. Mayor Richard Daley set loose officers armed with tear gas and billy-clubs. If Yippies believed that the televised incident would turn ordinary Americans against the Establishment ("The whole world is watching!"), they could not have been more wrong. Most suburbanites, however rebellious in their own youth, viewed Daley's reaction as a necessary move to keep chaos from overtaking the streets of America.

As always, popular culture reflected the temper of the times. TV's *Dragnet* (1955–59) — a hit during the McCarthy era, with Jack Webb as a no-nonsense ultra-conservative cop — had disappeared as the liberal Kennedy era began. Now, NBC revived *Dragnet* to great success with a Silent Majority audience that abandoned the movies (all at once dominated by youth films: *Bonnie and Clyde, The Graduate, Easy Rider*) for the medium they had, in the mid–'50s, despised: Television, which then belonged to their "square" parents. They had become what they once loathed; now, Mom and Dad's hero, Sgt. Joe Friday, was embraced as their own. Like Nixon, Webb offered a *faux* dream of the 1950s as a simpler, better era. So did, of all people, Elvis — one-time symbol of social, political and cultural tumult. All was forgiven as Presley came to represent "the good old days."

Shortly, the once unthinkable happened: Elvis, arriving unannounced at the White House (December 21, 1969), was embraced by the president. The two shared their intense dislike of "The Drug Culture, Hippie Elements, the SDS, etc."[4] Presley asked for an official badge so he could personally go after their common enemies; Nixon humored one of the few stars other than Webb and John Wayne to support him.[5] Neither Elvis nor Nixon had changed much since the vice-president damned Presley in public, though the world around them had. That shift in sensibility tossed the two one-time opposites together as similar symbols of what (despite the Cold War, a polio epidemic, racial unrest, generational conflict and McCarthy-inspired madness, among the ugliest elements) now came to be considered an American golden age — the "happy days," as a popular 1970s TV sitcom would put it.

On that upcoming show, "Fonzie" (Henry Winkler) wore a leather jacket. In the mythic rather than realistic vision of *Happy Days*, this rock 'n' roller was welcomed into a conventional home by "The Cunninghams." This revisionist (and distorted) notion of the 1950s had been preceded by Elvis' Comeback Special; at the time, Priscilla marveled that Elvis appeared in "a look we hadn't seen in years."[6] At that moment, "the nostalgia movement" was born. Shortly, *Grease* (a loving tribute to the '50s) premiered on Broadway; George Lucas' *American Graffiti* (1973) and TV's *Happy Days* (1974–80) would follow.

Members of the late–'60s Youth Movement who watched the Comeback Special viewed it as final proof that Presley was now utterly irrelevant:

> Elvis was sexy and ... twisting those still tantalizing hips ... [but he] was way too polite ... too mainstream, for a generation turned on by the subversive sexuality of crotch-grabbing, lip-smacking performers like Jim Morrison and Mick Jagger.[7]

Elvis was what he'd always been; he had not toned down his act to be acceptable. What had changed was the context in which he appeared. In fact, the show hardly qualified as a "comeback" in any ordinary sense. For Elvis displayed an irony about his own image that suggested a new awareness of his sexiness, and a humorous angle on it. Early Elvis always seemed something of a deer caught in the headlights. Now, he displayed a savvy self-consciousness as to his strutting style. Elvis winked at the audience to let everyone know he was having great fun with this act, with them, but most of all with *himself*. His 1956 TV appearances thrust "modernism" upon a public not ready for it; in 1968, Elvis introduced "post-modernism": everything written in italics, played with such arch seriousness it all becomes a put-on.[8] To burlesque his act while performing it was to deconstruct his myth; movements that could (and had) been described as silly by sophisticates were rendered smart by a knowing context.

But if fans expected black leather to be his costume from then on, they were wrong. When Elvis shortly embarked on a Vegas career, the 1950s biker aura would be discarded for a new fashion statement as the one-time rough rebel chose to emulate an earlier era's "softest" star, Liberace.

Woodstock West: *Elvis: That's the Way It Is* (1970)

Presley approached Las Vegas as he did the (in his mind) unknowable "other" sex: with heightened anticipation, affected bravado and much inner trepidation. Like Debra Paget, his original leading lady, this city had early on rejected him. On April 23, 1956, Elvis began what was to have been a four-week stint. But the "Vegas audience was older and more staid than most, with not a teenager in sight. Elvis played for only a week before his contract was broken by mutual consent."[9] The experience left him in a surly mood, if soon heartened to learn that "Heartbreak Hotel" had hit the top of the charts — teens supporting him despite their parents failing to yet "get it." Show biz insiders tagged the booking as "premature." Elvis seemingly turned his back on Vegas; actually, he bided his time.

He returned to shoot *Viva Las Vegas* (playing an outsider who by film's end is accepted) in 1964 and several years thereafter to get married. Thirteen years following his only significant failure, Elvis returned, a conquering hero of myth, to finally win over this bitch goddess of success, making Vegas over in his own image — precisely as he, Pygmalion-like, had turned the malleable Priscilla into a virtual redux of Paget-Galatea. Presley opened at the International Hotel on July 26, 1969, to an audience largely composed of members of the Silent Majority. They opened their arms and poured out their hearts to him. Fifteen years after their own youth rebellion, this was "a time for baby-boomers to face the unlikely but unavoidable fact: We were about to become the grown-ups."[10] Elvis was what they wanted to catch in Vegas, even as their parents came to Sin City a decade earlier to see and hear a great star who recalled their own 1940s youth: Frank Sinatra.

One rock historian has noted of Elvis' Vegas opening, "It was as if the audience had fallen through a time warp, leaving the '60s for the '50s ... on the biting edge of memory that went with high school and the beginnings of rock 'n' roll."[11] Yesteryear's radicals now embodied a reactionary agenda. Significant too was an opportune bit of timing. Even as Elvis' show unfolded in the parched Nevada heat, thousands of hippies, for whom Elvis was as "out of it" as Sinatra had been to the early Presley fan base, converged on Max Yasgur's farm in upstate New York to celebrate three days of sex, drugs, and rock 'n' roll — the emerging musical forms Elvis and his fans rejected. Here were a pair of pop-culture polar opposites, two antithetical musical events which symbolized a bitterly divided America: liberals who hoped, if naively, to begin a Greening of America[12] and forge a more enlightened peace and love future; traditionalists who hoped to return to the way we were — or wanted, with naïve earnestness, to believe we once had been.

In yet another example of unconscious opportunity, a film crew led by Denis Sanders captured Elvis' anti–Woodstock West (a celebration of the commerciality that early rock had degenerated into) even as another, led by Michael Wadleigh, immortalized the "new" music that seemed impervious to any such corporate co-opting. Time would prove that not to be true, as late-'60s rock songs were sold to producers of TV commercials. At the moment, though, the two rock-documentaries appeared to be a pair of opposing cinematic bookends, released a year after the two parallel events, proving the polarization of a once universal moviegoing audience as the film played to two strikingly different American sub-cultures.

Over an initially black screen we hear crowds of fans scream for, and at, Elvis. The image brightens to reveal a mostly female fan base, and not simply an "older" audience. There are elderly women, many middle-aged women, and teenagers. Even small children whoop it up for the star. What ties them together isn't the overstated distinction between young and old but values. All are Middle American types; the youngest females wear their hair in styles that appear a decade behind the times, not a single scruffy hippie (of any age) in sight. (In *Woodstock*, virtually all participants were longhairs, many notably above the age of 30.) Men in Elvis' audience wear neat, gaudy, off-the-rack jackets and gauche ties. Multi-screen cameras (identical to those employed by Wadleigh) capture Elvis gyrating in a white jumpsuit as he sings "Tiger Man"— he long since nicknamed the King, Vegas a chrome jungle.

Like *Woodstock*, this film does not follow a linear approach. Rather, the moviemakers chose to fragment the experience, bouncing back and forth in "stream of consciousness" style to convey the way this event would be remembered in the minds of those who attended. So suddenly we're back at the MGM rehearsal. Elvis directly addresses the camera, suggesting this is not only a movie of his concert and the days leading up to it but a movie about the making of the movie of that event. We notice that his sideburns are not only back but bigger than ever, as if intended to affront — not suburbanites who grew angry at anything Southern in 1955, rather the radical youth who butted heads with sideburned Southern cops during the Civil Rights marches of the late '60s. Elvis does rehearse several late–'60s songs, including "(It's Only) Words"; they are hippie, not yippie, love ballads, not political — bubble gum music knock-offs of the more authentic and profound music from that era. As to which pole of America Elvis associates with — straggly bikers like those played by Dennis Hopper and Peter Fonda in *Easy Rider* (1969), or the truckers who shoot them down at film's end — Elvis holds his guitar up to the camera, pretending it's a gun which he, grinning, fires at us.

Elvis drives his own limo onto the Hollywood lot where he's greeted by an elderly guard. The man clearly hails from the days when Clark Gable was known as this studio's "King"; Elvis, then an outsider, now holds that distinction. Huge signs proclaiming ELVIS are plastered all alongside the buildings of an otherwise deserted studio; this was the year when MGM auctioned off properties, even Dorothy's ruby slippers from *The Wizard of Oz*. Sound stages are empty until Elvis, last vestige of a fast-fading past, steps onto one to rehearse. Film editors Henry Berman and George Folsey, Jr., cut away to interviews with fans, young and old, black and white, congregating for the show's Vegas opening. A young blonde teenager, in town to cover the show for the youth-oriented music rag *Tiger Beat*, sings Elvis' praises. She looks like a girl from the late '50s, oblivious to all that's happened to others of her age, happy to remain so.

The songs heard in rehearsal make clear (as does the white jumpsuit with gold rhinestones and long fringe) that the show is intended as a departure from the past, which he had apotheosized in the Comeback Special. Elvis covers oldies by Ray Charles ("What'd I Say?") and new tunes from B. J. Thomas ("I Just Can't Help Believin'"). While he and a small combo go through the motions, director Sanders introduces the Vegas team that will prepare the hotel for an onslaught of international fans. The hotel president brings up a key Elvis theme when he talks about this venture: "We pay Elvis a goodly sum of *money*, but he's worth every penny of it." The question is whether the Presley persona who in films like *Lovin' You* refused to become a rhinestone cowboy and make big bucks has finally "wised up" or ultimately "sold out."

Not all the songs are without merit. One worthy number is "Bridge Over Troubled Water." Simon and Garfunkel were unique among popular 1960s performers in that their numbers have little to do with the protest movement, rather written in the form of folk songs from an earlier era — something Elvis had always been comfortable with. We notice that he (officially or otherwise) produces as well as stars in the show. During rehearsals, Presley halts the performance to instruct his back-up artists as to how they should approach a melody or emphasize a rhythm. We note the qualities that make Elvis, like performers as diverse as Sinatra and Harry Belafonte, a true performance artist (rather than a mere entertainer) even though he doesn't write his own material. It's recently become a much overused phrase, owing to Paula Abdul on *American Idol*, but Elvis makes each song his own. When performed by Elvis, a number written by someone else takes on autobiographical elements, much in the manner that "My Way" (written by Paul Anka, made famous by Sinatra) appeared to be an autobiographical statement from that star. "You've Lost That Lovin' Feeling," a classic by the Righteous Brothers, takes on additional meaning as we sense Elvis is here singing about Priscilla.

Always, there are cutaways to other areas of interest. The hotel's P.R. man asserts that no Vegas star ever equaled Elvis in terms of box office draw, though the runner-ups are Sinatra and Martin — Elvis' idols, both of whom he has now surpassed in popularity. We are whisked to the Cupid Wedding Chapel, where a preacher tells a young couple how necessary it is to keep *romance* alive for their marriage to succeed. Interviewed, they reveal that they planned the wedding around seeing Elvis. In him, religion and romance fuse. These two young people represent the majority of American youth — unchanged in attitude by all that had happened in the past few years, as is Elvis himself.

Seating arrangements, as outlined by the hotel's team, look like battle strategies for a full-scale war. As the opening night audience arrives (first we see a nervous Elvis pacing in a room), several bona fide superstars (Cary Grant, Sammy Davis, Jr.) are among them. Mostly the guests — singer-dancer Charo, stand-up comic Norm Crosby, actress Juliet Prowse — look like refugees from *The Hollywood Squares*, has-beens and wannabes. The second half of the film consists of the concert itself. Presley assumes (essentially for the first time) "The Elvis Stance": back arched forward, legs spread far and wide, maintaining a precarious balance as he appears ready to, in an oddly erotic gesture, swallow the mike he holds before him like some immense musical member.

The idea that Elvis is not a sex symbol per se, though sexy and a symbol, is driven home. "In a sense, I love Elvis," a fan explains, describing him less like a potential husband than as "a member of the family." Elvis can arouse her with movements and gestures, but must always remain off-limits — the very image his screen persona took on in the final films. The success of his renditions derive less from calculated technique (though his technique is flawless) than the *emotion* (his hallmark from Day One), suggesting again that this is self-expression, shared with a sympathetic group of friends, as to his post–Priscilla lost soul. This holds true for the new record release that he performs: "I've Lost You." To borrow from Blake, the Comeback Special offered Elvis's Songs of Innocence; the live concert allows him to share his Songs of Experience.

Elvis falls into a fit of passion, more spiritual than sexual, as such the ultimate expression of the intense emotion that always motored his music. He appears to have entered another dimension entirely, a metaphysical plane of existence we mere mortals can but marvel at. But this isn't all earnestness; the self-satiric attitude returns, notably when Elvis' mike fails to work. Rather than grow flustered upon realizing that the audience can't hear him, he turns the situation into an impromptu comedy skit, borrowing the mike of every back-up band member. Elvis becomes the pop star incarnate, expressing "the revolutionary (social and cultural, if decidedly not political) reaction to officialdom; the clown stressing the wonder and whimsy of life."[13] When his African-American back-up girls giggle, Elvis — with perfect timing — considers them in mock disdain before asserting, "I'm gonna bring in the *Supremes* tomorrow night, y'know." They laugh; we know it's all in fun. We also know that these girls, the Sweet Inspirations, are Supremes clones — adding another dimension to the wit, while deconstructing the gag Elvis has come up with, then deftly delivered.

Then it's time for something old and something new. He sings his original Elvis Cinema hit, "Love Me Tender," now doing so while kissing as many women in the front rows as possible. One hops up on-stage and puts a loving stranglehold on him until gently pried away by a security guard. Here's the stud show, from that man who had trouble consummating relationships with women in his private life, performed bigger and better than ever. It's accepted as the real thing — theater as life — by adoring female fans who either missed the self-revelatory implications contained in film after film or slipped into denial about what their beloved star had admitted in his screen work about his own limitations. The actuality of Elvis, revealed by Priscilla in her book, could only disappoint; the dream of Elvis — best left like figures on a Grecian urn unfulfilled — tantalizing forever, so long as the passion remains unfulfilled. "Heard melodies are sweet," Keats wrote; those unheard? "Sweeter"! The songs Elvis sang must be heard. The song that is Elvis? Best left unknown, or — as for those in this audience — fleetingly glimpsed in passing, "known" only as a brief brush of parted lips against his moist mouth.

In keeping with the theme of many films, particularly the latter ones, Elvis makes it a point to pick out and kiss all the female *children*— appearing far more comfortable when kissing them (here, he's clearly the aggressor) than when being kissed by adult women of various ages. As in the films, he immediately becomes the passive acceptor of their kisses, as overwhelmed and intimidated by grown women as he is in control, the master, with little girls. "He's a very *religious* boy," an elderly lady fan notes, pointing out that he's very kind to his parents — apparently unaware or unconcerned that Gladys died more than a decade earlier. The Elvis of her imagination is the opposite of everything she most detests: all the acid rockers then converging on the nation's much despised-feared Eastern edge. If the blue states-red states dichotomy did not already exist, it began here. Ironically, such country people were the ones who, early on, most detested Elvis. They've long since done a total turnabout — he a hillbilly Hamlet, beloved by the motley multitude ... a mythic hero strutting and swaggering in butch garb, setting the pace for such gender-unidentifiable stars of country-rock as k d lang.

Toward the concert's end, there is a medley of oldies: "Heartbreak Hotel," "One Night With You," "Blue Suede Shoes," "All Shook Up," etc. That this is now, not then, is made clear when director Sanders captures fans in freeze-frame shots, which in 1969-70 American moviemakers begged and/or borrowed from French *nouvelle vogue* experimentations of the early 1960s — once radical styles now co-opted by commerciality, much like the once-raw Elvis himself. The camera zooms in and out as he wildly gyrates during his final number. The filmmaker's technique embodies the rhythms of Elvis's movements, style finally at one with substance, self finally conjoined with society. When all is said and done, Presley stretches his arms outward, upward — looking for a moment like Jesus on the cross. If once his show "died" here, he has clearly risen to live again.

Just Like in the Movies: *Elvis on Tour* (1972)

The Comeback Special offered an apotheosis of all that had gone before, opening the way for a new beginning. Elvis now abandoned the black leather jacket, even as it finally became respectable, for a sequined jumpsuit that the late-'60s–early-'70s Yippies (who held early Elvis in high esteem) considered retro in the worst sense. Even as he permanently cut his ties to the Youth Movement, Presley emerged as "the biggest thing ever in show business."[14] For some, that moment signaled the death of rock 'n' roll — at least in the pure, anti-pop sense of early hillbilly, rhythm 'n' blues and Big Beat music, once accepted (if not necessarily intended) as an "alternative" to pre-existing Tin Pan Alley. Conversely, it can be accepted as the moment when rock was (re)born into an identity it had struggled toward all along as the essence of, and next step for, American Pop. This organic tradition evolved through folk and gospel to ragtime, then jazz and finally rock 'n' roll.

At this point, rock did become part of the American Establishment, as Elvis himself had over the years. And, as his new garb and latest venue made clear, this represented his wave of the future. There was no need to fear any longer that an audience in Las Vegas or any other American community would reject Presley for singing "Heartbreak Hotel" or "Teddy Bear." As he left Sin

City a conqueror, embarking on his concert tour across the country, auditoriums sold out shortly after his Second Coming was announced. Fans, many more conservative now than Presley himself, anticipated a glitzy, non-politicized show. Elvis did still occasionally sing about civil rights, as in his final masterpiece, "In the Ghetto." Largely, though, that battle had been won; hatred for hippies and the Drug Culture now took the place, on the part of bigots, for any hostility toward blacks — so potent during the mid–'60s, when Sammy Davis, Jr., met armed resistance while attempting to perform in the Deep South. There was no such reaction when that star returned in the mid–'70s.

An acceptance of racial minorities, however begrudging, had worked its way into the mainstream. When Elvis sang "In the Ghetto," few if any were willing to complain, other than a few hardcore Klansmen (by now marginalized even in rural Mississippi). Elvis performed tributes to his country and (the case with "American Trilogy") the need to heal old wounds. That had become even more difficult to achieve following the two tumultuous years that passed between the release of his concert films. For months, the Pentagon Papers dominated the news. Embarrassment to the military-industrial complex did not, however, lead to a new wave of student protest. Officially, the war wasn't over, yet draft calls diminished, then disappeared after Nixon augmented an all-volunteer army. The moment that happened, virtually all campus radicalism came to a halt. Other than a few diehard peaceniks, university students turned instead to such earlier pastimes as college football and new examples of mindless fun like "streaking" nude across campuses.

Just as the nation finally seemed likely to calm down, life returning to some sense of normalcy, Watergate broke. A desperate attempt to cover up the June 17, 1972, break-in at the Democrats' campaign headquarters by "plumbers" who owed allegiance to the Nixon campaign, and the entire array of illegal activities out of which it had come, kept the Watergate crime out of the news until after Nixon won a sweeping victory at the polls. *Washington Post* reporters Bob Woodward and Carl Bernstein continued a relentless investigation. Unfolding information was broadcast all day long; in the process, TV news transformed from a minor money-losing network responsibility to a major undertaking and source of revenue as truth did indeed prove to be stranger than fiction. Nixon resigned in early August 1973; his rabble-rousing vice-president Agnew, who once dismissively told reporters he didn't need to investigate ghettoes because "If you've seen one slum, you've seen 'em all," had already been forced out of office owing to varied financial scandals.

America had become the poisoned city of ancient myth, desperate for a catharsis. Squeaky-clean Republican Gerald Ford was appointed president in hopes that he could start fresh. But when he extended a full pardon to Nixon, the public felt that it had again been betrayed, setting the stage for his loss to Democrat Jimmy Carter in 1976.

Where did Elvis fit in with all of this? Once more, he served as a transitional figure for the passing of a torch. Presley had aligned himself with Nixon, yet it has been argued that without Elvis making everything Southern acceptable to the American majority, first Carter, then Bill Clinton could never have attained the presidency.[15] During the difficult days between the Watergate break-in and Nixon's resignation, Presley's concert tour provided precisely what the public needed: An assurance that, in spite of chaotic changes, coming at us with Future Shock frequency, at least one thing in America never changed. Fans could hang onto Elvis as a port in the storm, an old oak holding firm in hurricane winds. Elvis Presley, in 1955 the most divisive element in America, was now the only person (other than that other symbol of cowboy values John Wayne) whom the vast middle class could latch onto as a symbol of undying tradition. But these were men as well as symbols, so die they did — and within a short time of one another only a few years later. When that occurred, the public scrambled to find some alternative person who could reassure them that the simple Western values were not now gone. They found it in Ronald Reagan, who campaigned for the presidency wearing a cowboy hat identical to the one Elvis sported in so many films. Reagan posed in front of the Texas Alamo, which had provided Wayne with the subject of his most deeply personal film.

Despite its title, *Elvis on Tour* is something more than a concert film. Beyond that, producer Pierre Adidge and director Robert Abel determined to also include other elements so as to expand their film's ambitions. Featured are candid interviews with Elvis, employed as voice-over narration(s) for images of the star and his entourage traveling from one city to another, alternately clowning around and seriously rehearsing before a show. Additionally, there are old family photographs that unexpectedly appear, setting the 37-year-old star against pristine images of his childhood in rural Tennessee, in some cases lovingly posed with his parents. In retrospect, one gets the sense that everyone involved understood on some level that this did indeed mark the onset of endgame.

Serving a similar purpose is black-and-white footage from Elvis' early appearances, most notably on *The Ed Sullivan Show*. These grainy images contrast the once sleek, unspoiled country-boy in rural hepcat clothing with the middle-aged man now singing those same songs, wearing a white costume adorned with loud spangles and colorful ornaments. Fortunately, the filmmakers do not intrude in any obvious way with commentary, allowing vivid iconography to speak for itself. Elvis's metamorphosis from rockabilly artist to Liberace-like entertainer was lost on the film's primary audience, hardcore

Presley fans; their devotion helped establish *Elvis on Tour* as a cost-effective #13 on *Variety*'s list of top-grossing films for the year.[16]

To heighten the implied contrast between then and now, the film begins with a family portrait, recalling the poor Southern roots from which Elvis derived. "Johnny B. Goode" is heard over the opening credits. The effect is to recall our collective memory of the young Presley as a white Chuck Berry. Use of the split-screen technique reminds us that the content, tone and intent of this work — concurrent with its early-'70s filmmaking style — belong to a notably different era from that during which "the new music" was born.

In San Antonio, Jackie Kahane, a tuxedo-attired stand-up comic, steps on stage, telling the kind of old, forced jokes that earned Milton Berle an unflattering epithet, "The Thief of Badgag." Watching a commercial hack flattering an overdressed audience of bald men and silver-haired women sets the pace for a musical performance that has less to do with the bold contemporary rockers Elvis inspired than the pop stars who once cruelly dismissed him — but whose company he had always aspired to belong to, and now did. From the moment he steps on stage, it's evident that Presley wants to be liked, accepted. "I've got to please the crowd," he mumbles before beginning his act, "make 'em happy" — this from a performer who once gleefully left crowds all shook up.

An overblown orchestral arrangement accompanies the famed Presley strut into the eager live-audience's line of vision; the Sweet Inspirations augment his performance of the first offering, "See See Rider." In the background, perhaps surprisingly, we note varied musicians including long-haired types who might seem more likely to be jamming along with Crosby, Stills and Nash in a Woodstock-style natural setting. But that event was now ancient history; the dream of a New America died somewhere between the deadly violence at Altamont's rock concert and George McGovern's loss to Nixon. No one had been a more ready symbol of the late-'60s longhair than Neil Young; now he identified himself as a political conservative, though his locks were not shorn. The effect of Elvis' latest concert film, then, is to collapse concurrent musical styles into one another. Presley comes off less like his old self than a riff on Tom Jones — who had made his reputation during the '60s as a Welsh variation on Presley. At this moment, Elvis is no longer part of American pop music — he *is* American pop music!

Slow-motion effects and extreme close-ups on his still beautiful if now plump face allow for a sense that, in this film's context, the live-on-stage event has been modified by cinematic experience. Those of us watching (the movie, not the concert) catch significant details lost on the vast crowd, owing to their physical distance (they are in an immense auditorium) from their object of worship. When Elvis sings "Separate Ways," his eyes clouding over as he comes close to tears, there can be little doubt that, like a Method actor, Elvis wrings stirring emotions with that velvet voice from his own estranged spousal situation. At one of the countless airports we see Presley and company coming from and going to places that once considered him a public menace; they now gleefully open their gates to an authentic all–American populist hero, and middle-aged women scream as they did long ago. Yet the edge is off such reaction. Elvis continued to remain sexy, though he no longer seems sexual. "Don't Be Cruel" and "That's All Right (Mama)" let us grasp how non-incendiary the once-seemingly revolutionary numbers are, after the world has experienced Jimi Hendrix and Janis Joplin.

When Elvis performs covers of Blood, Sweat and Tears, he appears less to be joining (via music) the current youth culture than to mainstream their work in the manner his own once-radical numbers were reduced to elevator music on TV's *Your Hit Parade*. How strange then to see father Vernon talking about how Elvis was "wild in the early days." Here, he only appears tired, desperate to satisfy. A nostalgic montage offers varied images of the original longhair having his head shaved for entrance into the Army. "You'll always be number one," a Rhinestone cowgirl muses, "and never grow old." Elsewhere, an elderly lady who might have been lifted from Grant Wood's "American Gothic" stares, her neutral face refusing to reveal whether she's thrilled, offended or simply dazed by the proceedings. As the show progresses, Elvis slips into religious numbers, in particular those gospel classics that originally inspired him. "Rock My Soul" suggests that his once-controversial gyrations were only his own attempts at wriggling himself into salvation. Now a flesh-and-blood incarnation of the plastic Jesus on the dashboard of some clueless hick's rig, Elvis performs "Amen," the song Sidney Poitier did in *Lilies of the Field* (1963), Elvis cementing his religiosity with the civil rights element that always lent him social substance.

Finally, Elvis takes time to bend down to the women who crowd his stage, kissing a few. Significantly, one of the chosen sighs, "Just like in the movies!" She, for a moment, is Ann-Margret, Nancy Sinatra and Shelley Fabares all rolled into one; her fantasy (to be kissed by the King) incarnated as fleeting actuality. Fittingly, then, the filmmakers cut across the entire canon of Elvis Cinema, focusing on shots in which he puckered up for each of his leading ladies — then returning to the woman who (as her "live" kiss is captured for the Elvis on Tour film) becomes the latest. Her dream — the dream of every young woman of her generation — has just come true. For one wonderful moment — ephemeral at the concert, immortalized for all time on celluloid — she became "the girl who kissed Elvis," a ritual as essential to his movies as the inevitable fistfight with some rowdy guy.

This is that splendid if (as F. Scott Fitzgerald once wrote) "transitory enchanted moment" when the ideal becomes real, then is gone — except in the memory, as imagination reconstructs the experience each time it is recalled. The elusive star slips into a humble freight elevator. A loud voice announces, "Elvis has left the building." As accompaniment to the final image of Elvis Presley in any film made during his lifetime, that phrase takes on added if entirely unconscious resonance.

"50 Million Elvis Fans Can't Be Wrong!": Presley Movies and American Popular Culture

"There is always one moment in childhood," novelist Graham Greene wrote, "when the door opens and lets the future in." For the postwar generation, that wrinkle in time occurred January 28, 1956; with the first glimpse of Elvis on national TV, the Memphis Cat could be seen as well as heard. Those in control of that medium soon made the decision to eliminate, via close-ups on his face, what the children of affluence most wanted to see — a poor (for the moment) country yokel, gleefully shattering their suburbanite sense of privilege with a striking reminder of an earlier America. This icon was now presented in revised form via the contemporary technology of an electric rather than acoustic guitar. Not to be stymied, teenagers trundled off to see him at the movies and (in shrinking numbers) continued to do so for 15 years.

The passage of time eventually rendered those people dittos of that TV-addicted Establishment they once despised. Gradually, they turned theaters over to a new generation of youth and instead watched Elvis, now rendered tame via context and contrast, on television — where once-raunchy movements, displayed in what now were considered "old" movies, could be shown as family fare on Sunday afternoons. Such endless recycling of the musicals keeps the legend alive today. If *only*, critical observers cry, if *only* he had stood up to the colonel back in 1956! Then, the body of work would be composed of artistic gems rather than embarrassing artifacts — sad, silly reminders of a serious career we didn't get to witness. The true shame, many argue, is that Presley did indeed have offers for work in prestige products. His was less a tragedy of fate (a great potential talent offered nothing but junk) than an internal flaw (lack of courage to seize the day).

Here then is an alternative filmography, a glimpse of the road not taken....

273

In 1956, Elvis made his screen debut in Joseph Anthony's film version of N. Richard Nash's popular drama *The Rainmaker*, playing the youngest brother of Katharine Hepburn who, on her parched ranch, falls in love with the title character (Burt Lancaster). Secretly, Elvis dreamed of someday doing the male lead. After the opening credits listed the bulk of the cast, he had the screen to himself for a title that read, "Introducing Elvis Presley." Soon thereafter, he stepped into Joshua Logan's production of *Bus Stop* opposite Marilyn Monroe. Elvis took second-billing to that star (her name above the title, his below it) in a part that would have been James Dean's were he still alive. Next came *Thunder Road*. This might have seemed a letdown (a blood 'n' thunder drive-in flick about moonshiners) except Elvis shared *above*-the-title billing alongside Robert Mitchum, producer-star and one of those "non-smiling" screen idols of Elvis' youth. He played Mitchum's younger brother; at that moment, his sexy-sensitive rebel image crystallized, particularly after the film proved a box office sensation. Each star had a hit record with the title tune.

Now in demand by top producers, Elvis portrayed a country singer whose radio popularity puts him in a position to influence politics in the Budd Schulberg–scripted, Elia Kazan–directed *A Face in the Crowd* (1958), his first lead. Elvis embodied a guitar-strumming incarnation of Orpheus, doomed poet-hero of Greek myth, decked out in a snakeskin jacket for Sidney Lumet's *The Fugitive Kind* (1959), derived from a Tennessee Williams play. He starred opposite (and was billed above) Academy Award–winning actresses Joanne Woodward and Anna Magnani, making clear that Elvis was no mere passing fancy. If anyone still harbored doubts, he dispelled them after receiving an Oscar nomination for Best Actor opposite Elizabeth Taylor in Richard Brooks' adaptation of Williams' *Cat on a Hot Tin Roof*. Presley was highly convincing as "Brick," a seeming Southern stud inwardly confused as to sexual identity.

Our imaginary construction of Elvis' film career continues....

Having achieved what he set out to prove — that he could hold his own on film without singing — Elvis now felt established enough to finally appear in a musical. He perfectly embodied the title character in Melvin Frank's version of Al Capp's *Li'l Abner*. This was swiftly followed by a serious drama about the birth of modern music; in *All the Fine Young Cannibals*, Elvis played a musician based on Chet Atkins, starring opposite Natalie Wood. Presley's deep desire to become a cowboy star was finally realized when he agreed to take third billing in two decidedly different A-list Westerns. In John Huston's *The Misfits*, Elvis played "Perce," a sensitive wrangler role that would have gone to Montgomery Clift had he been in better health. Starring Clark Gable and Marilyn Monroe, the movie's advertising campaign played off the iconography: "Two 'Kings' and the Queen!" No sooner had Elvis completed that grim, downbeat contemporary oater than he headed for Arizona to shoot the light-hearted *Rio Bravo* for Howard Hawks. As the surly young sidekick of John Wayne, Elvis also got to sing a duet with another of his early idols, Dean Martin.

Elvis passed on offers to do several more Westerns, including *The Left Handed Gun* (also originally intended for James Dean) for fear he would become typecast. Following the lead of Kirk Douglas and Paul Newman, he felt that it was better to return on occasion to Western roles without painting himself into a corner and being limited to that genre. He signed for another musical, again appearing opposite sometimes-girlfriend Natalie Wood in Robert Wise's *West Side Story* (1961). His only competition for the status of most talented star to emerge from the early rock 'n' roll era, Bobby Darin, played Tony's friend Riff. They were together a year later in Jose Ferrer's remake of the durable *State Fair* (1962), Elvis as a country boy (romanced by the more experienced Ann-Margret), Bobby a city slicker who falls for Elvis' younger sister, Pamela Tiffin. That was followed in 1963 by a third musical, Elvis again appearing opposite Ann-Margret, this time their roles reversed: She played the virginal girl-next-door and he satirized himself as a womanizing rock 'n' roll star about to be inducted into the Army in *Bye Bye Birdie.* The leads were Janet Leigh and Dick Van Dyke; Elvis accepted "also starring" billing, apart from the rest of the cast. One song, "I've Got a Lot of Livin' to Do," became a huge hit.

Again he took "special billing" in *Captain Newman, M.D.*, a black comedy about life in a military sanitarium starring Gregory Peck and another of Elvis' early idols, Tony Curtis; Elvis was cast as an emotionally disturbed, guitar-strumming G.I. For his efforts, Presley received his second Oscar nomination, this time for Best Actor in a Supporting Role. One year earlier, he played the male lead opposite (with top billing over) esteemed actress Geraldine Page in both *Sweet Bird of Youth* (Elvis had displaced Brando as the interpreter of choice for Williams' heroes) and *Toys in the Attic*, from a Lillian Hellman play. The films allowed him to share romantic scenes with Shirley Knight and Yvette Mimieux. He next starred opposite Lee Remick in Robert Mulligan's *Baby the Rain Must Fall*, intriguingly cast as an Elvis wannabe; the title song provided yet another hit record.

Now it was time to return to his most beloved genre. In the superproduction *How the West Was Won* (1963), Elvis accepted alphabetical billing but had the virtual lead as a Civil War vet who becomes a legendary lawman on the final frontier; the film included Wayne, James Stewart and Henry Fonda in supporting roles. Among the gargantuan work's three directors was John Ford, the Frederic Remington of film; this was among his final works. Ford would shortly retire as, in the altering cultural landscape of the '60s, the new American sensibility demanded a new kind of Western. Elvis played the first of that decade's anti-heroes: Hud Bannon, a cynical rancher, in Martin Ritt's adaptation of Larry McMurtry's *Horseman Pass By*. Over the next several years, Elvis appeared in a succession of major league Westerns. He was "the Ringo Kid," the part that made Wayne a star a quarter-century earlier, in Gordon Douglas' remake of *Stagecoach*. Elvis re-teamed with Wayne for Henry Hathaway's *True Grit* as a Texas Ranger who helps an aged marshal round up outlaws; he also agreed to sing the title song over the opening credits. Firmly established as a Western hero but not wanting to desert his musical origins, Elvis combined the two in Logan's *Paint Your Wagon* (1969), an epic musical-Western. He co-starred with Lee Marvin opposite Jean Seberg; his inspiring rendition of "They Call the Wind Maria" resulted in yet another hit record.

Now our Twilight Zone-*ish journey into that fifth dimensional career which Presley passed on draws to its conclusion....*

Elvis' now firmly established iconography as a Western hero added an extra dimension to his casting in John Schlesinger's *Midnight Cowboy*. Presley played a would-be Texas stud who heads for Manhattan to service the needy women he believes are awaiting him there, only to be reduced to a male street hustler. Elvis sang several Harry Nilsson songs, including "Everybody's Talkin' (At Me)."

Though at the height of his powers, Elvis grew uncomfortable with Hollywood's direction during the 1970s. His traditionalist views didn't jell with the new Ratings System (installed in 1969), which allowed for nudity, rough language and violence. So Presley was happy to return to live concerts, in Vegas and on tour, where he enjoyed great success. He made only one other film, *A Star Is Born* (1976), playing opposite (and accepting second billing to) Barbra Streisand — Elvis effectively cast as a fading star who must make room for the next generation. If Oscar eluded him, Elvis did receive a pair of Emmys for his highly acclaimed performances in two upscale made-for-TV movies: the remake of *A Streetcar Named Desire*, in which he tackled Brando's star-making role (and made it his own) opposite Ann-Margret and Tuesday Weld as Blanche and Stella, respectively; and the lead in a musical broadcast based on Broadway's *40 Degrees in the Shade*— Elvis at last getting to play "The Rainmaker."

That imagined film career certainly seems a happy alternative to the "travelogues with music." According to all conventional standards of good taste, such work done by other stars resulted in great and near-great films or, at the least, ambitious failures. The critical establishment, if once (long ago) divided over the man's music, has always expressed unanimity as to his movies: "brain rotting"[1]; "low-mediocre"[2]; "numbingly stupid."[3] Such statements hail not from those who come to bury Presley but to praise him as a musical genius, the key figure between Sinatra and Dylan. Finally, the ultimate put-down: "His movies made millions but could not be defended on artistic grounds."[4] That only begs the question: *who*se artistic grounds? Those of upper-middlebrow types who dictate what is momentarily considered "classy" at the time of initial appearance? (Such standards were as dismissive of Shake-spearean theater and Italian opera in their original eras as Presley's musicals in his time.) The elitist view has always held that anything beloved by the masses can't be good. Ortega y Gasset, long ranked as the leading spokesman for such a position, claimed that "the masses not only vulgarize and dehuman-ize but actually destroy art."[5] By that standard, the coda employed to defend Presley in the early days ought to be reversed: 50 million Elvis fans can't be *right*!

Even in the twenty-first century, as Stephen King noted, there are many "folks who believe art should be work and see entertainment as subversive."[6] But if we accept *varied* definitions as to what constitutes art, we will perceive the situation in a different light. Nineteen hundred and sixty-five was the year when Matthew Arnold's notion of "high seriousness," since 1880 set in stone as the *only* acceptable definition of true art, gave way to a diversity, allowing for the frivolous which provides fun. Poetry (or any art form), Arnold once claimed, *must* offer "a criticism of life."[7] Perhaps that statement would best be taken as *a* description of the only sort of art a classicist admires. This hardly rules out an alternative (i.e., romantic) description — one which *celebrates* life, accepts (and represents) it warts and all, rather than longs to improve what we discover in the world around us. The works of Walt Whitman (or for that matter Walt Disney), worthless to the classical mind, are all-important to the romantic sensibility — and to the populist. The point isn't that Arnold's notion should be rejected, only that other attitudes ought to also be expressed and heard.

So consider an alternative ideology as to what constitutes art: "intuitive apprehension," "self-objectification of feeling," "pattern informed by sensibil-ity," "liberation of personality," "man speaking to men," "an act of love toward humanity," "the direct measure of spiritual vision."[8] Fishwick was here writ-ing in general terms about new directions in art; he might well have been speak-ing specifically of Elvis.

From Plato through Arnold to Gasset, an idealistic definition of art has called for a "study and pursuit of perfection ... beauty and intelligence ... sweetness and light."[9] Art should make us "better" (or at least set out to do so) via exposure to the finer things in life; art's greatest function, to serve as a brave bulwark against the ordinary — the low culture of chaos as opposed to high culture of the civilized, cliquish *cogniscenti*, the self-appointed elite.

But beginning early in the twentieth century, and particularly in the mid–'60s, fresh aesthetics and emerging attitudes, evolving in response to an altering zeitgeist, reacted against Arnold's (arguably) outworn values. Rebel critics began to question what truly did constitute those finer things in life; whether exposure to ballet, for instance, could make us "better people" than those who chose instead to head for the Peppermint Lounge and watch hipsters perform the Twist.

This was not so new as it first seemed. From Parmenides to Susan Sontag, there has always been a parallel line of celebratory rather than critical voices crying out in the wilderness. They express a notion of art that embraces rather than rejects "the meanest things" in life, finding not only pleasure but value: Whitman celebrating his own self; Warhol and Lichtenstein insisting we ought to perceive soup cans and comic strip panels as something of value. Meaningful elements in our pop landscape, so obvious and all-present, glanced at on such an everyday basis (familiarity does breed contempt!) that our brains ignore what our eyes report as we learn *not* to see them. But which ought to be granted the respect of our choosing to actually look, and perhaps finally see with eyes and brains both, that there is more here than a cursory glance might lead us to believe. After all, "nothing begins as art. Objects come into being as something to be measured on the scale of desirability."[10]

In truth, what was more desirable, between 1955 and 1970, than Presley's music and movies, as record sales and box office returns made clear at the time. And which CD and DVD sales today continue to validate. The only thing the music failed to earn early on was some measure of critical respect, though that has long since come. Not, however, the movies. Difficult though it may be to believe, it isn't entirely impossible that the 33 silly musicals, tripey travelogues and youth exploitation flicks may achieve an aura of worthiness. This volume has attempted to provide a tip for the iceberg which may eventually prove itself big enough to transform our collective vision of Presley's unpretentious films into an oeuvre known as Elvis Cinema.

Warhol, Lichtenstein and their crowd achieved respect for Campbell's, Coca-Cola and *Batman* by yanking them out of their everyday environment, setting such stuff on the pedestals and walls of edgy galleries, then in due time legitimate museums. My purpose has been to likewise pull Presley's films out of their obvious position in our pop culture world (channel-surf through cable TV and you'll find one playing at almost any hour of every day), then reset them in the heady world of an academic tome in hopes that perceiving the "flicks" in such a radically removed situation will kick-start a new way of looking at them.

After all, what is art, according to a less idealistic, more realistic definition, than popular pieces of seemingly ephemeral entertainment which, perhaps to the surprise of everyone, have passed the test of time and remain with us still? Or, to return to an earlier theme, "the finer things in life" are the ones we enjoyed most, on instinct, not those we were told by our "betters" that, if we had class, we should "appreciate." The omnipresence of the Presley films proves they pass the test of time, in a way that works with loftier ambitions often fail to do. For instance: In 1958, few Hollywood productions were as eagerly anticipated as *A Farewell to Arms*: based on a Hemingway novel, produced by *Gone with the Wind*'s David O. Selznick, starring Oscar winner Jennifer Jones, directed by the esteemed Charles Vidor. The film was attended in its time by those very suburbanites who would never have considered going to see Elvis in *King Creole*, leaving that to their crazy teenage kids or adult members of the lower classes. Today, that dull, overblown, uninvolving rendering of *A Farewell to Arms* appears all but non-existent. The film never shows on TV because the public doesn't care to watch it. Nor is it revered by academics, who don't screen it in university film seminars. *King Creole*, an exploitation flick that played second-string theaters? The recent DVD reissue sold out; professors use it to demonstrate everything from the vision of women in the 1950s to the relationship between folk and jazz and early rock 'n' roll, now a subject of academic interest.

"Opinion," Schopenhauer wrote, "is like a pendulum and obeys the same law." My intent has been to initiate a pendulum swing away from the overriding opinion as to Presley's musicals. "The movies are [merely] a parody of the myth that in other ways he seemed to fulfill," Van K. Brock has written.[11] Inarguable? Perhaps. Yet couldn't the essential truth of this statement be allowed a positive rather than negative spin — viewed not as the intended criticism but a tribute? *He never forgot where he came from!* Them thar people in New York and Hollywood didn't change him none. Elvis could have opted for those upscale projects that appealed to a suburban audience. Instead, he made movies which, following brief popularity with 1950s teens, settled down to comfortably entertain a target audience of farming folk in the rural South and blue collar workers in the industrial North —*his* "people"; Elvis people!

Perhaps the colonel didn't make him do it after all; maybe Elvis opted for such films to remain true to his all-important promise to the Memphis fans following his embarrassing appearance in a tux on Steve Allen's TV show. To have done *West Side Story* would have signified that Elvis had changed, gotten "classy," would in time don another tux for the Oscars. He couldn't let that happen, so he made *Kissin' Cousins* instead. Rather than sell out his base to become "respectable," Elvis — always an incarnation of the ancient mythic hero — gave up his potential for growth to remain true to his word ... and his world. This is affirmed less by the music (which did become mainstream) than the movies. As to Brock's chosen term "parody," doesn't that actually indicate Elvis' post-modernism, a smart approach taken toward silly material that redeems it? A sly deconstruction of his own somewhat absurd image to deflate any and all pretensions?

"The real significance of his movies," Brock can scoff,

> is in how little they contributed to him as a human being, how little he learned, and how much they reduced his [musical] achievement and put him back in his place as, to paraphrase his words, this Southerner always singing to dogs and children.[12]

If "contribute" means to "facilitate growth," isn't the essence of Elvis — his basic values — a *rejection* of just such growth? By putting him "back in his place as this Southerner," didn't the films prove that he remained true to his promise, "didn't change none"? Rather, he changed the world: Elvis would not adjust to Vegas after his initial failing; true to country roots, he changed the nation's tastes, then triumphantly returned to Vegas where, still the good ol' boy he'd always been, he was now welcomed, the hillbilly having over the years countrified the entire country.

Elvis' films were, between 1956 and 1969, the equivalent of such déclassé entertainment as the rural comedies of the summer tent circuit and the hard-laugh hillbilly antics of the first flickers. Toby (on-stage) naturally metamorphosed into "Uncle Josh" (on-screen). Later, into the sub-literary shenanigans of Erskine Caldwell's *Tobacco Road* denizens. And, in more polite writing about rubes, the dumb-like-foxes rednecks who haunt Faulkner's Yoknapatawpha County. Then on to Toby's darker incarnation as Stanley in *Streetcar*; eventually, the most light-hearted version of all as Jed Clampett's son Jethro, not lettin' no one change him none though he now lives in Beverly Hills.

And, most notably, in the Presley musicals. He could be the country Candide, a backwoods innocent, in one; a localized Loki, the rube as trickster, in the next. In this light, the films' utter failure to satisfy, on any (conventional) critical level, does not negate their significance as a body of work, in terms of what they tell us about this unique and yet universal person. The early ones reveal the country boy who, Gatsby-like, sprang from "a platonic conception of himself," achieving his dream of commercial success — his unique version of the greater American dream — in a remarkably short time. If he momentarily appears epic, that's but a fleeting illusion. He wants to win the dream girl, and in a sense does, though (as the middle films, reflecting his life, make clear) realistic achievement of a double for the woman he loved and lost does not satisfy. He wanted not a real girl, however beautiful, but to actualize his impossible romantic dream of her as perfect; unfortunately, perfection cannot exist in the real world. Let down by all he's achieved and like that other dark artistic American icon of the unique South, Edgar Allan

Poe, Elvis hopes to put off consummation forever with his child bride in the final films, just as (late in his own life) he ruins the relationship, searching for his lost love in ever younger girls.

One ongoing way of determining if any work qualifies as art is whether or not it imparts an emotional autobiography of the human who creates it; by that standard, Elvis Cinema does indeed rate as art in a way those loftier films he passed on would not. His appearance in any or all of them would have been entirely arbitrary, based on the relative worth at that one moment in time of the individual project, not whether it would have allowed for self-expression. How, for example, can we grasp the significance of Elvis in the Oval Office with Nixon, hesitating to leave until the president turned over his cufflinks (of all things) to Jerry Schilling and Sonny West, Memphis Mafiosos who accompanied him on that bizarre journey? By watching *Jailhouse Rock*, discovering there the significance such items had for the man who would be King. "The only kind of music he wasn't terribly fond of was jazz," Priscilla once noted.[13] She appears stumped as to where the answer lies, yet we can find the reason in that film's suburban party.

Priscilla's autobiography reveals with touching honesty her deep desire to make sense of what went wrong with their marriage; she only needed to watch *Double Trouble* to discover her husband's open admission as to his obsession with underage girls. This, as opposed to his fear of consummation when his "live-in Lolita"[14] (at age 14 sexually toyed with, though never violated, both on-screen and in real life) did indeed reach legal age:

> I begged him to consummate our love.... "No. Someday we will, Priscilla, but not now. You're just too young."[15]

Two years later, Priscilla by her own admission lived a bizarre double life, wholesome schoolgirl at the aptly named Emmaculate Conception by day, black-lace quasi-lover by night, providing him with the satisfaction he still steadfastly denied her:

> Not yet, not now. We have a lot to look forward to. I'm not going to spoil you. I just want to keep you the way you are for now. There'll be a right time and place, and when the moment comes, I'll know it.[16]

Jill Conway in *Double Trouble* could, like Priscilla, admit about Elvis' character, Guy Lambert, in that highly revealing film:

> I don't think he really knew what to do with me. After all, Elvis had protected me and saved me for so long. He was now understandably hesitant about fulfilling all his promises about how very good this moment was going to be.[17]

Then came the moment that could be put off no longer. Following the Vegas wedding, "he carried me across the threshold of our house singing 'The

Hawaiian Wedding Song.'"[18] Perhaps Priscilla remained unconscious of the extremes to which Elvis would go to stage his own actual wedding so it would combine the best qualities of those which end *Blue Hawaii* and *Viva Las Vegas,* life now imitating art instead of the other way around. And do so for a woman born with a natural resemblance to actress Debra Paget whom Elvis had lost both on-screen and off- in 1956. A resemblance that Elvis, like "Scottie" in Hitchcock's *Vertigo* (1958), consciously heightened over the years, emphasizing all the more as the moment of full, final consummation became unavoidable. This, despite his desire to put this actualization off for as long as possible, knowing as he did that reality, however pleasurable, can never live up to a romantic egoist's impossible dream.

In addition to the creative expression of self, another means of deciding whether or not a piece of entertainment makes the great crossover to true art relates to its social significance. Such is also reflected in Presley's movies, for the world around him changes, as it must, with each successive film. Step by step, we note the shifting of what constituted America between 1955 and 1970, along with Elvis' moral vision of it. (We actually do see a change in tone from celebratory of the late 1950s and early '60s scene to what Arnold would have considered a "criticism" of the late 1960s-early '70s zeitgeist.) Those supposedly marginal movies in retrospect provide an ongoing, organic oeuvre filled with self-revelation and social commentary. "They all have two things in common," Stanley Booth can scoff; "None lost money, none is contingent at any point upon reality."[19] Some did indeed lose money, particularly the latter entries; if they hadn't, Hollywood would never have stopped making them. More important, how does one define reality? That's proven as difficult as defining art.

On the surface, it's true that the films create a colorful fantasy world. But if the invention of an alternative reality negates a work's quality, then we aren't justified in our ongoing respect for Jonathan Swift, Lewis Carroll, Frank Baum and filmmakers as disparate as George Lucas and Federico Fellini. Isn't a third aspect of art the creation of an alternative universe in one's chosen medium of expression? Or (to switch to popular culture rather than the classical canon) Tex Avery's off-the-wall MGM cartoon shorts. Are Andrew Wyeth's paintings of more value than Picasso's simply because they can more accurately be described as "realistic"? In the fine arts, we would consider such a pronouncement to be naïve, and rightly so. Why not disparage such narrowness in the realm of cinema?

As to Presley's films, Greil Marcus appears one of the few observers who "gets it": "Elvis' blues were a set of musical adventures, and as a blues-singing swashbuckler, his style owed as much to Errol Flynn as it did to Arthur Crudup. It made sense to make movies out of it."[20] By that line of reasoning, Elvis made the only movies that could have ever naturally emerged from his unique sensibility — movies which reflect rather than undermine his musical base. Seeing is believing, Biskind has reminded us in referring to other films of the '50s; without the movies, we could not have seen (thus believed) Elvis. They are inseparable, not apart, from his greatness.

Still, as King points out about American pop culture in general, "There are plenty of people who see this beautiful junk-shop carnival as lowbrow, thoughtless, ruinous, even vicious."[21] For those who cling to conventional tastes, the claim that *Follow That Dream* and *Fun in Acapulco* may be more significant relics of the early '60s than *Advise and Consent* or *The Night of the Iguana* remains inconceivable, laughable, virtually impossible. Still, the "mindless musicals" stand the test of time in a way that many of that era's elevated, ambitious films do not.

However admired *Becket* was in 1964, it owns no significant place in our contemporary culture. *Viva Las Vegas* is another matter. It has become a cultural touchstone; TV advertisements and major motion pictures (including *The Big Lebowsky* by the Coen Brothers, 1998) employ it as a point of reference. Virtually no one fails to get such references. Simply, a shaking-out process in the arts allows us to discern the wheat from the chaff; often, each turns out to be the opposite of what it initially seemed. Susan Sontag and Marshall McLuhan were the pop-culture prophets who fully and forcefully expressed such attitudes during the tumultuous cultural revolution that was the '60s. Forerunners included Harold Rosenberg who, in *The Tradition of the New* (1959), related modern media forms and all of pop culture to our lives rather than writing them off as temporary fads. He paved the way for perception of supposed junk and ephemera as the works that ultimately matter the most; those elements in our culture that define the age in which they were created in a way that more polite forms do not.

Properly understood, Presley's pictures appeared in our pop culture during a period of radical transition from one America to another. They premiered in a grind circuit context that caused them to be perceived as some radical alternative to then-typical Hollywood fare. That America disappeared as we evolved (or de-evolved) into a nation devastated by political assassinations, an un-winnable war in Vietnam, the Watergate scandal and resignation of a president, revelations of pollution in our environment, the descent into a drug culture, and an overturning of every idea as to what constituted acceptable public behavior. Viewed today, Elvis' musicals, however humble, project the last hoarse, hollow, reactionary gasp of Hollywood's old-fashioned approach and traditional values. The great irony: that Presley also set into motion the forces that would destroy the very Establishment he so admired — this only adding to his tragic as well as mythic image.

Approaching Elvis Cinema from this perspective, we may well conclude the opposite of what's always been assumed about them. Perhaps Presley didn't follow his worst instincts upon arriving in L.A. but his *best*, forsaking quasi-elitist projects for ones more in tune with the people (and his own populist spirit) than the critics, the Academy and staid, self-satisfied suburbanites. Fortunate, then, that we will always have *Loving You*, *Viva Las Vegas* and all the others. Without them, their continued availability and the unrelenting interest in them, the legend of Elvis might very possibly not exist, at least not with the potency that it currently knows. Even if we are willing to admit that, on any conventional level of judgment, they are mostly awful films, we can counter by insisting that their greatness can't be calculated by narrow standards.

Ought we then to announce that all those reviewers for daily newspapers were wrong — that, say, *Kissin' Cousins* is actually a misunderstood masterpiece? Not necessarily, and certainly not for the multitude of middlebrow filmgoers, past and present. For them, what has come to be thought of as the Ebert-Roeper thumbs up/down approach (the quality of a film is judged as to whether it's deemed worthy of the average person paying for a ticket) remains the right mode of criticism. Yet if we have learned anything from recent social, cultural and political transformations, it is that diversity ought to be celebrated in *all* things: lifestyle, gender, religion, of course, but also the appreciation of art and/or entertainment. There are other inroads into a film, equally valid to the overriding one, these based on alternative aesthetics that may better serve specific minorities of movie buffs, each with its own values and esoteric tastes that cause what's largely considered to be a "bad" film "good," and vice versa. Such varied means of evaluating movies as auteurism, structuralism, semiotics, Marxism, feminism, queer studies, camp and a dozen other competing approaches drive home this point. If we approach even the shoddiest Presley vehicle (the aforementioned *Kissin' Cousins* a fitting example), we may find something of value beneath all the crassness and cornpone as a work that initially seems devoid of ideology emerges as a political tract.

To borrow from McLuhan, the message comes in realizing that, any obvious limitations as to production values of any one film set aside, they reveal Elvis' own inner self far more than he apparently understood while reflecting the society which produced, adored, damned, accepted, then came to worship him; and that, like the chintz art of the early twentieth century — scorned by people of good taste at the time, now considered precious artifacts — they were realized in a style which, carefully considered, can't be analyzed apart from its substance. Those two aspects, fully understood, must — if the work truly qualifies as art — exist as mirror images of one another. This holds true not only in Elvis Cinema but all popular culture and, for that matter, the vaster realms of art and entertainment.

Notes

Introduction: All Singing! All Talking! All Dancing!

1. Michael Heatley, ed., *The Ultimate Encyclopedia of Rock* (New York: HarperCollins Publishers, Inc., 1993), pp. 218–19.

2. Dave McAleer, *The All Music Book of Hit Singles* (San Francisco: Miller Freeman Books, 1994), pp. 25 & 33.

3. Erika Doss, *Elvis Culture: Fans, Faith, & Images* (Lawrence, KS: University Press of Kansas, 1999).

4. Two documentaries, *Elvis: That's the Way It Is* (1970) and *Elvis On Tour* (1973), would follow in his lifetime, as well as numerous pseudo-documentaries and dramatic re-enactments produced after Presley's death.

5. Steven Zmijewsky and Boris Zmijewsky, *Elvis. The Films and Career of Elvis Presley* (Secaucus, N.J.: Citadel Press, 1976).

6. Zmijewsky, p. 80.

7. Zmijewsky, p. 81

8. Doss, p. 141.

9. Moira Walsh, *America*, 97:472, August 3, 1957.

10. Unsigned, *Time*, 83:86, May 29, 1964.

11. Albert Goldman, *Elvis* (New York: McGraw-Hill, 1981), p. 133–35.

12. Peter Guralnick, *Careless Love: The Unmaking of Elvis Presley* (Boston: Little, Brown, 1999), p. 123.

13. Guralnick, p. 123.

14. Guralnick, p. 75.

15. Benita Eisler, *Private Lives: Men and Women of the Fifties* (New York: Franklin Watts, 1986), p. 337.

16. Doss, p. 139.

17. Greil Marcus, *Dead Elvis: A Chronicle of a Cultural Obsession* (New York: Doubleday, 1991), p. xxl.

18. David Halberstam, *The Fifties* (New York: Ballantine Books, 1994), p. 457.

19. Alanna Nash, *Aaron Elvis Presley: Revelations from the Memphis Mafia* (New York: HarperCollins Publishers, Inc., 1995), p. 86.

20. Halberstam, p. 457.

21. Quoted in Halberstam, p. 477.

22. Guralnick, p. 133.

23. Halberstam, p. 477.

24. J. Ronald Oakley, *God's Country: America in the Fifties* (New York: W.W. Norton & Company, Inc., 1986), p. 276.

25. Oakley, p. 278.

26. James L. Neibaur, *Tough Guy: The American Movie Macho* (Jefferson, N.C.: McFarland, 1989), p. 190.

27. George Melly, *Revolt into Style: The Pop Arts* (New York: Anchor, 1971), p. 37–38.

28. Kevin Quain, ed., *The Elvis Reader: Texts and Sources on the King of Rock'n'Roll* (New York: St. Martin's Press, 1992), p. 255.

29. Louis Giannetti, *Understanding Movies*, Eighth Edition (Upper Saddle River, N.J.: Prentice-Hall, 1999), p. 80.

30. Doss, p. 52.

31. Review of *Speedway*, *The New York Times*, 43:1, June 14, 1968.

32. Elvis, quoted in Halberstam, pp. 478–79.

33. Doss, p. 13.

34. Doss, p. 13.

35. Egill "Budd" Krogh, *The Day Elvis Met Nixon* (Bellvue, WA: Pejama Press, 1994).

36. Eisler, p. 174.

37. Warren I. Susman, *Culture as History: The Transformation of American Society in the 20th Century* (New York: Pantheon Books, 1984), p. 32.

38. Eisler, p. 69.

39. Alvin Toffler, *Future Shock* (New York: Random House, 1970).

1. Elvis Died for Your Sins

1. Marcus, p. 92.
2. Halberstam, p. 164.
3. Eisler, p. 37.
4. Oakley, p. 88, also see Susman, p. 32.
5. Halberstam, p. 91.
6. Oakley, p. 121.
7. Elvis at once incarnates on-screen his own rural (farmer) rather than western (cowboy) past, see Van K. Brock, "Images of Elvis, the South, and America," found in both Jac Tharpe, *Elvis: Images and Fancies* (Jackson University Press of Mississippi, 1977), and *Reader*, pp. 126–58), also, May Mann, *The Private Elvis* (New York: Kangaroo Books/Pocket Books, 1975), particularly pages 142–47.
8. James and Annette Baxter, "The Man in the Blue Suede Shoes," *Harper's* magazine, 1958, reprinted in *Reader*, p. 33.
9. Kael, quoted in Halberstam, p. 484.
10. Peter Biskind, *Seeing Is Believing: How Hollywood Taught Us to Stop Worrying and Love the Fifties* (New York: Pantheon Books, 1983), particularly pp. 34–44, 197–227, 278–84.
11. Guralnick, p. 61.
12. Clark Porteous, *Memphis Press Scimitar*, August 17, 1977, also in *Reader*, p. 50.
13. Jay Cocks, *Time*, August 29, 1977, also in *Reader*, p. 59.
14. Halberstam, p. 458.
15. Priscilla Beaulieu Presley (with Sandra Harmon), *Elvis and Me* (New York: Berkley, 1985), p. 33.
16. William Steif, "What Makes Elvis Presley Tick — No. 3, the Pelvis Explains that 'Vulgar' Style," *San Francisco News*, October 17, 1956, p. 3.
17. Baxter, *Reader*, p. 32.
18. Presley, p. 23.
19. Cocks, *Reader*, p. 61.
20. Goldman, p. 183.
21. Jack Kroll, "The Heartbreak Kid," *Newsweek* (August 29, 1977), reprinted in *Reader*, p. 68.
22. Linda Ray Pratt, "Elvis, or the Ironies of a Southern Identity," *Southern Quarterly*, 1979, reprinted (among many other places) in *Reader*, p. 93.
23. "Mr. Harper," "Elvis the Indigenous," *Harper's* magazine, April 1957, reprinted in *Reader*, p. 37.
24. "Mr. Harper," *Reader*, p. 37.
25. Elvis Presley's permanent F.B.I. file. Washington, D.C.
26. Marcus, p. 126.
27. Ted Harrison, *Elvis People: The Cult of the King* (New York: HarperCollins, 1993), p. 9.
28. Ron Rosenbaum, "Among the Believers," *The New York Times Magazine*, September 24, 1995, p. 50–57, 62 & 64, also see missive quoted by Peter Whitmer in *The Inner Elvis: A Psychological Biography of Elvis Aaron Presley* (New York: Hyperion, 1996), p. 198.

2. Alive and Well in TV Land

1. Eisler, p. 69
2. Maureen Orth, "All Shook Up," *Newsweek*, August 29, 1977, reprinted in *Reader*, p. 64.
3. Oakley, p. 99.
4. Quoted in Halberstam, p. 474.
5. Douglas T. Miller and Marion Nowak, *The Fifties: The Way We Really Were* (Garden City, N.Y.: Doubleday, 1977), p. 414.
6. Eisler, p. 92.
7. Halberstam, p. 24.
8. Baxter, *Reader*, p. 33.
9. Halberstam, p. 269.
10. Joyce Johnson, *Minor Characters* (Boston: Houghton Mifflin, 1983), p. 27.
11. Jack Kerouac, *On the Road* (New York: NAL/Dutton, 1958), p. 5.
12. Michael Wood, *America in the Movies* (New York: Basic Books, 1975), p. 39.
13. Doss, quoting numerous popular journalists of 1956, p. 6.
14. Greil Marcus, *Mystery Train: Images of America in Rock and Roll Music* (New York: E.P. Dutton, 1982), p. 189.
15. Halberstam, p. 479.
16. Norman Mailer, "The White Negro," reprinted in *Advertisements for Myself* (New York: G.P. Putnam, 1959).
17. Eisler, 97.
18. Goldman, p. 34, see also Presley, particularly pages 32–46 & 54–63.
19. Doss, p. 144.
20. Melly, p. 34–35.
21. Eisler, p. 171.
22. Eustace Chesser, *Love Without Fear: How to Achieve Sex Happiness* (London: Rich and Cowan Publishers, 1941), p. 82.
23. Nash, p. 121.
24. Patsy Guy Hammontree, *Elvis Presley: A Bio-Bibliography* (Westport, CT: Greenwood Press, 1985), p. 188.
25. Richard Schickel, *The Disney Version: The Life, Times, Art and Commerce of Walt Disney* (New York: Simon and Schuster, 1968), pp. 176–77.
26. Halberstam, p. 478.
27. Baxter, *Reader*, p. 32.
28. Doss, p. 128.
29. Mojo Nixon, *Reader*, p. xiv.
30. Cocks, *Reader*, p. 58.
31. Nicholas von Hoffman, *We Are the People*

Our Parents Warned Us Against (Chicago: Ivan R. Dee, Inc./Elephant Paperbacks, 1968).
32. Halberstam, p. 479.
33. Halberstam, p. 422.
34. Kroll, *Reader*, p. 69.
35. Biskind, p. 37.

3. Of Music and Money

1. McAleer, p. 39.
2. Oakley, p. 333.
3. Oakley, p. 332.
4. Doss, p. 39.
5. Betty Friedan, *The Feminine Mystique* (New York: Dell Publishing, 1963).
6. Miller and Nowak, p. 334.
7. Goldman, p. 47.
8. Nash, p. 85.
9. Eisler, p. 230.
10. Tom Thatcher, quoted by Julia Aparin, "He Never Got Above His Raising: An Ethnographic Study of Working Class Response to Elvis Presley"; Ph.D. dissertation (unpublished), University of Pennsylvania, 1988, pp. 73–76.
11. Eisler, p. 223.
12. Halberstam, p. 358.
13. Friedrich William Nietzsche, *Santliche Werke in Zwolf Banden* (Stutgart: A. Kroner, 1964–65), Vol. 6, p. 293.
14. Presley, p. 138.
15. Halberstam, p. 479.
16. Peter Guralnick, *Last Train to Memphis: The Rise of Elvis Presley* (Boston: Little, Brown, 1994), p. 411–12.
17. Nash, p. 87.
18. Nash, p. 196.
19. Eisler, pp. 337–38.
20. Eisler, p. 229.

4. Fathers and Sons

1. Doss, p. 168.
2. Halberstam, p. 456.
3. Halberstam, p. 459.
4. Halberstam, p. 460.
5. Guralnick, *Last Train*, p. 47.
6. Halberstam, p. 461.
7. Public statement, circa 1965.
8. Trent Hill, "The Enemy Within: Censorship in Rock Music in the 1950s," *South Atlantic Quarterly* 90 (1991), p. 691.
9. Eisler, p. 132.
10. Doss, p. 168.
11. Halberstam, p. 472.
12. Doss, p. 168, also see Adam Parfrey, "The Girlfriend Who Last Saw Elvis Alive Fan Club," and Debby Wimer, "Spanish Eyes," *Cult Rap-ture*, Adam Parfrey, editor (Portland: Feral House, 1995), pp. 62–91.
13. Halberstam, p. 477.
14. Goldman, p. 152.
15. Doss, p. 120.
16. Michael Fordham and Roger Hobdell, editors, *Freud, Jung, Klein—The Fenceless Field: Essays on Psychoanalysis and Analytic Psychology* (London: Routledge, 1998).
17. Doss, p. 151.
18. Biskind, p. 199.
19. David A. Stanley, *The Elvis Encyclopedia* (North Dighton, MA: World Publications/JG Press, 2002), p. 19.
20. Biskind, p. 197.
21. Jerry Osborne, *Elvis: Word for Word* (New York: Harmony Books, 1999), p. 3.
22. Schickel, p. 176.

5. You Can't Go Home Again

1. Doss, p. 14.
2. Lennon, quoted by Sandra Choron and Bob Oskam in *Elvis! The Last Word* (New York: Citadel Press, 1991), p. 33.
3. Stanley, p. 173.
4. George Kennan ("X"), "The Sources of Soviet Conflict," *Foreign Affairs*, July 1947, pp. 580–82.
5. Doss, p. 14.
6. Joseph M. Boggs, *The Art of Watching Films*, Fourth Edition (California: Mayfield Publishing Company, 1996), in particular pages 135–46.
7. Joni Mabe, *Everything Elvis* (New York: Thunder Mountain Press, 1998), pp. 46–48.
8. Vernon Chadwick, *In Search of Elvis: Music, Race, Art, Religion* (Reprint: Westview, CT: Greenwood, 1997), p. 127.
9. Laura Mulvey, "Visual Pleasure and Narrative Cinema," *Screen* 16.3 (Autumn 1975), pp. 6–18.
10. H. J. C. Grierson, "Classical and Romantic," pp. 20–33, and T. E. Hulme, "Romanticism and Classicism," pp. 34–44, in *Romanticism: Points of View*, Robert F. Gleckner and Gerald E. Enscoe, eds. Upper Saddle River, N.J.: Prentice-Hall, 1962.
11. Eisler, p. 304.
12. Quain, *Reader*, p. xx.
13. William H. Whyte, Jr., "The Outsize Life," *Fortune*, July 1955, p. 63.
14. Eisler, p. 86.
15. "Americans on the Move to New Jobs, New Places," *Life*, February 3, 1951, p. 36.
16. Whyte, "The Outsize Life," p. 85.
17. Dominic Cavallo, *A Fiction of the Past* (New York: St. Martin's Press, 1999), p. 34.

18. "The Careful Young Men," *The Nation*, March 1957, pp. 197–208.

19. Eisler, p. 240.

20. Goldstein, p. 37

21. *The Nation*, 1955.

22. Eisler, p. 29.

23. Benjamin Spock, *The Common Sense Book of Baby and Child Care* (New York: Duell, Sloan and Pearce, 1946), p. 1.

24. Eisler, p. 35.

25. Philip Wylie, *A Generation of Vipers* (New York: Rinehart Publishing, 1942).

26. Peter Wicke, quoted in Steven Watts, *The Magic Kingdom*, p. 58.

27. Dale Carnegie, quoted in Watts, p. 58.

28. Paul Goodman, *Growing Up Absurd: Problems of Youth in the Organized Society* (New York: Random House, 1960).

29. Louis Giannetti, *Understanding Movies*, Seventh Edition (Upper Saddle River, N.J.: Prentice-Hall, 1996), pp. 397–406.

30. Cavallo, p. 8.

31. Cole, quoted by Mildred Gilman, "Why Can't They Wait to Wed?," *Parents Magazine*, November 1958, p. 47.

6. Mired in the '50s

1. Eisler, p. 7.

2. Norman Mailer, "David Riesman Reconsidered," *Dissent* (Autumn 1954), pp. 358–59.

3. Stanley Aronowitz, p. 191.

4. Osborne, p. 151.

5. *Saturday Review*, December 1960.

6. Halberstam, p. 482.

7. Eisler, p. 260.

8. Doss, p. 123–24.

9. *Time*, December 1960.

10. Camille Paglia, *Sexual Personae: Art and Decadence from Nefertiti to Emily Dickinson* (New York: Vintage, 1990), p. 115.

11. Philip French, *Westerns: Aspects of a Movie Genre* (New York: The Viking Press), p. 80–81.

12. Biskind, p. 229.

13. French, p. 77.

14. Doss, p. 135.

15. Doss, p. 176.

16. Biskind, p. 238.

17. L. Berg and R. Street, *Sex: Methods and Manners* (New York: Archer House, 1953), p. 14.

18. Halberstam, p. 486.

19. Serling, quoted in Halberstam, p. 484.

20. Halberstam, p. 666.

21. Mercy Anne Wright, quoted in Peter Joseph, *Good Times: An Oral History of America in the Nineteen Sixties* (New York: Charterhouse, 1973), p. 359.

22. Lou Smith, quoted in *Good Times*, p. 200, also see pp. 198–201 for complete context.

23. Ray, quoted in Halberstam, p. 485.

24. Halberstam, p. 480.

25. *Reader*, p. 42.

26. Roy Blount, Jr., "Elvis," *Esquire*, December, 1983, reprinted in *Reader*, p. 77.

27. Charles Wolfe, in "Presley and the Gospel Tradition" in *Elvis: Images and Fancies*, edited by Jac Tharpe (Jackson: University Press of Mississippi, 1977).

28. Eisler, p. 129.

29. Eisler, pp. 54–55.

30. "Mike," quoted in Eisler, p. 130.

31. Anthony Storr, *Freud and Jung* (New York: Barnes and Noble Books/Oxford University Press, 1989/1994), p. 24.

32. Osborne, p. 91.

33. *Good Times*, pp. 193–97.

34. Ibid.

35. *Good Times*, p. 201.

36. Ibid.

37. Eisler, p. 337.

38. Eisler, p. 337–38.

39. Biskind, p. 206.

40. William H. Whyte, Jr., *The Organization Man* (Garden City, NY: Doubleday, Anchor Books, 1957), pp. 440–45.

7. Poor White Trash

1. Robert Pattison, *The Triumph of Vulgarity* (New York: Oxford University Press, 1967), p. 104.

2. Elmore Messer Matthews, *Neighbor and Kin: Life in a Tennessee Ridge Community* (Nashville: Vanderbilt University Press, 1966).

3. Presley, p. 155.

4. Halberstam, p. 211.

5. Halberstam, p. 207.

6. Halberstam, p. 214.

7. Halberstam, p. 214.

8. Doss, p. 13.

9. Wendy Steiner, *The Scandal of Pleasure: Art in an Age of Fundamentalism* (Chicago: University of Chicago Press, 1995), p. 156.

10. Fishwick, p. 67.

11. Albert F. McLean, *American Vaudeville as Ritual* (Lexington: University of Kentucky Press, 1965), p. 23.

12. Fishwick, p. 68.

13. David Roediger, *The Wages of Whiteness: Race and the Making of the American Working Class* (New York: Verso, 1991), p. 19.

14. Hundley, quoted by Torr, p. 42.

15. Malcolm Forbes, quoted in *Good Times*, p. 65.

16. Forbes, *Good Times*, p. 64.

17. Tad Friend, "White Trash Nation," *New York*, August 22, 1994.

18. Julia Aparin, "He Never Got Above His Raising: An Ethnographic Study of Working Class Response to Elvis Presley," Ph.D. dissertation (unpublished), University of Pennsylvania, 1988.
19. Dave Marsh, *Elvis* (New York: Thunder's Mouth Press, 1982), p. 1.
20. Fishwick, p. 26.
21. Frederick Jackson Turner, *The Frontier in American History* (New York: Henry Holt, 1990).
22. Fishwick, p. 25.
23. Halberstam, p. 268–69.
24. Schickel, p. 177.
25. F. Scott Fitzgerald, *The Great Gatsby* (New York: Scribner's, 1925), p. 198.
26. Presley, p. 23.
27. Presley, p. 24.
28. Presley, p. 27.
29. Presley, p. 29.
30. Eisler, p. 64.
31. Whyte, p. 63.
32. Roche, quoted in *Good Times*, p. 252.
33. Nash, p. 321.
34. Presley, p. 190.
35. "The Protestant Ethic and the Popular Idol in America: A Case Study," *Social Compass* 15.1 (1968), 45–69.
36. Joseph, p. xxxii.
37. Richard Corliss, "The King Is Dead — Or Is He?," *Time* magazine, October 10, 1988, reprinted in *Reader*, pp. 79–81.
38. Halberstam, p. 142.
39. Presley, p. 121.
40. Rich Cohen, *Tough Jews* (New York: Simon & Schuster, 1997).
41. Eisler, p. 52.
42. Stanley, p. 178.
43. Gerry McLafferty, *Elvis Presley in Hollywood: Celluloid Sell-Out* (London: Robert Hale, 1989), p. 13.
44. Halberstam, p. 244.
45. Califano, quoted in *Good Times*, p. 243.
46. George Meany, *Good Times*, p. 224.
47. Karen Armstrong, "Elvis Presley and American Culture," *Suomen Antropologi* 18.1 (January 1993), pp. 10–11.
48. Fishwick, p. 69.
49. Fishwick, p. 67.
50. Halberstam, p. 698.
51. Halberstam, p. 699–700.
52. Halberstam, p. 698.
53. Halberstam, p. 699–700.
54. Torr, p. 31.
55. Nash, p. 91.
56. L. P. Hartley, quoted in Torr.
57. Fishwick, p. 66.
58. Presley, p. 144.
59. Friend, ibid.

8. The Sexual Revolution

1. Halberstam, p. 871.
2. Arthur Schlesinger, "The New Mood in Politics," *The Politics of Hope* (Boston: Houghton Mifflin, 1962–3), p. 86.
3. Robert Middleton, "All Shook Up?," *Reader*, p. 6.
4. Chubby Checker, quoted in *Good Times*, p. 151.
5. Ibid.
6. Eisler, p. 121.
7. Eisler, p. 126.
8. Eisler, p. 128.
9. Halberstam, p. 321.
10. Eisler, p. 4.
11. Eisler, p. 5.
12. Obst, p. 120.
13. Eisler, p. 29.
14. Stanley, pp. 179 & 181.
15. Guralnick, p. 122.
16. Michael Wood, p. 39.
17. "The Playboy Philosophy," as outlined in *Playboy* magazine's pages in monthly installments between 1961–65.
18. Thomas Weyr, *Reaching for Paradise: The Playboy Vision of America* (New York: Times Books, 1978), pp. 77–79.
19. Barbara Ehrenreich, *The Hearts of Men: American Dreams and the Flight from Commitment* (New York: Anchor Press/Doubleday, 1983).
20. Doss, p. 4.
21. Doss, p. 6.
22. Mary Hancock Hinds, *Infinite Elvis: An Annotated Bibliography* (Chicago: Chicago Review Press/A Cappella Books, 2001), p. 4.
23. Abigail van Buren, *Good Times*, pp. 139–40.
24. Torr, p. 29.
25. Presley, p. 121–43.
26. Carol Doda, quoted in *Good Times*, p. 260.
27. Doda, *Good Times*, p. 260.
28. Red West, Sonny West, and Dave Hebler, as told to Steve Dunleary, *Elvis: What Happened?* (New York: Ballantine Books, 1977), p. 47.
29. Robin Wood, *Hitchcock's Films*.
30. Whitmer, p. 28.
31. Goldman, p. 141.
32. Ibid.

9. Up the Establishment!

1. Andrew Clements, "The Quiff That Roared," *The Guardian* (July 18, 1997), T2.
2. Abbie Hoffman, "Too Soon the Hero," *Crawdaddy* (November 1977), p. 39–41.
3. Nash, p. 303.
4. Marty Lacker, quoted in Nash, p. 301.

5. "1955: The Beginning of Our Own Time," *South Atlantic Quarterly* 73.4 (1974), pp. 426–44.

6. Elia Kazan, *A Life* (New York: Knopf, 1988), p. 91.

7. Doss, p. 187–88.

8. Doss, p. 191.

9. Stanley Rothman and S. Robert Lichter, *Roots of Radicalism: Jews, Christians, and the New Left*. New York: Oxford University Press, 1982), p. 400.

10. Nash, p. 42.

11. Doss, p. 208.

12. "Potshots at Elvis" by Frye Gaillard in *Race, Rock and Religion: Profiles from a Southern Journalist*, Charlotte, NC: East Woods Press, 1982, p. 73.

13. Halberstam, p. 101.

14. Porteous, p. 54.

15. Cocks, *Reader*, p. 60.

16. Nash, p. 57.

17. Presley, p. 141–78.

18. Doss, p. 258.

19. James A. Miller, *Flowers in the Dustbin: The Rise of Rock and Roll, 1947–1977* (New York: Simon and Schuster, 1999), p. 34.

20. Quoted in Torr, p. 121.

21. Presley, p. 46.

22. *Good Times*, p. 139.

23. *Good Times*, p. 140.

24. Peter Harry Brown and Pat H. Broeske, *Down at the End of Lonely Street* (New York: Dutton/Penguin Putnam, 1997), p. 41.

25. David P. Szatmary, *A Time to Rock: A Social History of Rock'n'Roll* (New York: Music Sales Corporation/Prentice-Hall, 1996), p. 39.

26. Middleton, *Reader*, p. 12.

27. Cavallo, p. 9.

28. Godfrey Hodgson, *America in Our Time: From World War II to Nixon* (New York: Doubleday, 1976), pp. 351–52.

29. Paul Potter, "Student Discontent and Campus Reform," *Papers of Students for a Democratic Society*, State Historical Society of Wisconsin (Social Action Collection). Microfilm, reel 4, series 2A, no. 29 (July 1965), 15.

30. Doss, p. 112.

31. Joseph, p. xiv.

32. Doss, p. 105.

33. Nash, p. 192.

34. Nash, p. 341.

35. Nash, p. 228.

36. Tony Zoppie, "Presley Thrills Crowd of 26,500," *Dallas Morning News*, October 12, 1956.

37. *Life*, August 27, 1956, pp. 101–09.

38. Nash, p. 221.

39. Tempest Storm, "The Lady Is a Vamp," *Cosmopolitan* (March 1988), pp. 152–55.

40. Paul Willis, *Profane Culture* (London: Routledge and Kegan Paul, 1978), p. 71.

41. Doss, p. 126, and Hanson, "Pleasure, Ambivalence, Identification" in *Babel and Babylon: Spectatorship in American Silent Film* (Cambridge, MA: Harvard University Press, 1991), p. 55.

42. Marge Crumbaker and Gabe Tucker, *Up and Down With Elvis Presley* (New York: Putnam's, 1981).

43. Jonathan Buckley and Mark Ellingham, editors, *Rock: The Rough Guide* (London: Rough Guides/Penguin, 1996), pp. 106–99.

44. Eric Lott, *Love and Theft: Blackface Minstrelsy and the American Working Class* (New York: Oxford University Press, 1993), p. 92.

45. George Lipsitz, *Time Passages: Collective Memory and American Popular Culture* (Minneapolis: University of Minnesota Press, 1990), p. xiv.

46. Quain, p. 255.

10. From Marginalization to Mainstream

1. Nash, p. 340.

2. Ibid.

3. Dick McDonald, quoted by John Love in *McDonald's: Behind the Arches* (New York: Bantam, 1986), p. 14.

4. Halberstam, p. 140.

5. Kazan, p. 537.

6. Fike, quoted in Nash, p. 535.

7. Smith, quoted in Nash, p. 512.

8. Fike, quoted in Nash, p. 199.

9. Doss, p. 141.

10. Stanley, p. 65.

11. Lana Wood, *Natalie: A Memoir by Her Sister* (New York: Dell, 1985).

12. Goldman, p. 79.

13. Dan Kiley, *The Peter Pan Syndrome: Men Who Have Never Grown Up* (Dresden, TN: Avon Books, 1995).

14. Presley, p. 28.

15. Presley, p. 31.

16. Presley, p. 33.

17. Presley, p. 44.

18. Presley, p. 15.

19. Presley, p. 162.

20. Presley, p. 191.

21. Quoted in Halberstam, p. 625.

22. Quoted in *Good Times*, p. 75

23. Doss, p. 124, also see "Elvis Alive?: The Ideology of American Consumerism," *Journal of Popular Culture* 24 (Winter 1990), pp. 11–19.

24. Presley, p. 15.

25. Melly, pp. 37–38.

26. Of course, not *all* American males "flirted" with this philosophy, still, between (roughly) 1960–65, the immense popularity of the maga-

zine with male readers certainly did impact on standards of sexual identity and the self-image of the reader, as the once-popular (then oft-satirized) self-promotional page "What Sort of Man Reads *Playboy?*" attested.
27. Presley, p. 137.
28. Goldman, p. 96.

11. A Mid–'60s Masterpiece

1. Halberstam, p. 506.
2. Doss, p. 259.
3. Halberstam, p. 714.
4. James Reed, *From Private Vice to Public Virtue* (New York: Basic Books, 1978), p. 321.
5. Middleton, *Reader*, p. 6.
6. Halberstam, p. 507.
7. Hunter S. Thompson, *Fear and Loathing in Las Vegas* (New York: Modern Library, 2005 reprint), p. 156.
8. Sonya Sayres, Anders Stephanson, Stanley Aronowitz and Fredric Jameson, editors, *The 60s Without Apology* (Minneapolis: University of Minnesota Press, 1984), p. 26.
9. Doss, p. 133.
10. Pauline Kael, *For Keeps: 30 Years at the Movies* (New York: Dutton, 1994), p. 137.
11. Dodge, quoted by Madeleine Gray, *Margaret Sanger: A Biography of the Champion of Birth Control* (New York: R. Malek, 1979), pp. 58–59.
12. Margaret Mead, "Marrying in Haste in College," *Columbia University Forum*, Spring 1960, p. 31.
13. Halberstam, p. 598.
14. Ferdinand Lundberg and Marynia Farnham, *Modern Woman: The Lost Sex* (New York: Harper and Brothers, 1947), p. 41.
15. Review in *Time*, May 29, 1964.
16. Cavallo, p. 9.
17. Daniel Miller and Guy Swanson, *The Changing American Parent* (New York: Wiley, 1958), p. 41.
18. Fred MacDonald, *Who Shot the Sheriff?*, (Westport, CT: Greenwood/Praeger, 1986), pp. 51–52.
19. Midge Decter, *The New Chastity* (New York: Berkley/Medallion Books, 1973), p. 71.
20. Thompson, p. 42.
21. Nash, p. 342.
22. Peter Conrad, *Modern Times/Modern Places* (New York: Alfred A. Knopf, 1999), p. 278.
23. Presley, p. 82.
24. Review in *Time* magazine, May 29, 1964.
25. "Elvis Dorado: The True Romance of *Viva Las Vegas*," *Film Comment* (July–August 1994), pp. 45–46.
26. Ibid.

27. Fishwick, p. 9.
28. *Entertainment Weekly*, January 10, 2005, p. 18.
29. Ibid.
30. John Kouwenhoven, *Made in America* (New York: Doubleday, 1948), p. 125.
31. Fishwick, p. 46.
32. Susan Sontag, *Against Interpretation* (New York: Dell Publishing, 1969 reprint), p. 276.

12. Out of It

1. Garcia, quoted in *Good Times*, p. 188.
2. "Changing Agricultural Magic in Southern Illinois: A Synthetic Analysis of Folk-Urban Transition," *Social Forces* 22, 1943, pp. 98–106.
3. Howard Odum, p. 47.
4. Fishwick, p. 2.
5. Gleason, quoted in *Good Times*, p. 91.
6. Halberstam, p. 369.
7. Cavallo, p. 121.
8. Gleason, p. 92.
9. Cavallo, p. 176.
10. Cavallo, p. 92.
11. Quoted in *Good Times*, p. 242.
12. Doss, p. 154.
13. Nash, p. 412.
14. Doss, p. 127.
15. Quoted by Doss, p. 156.
16. Mulvey, ibid.
17. Presley, p. 259.
18. Biskind, p. 279.
19. Robert Sklar, "Red River — Empire to the West," *Cineaste* 9 (Fall 1978): pp. 14–19.
20. Doss, p. 127.
21. Whitmer, 192.
22. Presley, p. 308.
23. Doss, p. 154.

13. Everything New Is Old Again

1. Nash, p. 96.
2. Goldman, p. 323.
3. Doss, p. 127.
4. Karal Ann Marling, "When Elvis Cut His Hair: The Meaning of Mobility," *As Seen on TV: The Visual Culture of Everyday Life in the 1950s* (Cambridge, MA: Harvard University Press, 1994).
5. Marjorie Graber, "The Transvestite Continuum: Liberace-Valentino-Elvis," *Vested Interests: Cross-Dressing and Cultural Anxiety* (New York: HarperPerennial, 1993), p. 372.
6. Presley, p. 107.
7. Presley, p. 107.

8. Fishwick, p. 2.

9. Fishwick, p. 1.

10. Robert Meredith, *American Studies: Essays on Theory and Method* (Columbus, OH: Charles E. Merrill, 1968), p. xii.

11. Sidney Finkelstein, *How Music Expresses Ideas* (New York: International Publishers, 1952).

12. Hinds, p. 225.

13. Sontag, p. 289.

14. Sontag, p. 279.

15. Sontag, p. 280.

16. J. S. Reed, p. 74.

14. Hot Wheels and Wild Women

1. Conrad, p. 91.

2. Conrad, p. 92.

3. Conrad, p. 92.

4. Conrad, p. 92.

5. Conrad, p. 94.

6. Halberstam, p. 126.

7. Halberstam, p. 123.

8. Halberstam, p. 120.

9. Halberstam, p. 127.

10. Halberstam, p. 126.

11. Thomas Hine, *Populuxe* (New York: Knopf, 1986), p. 93.

12. B. A. Botkin, "Icon on Wheels: Supericon of Popular Culture" in Marshall Fishwick and Ray B. Browne, editors, *Icons of Popular Culture* (Bowling Green, OH: Bowling Green University Popular Press, 1970), p. 61.

13. John Egerton, "Elvis Lives! The Stuff That Myths Are Made Of," *The Progressive* (March 1979), pp. 2–23.

14. Fishwick, p. 25.

15. Botkin, p. 47.

16. Fishwick, p. 53.

17. Gilbert B. Rodman, *Elvis After Elvis: The Posthumous Career of a Living Legend* (London, New York: Routledge, 1996), p. 31.

18. Botkin, p. 59

19. Reed, "Elvis in Hollywood" in Torr, p. 53.

20. Waldo Frank, *In the American Jungle* (New York: Farrar and Rinehart, 1937), p. 50.

21. In particular, see Karen Armstrong and Jon Katz, "Why Elvis Matters," *Wired* (April 1995), pp. 10–105, Mary and Patsy Lacker with Leslie S. Smith, *Portrait of a Friend* (Memphis: Wimmer Brothers Books, 1979), and (no author given) *All the King's Things: The Ultimate Elvis Memorabilia Book* (San Francisco: Bluewood Books, 1993).

22. Eisler, p. 183.

23. Harry M. Benshoff and Sean Griffin, *America on Film: Representing Race, Class, Gender, and Sexuality at the Movies* (Madden, MA: Blackwell Publishing, 2004), p. 233.

24. Ibid.

25. Ibid.

26. David R. Shumway, "Watching Elvid: The Male Rock Star as Object of the Gaze," included in *The Other Fifties* (Joel Foreman, ed.): University of Illinois Press, 1997).

27. Mulvey, Ibid.

28. Benshoff and Griffin, pp. 233–35.

29. Robert H. Boyle, "The Car Cult from Rumpsville," *Sports Illustrated*, April 24, 1961, pp. 70–71.

30. Botkin, p. 48.

31. Fishwick, p. 76.

32. Stephen L. Harris and Gloria Platzner, *Classical Mythology: Images and Insights*, second edition (Mountain View, CA: Mayfield Publishing, 1998), p. 966.

33. James Miller, p. 18.

34. Presley, p. 101.

35. Doss, p. 138.

36. Nash, p. 366.

37. Goldman, p. 199.

38. Guralnick, p. 43.

39. Nash, p. 226.

40. West, West and Hebler, pp. 101–24.

41. Stanley, p. 195.

42. Stanley, p. 183.

43. Paul Demko, "Elvis Lives! (in Philanthropy)" in *The Chronicle of Philanthropy* (May 2, 1996), p. 30.

44. Halberstam, p. 488.

45. Ralph Nader, *Unsafe at Any Speed* (New York: Grossman, 1965).

46. Botkin, p. 59.

47. Grace and Fred M. Hechinger, "Serious Epidemic of 'Automania,'" *The New York Times Magazine*, August 11, 1963, p. 18.

48. Robert H. Boyle, "The Car Cult from Rumpsville," *Sports Illustrated*, April 24, 1961, pp. 70–71.

49. Botkin, p. 58.

50. Botkin, p. 58.

15. The Summer of Love

1. Aronowitz, pp. 24–25.

2. Mills, p. 55.

3. *Encyclopedia*, pp. 189, 191.

4. Eisler, p. 72.

5. Fishwick, p. 84.

6. Daniel Boorstin, *The Image: A Guide to Pseudo-Events in America* (Harper Colophon Books, 1964).

7. Nash, p. 92.

8. Wood, p. 122.

9. See "Elvis and the Frauleins," *Look* (December 23, 1958), pp. 113–15, and *Private Pres-*

ley: Elvis in Germany—The Missing Years (Weert, Netherlands: Uitgeverij B.V., 1993), pp. 37–39.
10. Priscilla, p. 130.

16. The Cowboy Way

1. Sorenson, *Good Times*, p. 145.
2. Turner, op. cit.
3. Norman Mailer, *Why Are We in Vietnam?* (New York: Berkley, 1968), op. cit.
4. Giannetti, p. 68.
5. Presley, p. 191.
6. John Finlator, "Elvis" in *The Drugged Nation: A Narc's Story* (New York: Simon and Schuster, 1973), Connie Kirchberg and Marc Hendrickx, *Elvis Presley, Richard Nixon, and the American Dream* (Jefferson, NC: McFarland, 1999), and Douglas Brinkley, "Dept. of Missed Opportunities: The White House–Graceland Connection That Might Have Saved Elvis" in "Talk of the Town" column, *The New Yorker* (August 18, 1997).
7. Stanley, p. 33.

17. The Last Temptation(s) of Elvis

1. Norman Podhoretz, "The Know-Nothing Bohemians," *Doings and Undoings: The Fifties and After in American Writing* (New York: Farrar, Strauss, 1964), pp. 144–57.
2. John Sharnik, "The War of the Generations," *House and Garden* (October 1956), pp. 40–41.
3. Terry Anderson, *The Movement and the Sixties* (New York: Oxford University Press, 1995), p. 135.
4. Cavallo, p. 9.
5. Arthur Schlesinger, Jr., "The Crisis of American Masculinity," *The Politics of Hope* (Boston: Houghton Mifflin, 1963), pp. 238–39.
6. Cavallo, p. 2.
7. Quoted in Halberstam, p. 527.
8. Cavallo, p. 9.
9. Joseph Veroff, Elizabeth Douvan and Richard A. Kulka, *The Inner American* (New York: Basic Books, 1981), p. 23.
10. Presley, p. 141.
11. Lloyd Grossman, *A Social History of Rock Music: From Greasers to Glitter Rock* (New York: McKay, 1976), pp. 41–43.
12. Joseph Campbell, *The Power of Myth* (New York: Doubleday, 1988).
13. "Death, Resurrection and Transfiguration: The Religious Folklore in Elvis Presley Shrines and Souvenirs," *International Folklore Review* (1987), p. 95.

14. Presley, p. 99.
15. Adam Wong, *The Importance of Elvis Presley* (Lucent Books, 1997), p. 19.
16. "All Things Considered" on National Public Radio, May 28, 1999.
17. Fishwick, p. 30.
18. "The Iconography of Elvis" by Charles Reagan Wilson, Ph.D., in *Judgment and Grace in Dixie: Southern Faiths from Faulkner to Elvis* (Athens, GA and London: University of Georgia Press, 1995), pp. 136–37.
19. Joan Turner Beifuss, "Elvis: They Still Love Him Tender," *National Catholic Reporter* (September 10, 1982), p. 19.
20. Richard Cooper, "Did the Devil Send Elvis Presley?," *True Strange* 3 (May-June, 1957), p. 21.
21. Presley, p. 199.

18. Pilgrim's Progress

1. Fishwick, p. 54.
2. Harvey Cox, *The Secular City* (New York: McMillan, 1966), p. 50.
3. Fishwick, p. 11.
4. Harrison, p. 21.
5. Ibid.
6. Fishwick, p. 96.
7. Jesse Stearn and Larry Geller, *The Truth About Elvis* (New York: Jove Publications, 1980).
8. Larry Geller and Joel Spector with Patricia Romanowski, *If I Can Dream: Elvis's Own Story* (New York: Simon and Schuster, 1989).
9. Presley, p. 204.
10. Sammy Davis, Jr., quoted in "Presley Show Impresses Even the Celebrities," *Elvis Album*, ed. DeNight, Fox and Riff, 251.
11. "His Truth Goes Marching On: Elvis Presley and the Pilgrimage to Graceland," *Pilgrimage in Popular Culture*, eds. Ian Reader and Tony Walter (London: Macmillan Press, 1993), pp. 103–04.
12. Doss, p. 135.
13. The Reverend Martin R. Long, *God's Works Through Elvis* (Hicksville, NY: Exposition Press, 1979).
14. Quoted in *I Am Elvis*, p. 58.
15. Demko, "Elvis Lives! (in Philanthropy)," p. 30.
16. Doss, p. 108.
17. Fishwick, p. 2.
18. Fishwick, p. 3.
19. John Daniel Sumner, legendary gospel performer.
Quoted by Charles Wolfe in "Presley and the Gospel Tradition" in *Elvis: Images and Fancies*.
20. Hammontree, p. 64.
21. Doss, p. 88
22. *Reader*, p. 56.

23. J. B. Priestley, *Literature and Western Man*, quoted in Fishwick, p. 97.
24. Kesey, quoted in *Good Times*, p. 386.
25. Bond, quoted in *Good Times*, p. 68.
26. Smith, quoted in *Good Times*, p. 201.
27. Bond, *Good Times*, p. 69.
28. Lula Belle Weathersby, quoted in *Good Times*, p. 296.
29. *Good Times*, p. 413.
30. *Good Times*, p. 414.
31. Stearn and Geller, Ibid.
32. Presley, p. 204.
33. Doss, p. 215.
34. Doss, p. 106.
35. Doss, p. 76.
36. Cass Hunnicutt, quoted by Eisler, p. 338.
37. Isaacks, quoted in Doss, 105
38. Fishwick, p. 96.
39. Wolfe, *Reader*, p. 18.
40. *Good Times*, p. 157.
41. Fishwick, p. 97.
42. Fishwick, p. 95.
43. Fishwick, p. 54.
44. Doss, p. 74.
45. Doss, p. 74.
46. J.W. Davidson, Alfred Hecht and Herbert A. Whitney, "The Pilgrimage to Graceland," *Pilgrimage in the United States*, G. Rinschede and S. Bbhardwaj, eds., (Publisher: 1990), pp. 229–52.
47. Martin Filler, "Elvis Presley's Graceland: An American Shrine," *House and Garden* (March 1984), p. 140–47.
48. J. A. Mille.
49. Eisler, p. 338.

19. Nostalgia Ain't What It Used to Be

1. Stanley, p. 85.
2. Ibid, p. 87.
3. Patricia Jobe Pierce, *The Ultimate Elvis: Elvis Presley Day by Day* (New York: Simon and Schuster, 1994), p. 15.
4. *Encyclopedia*, p. 101.
5. "John Finlator, The Guy Who Gave Elvis a Badge for Nixon," in *The Drugged Nation: A Narc's Story* (New York: Simon and Schuster, 1973), pp. 102–05.
6. Presley, p. 91.
7. Doss, p. 22
8. Thomas C. Carlson, "Ad Hoc Rock: Elvis and the Aesthetics of Postmodernism" (*Studies in Popular Culture* XVI.2, April 1994), pp. 40–50.
9. Rupert Matthews, *Elvis* (New York: Gramercy, 1998), p. 121.
10. Obst, p. 252.
11. Jerry Hopkins, *Elvis: A Biography* (New York: Simon & Schuster, 1971), op. cit.
12. *The Greening of America*.
13. Fishwick, p. 10.
14. Jeff Pike, *The Death of Rock'n'Roll: Untimely Demises, Morbid Preoccupations, and Premature Forecasts of Doom in Pop Music* (Boston: Faber and Faber, 1993), p. 60.

Conclusion: "50 Million Elvis Fans Can't Be Wrong!"

1. Cocks, *Reader*, p. 60.
2. Corliss, *Reader*, p. 81.
3. Pratt, *Reader*, p. 96.
4. Pratt, *Reader*, p. 97.
5. Fishwick, p. 16.
6. Paul Morrissey, *Good Times*, pp. 278–80.
7. Walter Sutton and Richard Foster, *Modern Criticism: Theory and Practice* (New York: Odyssey Press, 1963), p. 95.
8. Fishwick, p. 58.
9. Matthew Arnold, *Culture and Anarchy*, reprinted 1966, p. 113.
10. Fishwick, p. 59.
11. Brock, *Reader*, p. 138.
12. Brock, *Reader*, p. 138.
13. Presley, p. 99.
14. Presley, p. 22.
15. Presley, p. 39.
16. Presley, p. 74.
17. Presley, p. 239.
18. Presley, p. 158.
19. Booth, "A Hound Dog, to the Manor Born," *Esquire* (February, 1968).
20. Greil Marcus, *Mystery Train* (New York: E.P. Dutton, 1982), p. 139.
21. Ibid,

Bibliography

Hundreds of books were consulted during the preparation of this volume, and many indirectly influenced its writing. The following list consists solely of works that were directly cited at least once in the text.

A. Presley Specific Sources

The following books, periodical articles (signed and unsigned), doctoral dissertations, pamphlets, obituaries, appreciations, etc., served as key resources for background material on the life, career, and legacy of Elvis Presley. Though numerous others were consulted during the writing of this book, each of these is cited at least once in the notes.

All the King's Things: The Ultimate Elvis Memorabilia Book. San Francisco: Bluewood Books, 1993.

"All Things Considered," National Public Radio, May 28, 1999.

"Americans on the Move to New Jobs, New Places." *Life*, February 3, 1951.

Aparin, Julia. "He Never Got Above His Raising: An Ethnographic Study of Working Class Response to Elvis Presley." Ph.D. dissertation (unpublished). Philadelphia: University of Pennsylvania, 1988.

Armstrong, Karen. "Elvis Presley and American Culture." *Suomen Antropologi* 18.1 (January 1993).

Armstrong, Karen, and Jon Katz. "Why Elvis Matters." *Wired*, April 1995.

Baxter, James, and Annette Baxter. "The Man in the Blue Suede Shoes." *Harper's*, 1958.

"The Beginning of Our Own Time." *South Atlantic Quarterly*, 73.4 (1974).

Beifuss, Joan Turner. "Elvis: They Still Love Him Tender." *National Catholic Reporter*, September 10, 1982.

Blount, Roy Jr. "Elvis." *Esquire*, December 1983.

Brinkley, Douglas. "Dept. of Missed Opportunities: The White House-Graceland Connection That Might Have Saved Elvis." "Talk of the Town," *The New Yorker*, August 18, 1997.

Broeske, Pat H., and Peter Harry Brown. "Epilogue: Long Live the King." *Down at the End of Lonely Street*. New York: Dutton/Penguin Putnam, 1997.

"The Careful Young Men." *The Nation*, March 1957.

Carlson, Thomas C. "Ad Hoc Rock: Elvis and the Aesthetics of Postmodernism." *Studies in Popular Culture*, XVI.2, 1994.

Chadwick, Vernon. *In Search of Elvis: Music, Race, Art, Religion* (paper). Delivered at Westview, CT, 1997.

"Changing Agricultural Music in Southern Illinois: A Synthetic Analysis of Folk-Urban Transition." *Social Forces* 22, 1943.

Choron, Sandra, and Bob Oskam. *Elvis: The Last Word*. New York: Citadel Press, 1991.

Clements, Andrews. "The Quiff That Roared." *The Guardian*, U.K., July 18, 1997.

Cocks, Jay. *Time*, August 29, 1977.

Cooper, Richard. "Did the Devil Send Elvis Presley?" *True Strange* 3, May/June 1957.

Corliss, Richard. "The King Is Dead — Or Is He?" *Time*, October 10, 1988.

Crumbaker, Marge, and Gabe Tucker. *Up and Down With Elvis Presley*. New York: G.P. Putnam's, 1981.

Davidson, J.W., Alfie Hecht, and Herbert A. Whitney. "The Pilgrimate to Graceland." *Pilgrimage in the United States*, 1990.

"Death, Resurrection and Transfiguration: The Religious Folklore in Elvis Presley Shrines and Souvenirs." *International Folklore Review*, 1987.

Demko, Paul. "Elvis Lives! (In Philanthropy)." *The Chronicle of Philanthropy*, May 2, 1966.

Doss, Erica. *Elvis Culture*. Lawrence: University Press of Kansas, 1999.

Egerton, John. "Elvis Lives: The Stuff That Dreams Are Made Of." *The Progressive*, March 1979.

"Elvis Alive?: The Ideology of American Consumerism." *Journal of Popular Culture* 24, Winter 1990.

"Elvis and the Frauleins." *Look*, December 23, 1958.

"Elvis Dorado: The True Romance of *Viva Las Vegas*." *Film Comment*, July/August 1994.

"Elvis the Indigenous." *Harper's*, April 1957.

Entertainment Weekly, January 10, 2005.

Filler, Martin. "Elvis Presley's Graceland: An American Shrine." *House and Garden*, March 1984.

Gaillard, Frye. "Potshots at Elvis." *Race, Rock and Religion: Profiles from a Southern Journalist*. Charlotte, NC: East Woods Press, 1982.

Geller, Larry, and Joel Spector (with Patricia Romanowski). *If I Can Dream: Elvis's Own Story*. New York: Simon and Schuster, 1989.

Goldman, Albert. *Elvis*. New York: McGraw-Hill, 1981.

Guralnick, Peter. *Careless Love: The Unmaking of Elvis Presley*. Boston: Little, Brown, 1999.

Guralnick, Peter. *Last Train to Memphis: The Rise of Elvis Presley*. New York: Little, Brown, 1999.

Hammontree, Patsy Guy. *Elvis Presley: A Bio-Bibliography*. Westport, CT: Greenwood Press, 1985.

Harrison, Ted. *Elvis People: The Cult of the King*. New York: HarperCollins, 1993.

Hinds, Mary Hancock. *Infinite Elvis: An Annotated Bibliography*. Chicago: Chicago Review Press/A Cappella Books, 2001.

Hoffman, Abbie. "Too Soon the Hero." *Crawdaddy*, November 1977.

Hopkins, Jerry. *Elvis: A Biography*. New York: Simon and Schuster, 1971.

"A Hound Dog, To The Manor Born." *Esquire*, February 1968.

Kirchberg, Connie, and Marc Hendricks. *Elvis Presley, Richard Nixon, and the American Dream*. Jefferson, NC: McFarland, 1999.

Krogh, Egill "Budd." *The Day Elvis Met Nixon*. Bellvue, WA: Pejama Press, 1994.

Kroll, Jack. "The Heartbreak Kid." *Newsweek*, August 29, 1977.

Lacker, Marty, and Patsy Lacker (with Leslie S. Smith). *Portrait of a Friend*. Memphis, TN: Wimmer Brothers Books, 1979.

Life. August 27, 1956.

Long, Rev. Martin R. *God's Works Through Elvis*. Hicksville, NY: Exposition Press, 1979.

Marling, Karal Ann. "When Elvis Cut His Hair: The Meaning of Mobility." *As Seen on*

TV: The Visual Culture of Everyday Life in the 1950s. Cambridge, MA: Harvard University Press, 1994.

Marsh, Dave. *Elvis.* New York: Thunder's Mouth Press, 1982.

Marcus, Greil. *Dead Elvis: A Chronicle of a Cultural Obsession.* New York: Doubleday, 1991.

Matthews, Rupert. *Elvis.* New York: Gramercy, 1998.

McLafferty, Gerry. *Elvis Presley in Hollywood: Celluloid Sell-Out.* London: Robert Hale, 1989.

"Mr. Harper." *Harper's,* April 1957.

Nash, Alanna. *Aaron Elvis Presley: Revelations From the Memphis Mafia.* New York: Harper-Collins, 1995.

New York Times review of *Speedway,* 43:1, June 14, 1968.

Orth, Maureen. "All Shook Up." *Newsweek,* August 29, 1977.

Osborne, Jerry. *Elvis: Word by Word.* New York: Harmony Books, 1999.

Porteous, Clark. *Memphis Press Scimitar,* August 17, 1977.

Pratt, Linda Ray. "Elvis, or The Ironies of a Southern Identity." *Southern Quarterly,* 1979.

Presley, Priscilla Beaulieu (with Sandra Harmon). *Elvis and Me.* New York: Berkley, 1985.

"The Protestant Ethic and the Popular Idol in America: A Case Study." *Social Compass,* 15.1 (1968).

Quain, Kevin (ed.). *The Elvis Reader: Texts and Sources on the King of Rock'n'Roll.* New York: St. Martin's Press, 1992.

Ridge, Millie. *Elvis Album.* Lincolnwood, IL: Publications International, 1997.

Rodman, Gilbert. *Elvis After Elvis: The Posthumous Career of a Living Legend.* London and New York: Routledge, 1996.

Rosenbaum, Ron. "Among the Believers." *The New York Times (Sunday) Magazine,* September 24, 1995.

Saturday Review critique of *Flaming Star,* December 1960.

Stanley, David A. *The Elvis Encyclopedia: The Complete and Definitive Reference Book on The King of Rock & Roll.* North Dighton, MA: World/JG Press, 2002.

Steiff, William. "What Makes Elvis Presley Tick — No. 3, the Pelvis Explains That 'Vulgar' Style." *San Francisco News,* October 17, 1956.

Stern, Jess, and Larry Geller. *The Truth About Elvis.* New York: Jove, 1980.

Tharpe, Jac (ed.) *Elvis: Images and Fancies.* Jackson: University of Mississippi Press, 1977.

Time, 83:86, May 29, 1964.

West, Red, Sonny West, and Dave Hebler (as told to Steve Dunleavy). *Elvis: What Happened?* New York: Ballantine Books, 1977.

Whitmer, Peter. *The Inner Elvis: A Psychological Biography of Elvis Aaron Presley.* New York: Hyperion, 1996.

Wilson, Dr. Charles Reagan. "The Iconography of Elvis." In *Judgment and Grace in Dixie: Southern Faiths from Faulkner to Elvis.* Athens and London: University of Georgia Press, 1995.

Wood, Lana. *Natalie: A Memoir By Her Sister.* New York: Dell, 1985.

Woog, Adam. *The Importance of Elvis Presley.* San Diego: Lucent Books, 1997.

Zmijewsky, Steven, and Boris Zmijewsky. *Elvis: The Films and Career of Elvis Presley.* Secaucus, NJ: Citadel Press, 1976.

Zoppie, Tony. "Presley Thrills Crowd of 26,500." *Dallas Morning News,* October 12, 1956.

B. General Sources (Sociological and Historical)

The following nonfiction books, novels, articles, etc., were consulted during the writing of this book for information about the transitional period in American life and letters between 1955 and 1970, as well as earlier works that contributed to the modern vision.

Anderson, Terry. *The Movement and The Sixties*. New York: Oxford University Press, 1995.

Berg, L., and R. Street. *Sex: Methods and Manners*. New York: Archer House, 1953.

Cavello, Dominic. *A Fiction of the Past*. New York: St. Martin's Press, 1999.

Cohen, Rich. *Tough Jews*. New York: Simon and Schuster, 1997.

Conrad, Peter. *Modern Times/Modern Places*. New York: Alfred A. Knopf, 1999.

Cox, Harvey. *The Secular City*. New York: Macmillan, 1966.

Decter, Midge. *The New Chastity*. New York: Berkley/Medallion Books, 1973.

Ehrenreich, Barbara. *The Hearts of Men: American Dreams and the Flight from Commitment*. New York: Anchor Press/Doubleday, 1983.

Eisler, Benita. *Private Lives: Men and Women of the Fifties*. New York: Franklin Watts, 1986.

Eustace, Chesser. *Love Without Fear: How to Achieve Sex Happiness*. London: Rich and Cowan, 1941.

Finlater, John. *The Drugged Nation: A Narc's Story*. New York: Simon and Schuster, 1973.

Fitzgerald, F. Scott. *The Great Gatsby*. New York: Scribner's, 1925.

Fordham, Michael, and Roger Hobdell (eds.) *Freud, Jung, Klein—The Fenceless Field: Essays on Psychoanalysis*. London: Routledge, 1998.

Foreman, Joel (ed.) The Other Fifties: *Interrogating Mid-century American Icons*. Urbana and Chicago: The University of Illinois Press, 1997.

Friedan, Betty. *The Feminine Mystique*. New York: Dell, 1963.

Gilman, Mildred. "Why Can't They Wait to Wed?" *Parents Magazine*, November 1958.

Gleckner, Robert, and Gerald E. Enscoe (eds.). *Romanticism: Points of View*. New Jersey: Prentice-Hall, 1962.

Goodman, Paul. *Growing Up Absurd: Problems of Youth in the Organized Society*. New York: Random House, 1960.

Gray, Madeleine. *Margaret Sanger: A Biography of the Champion of Birth Control*. New York: R. Malek, 1979.

Halberstam, David. *The Fifties*. New York: Ballantine Books, 1994.

Hefner, Hugh. *The Playboy Philosophy*. *Playboy* magazine, December 1962–May 1966 (total: 25 articles).

Hine, Thomas. *Populxe*. New York: Knopf, 1986.

Hodgson, Godfrey. *America in Our Time: From World War II to Nixon*. New York: Doubleday, 1976.

Hoffman, Nicholas von. *We Are the People our Parents Warned Us Against*. Chicago: Ivan R. Dee/Elephant Paperbacks, 1968.

Johnson, Joyce. *Minor Characters*. Boston: Houghton Mifflin, 1983.

Joseph, Peter. *Good Times: An Oral History of America in the Nineteen Sixties*. New York: Charterhouse, 1973.

Kennan, George. "The Sources of Soviet Conflict." *Foreign Affairs*, July 1947.

Kerouac, Jack. *On The Road*. New York: NAL/Dutton, 1958.

Kiley, Dan. *The Peter Pan Syndrome: Men Who Have Never Grown Up*. New York: Dodd, Mead, 1983 (Avon Reprint, 1995).

Love, John. *McDonald's: Behind The Arches*. New York: Bantam, 1986.

Lundberg, Ferdinand, and Marynia Farnham. *Modern Woman: The Lost Sex*. New York: Harper Brothers, 1947.

Mailer, Norman. "David Riesman Reconsidered." *Dissent*, Autumn 1954.

Mailer, Norman. "The White Negro." *Advertisements for Myself*. New York: G. P. Putnam, 1959.

Mailer, Norman. *Why Are We In Vietnam*? New York: Berkley, 1968.

Matthews, Elmore Messer. *Neighbor and Kin: Life in a Tennessee Ridge Community*. Nashville: Vanderbilt University Press, 1966.

McLean, Albert F. *American Vaudeville as Ritual*. Lexington: University of Kentucky Press, 1965.

Mead, Margaret. "Marrying in Haste in College." *Columbia University Forum*, Spring 1960.

Miller, Daniel, and Guy Swanson. *The Changing American Parent*. New York: Wiley, 1958.

Miller, Douglas T., and Marion Nowak. *The Fifties: The Way We Really Were*. Garden City, N.Y.: Doubleday, 1977.

Nader, Ralph. *Unsafe at Any Speed*. New York: Grossman, 1965.

Nietzsche, Friedrich William. *Stanliche Werke in Zwolf Banden*. Statgart: A. Kroner, 1964–65 (reissue dates).

Oakley, J. Ronald. *God's Country: America in the Fifties*. New York: W.W. Norton, 1986.

Podhoretz, Norman. "The Know-Nothing Bohemians." *Doings and Undoings: The Fifties and After in American Writing*. New York: Farrar, Strauss, 1964.

Potter, Paul. "Student Discontent and Campus Reform." *Papers of Students for a Democratic Society*. State Historical Society of Wisconsin (Social Action Collection); Microfilm, reel 4, series 2A, no. 29 July 1965.

Reed, James. *From Private Vice to Public Virtue*. New York: Basic Books, 1978.

Reich, Charles A. *The Greening of America*. New York: Bantam, 1971.

Roediger, David. *The Wages of Whiteness: Race and the Making of the American Working Class*. New York: Verso, 1991.

Rothman, Stanley, and Robert S. Lichter. *Roots of Radicalism: Jews, Christians, and The New Left*. New York: Oxford University Press, 1982.

Sayres, Sonya, Andrew Stephenson, Stanley Aranowitz, and Fredric Jameson (eds.) *The '60s Without Apology*. Minneapolis: University of Minnesota Press, 1984.

Schlesinger, Arthur. *The Politics of Hope*. Boston: Houghton Mifflin, 1962–63.

Sharnik, John. "The War of the Generations." *House and Garden*, October 1956.

Spock, Benjamin. *The Common Sense Book of Baby and Child Care*. New York: Duell, Sloan and Pearce, 1946.

Storr, Anthony. *Freud and Jung*. New York: Barnes and Noble Books/Oxford University Press, 1989/1994.

Susman, Warren I. *Culture as History: The Transformation of American Society in the 20th Century*. New York: Pantheon Books, 1984.

Thompson, Hunter S. *Fear and Loathing in Las Vegas*. New York: Modern Library, 2005 (reprint).

Toffler, Alvin. *Future Shock*. New York: Random House, 1970.

Turner, Frederick Jackson. *The Frontier in American History*. New York: Henry Holt, 1990 (reprint).

Veroff, Joseph, Elizabeth Douvan, and Richard A. Kulka. *The Inner American: A Self-Portrait from 1957 to 1976*. New York: Basic Books, 1981.

Waldo, Frank David. *In the American Jungle, 1925–1936*. New York: Farrar and Rinehart, 1937.

Walsh, Moira. *America*: 97:472; August 3, 1957.

Weyr, Thomas. *Reaching for Paradise: The Playboy Vision of America*. New York: Times Books, 1978.

Whyte, William H., Jr. *The Organization Man*. New York: Doubleday, Anchor Books, 1957.

Whyte, William. "The Outsize Life." *Fortune*, July 1955.

Wylie, Philip. *A Generation of Vipers*. New York: Rinehart, 1942.

C. Additional Sources (Pop Aesthetics and the Arts)

The following works were consulted for information about American popular culture, including both rock 'n' roll music and the popular cinema, as well as key concepts that earlier set the pace for "modernity" in entertainment and the arts.

Arnold, Matthew. *Culture and Anarchy*. Minneapolis: H. W. Wilson, 1903 (reprinted 1966).

Benshoff, Harry M., and Sean Griffin. *America on Film: Representing Race, Class, Gender, and Sexuality at the Movies*. Madden, MA: Blackwell, 2004.

Biskind, Peter. *Seeing Is Believing: How Hollywood Taught Us to Stop Worrying and Love the Fifties*. New York: Pantheon Books, 1983.

Boggs, Joseph M. *The Art of Watching Films* (Fourth Edition). Palo Alto, CA: Mayfield, 1966.

Boorstin, Daniel. *The Image: A Guide to Pseudo-Events in America*. New York: Harper Colophon Books, 1964.

Boyle, Robert H. "the Car Cult from Rumpsville." *Sports Illustrated*, April 24, 1961.

Buckley, Jonathan, and Mark Ellingham. *Rock: The Rough Guide*. London: Rough Guides/Penguin, 1996.

Campbell, Joseph. *The Power of Myth*. New York: Doubleday, 1988.

Fishwick, Marshall. *Parameters of Popular Culture*. Bowling Green, OH: Popular Press, 1974.

Fishwick, Marshall, and Ray B. Browne (eds.). *Icons of Popular Culture*. Bowling Green, OH: Popular Press, 1970.

Finkelstein, Sidney. *How Music Expresses Ideas*. New York: International, 1952.

French, Philip. *Westerns: Aspects of a Movie Genre*. New York: Viking Press, 1973.

Friend, Tad. "White Trash Nation." *New York*, August 22, 1994.

Giannetti, Louis. *Understanding Movies*. Eighth Edition Upper Saddle River, NJ: Prentice-Hall, 1999.

Graber, Marjorie. "The Transvestite Continuum: Liberace-Valentino-Elvis." *Vested Interests: Cross-Dressing and Cultural Anxiety*. New York: HarperPerennial, 1993.

Grossman, Lloyd. *A Social History of Rock Music: From Greasers to Glitter Rock*. New York: McCay, 1976.

Hansen, Miriam. *Babel and Babylon: Spectatorship in American Silent Film*. Cambridge, MA: Harvard University Press, 1991.

Harris, Stephen L., and Gloria Platzner. *Classical Mythology: Images and Insights* (second edition). Mountain View, CA; Mayfield, 1998.

Heathey, Michael (ed.) *The Ultimate Encyclopedia of Rock*. New York: HarperCollins, 1993.

Hechinger, Grace, and Fred M. Hechinger. "Serious Epidemic of Automania." *The New York Times Magazine*. August 11, 1963.

Hill, Trent. "The Enemy Within: Censorship in Rock Music in the 1950s." *South Atlantic Quarterly*, 90, 1991.

Kael, Pauline. *For Keeps: 30 Years at the Movies*. New York: Dutton, 1994.

Kouwenhoven, John. *Made in America: The Arts in Modern Civilization*. New York: Doubleday, 1948.

Lipsitz, George. *Time Passages: Collective Memory and American Popular Culture*. Minneapolis: University of Minnesota Press, 1990.

Lott, Eric. *Love and Theft: Blackface Minstrelsy and The American Working Class*. New York: Oxford University Press, 1993.

Marcus, Greil. *Mystery Train: Images of America in Rock and Roll Music*. New York: Dutton, 1982.

McAleer, Dave. *The All Music Book of Hit Singles*. San Francisco: Miller Freeman Books, 1994.

MacDonald, Fred J. *Who Shot the Sheriff?* Westport, CT: Greenwood/Prager, 1986.

Melly, George. *Revolt into Style: The Pop Arts*. New York: Anchor, 1971.

Meredith, Robert. *American Studies: Essays on Theory and Method*. Columbus, OH: Charles E. Merrill, 1968.

Miller, James A. *Flowers in the Dustbin: The Rise of Rock and Roll, 1947–1977*. New York: Simon and Schuster, 1999.

Mulvey, Laura. "Visual Pleasure and Narrative Cinema." *Screen* 16.3, Autumn 1975.

Neibaur, James L. *Tough Guy: The American Movie Macho.* Jefferson, NC: McFarland, 1989.

Paglia, Camille. *Sexual Personae: Art from Nefertiri to Emily Dickinson.* New York: Vintage, 1990.

Parfrey, Adam (ed.) *Cult Rapture.* Portland: Feral House, 1995.

Pattison, Robert. *The Triumph of Vulgarity: Rock Music in the Mirror of Romanticism.* New York: Oxford University Press, 1987.

Pike, Jeff. *The Death of Rock'n'Roll: Untimely Demises, Morbid Preoccupations, and Premature Forecasts of Doom in Pop Music.* Boston: Faber and Faber, 1993.

Reader, Ian, and Tony Walter. *Pilgrimage in Popular Culture.* London: Macmillan, 1993.

Schickel, Richard. *The Disney Version: The Life, Times, Art and Commerce of Walt Disney.* New York: Simon and Schuster, 1968.

Sklar, Robert. "Red River — Empire to the West." *Cineaste* 9, Fall 1978.

Sontag, Susan. *Against Interpretation.* New York: Dell, 1969 (reprint).

Steiner, Wendy. *The Scandal of Pleasure: Art in the Age of Fundamentalism.* Chicago: University of Chicago Press, 1995.

Storm, Tempest. "The Lady Is a Vamp." *Cosmopolitan*, March 1988.

Sutton, Walter, and Richard Foster. *Modern Criticism: Theory and Practice.* New York: Odyssey Press, 1963.

Szatmary, David P. *A Time to Rock: A Social History of Rock'n'Roll.* New York: Music Sales Corporation/ Prentice-Hall, 1996.

Watts, Steven. *The Magic Kingdom: Walt Disney and the American Way of Life.* Boston: Houghton-Mifflin, 1997.

Willis, Paul. *Profane Culture.* London: Routledge & Kegan Paul, 1978.

Wood, Michael. *America in the Movies.* New York: Basic Books, 1975.

Index